John Edward Bunch II 121,979 words.
Black Dragon
Lifer
Retired National President
Former National Enforcer
Former East Coast Regional President
Original 7/President Atlanta Chapter
Mighty Black Sabbath MC Nation
A Breed Apart
Since 1974 and Still Strong……….///
www.bikerliberty.com
Host Black Dragon Biker TV YouTube
Host Black Dragon Biker Facebook
Host BlackDragonBikerTV Instagram
Host BlackDragonBikerTV TikTok
X.COM @jbunchii
Host The Dragon's Lair Motorcycle Chaos Podcast – Spreaker.com
Sales/Advertising 404.692.0336
blackdragon@blacksabbathmc.com
Bunch Media Group
P.O. 931792
Norcross, Ga 30003

The MC Social Construct!

Edited by
- Christin Chapman

Cover design by

- Black Dragon

First Edition, First Printing March 2025

Motorcycle Club Protocol 101

"The social construct of motorcycle club life, rules, traditions, history, politics, and modus operandi"

By, John Edward Bunch II 'Black Dragon' BSFFBS

Motorcycle Club Protocol 101 "The Social Construct of motorcycle club life, rules, traditions, history, and modus operandi" is the seventh book in the Motorcycle Club Bible series. This manual teaches hang-arounds, prospects, and full patch members of motorcycle clubs the history, protocols, rules, and principles of the motorcycle clubs set - thus, empowering them to successfully navigate its social and political climate.

Bunch Media Group
Motorcycle Club Education Division
Copyright © 2025 by John E. Bunch II/Bunch Publishing/ Bunch Media Group

All rights reserved, including the right to reproduce this book or portions thereof in any form whatsoever without expressed written authorization from the author. For information, address Bunch Media Group P.O. 931792, Norcross Georgia 30003. Written and printed in the United States of America in Tucker, Georgia, utilizing American ingenuity, pride, and workmanship.

Library of Congress Control Number: **2025903866**
International Standard Book Number: **978-0-9974322-9-9**

◊◊◊

For information about special discounts for bulk purchases or club purchases please contact Bunch Media Group at 404.692.0336 or blackdragon@blacksabbathmc.com.

Black Dragon can speak at your live events, host your annual, teach at your MC protocol training sessions, or host your live events. For more information or to book an event contact Bunch Media Group at 404.692.0336 or blackdragon@blacksabbathmc.com.
BlackDragonBikerTV - Instagram
Black Dragon Biker TV - YouTube
Black Dragon Biker - Facebook
BlackDragonBikerTV - TikTok
The Dragon's Lair Motorcycle Chaos Podcast
www.blackdragonsgear.com
www.bikerliberty.com

◊◊◊

Some sections of this book were researched with the assistance of the Artificial Intelligence platform ChatGPT and others.

Acknowledgements:
Above all, I thank God. To Him be the glory.
To my love and my rock Tahmehrah 'Tia' Purdue.
To my editor Christin Chapman, thanks for sticking with me for five months on this one. We've done it again!
To my beloved mother Anese Yvonne Bunch
To my beloved Aunt Bernita Hall

These people have helped me to develop & grow through the years, so I would like to send them an honorable mention:
Invader Shaggy 1%er, Invaders MC
James Heavy Evans, Soul Brothers MC Founder (RIP)
White Boy Art, Chosen Few MC (RIP)
Boar 1%er, Sons of Silence MC
BANDIDO Kenneth 1%ER, Bandidos MC
Dolla Bill 1%er, Outcast MC
Eddie Kane 1%er, Outcast MC
Cell Block 1%er, Outcast MC
Big Bone 1%er, Outcast MC
Archbishop 1%er, Outcast MC
Big FU 1%er, Outcast MC
Knowledge 1%er, Outcast MC
Skull 1%er, Outcast MC
Uncle Chucky, Outcast MC
Bolo 1%er, Outcast MC
PNut 1%er, Outcast MC
Tarzan 1%er, Outcast MC
Nakita 1%er, Wheels of Soul MC
JRock 1%er, Wheels of Soul MC
Teddy Bear 1%er, Sin City Deciples MC
Chuck 1%er, Thunderguards MC
Rice 1%er, Thunderguards MC
Big Caz 1%er, Thunderguards MC Ret
Dark Shadow 1%er, Thunderguards MC
Seven 1%er, Thunderguards MC
Reef "the guy who likes to ride his motorcycle"
Miles 1%er, Chosen Few MC Texas
DJ, Chosen Few MC Texas (taught me as a prospect)

Motorcycle Club Protocol 101

Doc 1%er, Chosen Few MC California
Black Ice 1%er, Chosen Few MC Georgia
Milcc 1%er, Chosen Few MC California
Born 1%er, Rolling Knights MC, Oklahoma
FUBAR 1%er, Highway Men MC Michigan
Guns, Cycle Kings MC Atlanta, GA
Snow Man, Rare Breed MC Atlanta, GA
Sexy Ass Teacher (SAT), Chaser, Black Pearls MC
Goose, Black Sabbath MC, Topeka
Hog Man, Black Sabbath MC former Nat. VP
Big Dale, Black Sabbath MC I.E., California founder
Black Sheep, Black Sabbath MC Ronin
El Chappo, Black Sabbath MC Atlanta, GA
Black, Black Sabbath MC North Shore LA
Prime, Black Sabbath MC Jacksonville
Big Rob, Black Sabbath MC Macon, GA
Skeebo, Black Sabbath MC Macon, GA
Super Mario, Black Sabbath MC Macon, GA
Alcatraz, Black Sabbath MC Houston, TX
Nubia, Black Sabbath MC San Diego (RIP)
Papa Vern, Black Sabbath MC San Diego (RIP)
Eli, Black Sabbath MC San Diego (RIP)
Scrap Iron, Black Sabbath MC Little Rock, Arkansas
Doc, Black Sabbath MC Little Rock, Arkansas
Bull, Zodiacs MC San Diego (RIP)
Picture man Vapors, San Diego
Reka Rat, Black Sabbath MC Phoenix
Dana, Hawg Riders MC San Diego
Lawd Have Mercy, Hood Beast MC San Diego
Lion Lock, Regulators MC Atlanta, GA
Mad Dog, Regulators MC Atlanta, GA
Bug, Regulators MC Atlanta, GA
Lo-Ke, Regulators MC Atlanta
Guns, Cycle Kings MC Atlanta
Full Nelson, Cycle Kings MC, Atlanta
Sunz, Cycle Kings MC, Atlanta
Joker, Cycle Kings MC, Atlanta
Sweets, Cycle Kings MC Atlanta

P'can Man Cycle Kings MC, Atlanta (RIP)
Bad News, Midnight Star MC Denver
Alarce, Midnight Star MC Atlanta, GA
White Boy, Midnight Star MC Kansas (RIP)
Freight Train Golden Hawks MC Atlanta, GA
Big Dog, Front Runners MC Founder Atlanta
Goldie, 1 Down MC Founder Los Angeles
Gucci, Royal Aces MC San Diego
Frank, Royal Aces MC San Diego
Papa G, Royal Aces MC San Diego
Howie, Final Option MC San Diego
Crazee, Ebony Wheels MC Little Rock
Flatline, Gentlemen's MC Memphis
Kev, Forsaken MC New York City
Shari Joyner Robbins 'Dominatrix' Arkansas
Tin Man, Road Rangers MC Cleveland
Top Dollar, Flaming Knights MC Atlanta
Kingfish, Flaming Knights MC San Diego
BoBo, One Blood MC Jacksonville
Brother Bob, Truly Beloved MC San Diego

<u>Special Thanks to:</u>
AK, West Africa
Sven Black Forest Germany
Lubis Brazil Moto Clube podcast
Chucky South Africa
Bubby Love, V103 Radio Atlanta
Classy Nico, San Diego
OG Weasel, MC Protocol Expert
Rickey Gadsen, Racing Legend
Foxy, PROC GM
George Lestor, NCOM Founder
Hollywood James Macecari 1%er, Insane Throttle podcast
Dibber in the Wind Podcast United Kingdom
Mike Ball, Insane Wheels podcast
Michael Jarvie 1%er Outlaws MC ret. Biker News Canada podcast
David 'Lil Man' Calibozo 1%er Soul Brothers MC Nomad
Reggie Rock Bythewood, Biker Boyz Director

Paul Garnes, Producer Biker Boyz
Tammy Garnes, Producer Biker Boyz
Preach Leveque Vladimir Sucka Free MC Protocol Expert
Wild on Twos podcaster
Verrel Elizabeth Woods (Vera)
Adam Sandoval podcaster
Joe Yanny, Attorney at Law

Thank you to these Men who helped raise a fatherless boy:
Uncle J.P. William Hall (my entire life)
Ret. Lt. Col Robert Stinnett [silver star Vietnam] (ages 5 – 12)
Paul 'Pep' Perry (ages 25 – 62 -so far)

Thank You to My Staff:
Christin Chapman Editor-in-Chief
Jason 'Goose' Markey Producer
Melissa Ritchee, Senior Advisor/Overseer
Kenneth 'Gate Keeper' Lovejoy Producer
Brian J. Hass Master Videographer
Wolf the Red Discord Server Master
Ghost Eagle Advisor (writer)
Papa Renegade (writer)
Lavish T. Williams Co-host

My Blood Sisters:
Thea Lynn and son Michael
Lori Jean and children David, Jessica, Jasmine, Walter Jr.

My blood brothers:
Jon Pierre Bunch
David Edward Bunch

Foreword

I wrote this book from my 36 years of experience as an operator in the motorcycle club world since my introduction to the Black Sabbath Motorcycle Club in 1989. From a prospect I rose to the position of National President and spread my small MC from a mom-and-pop organization to a national motorcycle club recognized nationally from coast to coast. During that time, I have experienced joy, exhilaration, disappointment, and heartbreak. I have operated at the highest levels of my MC and have even had a National President of my beloved MC announce to the world that I had been put OUT BAD without a trial on social media in front of the entire world so that he and his interlopers could take over the nation I sacrificed a significant portion of my adult life building. I stand before you a fractured man with many lumps, bumps and bruises. I am not perfect by any means so I cannot present this book as some collection of factoids by some all-knowing motorcycle club being. Some of the knowledge I share in this book will be useful for some of you. Some of it will not. There are other interpretations out there. Find them all, weigh them all and take what is useful to you. This book is about MC protocol learned from my experiences of opening chapters from coast-to-coast. It is also written from my ten years of experience as the host of Black Dragon Biker TV which is an MC protocol and Biker News channel. In my capacity as host of that channel I have reported on and consulted motorcycle clubs and club bikers worldwide from riding clubs to one percent nations from Prospects to National Presidents. These are my qualifications. Finally, if you don't like this book write your own.

Black Dragon

◊◊◊

"If you don't have organization, you don't have an organization." Chuck 1% Thunderguards MC

"Do what is right not what you are able to do" Chuck 1% Thunderguards MC

A belief is not a fact, it is merely something you believe. It doesn't become a fact until it has been independently verified. Don't persecute your brothers based upon something you believe! Black Dragon

Who Should Read this Book?

This book should be read by motorcycle club members, officers, prospects, hang-arounds, and people who are interested in learning the social construct of motorcycle club life, rules, traditions, history, and modus operandi of biker clubs that operate on the biker set internally, among one another, and externally. You will also learn some of the intricacies of motorcycle club politics, and the biker set social construct. It will enhance your knowledge about the secretive societies of biker club nations and their associated communities.

- Presidents
- Vice Presidents
- Secretaries
- Business Managers
- Sgt at Arms
- Founders
- Members
- Prospects
- Probates
- Hang-Arounds

◊◊◊

When to Use this Book

Use this book as a reference manual to help you develop your knowledge and experience. In these chapters you will find valuable information that will prepare you to operate on the biker set smoothly and effectively! But keep in mind that no book can teach you everything you need to know about any subject. The greatest teacher is experience and learning through the process of applying theory to practice. You must collect data from your experiences then conduct analysis of that data and finally come to an interpretation. This book is only one step in that process. The biker set world can be dangerous for the ill-informed, hardheaded, naïve, or stupid. Even someone with as many years of experience as I have can wind up Out Bad without at trial. So, learn well and be wise. Good luck!

Motorcycle Club Protocol 101

"Don't do the right things because you are expecting people to be grateful rather do things right because they are the right thing to do! People are never grateful! If you do things right expecting people to be grateful, to recognize you for doing right, or to do the right things to you because you did the right things to them, you will be sorely disappointed. Take heart in the good things you do and move forward in them without expectation, in that way you will always be proud of the things you've done. In short, my son, if you move righteously on this Earth without expectation, you won't be disappointed by the shortcomings of people."

My mother, Anese Yvonne Jackson Bunch

Motorcycle Club Protocol 101

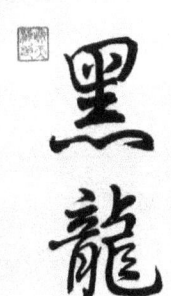

JBII

Table of Contents

CHAPTER ONE MOTORCYCLE CLUB PROTOCOL 36

Motorcycle Club Protocol 101 36

MC Protocol Differs Depending Upon Location 36

MC Protocol Constantly Evolves 37

Time, Distance & Shielding Knowledge, or Ignorance 38

CHAPTER TWO UNDERSTANDING THE MOTORCYCLE, MOTORCYCLE CLUB ORGANIZATION, & THE BIKER CLUB SET 41

The Biker Club Set 41

The History of the Motorcycle in the United States 42

Motorcycle Summary 45

The History of Motorcycle Clubs in the United States 45

Late 1800s to Early 1900s 46

Riding Enthusiasts Were First 46

Segregation in America Formed White & Black MC Sets 46

Exploratory Excursions Helped Form MCs 47

Motorcycle Racing Helped MCs 47

Community-Based Groups Helped Form MCs 47

Shared Mechanical Knowledge Helped Form MCs 47

Motorcycle Manufacturers and their Contribution to Establishing and Supporting MCs in the United States 48

Print Advertisements 50

The Formation of Formal Clubs and the First MC 51

Military Connection of Vets to MCs 52

MC Governing Bodies 53
M&ATA 54
1920s: 55
    Expansion of MCs 55
    The American Motorcyclist Association 57
1930s-1940s: 61
    Community Support in MCs 61
    Diamond 13 Patch, Southern California Outlaw Federation; "Outlaw" Biker Culture Begins 61
    Summary of the Diamond 13 Patch 63
    Support for Military Personnel World War II 63
    Post-WWII Disillusionment "Outlaw" MCs Strengthened 64
    The Hollister Riot of 1947 65
    Riverside Riot of 1947 72
    Riverside Riot of 1948 72
    Motorcycle Maintenance and Repairs: 74
    Recreational Riding and Group Tours: 74
    Friendship and Brotherhood: 75
1950s-1960s: 75
    A New Era in MCs 75
    Mainstream MCs 75
    Emergence of the OMC 1950s—1960s 76
The AMA Statement That Allegedly Birthed the 1% 79
    The 1% Diamond Created by the Hells Angels MC 80
    Outlaws MC the first to Wear Diamond on the East Coast 81

The 1%(er) Diamond Ultimate 1% OMC Symbol 81

OMCs Summary 82

The Rise of African American Clubs 40s – 60s 82

The Rise of African American "Outlaw" Culture 85

African American Outlaw Cultural Expression and Identity 85

The Influence of African American MCs on African American OMCs and 1%ers 85

African American OMCs and the 1% Diamond 86

Today's African American MCs and the AMA 94

African American Social and Political Climate: 94

Black Pride in African American OMCs 94

Community and Support Networks of Black OMCs 95

Cultural Impact and Representation of Black OMCs 95

Greaser Subculture: 95

The Bob-Job Era, 1946—1959 96

Motorcycle Racing 96

Motorcycle Culture in Popularity: 96

1970s-1980s 97

The Vietnam War and its Affect on OMCs 70s – 80s 97

The 1% OMC Wars 98

Hollywood Cashes in on 1% OMC Culture 99

Law Enforcement Crackdown 103

Chopper Subculture 104

Racing and Competitions 104

Safety and Legislation 105

1990s-Present 105

1% OMCs Exponential Growth... 105

1% OMC Conflicts and Violence... 106

1% OMC Law Enforcement Scrutiny 106

1% OMC Internal Changes and Leadership Shifts 107

1% OMC Global Reach 107

1% OMCs Influence on Popular Culture............................... 107

1% OMCs Decline in Numbers 107

1% OMCs Persistence and Resilience 107

1% OMCs Growth and Diversification.................................. 108

Popularity of Riding Groups 108

Women in Motorcycle Clubs.. 108

Riding for a Cause 109

Evolving Riding Styles and Subcultures................................ 109

Globalization of Traditional MCs, alternative Biker Groups and Law Enforcement MCs (LEMCs) 109

Technology and Social Media Impact 109

The Effect of the movie Biker Boyz on the Black biker set 110

History of MCs Summary 112

CHAPTER THREE *HOW DO MOTORCYCLE CLUBS OPERATE* 113

The Makeup of the MC 113

National Officers 114

Responsibilities of the Nationals.. 115

Leadership.. 115

Governance and Administration.. 115

- Communication and Representation 115
- Event Coordination and Planning 115
- Conflict Resolution 116
- Promoting Club Culture and Values 116
- Growth and Expansion 116
- Definition of a National MC 116
- "Chapter" versus "Charter" 117
- Chapter 117
- Charter: 117
- Definition of a Regional MC 118
- Definition of a Local MC 118
- Chapter President 119
- Chapter VP 120
- Chapter SAA/Enforcer 121
- Club Security 121
- Enforcing Club Rules 121
- Preserving Club Traditions and Protocols 121
- Managing Club Property 121
- External Relations and Security 122
- Conflict Resolution 122
- Ride Formation and Safety 122
- Chapter Secretary 123
- Meeting Coordination 123
- Meeting Minutes 123
- Club Correspondence 123

Club Records and Documentation 124

Membership Administration 124

Financial Record-Keeping 124

Reporting and Documentation 124

General Administration 125

Chapter Treasurer 125

Financial Record-Keeping: 125

Budget Planning 125

Membership Dues and Finances 125

Financial Reporting 126

Banking and Financial Transactions 126

Fundraising and Sponsorships 126

Financial Compliance 126

Financial Planning and Advice 127

Chapter Business Manager 127

Financial Management 127

Club Business Operations 128

Club Business Communication 128

Documentation and Record-Keeping 128

Business Contracts and Relations 128

Club Administration 129

Chapter Road Captain 129

Ride Planning 129

Pre-Ride Briefing 130

Leading the Ride 130

- Group Management 130
- Safety and Traffic Management 131
- Communication and Coordination 131
- Ensuring Rider Compliance 131
- Ride Evaluation 131
- Chapter Public Relations Officer (PRO) 132
- Media Relations 132
- Public Image Management 132
- Community Engagement 133
- Club Representation 133
- Online Presence and Social Media Management: 133
- Crisis Management 133
- Internal Communication 134
- Branding and Merchandising 134
- Nomad 134
- Representing the Club 135
- Building Relationships 135
- Support and Assistance 135
- Reporting and Communication 136
- Maintaining Club Standards 136
- Flexibility and Adaptability 136
- Nomad Chapters 136
- *99%er Clubs with Nomads 137
- *RCs, MMs, MAs, Motorsports clubs, etc. with Nomads 137
- Nomads Summary 137

Nomads with Little Experience 137

What is a Full Patch Brother 138

Club Loyalty 138

Club Unity and Brotherhood 138

Club Support and Participation 139

Club Security and Protection 139

Club Tradition, Etiquette and Protocol 139

Club Representation 139

Club Development and Growth 140

Club Unity in Conflict Resolution 140

Good Standing 140

What is an MC Prospect/Probate/Probationary 140

Club Familiarization 141

Club Support 141

Club Education 141

Club Integration 141

Club Loyalty 142

Club Contributions 142

Personal Development 142

Prospect Evaluation 142

Women's Auxiliary of an MC 144

Support Club Activities 144

Community Involvement 144

Social and Networking Activities: 145

Support for the Full Patch Brothers 145

Promoting the Club's Values 145
Fundraising and Financial Assistance 145
Communication and Coordination 145
Properties Of an MC 146
Properties of a Club Member 147
Support and Loyalty 147
Club Participation 147
Socializing and Networking 148
Community Engagement 148
Supporting Club Functions 148
Emotional and Physical Support 148
Respecting Club Hierarchy 148
Honorary Members of the MC 149
Recognition 149
Symbolic Inclusion 149
Association with the Club 149
Support and Representation 150
Relationship with Full Patch Members 150
Non-voting Status 150
Hang-arounds 151
Observation and Familiarization 151
Building Relationships 151
Club Etiquette and Respect 151
Support and Assistance 152
Getting Vetted 152

Brother Clubs of an MC 152
Mutual Relationship 153
Support and Association 153
Shared Values and Protocol 153
Patch or Colors 153
Relationship Dynamics 153
Autonomy and Independence 154
Support Clubs of an MC 154
Relationship with the Dominant MC 155
Support and Assistance 155
Patch or Colors 155
Hierarchy and Structure 155
Relationship Dynamics 155
Limited Autonomy 156
Social Clubs (SCs) on the Black biker set 156
Support Sponsoring Club Activities 157
Community Involvement 157
Social and Networking Activities 158
Support for the Full Patch Brothers of Their Sponsoring MC 158
Fundraising and Financial Assistance 158
Friend of the Club 158
Trusted and Respected Associate 159
Support and Camaraderie 159
Loyalty and Discretion 159
Mutual Respect and Trust 159

Limited Privileges 159
Recognized Affiliation 160
Club Supporters 160
Loyalty and Support 160
Respect for the MC 160
Representation 161
Relationship with Club Members 161
Mutual Respect and Trust 161
Limited Involvement 161
Summary of Motorcycle Club Operations 162

CHAPTER FOUR *BIKER CLUBS, SETS, RELATIONSHIPS, MC PROTOCOL, & MOVING AROUND* 163

Colors, Cuts, Patches, Sweaters, Serapes and Rags 163
   Traditional Patch Setup 164
   Post WWII, Disillusionment, Birth of the Three-Piece Patch .. 165
   One-Piece, Two-Piece Patches & Diamonds on Black Set 170
   Two-Piece Back Patches 171
   The MC Cube and Side Rockers 172
   Cut-Off Blue or Black Denim Cuts & Leather Cuts 175
   Patch Summary 177
A Deeper Look at the "Set" 177
Hierarchy of Clubs on the Set 178
   1% Outlaw Motorcycle Club (OMC) Nations 180
   1% MC Designated Support Clubs 180
   Supporter MCs 182

Outlaw, OMC, or Diamond MCs 182

Law Enforcement MC (LEMCs) 183

Traditional MCs / 99%ers 185

Veterans MC 186

Non-Traditional MCs 187

Female MCs 196

Motorsports Clubs (MSCs) 197

Riding Clubs 197

Patriot Guard Riders and Specialty Biker Groups 198

Motorcycle Organizations 200

Female Social Clubs 203

MC Hierarchy Summary 203

CHAPTER FIVE INTRA & INTER MC PROTOCOL 204

MC Protocol 204

Intra-club MC Protocol 204

Inter-Club MC Protocol 204

CHAPTER SIX INTRA-CLUB MC PROTOCOL 206

The Biker Club Code 208

Club Colors and Patches 209

Respect for Club Hierarchy 210

Club Meetings and Communication 211

Manage the Money 212

Dealing with the Patch Maker 213

Brotherhood's Responsibility When You go to Jail 213

Brotherhood's Responsibility When You go to the Hospital 214
Riding Formation and Etiquette 215
Club Events and Activities 216
Loyalty and Brotherhood 216
Club Disciplinary System 217
    Punishment 219
    Brother's Responsibility After Trial, Appeal, Punishment 220
    What to Do If Expelled/Dismissed from the MC 221
    Out Bad 222
Brother's Responsibility if the Club Violates Its Bylaws 224
Founding Members and Presidents Forever 224
The Biker Club Code Explained 225
    1. Maintaining Membership in Good Standing 225
    2. Protect Your MC brotherhood with all your might! 226
    3. One Patch One Vote 226
    4. All Grievances are Handled at the Table 226
    5. Never Sleep with Your Club Brother's Old Lady 226
    6. Always Show Respect to the Club's OGs and Severely Punish any brother who Disrespects them 227
    7. Never Discuss Club Business Outside of the Club 227
    8. Never Lie to a Club Brother or Officer 227
    9. Never Steal from Club Brothers or the Club 228
    10. Always Pay Back a Loan from a Club Brother or the Club 228

11. When Handling the Club's Money always get a Receipt 228

12. Never Exploit the Club for Personal Gain unless all Brothers Benefit Equally 228

13. Never get High in the Clubhouse 228

14. Never Make a Personal Fight a Club Fight 229

15. Never Allow the brothers to Die for what they believe, instead make the Enemy Die for what they Believe 229

16. One Fights We All Fight! Never Abandon a brother in Battle 229

17. No One Talks to Cops Without at least One Witness from the Club 230

18. No Brother Allows Rumors to Spread about Another Brother Not Present to Defend Himself................ 230

19. No Brother is Punished, Fined or Put Out Bad without a Trial 230

20. Never Break the Law in Club Colors 230

21. Never Incite a Club War without a War Counsel 231

22. Never Snitch on the Club or on a Club Brother.......... 231

23. If the Police Question the Club; No One Talks, we all Walk 231

24. Never Divulge Personal Information about a Club Brother for Any Reason......... 231

25. Never Allow a Club Brother to Speak Negatively Against the Club or its Officers in Public............ 231

26. Never Write Down Anything in Church that can be Used Against the Club in a court of Law 232

Intra MC Protocol Summary 232
CHAPTER SEVEN INTER-CLUB MC PROTOCOL 233
   Respect for Club Colors and Patches 233
      Returning a Club's Colors 234
   Permission and Courtesy While Traveling 234
   Pass Pin, Pass Thru Pin or Pass Through Pin 235
      How to Call Ahead 235
   Greetings and Acknowledgment 237
      Removing Helmet and Glasses 237
      Full Patch Greeting a Full Patch 237
      Whose Hand(s) do You Shake First 238
      Prospect Greeting a Full Patch 239
      Some 1%ers Won't Shake Your Hand 239
      Interrupting Two Full Patches Talking 240
      Embracing When Meeting 240
      The Term Brother 240
      Some Clubs Have Problems Meeting & Greeting Women in MCs 241
   Communication and Diplomacy in Settling Beefs 242
      Non-Interference Prevents Most Conflicts 242
      Don't Speak Negatively About Other MCs on the Set 242
      Have the Receipts or See them Before You Spread the Lie! .. 243
      What is a Receipt 243
      Who Uses Receipts 244
      Receipts vs Bullshit Subterfuge Designed to Confuse 244

Example of Bullshit Receipts 245
Protocol at Events 246
Elements of a Neutral Club 246
Avoidance of Territory Disputes 247
  The MC Sit-Down 248
Protocol for Two or More Clubs Riding Together 249
  Dominant Clubs Riding with Subordinate Clubs 249
Passing 1% and Other MCs 250
Patch Overs and Club Flips 251
Taking Former Members of Other Clubs 252
  Inter-club MC Protocol Summary 254
CHAPTER EIGHT HOW TO START A MOTORCYCLE CLUB 255
  Internal Challenges to Starting Your MC 255
  External Challenges to Starting Your MC 256
  There are Several Ways to Start an MC 259
  What is a Blessing 260
  Starting Your MC in Areas dominated by 1% OMC Nations .. 264
  Starting Your MC in Areas where there are NO 1%ers 274
  Starting Chapters of an Established MC 275
  AMA Affiliation 276
  Starting an LEMC 276
  Starting an MM 276
  Starting an OMC or 1% OMC 276
  Starting MCs in Countries Other Than the United States 277

Conclusion 277

CHAPTER NINE THE BYLAWS 279

    Study to Shew Thyself Approved 282

    Beware of Constructing Overly Rigid Bylaws 282

    Honor the Spirit of the Bylaws 283

CHAPTER TEN THE PROSPECT'S LIST OF 52 DO'S AND DON'TS 284

    Prospect's Bible 284

    1 Prospecting is Getting into The Habit of Prospecting 284

    2 Everyone Goes Through It 285

    3 Your Pride May Take a Few Hits 285

    4 Never Compromise Your Values 286

    5 Not Every Brother Who Wears the Patch Will Be Your Brother 287

    6 Give Prospecting Your Best Effort 287

        Take a Lesson from the US Navy Submarine Service 287

    7 Conduct Yourself Responsibly Publicly 289

    8. You Haven't Earned Your Way In Yet 291

        9A Take an Example from the Submarine Service 292

        9B Remember Jake Sawyer Hells Angels Nomad 294

    9C Always Display a Positive Attitude 295

    10 Participate as Much as You Think is Acceptable then Participate More 295

    11 If You See a Club Brother You Haven't Met Take the Initiative to Introduce Yourself 296

    12 Ask to Circulate and Greet Every Patch Holder 296

13 Anticipate Needs, Don't Wait to be Told 297

    13A Anticipatory Observation Skills 298

    Remember Jake Sawyer, the Hells Angels Nomad 298

14 Don't Get Overly Friendly with Any Non-Regular Acquaintance of the Club; CYA 299

15 Brothers' Information Stays in the MC 300

    15A The Day I Spoke on a Brother's Business 300

16 MC's Information Stays in the MC 302

    16A One Lies We All Lie 303

17 Stay Alert 305

    17A. Listen to Your "Somethings" 306

18 Conduct Yourself with the MC in Mind 306

19 We Don't Leave Folks Behind – Like the Military 306

    19A Don't Make Jazz's Mistake and Wander Off during Troubled Times 307

20 Alert the SAA or Senior Brother to Negative Vibes 308

21 Sobriety Helps You Keep your Eyes and Ears Open 308

22 You are a Prospect 24/7 308

23 You Are Every Brother's Prospect 309

24 Never Wear Your Colors Out of Your Area Without Your Sponsor's Approval and Never Out of State Unless You are with Your MC 309

25 Don't Interrupt Conversations Among Brothers 310

26 The Word "Gang" Should Never Be Uttered on the Set 311

27 Never Lie to a Member of Another Club 311

28 Show Equal Respect to Full Patch Brothers of Any Club 312

29 Always Carry Pen, Paper, Watch, and Calendar 312

30 Frequently Ask Full Patch Brothers How You Are Doing and If There Is Anything You Should Be Doing Differently 313

31 Never Ask When You May Be Getting Your Full Patch 313

32 Never Call a Full Patch Your "Brother" 313

33 Never Call a Full Patch or Prospect of Another MC "Brother" 314

34 Patches are Earned Not Given, No Royalty in MCs 314

35 Never Bring a Personal Friend or a Stranger Into the Presence of Your Prospective Brotherhood Without Permission 315

36 Never Turn your Back on a Patch Holder of Another MC 316

37 Always Show Respect and Courtesy to Patch Holders of Other Clubs 316

38 Avoid Pillow Talk like the Plague 316

39 Prospects Never Partake in Consuming Alcoholic Beverages at any Open Function 317

40 Prospects Never Partake in any Unnatural Drug 317

41 Never Acknowledge a Full Patch Brother's Woman Especially Upon First Meeting Her 317

42 Do Not Touch or Sit on a Patch Holder's Motorcycle Unless Invited 318

43 Prospect's Don't Pack But If You Do Turn her Cut Inside Out 319

44 Two Dudes Don't Ride on the Same Bike 319

45 It's Not an Insult Not to be Acknowledged on the Set 320

46 Learn Your Patch Parts and Colors 320

    46A Knowing Other Club's Patches and Meanings 321

47 A Prospect Must Do Anything a Full Patch Asks 322

48 Don't Touch Another Club's Colors 322

49 Prospects Must Show Sincere Interest in the Club 323

50 Stealing is Not an Option 323

51 Your Colors Should Never Touch the Ground 323

52 For Now, Just Follow the Rules & Bylaws 323

Summary 324

BEST OF LUCK PROSPECT! 324

CHAPTER ELEVEN DEALING WITH THE 1%, DOMINANTS, DIAMONDS, OUTLAWS, OMGS, AND THE LIKE 325

- A Quick Overview to Bring You Up-to-Speed 325

  - What are they called 325

  - 1% OMCs 325

  - Dominant OMCs 325

  - Outlaw Motorcycle Gangs (OMGs) Outlaw Motorcycle Clubs (OMCs) 326

  - Motorcycle Gang (MG) 328

  - Today's Diamond Clubs 329

  - Diamond 13 Racing MCs (RMC) 329

  - Other Kinds of Diamond Patches 329

  - Hierarchy Among the 1% 330

  - How Do 1% OMCs Control the MC Set 332

  - Getting a Blessing Today 333

  - Sponsoring MC (Brother Club) 334

  - Hard Colors vs Soft Colors 335

The 1% Clubhouse 336

Never Run Your Mouth Negative on the Set 345

Staying Sober at the 1% Clubhouse 346

CHAPTER TWELEVE MC PROTOCOL AND THE POLICE 347

After You're Arrested What should the Club Do for You 349

Assertion of Rights 352

Know Your Rights: A Detailed Guide to Protecting Yourself During Police Encounters 353

   If You Are Stopped for Questioning 353

   During a Traffic Stop 355

   If Police Approach You on the Street 357

   If Police Come to Your Home 358

   If You Are Arrested 359

   Understanding Probable Cause 361

   Final Note: The Balance Between Asserting Rights and Staying Safe 367

CHAPTER THIRTEEN MC PROTOCOL FOR FIRST EMERGENCY DEPARTMENT PERSONNEL 369

OMGs: Aspects of the 1%er Culture for ED Personnel 369

Suggested Modern Day Procedures for First Responders and ED Personnel Interfacing with MCs 384

   On the Accident/Incident Scene Be Calm, Professional and Show Respect 385

   First Responders Should Quickly Identify the Situation 385

   First Responders Should Focus on the individual 385

   First Responders Should Prepare for Insulting Iconology 386

First Responders Should Observe Body Language and Behavior on the Scene 387

First Responders Should Communicate effectively 387

First Responders Can Seek Backup from Club Officers 387

First Responders Should Remove Colors with Caution and Respect... 388

First Responders Should Respect Personal Space 390

First Responders Should Not Engage in Personal Opinions or Biases 390

First Responders Should Know the Local Landscape 390

CHAPTER FOURTEEN THE WAY FORWARD 391

Bibliography 393

Index: 404

Appendix A: Biker Set Readiness Test... 429

Appendix A: Brief History of the Mighty Black Sabbath Motorcycle Club Nation 438

Glossary... 454

CHAPTER ONE
MOTORCYCLE CLUB PROTOCOL

Motorcycle Club Protocol 101

All Motorcycle Club (MC) sets are governed by a set of rules known as "motorcycle club protocol" (MC protocol). MC protocol exists within the club to establish and define guidelines for conduct between members and outside the club with other MCs and their supporting organizations. To operate safely and freely on the MC set you must learn MC protocol and have a strong understanding of how it works in your area as well as the areas you visit or areas to which you may relocate. MC protocol is like politics and all politics are local. That is to say that what you can do in one place may or may not work in another. Regardless, a general understanding of MC protocol will give you the basics from which to work in understanding general protocol guidelines.

MC Protocol Differs Depending Upon Location

As a former National President, I established chapters of the Black Sabbath MC Nation nationally for nearly ten years. In each area, state, and region the rules necessary to accomplish this task were slightly different. For instance, establishing a chapter and getting it blessed varies greatly on the West Coast from getting a chapter up and running on the East Coast. Equally difficult and just as challenging, was getting a chapter established in the Midwest and the Dirty South. Further, as times changed, so did the rules for establishing clubs and chapters on the set in each region.

In 1999 when opening my first chapter away from the San Diego mother chapter, all I had to do was open a chapter in a new area and just popup. In some locations, you may have had to ask the dominant club in the area for a blessing, but by 2009, the Georgia

Council (GAC) was established on the Black biker club set, REQUIRING you to obtain a blessing from the council or from a dominant club to operate in peace and unmolested. Things had changed that much in just ten years. By 2015, there were so many dominant clubs spreading out in big cities you might have to get multiple blessings by multiple 1% nations to get a chapter or new MC up and running. Other cities adopted a confederation of clubs (COC) approach where you only had to go to one coalition or council to be accepted by all the clubs and dominants in your city or area.

MC Protocol Constantly Evolves

The rules for how clubs get along and maintain civil relationships are constantly evolving on the set. If you don't travel much, your knowledge of MC protocol may only be relevant in your area. Never make the mistake of thinking that just because you do things in your area a certain way, it's done the same way by MCs in other parts of the country or the world. MC protocol is essentially tribal rules of human interaction, so it is similar in all areas. But it is also different. When you travel don't assume. Always, look, listen, hear, watch, and learn. Ask questions, read, examine, and interpret! This book will provide a beginning. Your experience will provide the rest. Many haters will see you with this book and mock you. They will say that you can't learn MC protocol from a book. There is some truth to that. Like a doctor can't learn to be a surgeon from a book. He needs the combination of reading to learn the theory and then he needs to put the theory to practice so he can gain the experience. The combination leads to knowledge. I say challenge every word I have written in this book. Research each statement to prove the level of its accuracy. It is through this questioning that you will develop your own theory of MC protocol. Then put your theory to practice as you matriculate on the set. Ask questions of the OGs in your club and area so that you hear informed opinions bronzed by decades of living this lifestyle. Participate in club church, coalition meetings and attend runs, events, seminars and conferences. Organizations like NCOM (National Coalition of Motorcyclists), ABATE (American Brotherhood Aimed Towards Education), PROC (MC Professional Convention), AMA (American Motorcyclist Association), and your local COCs (Confederation of Clubs) are designed to educate and inform you. Utilize them to increase your exposure. Read everything you can get your hands on utilizing the internet, social media, libraries, news articles, and artificial intelligence. Study!

Time, Distance & Shielding Knowledge, or Ignorance

In the United States nuclear submarine Navy, we had a simple formula for limiting our exposure to radiation called "As Low As Reasonably Achievable" (ALARA). This formula uses time, distance, and shielding to limit an individual's exposure to the harmful rays of nuclear radiation:

- spend as little time exposed to it as possible (time)
- stay as far away from it as possible (distance)
- put as much shielding between you and it as possible (shielding)

The same formula can be said about learning and understanding MC protocol. If you don't want to know it, put as much time, distance, and shielding between you and it as you possibly can, and you will be guaranteed blissful ignorance. And many folks are incredibly happy with never actually knowing anything about what they claim to love or bear responsibility for protecting. You see it in your MC every day when you encounter brothers or sisters who have never even read their bylaws. Gleefully ignorant they are not even embarrassed when they ask you, "Is that in the bylaws?" They aren't even ashamed of themselves when you look at them out of the side of your eye with your eyebrows raised incredulously. And you think, "These people actually vote and are bold enough to run for office in the MC!?" And to imagine that if they won't even learn their own bylaws how in the hell can they plan to safely navigate the club through the shark infested waters of the biker club set with little more knowledge about MC protocol than a hangaround who shows up at the club on his first night? But these ignorant fools claim to know it all (here's where we get into the bliss of ignorance) and make decisions based on theories they have not put into practice. Then you find your club sitting in a terse meeting with a dominant MC wondering why your president thought it was okay to popup a new chapter in a state wearing unauthorized patches in denim cuts with that state's name as a bottom rocker talking about, "This is America and I'll do whatever I want," but never once explained to all the brothers he was responsible to protect the repercussions a move like that would bring. And the first time you are finding out about those repercussions is at this terse meeting with a menacing bunch of mean folks glaring at you angrily with looks that could kill—and that is when you realize, "This fool has no idea of what the fuck he's doing and he's about to get us all fucked up because he walked us in this meeting telling us it was okay to take our guns and cell phones off and leave them on our bikes like the dominant requested!" If you've ever found yourself in a meeting like that with an idiot in charge, you know exactly what I'm talking about! I chuckle to myself when I remember that I was once that idiot who led my men into a scenario that mirrored some of these elements. Take my word and learn from my mistakes - it wasn't pretty! The words, "Black Dragon, we brought you to this meeting to bust your head to the white meat if you don't walk in here talking some sense..." will forever reverberate in my memory. Especially when I realized I was the idiot who okayed my brothers to leave their cell phones and guns on our bikes when the 1% club demanded it! Let's just say, it made for an interesting afternoon. It was in that moment that I decided the "time, distance, and shielding" formula could be reversed. The more time you spent exposed to the MC lifestyle you claim to love, the less distance you put between you and it, the less shielding you put between you and it, and the more you will learn about it so that you will actually know what you are doing to protect those for whom you are responsible! In this book I will tell you about many of the things I've experienced and lessons I've learned the hard way—so that perhaps you can avoid learning them the hard way yourself. You may ask, "What makes me the expert?" Well, if you fail at something you can easily tell others what NOT to do! Or at least tell them what DIDN'T work for you. There will be many other points of view on this information I'm sharing with you. Some will disagree with a few things or with everything I have written. That's because others have had different experiences, and they should also write a book. In this book, these experiences are mine and mine alone. I share them without reservation.

Let's Go!

**Black Dragon
Lifer (36 Years)
Mighty Black Sabbath MC Nation
BSFFBS
Out Bad Breed**

◊◊◊

CHAPTER TWO
UNDERSTANDING THE MOTORCYCLE, MOTORCYCLE CLUB ORGANIZATION, & THE BIKER CLUB SET

The Biker Club Set

The biker club set is any part of the MC community that bikers in clubs (and occasionally non-affiliated bikers) hang out. It is important to understand the functions, traditions, history, and protocols that govern all biker club sets. It is also important to realize that biker club sets are still largely segregated by race across the United States. So, yes there is a Black biker set, White biker set, Hispanic biker set, Asian biker set, etc. And even though racism can run rampant on any or all these sets that doesn't stop members from each of these sets from getting along and hanging out together. They interact often with great respect due in large part to their adherence to MC protocol, which is a set of largely unwritten rules handed down from one MC generation to the next keeping alpha men in alpha clubs operating in peace (without violence for the most part) and in relative safety. Knowing how these sets operate allows you to matriculate safely among them. And if you are operating according to protocol, you can have lots of fun as this is an incredible lifestyle enjoyed by many bikers worldwide.

In this chapter we will look at general overall MC history throughout the US and how all clubs interconnect on every set. If you already know about these subjects skip ahead.

Now, since none of this would have been possible without the iron horse itself, I believe it is appropriate to start with the history of the motorcycle in the US.

Motorcycle Club Protocol 101
The History of the Motorcycle in the United States

A motorcycle, motorbike, bike, or trike (if 3-wheeled) is a two or three-wheeled motor vehicle steered by a handlebar from a saddle styled seat (Merriam-Webster) (Foale) (BMV) (Cossalter) (Britannica) (GovInfo). Motorcycle means a motor vehicle with motive power having a seat or saddle for the use of the rider and designed to travel on not more than three wheels in contact with the ground.

Motorcycles first appeared in the US in 1866 following the invention of the bicycle in 1817. The first motorcycle was driven by steam invented by Pierre Michaux in Paris. He called his motorcycle the Michaux-Perreaux steam velocipede (Burgess Wise). In 1866 one of his employees, Pierre Lallement, brought the design to the US (Fiedler).

Gottlieb Daimler and Wilhelm Maybach in Germany are widely credited with inventing the first internal combustion, petroleum fueled motorcycle in 1885, called the Daimler Reitwagen. In 1894, Hildebrand & Wolfmuller became the first series production motorcycle (Motorcycles).

The Orient-Astor became the first production motorcycle in the US built by Charles Metz in 1898 at his factory in Waltham MA.

By 1901, two of the biggest motorcycle brands in US history were born. Indian Motorcycle Manufacturing from Springfield MA and Harley Davidson Inc., from Milwaukee WI. Both companies survived *The Great Depression* even though most others did not. In 1941, following the attack of the Japanese on Pearl Harbor, the US was pushed into the Second World War. Motorcycles had replaced horses in infantry battalions and Harley-Davison was conscripted as the motorcycle supplier for the allied war efforts. Around 90,000 units of the 45cs Harley-Davidson WLA aka "The Liberator" were shipped to Europe and other war fronts (Motorcycles). Both companies are viable and operating today even though Indian went out of business in 1953; however, the name was purchased by Polaris in 2011, and Indian motorcycle manufacturing was back up and running. Similarly, Harley Davidson ran into financial troubles and to save it from liquidation in 1969 it was purchased by American Machine and Foundry (AMF) a sporting goods company known for producing bowling balls. Then production quality took a dive and AMF made many marketing and brand image mistakes (pissing off many Harley owners who protested AMF's every move), AMF sold Harley-Davidson back to a group of Harley-Davidson senior executives, including Willie G. Davidson, in 1981. Harley rebounded and went on to enjoy one of the strongest name brands in U.S. history but not before they worked hard to rid themselves of the anchor of the stigma of the outlaw bikers. In 1983, Harley-Davidson was able to successfully shed its past associations with outlaw biker culture with the establishment of the Harley Owners Group aka HOG (Sam). The riding club associates itself with various philanthropic efforts and with more than a million members worldwide, acts as a channel for the brand to interact with its fans and get their feedback. It also supports the US military by introducing a number of biking programs to honor veterans for their service (Sam). Today Harley-Davidson is the brand of choice mandated by thousands of motorcycle clubs across the country, however they are closely competing with the renewed Indian brand now owned by Polaris as of the writing of this book in 2025.

The Japanese motorcycle is a popular bike in the US that rose in popularity in the late 60s. The term Universal Japanese Motorcycle, or UJM was coined in the mid-70s because all major brands—Honda, Kawasaki, Yamaha, and Suzuki made similar bikes following the same form, function and quality. By the 60s Honda had set its sights on entering the US market. By this time, thanks to the prominence of outlaw motorcycle culture and supporting Hollywood productions, if someone owned a motorcycle, usually a Harley-Davidson or a Triumph, they were either considered to be a leather-clad ruffian from an illegal biker gang or a Rock-N-Roll star (Sam). They were also big, bulky machines that required constant maintenance and no one, besides the most ardent of enthusiasts would want to own (Sam). Honda rightfully speculated there was another market in the US and targeted them with the 'Super Cub' a small 50cc motorcycle for the masses (Sam); therefore, they enlisted Grey Advertising to create a marketing campaign with the slogan "You meet the nicest people on a Honda," targeting the average joe, housewives, young couples, students, working men etc. (Sam). By highlighting the fun, simple, low-cost nature of the Super Cub the campaign became so successful it captured 63% US motorcycle market share for Honda and is still analyzed in marketing case studies today (Sam). It also was paramount in erasing the motorcycle's deep-rooted image of rebellion and evil (Sam). In 1974 Honda introduced the Goldwing, coined as the world's biggest motorcycle," which has dominated the motorcycle touring industry for decades. By the 1980s, Japanese manufacturers began to diversify, building incredible street legal racing platforms, dirt bikes, enduros, and adventure travel bikes that have been wildly successful. They revolutionized the industry by creating motorcycles with better performance, reliability and equipment packages with a much cheaper price than the American and British manufacturers.. In the mid-90s, Japanese manufacturers went directly after the Harley-Davidson market by creating cruisers that closely resembled and sounded like traditional Harleys. Following their pattern of creating better performance, reliability, and equipment packages at a cheaper price caused those bikes to be wildly popular as well.

Motorcycle Summary

The motorcycle drives a spirit of adventure, travel, excitement, nomadism, and independence in bikers in the US and around the world. The insatiable passion of the lifestyle of folks who ride the steel has led to many communities sprouting to support life molded around riding these amazing machines. Many of these communities are the mighty MC nations of the world who live by the commandments dictated by this lifestyle. Those who haven't experienced the freedom of the ride will never understand the crazed obsession of those who ride year-round no matter what the weather—excruciating heat, relentless rain, sleet, or bone-chilling cold. They will never understand how we embrace the discomfort, bugs in our teeth, heatstroke, frostbite, heavy winds, or foggy highways. And despite their warnings that we are simply advancing our fates as "organ donors," we continue to ride! And we will ride for as long as we are blessed with the strength to keep the bike upright and hold on to the back of it!

The History of Motorcycle Clubs in the United States

Once motorcycles became commercially available, they instantly drew the reckless, thrill seekers, and adventurists of the day. These individuals (men and women alike) saw motorcycles as daredevil machines to race, test the limits of their skills, express their freedoms, chase their passions for adventure and for some they even became the vehicle upon which they experienced death. Another thing is for certain; where two or more kindred spirits are gathered to experience the lifestyle of motorcycling and share the passions of the love of the two-wheeled-life obsession, interests were sparked in forming closer bonds that quickly became riding groups, then MC extended families. The bonds, sealed by the shared love of life clinging to the backs of speeding steel, pushed individuals to share time in exclusive members-only organizations, which eventually became the first MCs, with many original MCs consisting of both male and female members. Let's take a look at the progression of MCs in the US:

Late 1800s to Early 1900s

Riding Enthusiasts Were First

In the late 1800s, bicycle and cycling clubs as well as independent cyclists became engrossed in the motorized bicycles that were soon to become motorcycles. Informal groups of these new motorcycle riders began to form as their popularity grew and enthusiasts sought opportunities to connect and ride together. These groups were comprised of individuals who shared the passion and vision for motorcycles, enjoyed riding together, exploring the countryside, and participating in early motorcycle races. They laid the foundation for the development of more structured MCs that were soon to follow.

Segregation in America Formed White & Black MC Sets

As America was racially segregated by Jim Crow laws at the time the White biker sets were formed for White Americans and the Black set was formed for African Americans. Other races were absorbed into one or the other or formed their own sets. For the most part, the White set was where most media attention has been focused over the decades such that most other sets are still unknown to the general public to this day. For instance, I still run into people that are absolutely surprised that there is such a thing as Black 1% clubs in the United States in 2025. This is interesting since there were Black 1%ers clubs in the first group of clubs ever to don the diamond. Consequently, the Black MC biker set went largely unknown, undocumented, and unrecognized until about 2002 when we filmed the movie Biker Boyz with Director Reggie Rock Bythewood. This iconic movie caused a country-wide migration of clubs on the Black biker club set that exploded the popularity of biking among African Americans.

Exploratory Excursions Helped Form MCs

Many early riders saw their machines as a means of exploration and adventure. Groups would gather to explore the countryside, rural areas, and scenic routes. These excursions allowed riders to share the joy of discovery and experience the thrill of riding together. Riders would often exchange information about roads, routes, and places of interest, fostering a sense of camaraderie and knowledge-sharing among participants.

Motorcycle Racing Helped MCs

Motorcycle racing played a significant role in the formation of informal riding groups. Early motorcycle enthusiasts were drawn to the thrill of competition and would come together to watch or participate in races. Racing events provided opportunities for riders to connect, exchange technical knowledge, and share their experiences. These gatherings often served as informal meeting points, laying the groundwork for future collaborations and the formation of more structured MCs.

Community-Based Groups Helped Form MCs

Communities and neighborhoods often contributed to the formation of many informal groups as riders who lived in the same area would organize rides, social events, or simply come together to enjoy the thrill of riding. These community-based groups promoted a sense of belonging as riders shared a common bond over their love for motorcycles and local ties.

Shared Mechanical Knowledge Helped Form MCs

Early motorcycles required regular maintenance and repairs, which provided a platform for riders to exchange technical knowledge and expertise in maintaining their machines. Members of these groups would gather to share tips, troubleshoot mechanical issues, and help one another with repairs. In the days before social media, these training opportunities had to occur in person. These personal interactions facilitated the exchange of skills within the community and strengthened the bonds between riders.

Motorcycle Manufacturers and their Contribution to Establishing and Supporting MCs in the United States

It was actually motorcycle manufacturers who played the first significant roles in aiding the establishment and growth of the early MCs in the US. During the early 20th century, when motorcycles became increasingly popular, manufacturers recognized the potential for creating brand loyalty and fostering a sense of community among riders. They also knew that their strong support of the sport of bike riding would directly result in more motorcycles being sold. They began sponsoring motorcycle riders and motorcycle clubs to stimulate, grow, and encourage the new passion that was taking place across America. They fostered the beginning of biker MC life in the following ways:

Product Development

Motorcycle manufacturers focused on creating dependable, powerful, and affordable machines that appealed to a wide range of riders. By making motorcycles more accessible to the general public, manufacturers helped to popularize the sport and laid the foundation for, and encouraged the formation of, riding groups and clubs.

Sponsorship and Support

Motorcycle manufacturers recognized the importance of promoting racing events to foster the competitive spirit among the riding community, intertwining the sport with their brand. By sponsoring races and racers, they were further establishing their brand with supporters and fans. These racing events not only showcased the capabilities of their motorcycles, but also brought riders together, providing the catalyst that led to the formation of the legendary racing motorcycle clubs of the twenties, thirties, and forties.

Promotion and Advertising

Early on, manufacturers used strategic marketing tactics to promote their motorcycles by depicting riders in groups to emphasize the sense of belonging and community that came with owning a motorcycle. By associating their brand with the idea of riding as a social activity, manufacturers helped popularize the concept of MCs.

Dealer Networks

With the establishment of extensive dealer networks, motorcycle manufacturers were able to provide community hubs. Dealerships became gathering places where riders could socialize, share stories, and exchange information further facilitating connections. By supporting dealer-sponsored events, such as group rides and rallies, manufacturers further strengthened the sense of community.

Dealer Technical Support

Manufacturers recognized the importance of rider skill and safety in promoting their motorcycles. To support riders, they offered technical assistance, training programs, and educational materials. They conducted workshops and training sessions to help riders improve their riding skills, understand motorcycle maintenance, and promote safe riding practices. This support encouraged the obsession of most organized clubs to focus on safety, proper maintenance, and skill development of their riders.

Community Engagement

Manufacturers organized rallies, events, and gatherings that brought riders together from various regions. These events provided opportunities for riders to network, socialize, and bond over their shared passion for motorcycles. Manufacturers often sponsored or participated in these events, further solidifying their connection to the motorcycle community and the pulse that drove their direction. The celebrated awards distributed at these events, including "Longest Distance Riders," "Best Dressed MC," "Most Attended MC," and "Best Looking Motorcycle" are still awarded in many MC annuals and cabarets today.

By designing and promoting motorcycles for a wide range of riders, hosting community-focused events, encouraging and emphasizing safety, knowledge, and skills, sponsoring racing events, and developing dealer networks manufacturers created a sense of identity and belonging among riders, laying the foundation for the formation and need for MCs.

Defining the Roles of Women in MCs

MCs were not always exclusively male in the early years. It wasn't until much later that the big clubs removed women from full patch membership. Many of the big clubs of yesteryear, including some top 1% OMCs actually had full patch female members. Motorcycle manufactures played a role in helping women achieve status and membership where it did occur. During the early 20th century, while limited, motorcycle manufacturers made a concerted effort to illustrate women riders in their advertisements and encourage women to participate in MCs in the following ways:

Print Advertisements

Although print advertisements in magazines, newspapers, and catalogs were primarily targeted towards males—with an emphasis on performance, technical aspects of their motorcycles, and appealing to the speed and adventure-seeking spirit—some ads sought to highlight the emerging trend of female riders, featuring women experiencing the lifestyle and adventure in the same manner as their male counterparts. Manufacturers published newsletters and sponsored sections in MC publications to feature stories and news related events relevant to motorcycle communities. These newsletters often highlighted women riders by promoting their accomplishments and involvement in MCs. With this positive representation, manufacturers aimed to inspire more women to join clubs.

Women's Auxiliary Groups of Riders

Several women's auxiliary groups, such as the Motor Maids of America (1940), began to form with the support of motorcycle manufacturers. These groups provided a platform for women to connect, share their experiences, and participate in club activities. Manufacturers recognized the importance of supporting these women's groups to promote female involvement in MCs. It was these women's auxiliary groups that took hold in the early MC culture.

Women's Riding Competitions

Motorcycle manufacturers sponsored women's competitions, such as endurance races, hill climbs, and motocross events. These sponsorships not only promoted the brand but also showcased women's riding skills and their involvement in the sport. By highlighting women's achievements in competitive settings, manufacturers aimed to inspire more women to engage in motorcycling.

The Formation of Formal Clubs and the First MC

The first documented MC in the United Kingdom was "The Motor Cycling Club (MCC)." It was founded in 1901 and may be the oldest pure MC in the world. The MCC still exists today, and hosts runs, race meetings, and reliability trials. The first documented MC in the United States was "Yonkers Motorcycle Club," established in 1903 in New York, however it originally started on November 19, 1879, as the Yonkers Bicycle Club. For that reason, it claims to be the oldest active motorcycle club in the world. The Portsmouth Motorcycle

Club also claims to be the nation's oldest club having been established as a "cycling" club in 1893 (Portsmouth Cycling Club). It changed its name in 1913 to MC. The San Francisco Motorcycle Club was founded in San Francisco, California in 1904. It has been in continuous operation since its inception making it the second or third oldest MC in the United States depending on how you define an MC. By the 1910s there were many more clubs and with more clubs came a greater formal structure. These clubs allowed riders to share knowledge and experiences related to riding skills, maintenance, and repair. Members could rely on the expertise and assistance of fellow club members, fostering a sense of community and mutual support. During this time, clubs organized group rides to provide opportunities to explore new areas, participate in social events, and experience the joy of riding together. The connections established in these club events transitioned from friendships into communal bonds with a tight-knit brotherhood.

Military Connection of Vets to MCs

During WII, motorcycles played a crucial role in military operations. The connection between motorcycles and the military influenced the formation of MCs, with many clubs having ties to military veterans. Military veterans who had served as motorcycle dispatch riders during the war often formed clubs upon returning to civilian life. These clubs allowed former servicemen to continue their passion for motorcycles and maintain the camaraderie they experienced in the military. Many who were mentally ill with what was then known as "combat fatigue" later to be known as post-traumatic stress disorder, found that MCs were the only place where they were understood by brothers that had experienced the same horrors in war. In those days, the military did not provide the kinds of support it does for war veterans today, so MCs offered not only a military connection and camaraderie but also a mental health connection and loving support that the government was slow to understand it needed to give. Returning vets brought military-like structure to MCs that originally started out as family clubs and gatherings of close-knit friends. These clubs introduced structure and command positions in the MC. Bylaws began to make MCs look, operate, and feel like the paramilitary organizations they operate as today.

MC Governing Bodies

With the establishment of organized clubs came the need for regulation, political action, and support within the growing motorcycling community. Consequently, this period witnessed the formation of regional and national MCs and the establishment of governing bodies to hold them accountable. The first were the Federation of American Motorcyclists (FAM) and the Motorcycle and Allied Trades Association (M&ATA).

FAM

The formation of the FAM can be traced to the New York Motorcycle Club which merged with the in 1903 (Motorcycle Club). Those members saw the need for a national motorcyclist organization. The enactment of the New York City law requiring the registration of motorcycles as motor vehicles, further signified the need to create such an organization. This law was seen as a direct act by the government to extract money and taxes from bikers and to create laws targeting them.

Club members and independent riders recognized that the need for organizations that centered on biker's rights would be required to adequately lobby and protect bikers against predatory laws, policies, and politics that targeted bikers and portrayed them in a negative light. Bikers have always been a wild and free loving people unconstrained by societal norms and impervious to fear and danger. They have been misunderstood and vilified from the moment they started riding their iron horses – a perception that is still prevalent today.

FAM officially formed during a meeting of 93 biker enthusiasts on 7 September 1908 in Brooklyn, New York. The meeting was chaired by George H. Perry and one notable attendee was George M. Hendee of the Indian Motorcycle Company, who brought 109 membership pledges from the New England area (AmericanMotorcyclist.com).

During this meeting, officers were appointed, including R.G. Betts of New York as president, committees were formed, and a constitution was drawn up. Article I, section 2 of the constitution stated:

> Its objects shall be to encourage the use of motorcycles and to promote the general interests of motorcycling; to ascertain, defend and protect the rights of motorcyclists; to facilitate touring; to assist in the good roads movement; and to advise and assist in the regulation of motorcycle racing and other competition in which motorcycles engage.

During its 16-year existence, FAM developed competition rules and rider classifications, dealt with restrictive ordinances in cities like Chicago, Illinois and Tacoma, Washington, and wrestled with funding and membership concerns. In 1915, FAM had 8,247 members; however, with the start of World War I the number of potential members decreased significantly causing the organization to go out of business in 1919 (AmericanMotorcyclist.com).

M&ATA

Throughout FAM's existence, one clear indication of the health and vitality of the fledgling American motorcycle industry was the formation of several trade associations. Among the earliest was the Motorcycle Manufacturers Association, formed in 1908, it was created to represent and regulate motorcycle manufacturers, accessory makers, and distributors. In November 1916, the M&ATA. was formed. (AmericanMotorcyclist.com).

When FAM eventually folded due to a decrease in membership, the M&ATA was left without a counterpart to represent the riders. Although M&ATA was controlled by the motorcycle industry, the M&ATA "Educational Committee" began registering riders and clubs to support motorcycle activities in 1919, while the "Competition Committee" managed the former FAM's racing responsibilities (AmericanMotorcyclist.com).

After five years of growth, the "Educational and Competition Committee" was named the "American Motorcycle Association" (AMA). The M&ATA later united with scooter trade representatives to become the MS&ATA. And in 1969, it merged with the West Coast Motorcycle Safety Council to form the Motorcycle Industry Council, which continues today.

1920s:

Expansion of MCs

The 1920s, marked a significant growth in the number of MCs as motorcycles gained widespread popularity as a mode of transportation and a symbol of freedom and adventure. Some of the reasons clubs enjoyed the increased popularity are as follows:

Increased Motorcycle Ownership

The 1920s witnessed a surge in motorcycle ownership, as motorcycles became more affordable and accessible to a broader range of people. This increase in ownership contributed to the growth of MCs, as more individuals sought opportunities to connect with fellow riders and enthusiasts. The availability of various motorcycle models and brands also added to the appeal, with riders forming clubs around specific motorcycle brands or types.

Regional and Local Clubs

As motorcycle ownership increased, regional and local MCs proliferated. These clubs catered to riders within specific geographic areas, providing a sense of community and camaraderie. Regional and local clubs organized regular rides, social events, and gatherings, offering riders the opportunity to connect, share experiences, and explore new destinations together. These clubs became important hubs for riders to exchange information, plan trips, and form lasting friendships.

Social and Recreational Activities

MCs in the 1920s focused not only on riding but also on socializing and recreational activities. Club members organized picnics, parties, dances, and other social events that allowed riders and their families to come together in a fun and festive atmosphere. These activities fostered strengthened the bonds between club members by providing opportunities for riders and their families to socialize, relax, and enjoy the company of like-minded individuals who shared a passion for motorcycles.

Motorcycle Tours and Endurance Runs

The 1920s saw the rise of motorcycle tours and endurance runs, which became popular activities among MC members. These events involved riding long distances, often crossing state lines, or exploring scenic routes. MCs organized and participated in these tours and endurance runs, which allowed riders to test their skills, experience the thrill of long-distance riding, and explore new areas.

Racing and Competitions

Club members participated in organized races, both on dirt tracks and road circuits, competing against one another and other clubs. Racing events provided an avenue for riders to showcase their skills, push the limits of their motorcycles, and gain recognition within the motorcycle community. It also allowed clubs to demonstrate their prowess and build relationships through friendly competition.

Supportive Community

MCs in the 1920s often provided support and assistance to their members. Riders would help one another with mechanical issues, offer advice on maintenance and repairs, and provide a network of support for any challenges or hardships faced by fellow club members. The sense of community within MCs extended beyond riding and social activities. Clubs acted as a support system for riders, creating a sense of belonging and solidarity among members. The expansion of MCs in the 1920s reflected the growing popularity of motorcycles as a mode of transportation and a source of recreation. Further providing riders with community, friendship, and adventure, contributing to the thriving motorcycle culture of the era.

The American Motorcyclist Association

The American Motorcyclist Association (AMA) was the next logical progression in governing bodies that would exist to police, support, and lobby for the biker clubs' communities. It was established in 1924. The AMA played a crucial role in providing support and structure to MCs, serving as a national governing body for motorcycle activities and competitions.

> "The slogan of the AMA will be: An Organized Minority Can Always Defeat an Unorganized Majority"
> (Western Motorcyclist and Bicyclist 1924).

The Motorcycle & Allied Trades Association (M&ATA) began registering riders in 1919, and by early 1924, it claimed about 10,000 members. On May 15 at a meeting in Cleveland, the directors of the M&ATA proposed to create the American Motorcyclist Association as a division of the M&ATA. The new AMA would control rider registration and activities, issue sanctions for national events, and served motorcycle industry members. Riders registered with the registered M&ATA were transferred to the AMA as charter members, while individual AMA membership dues were set at $1 per year. The motorcycle industry was represented in the AMA in three membership classes: "Class A," which included large motorcycle companies; "Class B," which included supply and accessory companies; and "Class C," which included motorcycle dealers (AmericanMotorcyclist.com, American Motorcyclist Association).

Membership growth was at the top of the early AMA's list of priorities. As Parsons stated in the May 20, 1924, issue of *Western Motorcyclist and Bicyclist*: "Plans are under way to start membership contests and build up the AMA to a live and active fighting organization for the benefit of the motorcycle riders of America. Instead of the 10,000 members now registered with the M&ATA, it is expected that the AMA will have a membership of 50,000." (AmericanMotorcyclist.com, American Motorcyclist Association)

Concerns about restrictive government action against the motorcycling community were among the primary reasons behind the creation of the AMA. In fact, laws and ordinances threatening the freedom of "motor bicyclists" were the impetus for the creation of many early motorcycling clubs and organizations. As an announcement in August 1903, before the creation of the Federation of American Motorcyclists (FAM), stated:

> "The particular character of the motor bicycle has left its status open to various definitions, and as a result ... laws applying to big motor cars are brought to bear on motorcycles with oppressive force .... To combat such measures, to insist that the highways are free to all alike, and that the right to use them is irrevocable, is one of the objects to be served by this organization. It is an object that should appeal to every motorcyclist with red blood in his veins."
> (AmericanMotorcyclist.com, American Motorcyclist Association)

It wasn't until a rash of legislation in the 1960s, though, that motorcycling organizations began to realize how important legislative activity would become to the future of the sport. At that time, the MS&ATA (Motor Scooter & Allied Trades Association) began to concentrate on government relations efforts on behalf of the motorcycle industry, while the AMA saw the need to focus on laws and regulations threatening riders. This led to the formation of the AMA's Legislative Department, with a mission to:

"... coordinate national legal activity against unconstitutional and discriminatory laws against motorcyclists, to serve as a sentinel on federal and state legislation affecting motorcyclists, and to be instrumental as a lobbying force for motorcyclists and motorcycling interests." (AmericanMotorcyclist.com, American Motorcyclist Association)

The AMA was a Whites-only organization from its inception in 1924 until the 1950s, not allowing African Americans to join for its first 30 years. A 1930 AMA membership application form, on display at the Harley-Davidson Museum, included the statement, "membership is limited to white persons only." This segregation occurred at a time in American history when many motorcycle dealerships refused to sell motorcycles to African American riders, but these policies did not stop them from biking. They found ways to get around such restrictions, purchased their bikes anyway and an entire segment of American bikers created their own biking culture. The Negro American biker set known today as the Black biker set was thus born. The Harley Davidson Museum exhibit has examples of distinctive uniforms worn by motorcycle clubs, both AMA sanctioned, and those from the separate culture of African American or racially desegregated clubs that proliferated as a consequence of the AMA segregation policy, such as the Berkeley Tigers MC from the San Francisco Bay Area (AmericanMotorcyclist.com, American Motorcyclist Association).

Prior to the acceptance of African American members, the term outlaw motorcycle club could refer to either a White counterculture biker club that was "uninterested in 'square' events and competitions", or else a club that accepted non-white members and was therefore not allowed to participate in the AMA. In the 1920s and 1930s, Black hill climbing racer William B. Johnson evaded the Whites-only restriction and obtained an AMA membership card, which allowed him to compete around the Northeastern United States and become perhaps the first African American AMA member (AmericanMotorcyclist.com, American Motorcyclist Association).

After the racist policy was abolished, AMA-sanctioned motorcycle clubs thrived in the era after World War II when motorcycle sales soared, and club membership appealed to "better-adjusted" American veterans who enjoyed group participation and operated under strict bylaws that held club meetings and riding events (AmericanMotorcyclist.com, American Motorcyclist Association).

In 1995, AMA President Ed Youngblood said that as a consequence of this racist policy from 1924 to the 1950s, African Americans continued to be underrepresented in AMA events for decades after the segregationist policy was rescinded. That year, Youngblood presented African American AMA member Norman Gaines in their membership advertisement in the campaign "I want to protect my rights as a motorcyclist. That's why I'm an AMA member" in both the AMA member magazine and *Motorcyclist* magazine.

Still little could be done to erase the stigma of the racist policies of the AMA among Black clubs on the Black biker set and therefore there was never a popular registering among them to participate in the AMA. The Black Biker set developed its own governing bodies, rules, regulations, racing events, and lobbying groups. Though the AMA has tried with various outreach programs to enlist African

American MCs among their ranks, however, these efforts have gone largely unnoticed and unappreciated, proving that old wounds heal slowly.

1930s-1940s:

Community Support in MCs

Despite the economic challenges of the Great Depression, MCs of the 1930s continued to contribute to their communities and provide a sense of unity and support for their members. These clubs played a vital role in maintaining the spirit of motorcycling during this tumultuous period in U.S. history. MCs organized charity rides and fundraising events in an effort to alleviate hardships for those affected by the Great Depression. These efforts allowed club members to use their passion for motorcycles to make a positive impact in their communities, showcasing the generosity and community spirit of MCs. They engaged in community service activities by volunteering for local initiatives and aiding during natural disasters or emergencies as well demonstrating the positive impact that they could have beyond their recreational activities.

Diamond 13 Patch, Southern California Outlaw Federation; "Outlaw" Biker Culture Begins

In the 1930s the AMA exuded dominance in two major areas of motorcycling that enjoyed the most popularity in American biker culture:
- management, sanctioning, and control of MCs
- hosting and management of motorcycling competition events such as hill climbing, track racing, and other biker competitive sports

As a result, the AMA became a powerful and rich organization that set strict rules that clubs were expected to follow. Including Clubs had to pay membership and monthly dues to belong. To protect their brand and maintain unchecked control the AMA also established strict rules of conduct and organizational compliance policies for professionalism to which the AMA would reward compliant clubs handsomely with cash payouts earned from winning races and from sponsoring AMA events which also saw lucrative profits. Unruly clubs were thrown out of the AMA structure and banished from participating, preventing them from enjoying their share of the profits. Even though AMA races and affiliation paid more than independent racing, remarkably, some MCs still opted out in protest. For many reasons, perhaps including the financial burden of paying dues during that time, many riders and clubs began to drift away from the AMA and resist it despite the consequences. The AMA's response was very negative. Seeing a threat to its dominance, it sought to shame, humiliate and discredit what it saw as defectors and possibly competitors. It claimed that those who didn't join were operating "illegal" and were nothing but a bunch of "Outlaws" referring to their nonconforming position. Even though at that time the term "Outlaw", when first used, didn't refer to a person or club being involved in criminal activity, the inference was still insulting. These comments sparked a natural split between the AMA and the "Outlaws" (Not to be confused with the Outlaws MC aka, American Outlaws Association founded in 1935 in McCook, Illinois). An entire counterculture movement sprung up that saw the AMA as the "establishment" and the "Outlaws" as the anti-establishment. These protestors revolted from AMA's rules and values and started their own racing clubs with their own rules. During this time the Southern California Outlaw Federation (S.C.O.F.) was born, defiantly embracing the offensive outlaw label, they started their own racing organization. These racing clubs were also known as "Outlaws". The AMA members clung to their culture and the "Outlaws" established theirs. The AMA was about professionalism and mutual respect, and the "Outlaws" were about the unruly opposite (Wikipedia Moonshiners MC).

Consequently, the need for a symbol to represent the "Outlaws" and visually set them apart from the AMA arose. In 1939 the S.C.O.F. awarded a trophy and the Diamond 13 patch to the "Top

13" racing clubs of that year. This patch became the representation of the new "Outlaw" culture. Thus, the Diamond 13 Outlaw patch was born paying tribute to the "Top 13" outlaw racing clubs of 1939 (Wikipedia Moonshiners MC) and the anti AMA culture they represented. Soon other defiant racing MCs and eventually traditional MCs joined this movement and began wearing the "Outlaw" patch. Some initially wore it as a square white patch with the 13 in it. You will see the plain square 13 patch in many early photos but eventually the outlaw icon became standardized as a diamond.

Summary of the Diamond 13 Patch

In summary the Diamond 13 was the first outlaw diamond but being an "Outlaw" during that time simply meant you were anti-establishment not a part of a criminal gang. The "Diamond 13" began as a movement that ultimately led to the anti-AMA patch still worn by many clubs today. It was used by the early "Outlaw" clubs as a protest symbol to show their separation from AMA clubs and their rejection of the AMA establishment and rules (MC Historian). The outlaw (anti-AMA) culture and the "Diamond 13" patch were the beginning of what would become the OMC culture that eventually led to the 1%(er) diamond.

Support for Military Personnel World War II

In the 1940s with WWII underway, many club members enlisted in the armed forces. Remaining club members and women's auxiliary groups worked to maintain connections with those serving overseas. They supported the war effort by sponsoring war bond drives and participating in activities to support their members serving abroad as well asl the local community. These efforts allowed club members to use their passion for motorcycles to make a positive impact in their communities as well as express their patriotic passion for our fighting men and women. Clubs organized care packages, sent letters, and held events to honor and support their fellow club members serving in the military, boosting morale and fostering a keen sense of community within the MC.

Post-WWII Disillusionment "Outlaw" MCs Strengthened

The aftermath of WWII in 1945 contributed even more to the emergence of the "Outlaw" mindset. Many veterans returning from the war struggled to reintegrate into society and felt disillusioned and disconnected. MCs, particularly the outlawed clubs, provided a sense of purpose and belonging by offering an outlet to rebel against societal norms and express their dissatisfaction not only with the AMA but with the status quo.

Post-WWII changed the character of MCs as returning veterans began joining established clubs and forming their own MCs. The ill-effects of PTSD and the ineffective way the military handled this disease turned out war veterans from the battlefields to the streets without mental health treatment or support. Subsequently, many felt abandoned, misunderstood and haunted by the atrocities they experienced at war. They sought out MCs because they offered the camaraderie and support they experienced in the military. The brotherhood of the clubs also offered them a family that understood the horrors of war. Veterans could commiserate together, slowly decompress and recover from their war experiences (heddels.com). The returning veterans brought a darkness to the biker set it hadn't seen previously as many of them were not ready for the festive, carefree atmosphere of so-called "family" clubs which were represented by the AMA. Many chose to quiet their demons with alcohol and drug fueled parties, cavorting with loose women, and exuding anti-social behavior used as coping mechanisms to handle their mental anguish. They too were not as interested in the AMA rules or dominance it had over MCs and racing. Their departure from the establishment was also exacerbated by the American government which had become very suspicious of men hanging in groups (heddels.com).

In an article written on Heddels.com the author explained,

"World War II marked the largest-ever mobilization of American men in history. A great equalizer, the war brought millions of men into contact with one another in unprecedented ways and in totally foreign contexts. But when the war was over, the American government did their best to shunt them into responsible, productive lives and careers [without treating them for their mental conditions]. A strange shift occurred in postwar America, where men were discouraged from associating too openly outside of work or school. Veterans were expected to marry, have children, don their gray flannel Don Draper-esque suits and live tame, little lives." There are a number of reasons that the establishment discouraged groups of men from gathering but increasingly rowdy, anti-social bikers in clubs quickly rose high on the government's target list (heddels.com)."

The Hollister Riot of 1947

Already under increasing scrutiny, MCs experienced a single event that changed society's view of them forever worldwide. The event was the Hollister Riot and in motorcycling history, over the past 100 years no incident has had the impact it has. Hollister is a small California town, with a population of about 4,500 at that time, that had been hosting the AMA's annual 'Gypsy Tour' since the 1930s but had canceled the event during the war. By 1945 WWII was over and in 1947 the town decided to bring the event back over the July 4th holiday. The turnout was far greater than expected. It is estimated that 4,900 motorcyclists descended on the quaint desert village (revzilla.com). The event drew bikers and MCs from all over California and from across the United States including 13 Rebels MC, Pissed Off Bastards of Bloomington MC, Boozefighters MC, Market Street Commandos MC, Top Hatters MC, Galloping Goose MC, Sharks MC, Salinas Ramblers MC, and Yellow Jackets MC (Wikipedia Hollister Riot) (Wikipedia Moonshiners MC). Initially the bikers were welcomed as their numbers meant a boom in business but once drunk, they began to overwhelm the town's seven-man police force with their drunken antics (Sam). They were fighting, throwing beer bottles, racing their bikes down the main street, running traffic lights, wrecking restaurants and bars (revzilla.com) (Wikipedia Hollister Riot). The hotels and other accommodations were sold out which led to bikers sleeping on sidewalks, in parks, in haystacks and on people's lawns (Wikipedia Hollister Riot). Police arrested many for drunkenness and indecent exposure but couldn't restore order. By the evening of July 4, "they were virtually out of control" (C.J. Doughty). The police tried to stop the bikers by threatening to use tear gas and arresting many for drunkenness. The bars tried to stop the men from drinking by refusing to sell beer and voluntarily closing two hours ahead of time (C.J. Doughty) (Sam). The local hospital was jammed with injured bikers and the police arrested so many revelers for a variety of offenses that a special night court was convened (revzilla). Two blocks of the main drag, San Benito Avenue, were cordoned off and all but ceded to the bikers (revzilla). A band was even summoned to play for them, and they danced amid discarded beer bottles (revzilla). By Sunday nearly 30 California Highway Patrol officers armed with tear-gas guns, who were called in to supplement the overmatched Hollister police force, were able to disperse the unruly bikers with a show of force and threats of tear gas (Sam). Finally, after two days, the partying calmed down. Though there were a lot of discarded beer bottles, there was no damage done to the town and no injuries to the citizens (C.J. Doughty) (MC Historian) (Sam) (Wikipedia Hollister Riot). All the cyclists were gone by Monday after the final races with a brazen explanation, "We like to show off. It's just a lot of fun" (revzilla). But Hollister's police chief took a different view, "It's just a hell of a mess," he said (revzilla).

The newspapers wasted no time spreading the story with articles hitting the papers by July 5th. The *Hollister Free Lance* was the first to send reporters to the scene (revzilla.com). Their reporters also fielded phone calls from newspapers across the country as word spread (revzilla.com). Bikers have opined throughout the ages that the press had sensationalized the events to make them look bad from the start. But author Jerry Smith in a July 04, 2022, article said that he put the biker's claims of sensationalism to the test (revzilla.com). He ordered microfilm from the *San Francisco Chronicle, Los Angeles Times, Chicago Daily Tribune*, and the *New York Times,* who reported on the event. "Not surprisingly, the farther the paper was from Hollister, the more perfunctory its accounts were," Smith said (Revzilla). He indicated the original stories were no big deal. He noted that those papers gave no more than 67 lines of copy to the story, and none ran photos. "Even the *Free Lance's* account was, for the most part accurately retold, not grossly exaggerated," he said (revzilla). The reporting also showed there was no consensus as to the severity of the event among the townspeople or officials as to just how bad the takeover was. Some condemned the bikers, while others, compared the event to the annual rodeo nearby and dismissed the Gypsy Tour as "noisy, often annoying, but… damage free"(revzilla). Smith's conclusion was that initially, the story went largely unnoticed even though it was covered nationally. It wasn't until the July 21, 1947, edition of Life magazine displayed on page 31, a photo taken at the event that all hell broke loose and the perceptions of MCs being friendly, family, AMA styled bikers changed to MCs being roving, biker, gangster, hoodlums, ready to take over a sleepy village town near you (revzilla.com). The photo, taken by professional photographer Barney Peterson of the *San Francisco Chronicle*, was shot in front of Johnny's Bar—now the famed location considered the birth-spot "ground zero" of a chain-of-events that would ultimately lead to the infamous 1% moniker attributed to today's OMCs and the development of the 1% diamond.

The photo depicted the image of a dirty, drunken biker splayed out on his motorcycle. He had a beer bottle in both hands, his cap sat crookedly on his head, his shirt was open with his chest exposed, his britches leg was pulled up over his dirty boot, his eyes were glazed, and he sat unsteady astride his motorcycle with a duffle bag under the seat and dusty saddlebags on the back fender. He appeared to be unstable on his bike and looked like he was about to fall off. It is said, "A picture can say 1,000 words" and nothing said, "Trouble making traveling vagabond on a motorcycle ready to take over your town," more than this one. Under the motorcycle were at least 20 beer bottles strewn from the front wheel to the floorboards. The whole presentation just looked like a damned hot mess! The biker's name was later revealed to be Eddie Davenport of the Tulare Riders MC who was from the Lemoore-Hanford-Tulare area (Sam) (C.J. Doughty) (Wikipedia Hollister Riot) (revzilla). The picture was published in the photojournalism section of *Life*, relying heavily on graphic images and explanatory text instead of an article with details (Dulaney). The picture served as a full-page article above a 115-word caption with the headline *"CYCLIST'S HOLIDAY He and friends terrorize town"* (Life). The teaser description said, "The Week's Events: on Fourth of July weekend 4,000 members of motorcycle club terrorize Hollister, California (Life)." The caption went on to say,

> "On the Fourth of July weekend 4,000 members of a motorcycle club roared into Hollister, Calif. For a three-day convention. They quickly tired of ordinary motorcycle thrills and turned to more exciting stunts. Racing their vehicles down the main street and through traffic lights, they rammed into restaurants and bars, breaking furniture and mirrors. Some rested awhile by the curb (above). Others hardly paused. Police arrested many for drunkenness and indecent exposure but could not restore order. Finally, after two days, the cyclists left with a brazen explanation. "We like to show off. It's just a lot of fun." But Hollister's police chief took a different view. Wailed he, "It's just one hell of a mess (Life)"

In stark contrast to Davenport, standing behind him, in the picture was a clean-looking Hollister townsman. He was also staring into the camera. He was not drunk or filthy; his eyes were focused showing that he was of a clear mind. The unmistakable conclusion drawn by the most casual of observers would be that normal town's people would be at the mercy of a horde of drunken hoodlums looking and acting like Davenport. The name of the man standing behind him in the picture is Augustus 'Gus' De Serpa (C.J. Doughty) (Sam) (Wikipedia Hollister Riot).

When news of rogue motorcyclists causing havoc in a small town hit it was not comforting to Americans still recovering from World War II and scared of the impending Cold War. The nation started to fear motorcycle "hoodlums" and their potential rampages (Wikipedia Hollister Riot).

The AMA was caught in a public relations (PR) nightmare as the notion that any minute, roving bands of ruthless motorcycle hoodlums, showing up to one of their events, might descend upon and devour townspeople. This caused towns across the US to cancel race meets which were AMA's bread and butter. It bore the brunt of attacks aimed at the bikers and came under fire as its image took an immediate dive along with the image of bikers generally. The AMA would spend the next few decades defending its image and the image of its bikers just from the events that happened at Hollister. As a result, it antagonized and discriminated against many of its riders who wore military styled jackets with club insignia and rode 'chopped' motorcycles by banning them from attending AMA-sanctioned motorcycle events, which drove even more of them to the rebelling "Outlaw's" side of MC'ing (revzilla.com).

Bikers and MCs were angry and blamed Peterson whom they accused of looking for the story and for staging the photo for sensationalism to sell papers, and there seems to be some credibility to that idea. De Serpa was working as a movie projectionist in the Granada Theatre on the night of Friday, July 4, and after his shift ended at 11 p.m. he walked over to San Benito Avenue to take in the spectacle the whole town was talking about (revzilla.com). "We went uptown, my former wife and I," recalled De Serpa, "to see all the excitement, and we ran into these people. They were on the sidewalk and there was a photographer. They started to scrape up the bottles with their feet, you know, from one side to another, and then they took the motorcycle and picked it up and set it right in the glass. (revzilla.com)" Of the man on the motorcycle, De Serpa said, "That's not his motorcycle, I can tell you that. He was just in the vicinity, and he was pretty well loaded. There was a bar right there, Johnny's Bar. I think he came wandering out of that bar, and they just got him to sit down there. I told my wife, 'That's not right; they shouldn't be doing that. Let's stand behind them so they won't take the picture.' I figured if I was behind them, they wouldn't take it. But he took a picture anyhow, this fellow did, he didn't care. And then after that, everybody went on about their business. (revzilla.com)"

Paul Brokaw, who, at the time was the editor of Motorcyclist, was up in arms about this kind of "yellow journalism." He wrote a letter to *Life* speculating on the authenticity of the photo. Brokaw's letter, published in *Life* stated,

> "Sirs: Words are difficult to express my shock in discovering that motorcyclist picture [see Life July 21, 1947: 31]. It was very obviously arranged and posed by an enterprising and unscrupulous photographer. We regretfully acknowledge that there was disorder in Hollister – not the acts of 4,000 motorcyclists, but rather of a small percentage of that number, aided by a much larger group of non-motorcycling hell-raisers and mercenary-minded barkeepers. We In no manner defend the culprits – in fact drastic action is under way to avoid recurrences of such antics. You have, however, in presentation of this obnoxious picture, seared a pitiful brand on the character of tens of thousands of innocent, clean-cut, respectable, law-abiding young men and women who are the true representatives of an admirable sport. Paul Brokaw Editor, Motorcyclist Los Angeles, Calf (Saia)"

Perhaps this letter was the true beginning of the term that would eventually become known as 1%er rather than the apocryphal statement attributed to the AMA.

Peterson's former colleagues at the *San Francisco Chronicle*, however, defended him. "Barney was not the type to fake a picture," recalled Jerry Telfer, a photo assignment editor who knew Peterson. "Barney was the kind of fellow who had a very keen sense of ethics, pictorial ethics as well as word ethics. (revzilla.com)"

Still the critics of the photo are steadfast in their belief that it was staged. One reason is because they can point to a second photo the *San Francisco Chronicle* published, at some point, of Davenport taken that night on the same bike perhaps seconds before or after the one that was first published. It absolutely looks staged. In it, eight more bottles are placed standing upright around the motorcycle. Davenport's feet are kicked up over the gas tank under the handlebars. Slung across his shoulder is his Tulare Riders MC jacket with his colors emblazoned on the back; Tulare Riders top rocker, a skull with wings as the center emblem, with the "M" and "C" opposite each side under each wing left and right. His name "Dave" is painted as the bottom rocker of the setup. The caption under the picture read,

> "A second shot, never published, indicates that someone, either the photographer or perhaps the rider, believed to be Tulare, California, resident Eddie Davenport, repositioned the empty beer bottles and the jacket, thereby creating the suspicions that the entire scene was posed (MC Historian)."

Whether the picture was staged or not, the article blew the event out of proportion and had a chilling effect which is what *Life* magazine was looking for by posting a full-page spread hoping to create more of a furor than the details of the event would have shown had they published it as a written article instead. Although eye-witness testimonies of attendees of the event such as that of De Serpa claim that the image was faked by the photographer, the strong nationwide influence of the magazine made sure that the news was a national sensation (Sam) which sold plenty of magazines while destroying the innocence of biker culture. The article was the inspiration for the 1953 film *"The Wild One"* which dramatized the Hollister Riot as a gathering of criminals and degenerates (heddels.com). As towns began to close down to bikers and their events more incidents happened to further shape the biker bad boy image.

Riverside Riot of 1947

Two months later the same clubs went to Riverside, California for the Labor Day weekend to another AMA-sanctioned event. As in Hollister over four thousand people, including bikers from out of town and local residents, took over the town's main street. Allegedly Riverside sheriff, Carl Rayburn, blamed a bunch of punk kids for disrupting his town, saying "They're rebels, they're outlaws," thus cementing the term (Wikipedia Pissed Off Bastrds of Bloomington MC). "Yellow journalism" again blew the event out of proportion scaring citizens with this new image of bikers and biker clubs which further infuriated the AMA with another PR nightmare.

Riverside Riot of 1948

One year later, the community of Riverside was, again, inundated by motorcyclists who allegedly turned a simple event into a riot. News articles of the day read, *"July 4 Riverside Riots, Motorcycle Hollister-like Exactly 1 year after the 1947 'Hollister Riot,"* "*July 4, 1948, an H&H Championship by the Riverside MC & AMA Sanctioned Caused Motorcycle Gangs of 'Hoodlums & Tramps' to invade Riverside, Cal. Causing destruction, rioting & deaths which resulted in many arrests,"* Another article started out with, *"Of concern to many is that this will further result in the on-going negative image of motorcyclists,"* (Kuhn). It was called the 1948 Riverside Riot. This so-called riot also resulted in a PR nightmare for the AMA and caused towns across the U.S. to cancel race meetings due to fear of roving bands of motorcycle hoodlums. Though many reports said the

Riverside police chief blamed the violence on visiting "Outlaws" the actual letter written by Riverside, county Undersheriff Roger L. Abbot, who worked for Rayburn, on July 17, 1948, gives an entirely different story:

"As beautiful and cultured Riverside, painfully emerges torn and bleeding from the wreckage and devastation of a three day 4th of July celebration of several thousand motorcycle enthusiasts attending the Novice, Amateur, and National Championship 100 mile motorcycle races held under the auspices of the Riverside County Sheriff's Training Center, Incorporated, sponsored by the Bombers Motorcycle Club of Riverside and sanctioned by the American Motorcycle Association, one asks, "Just what is the extent of damage caused by these hoodlums and tramps, these uncivilized demons, who ride exploding and fire-belching machines of destruction with abandon, hell-bent on destroying the property and persons of Riverside citizens, according to the newspapers?"

"All, an awning got torn on a down-town business house. A city park plunge office was entered and a flashlight stolen. Swimming suits were left lying on the bottom of the plunge. Motorcyclists? Maybe.

An automobile, driven by an impatient citizen was set upon by victims and their friends who resented being knocked down by this car and its driver when it was driven into their midst for failing to yield the right of way. The body of the car was dented and some of its glass was broken.

A bottle fell or was dropped out of a hotel window, a man's wallet was taken from his pocket, and three motorcycles were reported stolen, one of which has been recovered.

A city park official got a bloody nose during an altercation with a motorcyclist who wanted to sleep in the park, and who imbibed too freely. This motorcyclist submitted peacefully to arrest by an officer and has plead not guilty to charges of assault and battery. The courts must decide on the issue involved.

That is the official total of damage to persons and property in what the news papers have screamed nationally to be "a week-end of terror, resulting from an invasion of Riverside by hoodlums and their molls on motorcycles rioting in the streets and wrecking the city.

In order to clinch the matter, and to make sure that the wire services would carry the story to the entire nation, the news articles added the spicy bit that, "the invasion left forty-nine arrested and one killed". It was convenient to omit, for the sake of sensationalism, that this one person killed in all of Riverside County on that week-end was nearly a hundred miles from Riverside at the time he ran into a bridge abutment on the highway and was killed and at the time he ran into the abutment, according to authentic reports, was not going to or from the Rally in Riverside. As a matter of police record..."

Undersheriff Abbot ended his letter saying the newspaper accounts were neither honest nor factual and called for an honest press to engage motorcycling. Still, it didn't seem to matter what the truth was because the narrative was drawn. And MCs would play into this narrative as the decades progressed.

Motorcycle Maintenance and Repairs:

Throughout the 1930s and 1940s, MCs continued to provide assistance and expertise in motorcycle maintenance and repairs. The tight-knit community allowed riders to rely on fellow club members for guidance and support in keeping their motorcycles in good working condition. Club members would share tips, techniques, and knowledge about motorcycles, helping each other troubleshoot issues, perform repairs, and enhance their riding experience.

Recreational Riding and Group Tours:

Recreational riding remained an essential aspect of MC activities. Club members would organize group rides, exploring scenic routes, countryside areas, and landmarks. These rides provided an escape from the challenges of the times and offered riders an opportunity to enjoy the freedom and adventure that motorcycles provided. Group tours became popular, with riders venturing on longer journeys to new destinations.

Friendship and Brotherhood:

MCs continued to fostering strong bonds of friendship and brotherhood among members. Club meetings, social gatherings, and events created a sense of belonging and support within the motorcycle community. Club members relied on each other for companionship, shared experiences, and mutual support during challenging times. The camaraderie within these clubs helped riders forge lasting friendships that extended beyond their love for motorcycles.

1950s-1960s:

A New Era in MCs

During the 1950s and 1960s, MCs underwent significant changes in their culture and image. These decades witnessed the rise of various motorcycle subcultures, including both mainstream clubs and the birth of the more notorious OMCs.

Mainstream MCs

Mainstream MCs, such as those who were members of the AMA, continued to thrive during this period. These MCs focused on promoting motorcycle riding as a recreational activity, organizing group rides, social events, and local racing competitions. Mainstream clubs maintained a positive public image and adhered to rules and regulations set forth by governing bodies like the AMA, often participating in charity rides, parades, and community events, projecting a sense of camaraderie and community involvement.

Emergence of the OMC 1950s—1960s

The 1950s and 1960s saw MCs moving from "Outlaws" into true OMCs as they are known today. They gained notoriety and unwanted police scrutiny for their rebellious nature, compunction for violence and movement toward extensive criminal activities.

Outlaws MC

Not to be confused with outlaw MCs in general, in 1935 the Outlaws MC, incorporated as the American Outlaws Association (A.O.A), was founded in McCook, Illinois. It is the oldest OMC in the world. It was formed by Electro-Motive Company employees at Matilda's bar on Route 66 under John Davis (AOA Outlaws MC Wikipedia). Today it is the third-largest 1% OMC nation in the world.

Hells Angels MC

Though there are several theories about how the Hells Angels MC started a popular one states that in 1948 former members of the "Pissed Off Bastards of Bloomington" formed a new MC and took the name of the WWII 303rd bomber squadron Hells Angels, or from the Hell's Angels squadron of the Flying Tigers in China during WWII (Wikipedia Hells Angels MC) as the name of their new MC. The club brought many significant changes to how MCs operated as it was the first notarized and organized OMC, and biker clubs formed subsequently have imitated the Hells Angels' insignias, rules, doctrines and rituals around the world. With a membership of over 6,000, and 592 charters in 66 countries, the HAMC is the largest OMC in the world (Wikipedia Hells Angels MC). The Hells Angels claim to have invented the 1% patch and actually have what they claim to be an original picture of it, (Hells Angels Frisco Instagram) but more on that later.

Pagan's MC

In 1957 Pagan's MC was formed by Lou Dobkin in Prince George, Maryland. By 1959, originally clad in blue denim jackets and riding both Harley-Davidson's and Triumphs, they began to evolve along the lines of the one percenter MCs we know today (Pagan's MC Wikipedia). The club had an initial thirteen founding members and Pagan's started out from the beginning wearing denim jackets with embroidered insignia instead of the more standard three-piece patches utilized by most 1% OMC nations (Pagan's MC Wikipedia). According to Wikipedia the Pagan's also claim to have invented and adopted the 1%er patch, referencing newspaper articles of the time. The article went on to say the 1%er patch was quickly adopted by most other OMGs (Pagan's MC Wikipedia)

Bandidos MC

Bandidos MC also known as the Bandido Nation is an outlaw MC with worldwide membership (Bandidos MC Wikipedia). Formed in San Leon, Texas, in 1966 by 36-year-old dockworker Donald Eugene Chambers. He named the club in honor of Mexican bandits who lived by their own rules. He recruited members from biker bars local in Houston as well as in Corpus Christi, Galveston, and San Antonio. Bandidos MC is the second largest 1% OMC nation in the world (Bandidos MC Wikipedia). The Bandidos became an international MC in 1983 with the opening of their Sydney, Australia chapter. They ceded Quebec to the Hells Angels after the conclusion of the province's deadliest biker war in 2003 (Bandidos MC Wikipedia).

The Big Four/The Big Five

These four clubs (Outlaws, Hells Angels, Pagan's and Bandidos) are often referred to as the "Big Four," comprise the hierarchy of OMCs operating in the U.S. (Pagan's MC Wikipedia). However, some also include the Mongols MC or the Sons of Silence MC into this hierarchy, referring to the collective as the "Big Five."

Mongols MC

The Mongols MC also known as the Mongol Brotherhood or Mongol Nation, is an OMC formed in Montebello, California on December 5, 1969, with ten founding members, the majority of whom were Vietnam veterans (Mongols MC Wikipeda). The first national president, Louis Costello, named the club in honor of Genghis Khan and the Mongol Empire. The club's founders were reportedly a group of Hispanic bikers from East Los Angeles who formed the MC as an alternative to the Hells Angels, which did not allow non-White members at the time (Mongols MC Wikipeda). They voted to become an OMC in 1974. With chapters in 14 states and internationally 11 countries, the Mongols MC is the fifth-largest 1% OMC nation in the world (Mongols MC Wikipeda). The DOJ and ATF tried for years to use civil asset forfeiture laws to seize all rights to the Mongols' emblems and patches in order to forbid members from wearing them. In 2019 they lost the rights to their logo and patch to federal prosecutors when a jury found them guilty, but it was rebuffed by the Central District of California Court, concluding that seizure of their trademark violated the First Amendment right to free expression and the Eight Amendment protection from excessive punishment. The Department of Justice (DOJ) eventually classified them as an outlaw motorcycle gang (OMG) but still they were not able to shut down the club or take its patches.

Sons of Silence MC

The Sons of Silence MC, an international 1% OMC was founded in Niwot, Colorado in 1966 by Bruce Gale "The Dude" Richardson after serving in the U.S. Navy (Sons of Silence Wikipedia). Richardson later left the club and died of natural causes in Scottsbluff, Nebraska on March 26, 2013. Sons of Silence's national headquarters were moved to Colorado Springs. Leonard Lloyd "J.R." Reed, Jr., also a Navy veteran, succeeded Richardson as the national president in 1977 and held the position for twenty-two years. In the 1990s Reed and Richard Lester, an attorney and motorcyclist, formed the

Colorado Confederation of Clubs, which improved communication between motorcycle clubs and provided a means to avoid conflict. The Sons of Silence MC is the sixth largest 1% MC in the world behind the Hells Angels MC, Bandidos MC, Outlaws MC, Pagans MC and Mongols MC (Sons of Silence Wikipedia).

The AMA Statement That Allegedly Birthed the 1%

The AMA had been the spokes-organization of the MC community since 1924, and by the 1960s it was fighting stereotypes that had been formed against bikers and clubbers since the Hollister riot in 1947. As the AMA's organization of clubs continued to be maligned along with the OMCs and its brand continued to suffer it has been rumored that in 1960 William Berry, a former president of the AMA, said that 99% of motorcyclists were good, decent, law-abiding citizens and that the AMA's ranks of motorcycle clubs were not involved in the debacle of the Hollister riot (Dulaney). This is said to be the statement that led to the term 1% or 1%er that eventually became the calling cry of OMC nations which solidified the 1% diamond patch, and the three-piece patches used today. However, the AMA says it has no record of ever releasing such a statement. Tom Lindsay, the AMA's Public Information Director, said 'We [the American Motorcyclist Association] acknowledge that the term 'one-percenter' has long been (and likely will continue to be) attributed to the American Motorcyclist Association, but we've been unable to attribute its original use to an AMA official or published statement—so it's apocryphal.' What is true and what is rumor will never be known. What is certain is that a new symbol of the "Outlaw" biker club was to be born that would go beyond the diamond 13 and the three-piece back patch. It would be the diamond 1%(er) the ultimate symbol of OMC nations.

The 1% Diamond Created by the Hells Angels MC

The impetus for 1%ers to create the diamond may not have started with the AMA statement at all as the timeline for the development of the 1%er diamond is rumored to have occurred in late 1957 or early 1958. On the Hells Angels' Instagram and Facebook pages it is stated:

> "In late 1957, or early 1958, the President of the Frisco Hells Angels, Frank Sadilek, had a meeting with leaders of other motorcycle clubs in the Bay Area. At this meeting the 1% diamond was created. This hand drawn diamond was the very first one. All of the Clubs on this list are the first Clubs to consider themselves 1%ers. To everyone out there that considers themselves a 1%er and makes the choice to wear that diamond, know that The Hells Angels created it. (Hells Angels Frisco Instagram)"

In a picture circulated on the internet reported to be the original hand drawn design, the diamond closely resembles the United States Marine Corps 1st Marine Division's diamond insignia with an incredibly similar red "1" in the middle in nearly the same font. The % sign sits to the right of the red "1" about a quarter of the size. Under it are the capital letters ER. The name of the clubs who had come to the meeting and agreed to wear it were written on the picture along with the colors their diamonds would be:

- Roaring Twenties – Richmond Black on Red – 10
- Road Rats – Black on White
- Skull Riders White on Black 20
- ~~Gypsy Jokers Black on~~ (scratched out)
- Presidents Yellow on Red
- Gooses – Purple on Yellow
- Angels – Red on White
- Vampires – Green on White 30
- Rattlers – Orange on White 20
- Mofos – White on Green 12

On the back of the drawing further notes were listed:

- Angels 0 Red on White
- Vampires – Green on White
- Rattlers – Orange on White
- Presidents – Yellow on Red
- Roaring 20's – Black on Red
- Mofos – White on Green
- Skull Riders – White on Black
- Road Rats – Black on White
- Slo-Mo-Suns – Black on Yellow (~~Gold on Black~~)
- ~~Gypsy Jokers – White on Black~~
- ~~Skull Riders~~
- WEBB – Blue on Gold
- Sacramento – Purple on White
- Gene – Blue on White
- Willie Powell – Green on Purple
- Gooses – Purple on Yellow
- Links – Gold on Purple
- Black 13's – Red on Black ~~Black on Green~~

These clubs listed above are said to be the first to wear the diamond which Hells Angels MC claims started in California (Hells Angels Frisco Instagram).

Outlaws MC the first to Wear Diamond on the East Coast

According to Wikipedia, in 1963, the Outlaws MC begin wearing a diamond shaped 1%er patch, becoming the first club east of the Mississippi River to do so (AOA Outlaws MC Wikipedia).

The 1%(er) Diamond Ultimate 1% OMC Symbol

The "1%" or 1%er diamond patch is the ultimate symbol associated with OMCs and is worn as a badge of honor by members who consider themselves outside the bounds of mainstream society and reject its authority. It serves as a way for club members to differentiate themselves from mainstream motorcycle riders and to assert their independence, nonconformity and dominance.

Note: *It is worth noting that while the 1% patch represents the highest level an OMC can attain, not all members of these clubs engage in criminal activities. The patch is primarily a symbol of defiance, camaraderie, and a shared subculture, rather than an indicator of illegal behavior. However, it has been associated with the outlaw image and is often viewed with suspicion by law enforcement and the general public.*

OMCs Summary

In the 1950s and 1960s, OMCs became a symbol for the younger, rebellious generation. They were more concerned with having a good time than with carrying out ongoing criminal efforts. By the late 1960s things began to change. OMCs operated outside the boundaries of traditional MC culture creating a sense of fear and fascination in the public eye. In the late 1960s, they spawned imitators; larger groups absorbed smaller groups; and roaming members, called nomads, carried the seeds of the clubs forming new chapters and alliances. Organized structures were formalized, and club leaders emerged. Though OMCs were more capable of significant criminal activity in the 1960s, they lacked focus. They would get that focus starting in the next decade.

The Rise of African American Clubs 40s – 60s

African Americans have a long history of using motorcycles as a means of personal expression and freedom since the beginning of motorcycles in the country. Motorcycles provided a platform for African Americans to assert their independence and challenge societal norms. The first recorded African American MCs began to appear after WWII with African American veterans returning home from the war. In the late 40s and early 50s many of these MCs were formed as drill teams (HarleyLiberty.com and Walters). They would get together and perform group routines consisting of stunts, maneuvers, races, and trick riding. They held meets and competed for scores against other African American bikers in their own communities (HarleyLiberty.com and Walters).

Bessie Stringfield and the Iron Horse MC

Bessie Stringfield was an African American woman who was an important contributor to the country's biker culture as a woman biker and in many other important aspects. Her accomplishments were legendary, and she is still a highly celebrated figure on the Black biker set. On Harley-Davidson motorcycles, in the 1930s and '40s, she rode across the United States eight times including through the Jim Crow South, alone—without external support (Maisano). Often, she had to sleep on her motorcycle at a "filling station" as gas stations used to be called then, or in other places. "If you had black skin, you couldn't get a place to stay," Stringfield said. "I knew the Lord would take care of me and He did. If I found Black folks, I'd stay with them." During WWII she worked for the U.S. Army as a civilian motorcycle courier. Following the war, she founded Iron Horse MC and earned the nickname "The Motorcycle Queen of Miami" (Maisano). Iron Horse MC excelled at drill team routines and trick riding.

State Burners MC

The State Burners MC, still in existence today with various chapters on the East Coast, began in 1945 with three anonymous bikers in Atlantic City who enjoyed the sport of riding motorcycles (StateBurners-woodbridge.com). They would frequently cross the bridge that connected Philadelphia and New Jersey and do "burnouts" in the oil at the base of the bridge, originating from the name "Old Burners" (StateBurners-woodbridge.com). Every weekend Coffee, Cheyenne, Boddie, Spartacus, and Peter Gun rode to Philadelphia to party with Big Daddy, June and Maverick. Freddie "Coffee" Carter led the riders, who all enjoyed stunt riding. In November 1946, Freddie "Coffee" Carter founded an MC with seven original members who were known for racing, trick riding, partying and "burning rubber from state to state." Coffee decided to name the club "State Burner's MC (StateBurners-woodbridge.com)."

Cycle Queens of America MC

The Cycle Queens of America MC, was perhaps the first all-female mixed-race MC started in Philadelphia by African American women in 1955 (Woods). The Cycle Queens of America was founded to provide women with the opportunity to ride motorcycles and participate in the male dominated motorcycle culture (OLDEST.org). Cycle Queens of America was groundbreaking at the time because it challenged the gender stereotypes of the era and paved the way for women's participation in the sport of motorcycling (OLDEST.org). "We started because one of our members bought a motorcycle from a dealer whose wife was a Motor Maid. She tried to get her African American friend into the Motor Maids, but they were not having it, because America was segregated then, said Vera (Woods). "That's when we said we were starting our own MC, but we made the decision that we would be integrated unlike the other clubs. We had white women and others in our club and chapters across the country all the way to California, said Vera (Woods). Their uniforms were red and white, and they often won all of the AMA trophies at the gypsy tours (Woods) (Cycle Queens of America Wiki). Cycle Queens of America MC was an AMA chartered corporation (Cycle Queens of America Wiki).

The Rise of African American "Outlaw" Culture

Many of the early clubs rode full dressers, as they were called in the day, and though outlawed by the AMA, because of its "Whites only" policies, most of the early African American clubs operated like the family MCs and racing MCs recognized by the AMA. But a new wind was blowing for returning African American vets and the younger crowd joining clubs. This wind would blow in the embracement of outlaw MC "bad boy" counterculture among African American MCs. Many of these bikers favored the "chopped" style motorcycle instead of the full dressers, cutoff denim jackets and their swarthy "No one messes with me" attitude. This non-conformist movement among African American MCs truly represented the word "Outlaw!" And it would begin to take shape in the mid to late 1950s eventually leading some of them on the path from "Outlaw" clubs to becoming today's definition of OMCs and ultimately to becoming 1% OMC nations themselves.

African American Outlaw Cultural Expression and Identity

The "Outlaw" subculture offered an avenue for African American clubbers to embrace their identity, express their individuality, and form communities based on shared experiences and interests. The rise can be attributed to various factors, including social and cultural shifts, a desire to establish their own "Outlaw" biker culture apart from the culture of the established Black family clubs, drill teams, racing clubs, the AMA and White "Outlaws," a desire for autonomy, protection from Jim Crow laws in the deep South and a sense of community among African American club brothers.

The Influence of African American MCs on African American OMCs and 1%ers

Established "Family" clubs, traditional MCs and "Outlaw" African American MCs paved the way for the establishment of what would eventually become Black 1% OMC nations. On the East and West coasts these MCs would become legendary on the Black biker set. Some would die out, some would stay "Outlaws" and others, from that base, would become 1% OMC nations and spurn the birth of others. On the East Coast clubs like Iron Horse MC, State Burners MC, Hells Lovers MC, Sin City Deciples MC, Thunderguards MC, Outcast MC and Wheels of Soul MC, were putting it down. Meanwhile, on the West Coast the nation would witness Flamingos MC, Buffalo Riders MC, Star Riders MC, Cobras MC, King Cobras MC, Frisco Rattlers MC, East Bay Dragons MC, Chosen Few MC, Richmond Road Runners MC, Vagabonds MC, Choppers MC, and LA Defiant Ones MCs rise in stature.

African American OMCs and the 1% Diamond

When the Hells Angels designed the 1% diamond patch it is said they had a meeting with the worthy clubs in the area to disseminate it to those who could hold it down. Many of the White clubs adopted it, many Black clubs stayed far away from such an audacious symbol that would bring law enforcement scrutiny down on top of them (Lil-Man-1%er). Law enforcement intimidation and aggression was already high towards African American men during the beginning of the civil rights era in 1954, so it didn't make sense to a lot of African American OMCs to put that beacon on their chests. Though invited to wear it, most stayed away preferring the strategy of keeping a low profile. Decades later, this standard began to change among the new breed particularly as African American OMCs started to spread across the country to become national powers expanding beyond the state and regional powers they had been before. They were running into problems associated with not being recognized as true OMCs because the news media, Hollywood and folklore had largely omitted them from the historic narrative focusing instead on the glorification of the 1% diamond which was worn by all the top OMC White clubs. Proving that the strategy of keeping a low profile employed by the OGs of the African American clubs in the early years had worked! Most of America had no idea there were Black dominant OMCs out there regardless of the fact that some wore the 1%. Even long running television shows like "*Sons of Anarchy*" failed to include their stories. But with the expansionism of African American OMCs the new breed no longer wanted to maintain a low profile. They wanted to be seen and recognized by the 1% standard and began demanding their clubs embrace the symbol that indicated they controlled the landscape in their respective territories for all to see and understand. But there is still quite a bit of resistance in these clubs among the OGs and purists even today who still refuse to wear the 1% diamond. During a conversation I once had with an OG of a major African American 1% OMC, he said, "I was never and will never wear that [1% diamond]. Our thing was always to keep a low profile not broadcast to the world. If I'm riding next to a brother wearing that 1%er diamond, and we both get pulled over and the cops want to ask questions—it's going to be that 1%er diamond wearer that will draw his interest. He's going to tell me to keep on riding, but that 1%er cat will be held back for 'questioning.' Hell no, I'll never wear that. People know who we are—we don't need no diamond to tell them." Therefore, it is not uncommon to see hardliners in some of the old school African American 1% OMCs who still refuse to wear the diamonds although the younger members do.

Frisco Rattlers MC

By most accounts, the Frisco Rattlers in early 1954 was the first "Outlaw" and eventually the first African American 1% OMC, preferring more stripped-down versions of the Harley-Davidson over the full dresser [to become known as the chopper]. Their name is listed along with the first OMCs to ever wear the 1% diamond introduced by the Hells Angels in 1958.

Richmond Road Runners MC

Late 1955 would mark the first appearance of the Richmond Road Runners MC.

LA Defiant Ones (D.O.s)

One of the most continuously operated African American MCs would come out of the Watt's section of Los Angeles, The LA Defiant Ones MC, known as the "D.O.s" was established in 1959. It is an all-Black MC that requires its members to ride American made motorcycles only. The motto of the "L.A.D.O.s" is "The Power of Togetherness." John 'PeeWee' McCollum one of the godfathers of Black biker culture in LA, is a founding member of L.A. Defiant Ones MC, and served as the President for many years. Today the L.A.D.O. still holds an open house every Friday with drinks, food, dancing and brotherhood.

Chosen Few MC

The Chosen Few MC (CFMC) is the first mixed-race, however, predominantly African American 1% OMC in the US. It was established from the mind of "The Father" Lionel Ricks in Los Angeles, California, in 1959 who gathered a founding group of African American riders who shared a passion for motorcycles and brotherhood. The founding members were Lionel, Lil Frank, Roger, Hawk, Slim, Shirly Bates, and Champ (Chosen Few MC Wikipeda). The purpose of the club was to ride and enjoy the new Black biker set in Los Angeles and Oakland, California (Chosen Few MC Wikipeda). Their first White member joined in 1960. The Chosen Few MC played a significant role in shaping the Black OMC culture, particularly on the West coast. It also served as a pioneering club that paved the way for the establishment of other African American motorcycle clubs in subsequent years. Today the Chosen Few MC is a 1% OMC nation and has expanded nationally. Additional chapters have been established in various locations internationally to include chapters in the Philippines (ChatGPT Artificial Intelligence).

East Bay Dragons MC

The East Bay Dragons MC is an All-Black all-male, all-Harley Davidson riding MC founded in Oakland, California, by Tobie Gene Levingston in 1959 (East Bay Dragon MC Wikipedia). The son of sharecroppers, Levingston, moved from Louisiana to Oakland and wanted something to keep his younger brother and friends off the rough streets of Oakland so he created a car club (East Bay Dragon MC Wikipedia). The car club adopted the official name "Dragons Car Club" in 1958. After numerous brawls with local East and West Oakland street gangs the Oakland Police Department began a campaign of harassment against the club. Levingston considered disbanding the car club, but long-time friend Sonny Barger, founder of the Oakland chapter of the Hells Angels MC, suggested he switch the club to an MC because bikes were more discrete than cars, easier to maintain and cheaper to work on (East Bay Dragon MC Wikipedia). The East Bay Dragons MC was launched in 1959.

Vagabonds MC

The Vagabonds MC originated in 1966 in Oakland, California (Vagabonds MC Instagram). At one time their clubhouse was in Richmond California.

Choppers MC

The Choppers MC, an all-Black, all Harley, OMC originated in Los Angeles, California in 1996 (Choppers MC Instagram). It was formed by men who lived life on the other side of the law which is why they were outlaws (Dobbs). Many lived on the West side and were pimps and hustlers (Dobbs). In an interview with "Chopper Tuggy" he said, "We didn't have to put a 1% diamond on. Black men during that time already had a target on our backs. We didn't need one on our chests too. Plus, if you were wearing that diamond you weren't really riding cross-country much. If you tried you would get hassled the entire way. Besides, our patches on our backs told the story of our outlaw culture, if you were smart enough to recognize what you saw. First of all, our colors fall within an Interstate symbol which let you know we rode miles. There were 43 original members so there are 43 links in our chain. There is a lock on the end of that chain because there was a time that we wouldn't let any more than 43 members in the club. But there is also a key on the patch, above the helmet, to unlock the chain to allow members in and out. And the ape hanger handlebars meant that you were in an outlaw club at that time because only outlaws rode with those handlebars. The axes had two meanings. The first is what we called our bikes back then. We called them axes because they were chopped. And that was the second meaning of the axes. They stood for chopped motorcycles like all of ours were. The axes were a metaphor for chopping our bikes up and making them choppers. The helmet is because we wore helmets when no one else did. And one of our founding members was Bobby Johnson, who was once a member of Chosen Few and East Bay Dragons (Dobbs). If you knew us when you saw our patches you understood that we don't broadcast and never needed that 1% diamond. Because many of us were pimps and hustlers back in the day we were already outlaws anyway (Dobbs)." In 1970 one of the Bikeploitation films of the day was made about the club called "Black Angels MC" that had actual Choppers members in it.

Buffalo Riders MC

Buffalo Riders MC, not to be confused with Buffalo Soldiers MC, was founded sometime in the late 1940s to early 1950s in Los Angeles, California. They wore buffalo horns protruding out of their helmets (Dobbs).

Star Riders MC

The Star Riders MC was one of the biggest African American MCs in Los Angeles that was started sometime in the late 1940s to early 1950s. Some of the members were Silver Kid, Booker, Speedy High, Big Black Sam, JB, and Joe Willie Hall. They wore uniforms that were so sharp that they won all of the best dressed competitions back in the day (Dobbs)

Soul Brothers MC

The Soul Brothers MC was officially established in East Palo Alto, California in 1967 (onepercenterbikers.com). Leading up to the founding a small group of friends had been riding together for approximately three years prior. Making the club rather unique at the time was the fact that they were a mixed-race club from their inception, with a mix of black and white members from day one. Considering that this was the late 1960s, this was unusual for an OMC. The club's first official run was on Labor Day of 1967 with a total of 57 members participating (onepercenterbikers.com). The founding father was James "Heavy" Evans (Lil-Man-1%er)—whom I was blessed to spend an entire day with as a prospect somewhere in the desert at his clubhouse. He taught me so much on that day that I have carried with me to this day, some of which I convey to you in this manual. Therefore, his legend lives on as his knowledge continues to pass. The Soul Brothers today are a 1% OMC nation having put on the 1% diamond in the mid to late 2000s, with chapters spread nationwide.

Outcast MC

Across the United States there were many others such as the Outcast MC, established in 1969 in Detroit Michigan (Hughson). It also laid the foundation for the development of Black OMC culture in the East U.S. (ChatGPT Artificial Intelligence). It is an all-Black all-male, all-American made motorcycle 1% OMC that does not allow White male membership, founded by a group of rebellious black bikers who decided that freedom, non-conformity and brotherhood were not exclusive to Whites only (Hughson). At the time (and still today) blacks were not permitted to join white outlaw biker clubs, so out of necessity the Outcast MC was born (Hughson). Their motto is, "We ride for Piece" which is represented by a middle finger flying with wings on it. This was said to be their diamond for decades until they adopted the 1% diamond in the mid-2,000s. All motorcycles in their club must be painted black.

Wheels of Soul MC

The Wheels of Soul MC was established in Philadelphia, Pennsylvania, in 1967. It was founded by "Coffee" and a group of African American riders who shared a passion for motorcycles and brotherhood (Wheels of Soul MC Wikipedia). Though multiracial in its composition it operates primarily on the Black Biker set and is therefore considered an African American OMC. It has subsequently gained recognition as one of the prominent African American 1% OMCs in the United States (ChatGPT Artificial Intelligence). With one chapter in Puerto Rico and chapters in at least 25 states, they claim to be the first East Coast OMC to put on the 1% diamond on the Black MC set sometime in the early 1970s (Wheels of Soul MC Wikipedia).

Sin City Deciples

Sin City Deciples MC, also known as Sin City Nation, was founded in Gary, Indiana, in 1966. It was founded to allow minorities such as African American, and other racially segregated communities into the space held by traditional 1% outlaw all-white clubs (SCDNation.com). As one of the most well-known and oldest black outlaw motorcycle clubs in the United States, they have multiple chapters across the nation and have an additional presence in Canada, Europe, Asia, Australia, and South America. Additionally, the organization has many support clubs in across the U.S. in select states (Sin City MC Wikipedia). The club demands that its brothers ride American made steel such as Harley-Davidson motorcycles, however men who ride sport bikes can join their sibling club, Sin City Titans MC, which is their racing division (Sin City MC Wikipedia).

Hell's Lovers MC

Hell's Lovers MC is a multi-ethnic MC founded in Chicago in 1967. One of the first integrated biker clubs in Chicago, the club was founded by Frank "Claim-Jumper" Rios after he was denied membership in another motorcycle club possibly because he was a Mexican American, so he decided to start his own club along with friends including Andrew "Poolie" Poole (Hells Lovers MC Wikipedia) (One Percenter Bikers). Hell's Lovers are active in various US states. The club's motto is, "Death is my sidekick and the highway is my home." A 0% diamond is worn in place of the traditional 1% (Hells Lovers MC Wikipedia).

Thunderguards MC

The Thunderguards MC originated in 1965 in Wilmington, Delaware. One of the club's founders, "Buckie", was responsible for giving the club its name. The first members and founders of the Thunderguards were: Buckie, Junkyard, Fishman, Billy C., Charlie, Gordie, and Cuppie (Prezi.com). The group of men to join next were given the title of "7%ers", they were Big Leonard, Joe, Lensey, Marvin, Sonny, Sam and Soul man (One Percenter Bikers). Today the Thunderguards MC is a 1% OMC nation.

Today's African American MCs and the AMA

Many African Americans MCs refused to join after the AMA dropped its "White's only" policy because by then they had already established thriving communities, events, racing culture, traditions and customs and no longer needed what they had never received from the AMA in the first place. Consequently, even today African American clubs largely stay away from the AMA. In 1995, AMA President Ed Youngblood said that as a consequence of its racist policies from 1924 to the 1950's, Black MCs continued to be underrepresented in AMA events for decades after the segregationist policy was rescinded (AmericanMotorcyclist.com).

African American Social and Political Climate:

With the emerging civil rights movement of the 1950s and 1960s, segregation and the broader social and political climate played a significant role in the rise of Black OMCs. African Americans were fighting for equal rights, autonomy, and self-determination. OMCs offered a sense of empowerment and sometimes armed resistance against oppressive systems. They provided a space where Black riders could assert their freedom, challenge stereotypes, exude MC dominance within their regions, and create their own rules and standards. They could also rebel against society and "the Man."

Black Pride in African American OMCs

Throughout the 1950s and 1960s, Black OMCs fostered a sense of brotherhood, encouraged motorcycle riding, and represented Black pride and self-determination. Though they came after Black family clubs they assumed the mantle as the big brothers of the MC set, establishing themselves at the top of the food chain of MCs on equal footing with the White OMCs that ran White MCs on the "other side of the fence."

Community and Support Networks of Black OMCs

Black OMCs served as a community support network, offering camaraderie, mentorship, and resources to their members. They provided a sense of belonging and solidarity, especially in the face of racial discrimination and marginalization. Black OMCs organized rides, social events, and community outreach initiatives, contributing positively to their local communities and challenging negative stereotypes associated with traditional OMCs.

Cultural Impact and Representation of Black OMCs

The rise of Black OMCs many of which eventually became Black 1% OMCs, had a cultural impact in new areas of the U.S. as they spread across the country. They insisted that they alone act as the governing bodies of all Black and mixed raced predominately Black MCs and MC protocols were enacted that dictated when White diamonds had problems with Black 99%er MCs, they would settle those problems through Black OMCs first and not take direct action on Black and predominately mixed-race Black MCs. Thus, the emergence of Black OMCs played a significant role in diversifying the MC landscape and providing a space for Black riders to celebrate their identity, autonomy, and brotherhood in peace and safety.

Greaser Subculture:

The 1950s and 1960s saw the emergence of various motorcycle subcultures, each with their unique identity and style. One such notable subculture was the "greasers" or "rockers," characterized by their love for motorcycles, leather jackets, and rock 'n' roll music.

These subcultures had their own clubs and gatherings, often associated with a particular fashion style and rebellious attitude. They represented a countercultural movement, challenging societal norms and embracing a sense of freedom and nonconformity.

The Bob-Job Era, 1946—1959

Before there were choppers, there was the "bobber." A "bobber" is a motorcycle that has been "bobbed" (or relieved of excess weight by removing parts) with the intent of making the bike lighter and faster or at least to make it look better in the eyes of a rider seeking a more minimalist ride. In post–WWII United States, servicemen returning home from the war started removing all parts deemed too big, heavy, ugly, or not essential to the basic function of the motorcycle. This included fenders, turn indicators, and even front brakes. The large, spring-suspended saddles were also removed in order to sit as low as possible on the motorcycle's frame. These machines were lightened to improve performance for dirt-track racing and mud racing and were an important part of the hotrod culture that developed in this era (Chopper Wikipedia).

Motorcycle Racing

Motorcycle racing continued to be popular throughout the 1950s and 1960s. Road racing, motocross, and dirt track racing gained significant attention, with skilled riders competing in national and international competitions. The Isle of Man TT race continues to be a prestigious event attracting talented riders from around the world. Legendary racers such as Mike Hailwood, Giacomo Agostini, and Barry Sheene made their mark during this era, captivating motorcycle enthusiasts and inspiring a new generation of riders.

Motorcycle Culture in Popularity:

The 1950s and 1960s marked a period of increased popularity and fascination with motorcycles and motorcycle culture. The release of iconic films like "The Wild Ones" (1953) starring Marlon Brando and "Easy Rider" (1969) starring Peter Fonda and Dennis Hopper further fueled the interest in motorcycles and the rebellious image associated with them. Motorcycles became symbols of freedom, adventure, and individuality, attracting a wider range of enthusiasts and creating a sense of intrigue around MCs and the biker lifestyle. Overall, the 1950s and 1960s were a transformative period for MCs. Mainstream clubs continued to promote recreational riding and community engagement, while OMCs and MC subcultures challenged societal norms and captured public attention with their rebellious image. These decades laid the foundation for the diverse motorcycle culture we see today.

1970s-1980s

The 1970s and 1980s were marked by a mix of mainstream MCs, the increasing violence of OMCs, the rise of new motorcycle subcultures and the push for safety and legislation.

The Vietnam War and its Affect on OMCs 70s – 80s

During this time yet another US war would spit out its PTSD traumatized, untreated, and weary veterans from its battlefields to the streets of the US, who would eventually find homes in the country's OMCs (Shaggy 1%er). These returning soldiers did not come home to parades and heroes' welcomes instead they returned to protest marches and were spat upon while being called, "baby killers!" It was the conflict known as the Vietnam war and the illicit use of drugs on the battlefield also followed these vets home and brought the drug trade to the OMCs' doorsteps to support and fuel the habits many had developed while supporting their country. Many old-timers I've spoken with remarked, "This is when many 1%ers stopped being outlaws and started being gangsters and drug dealers (Shaggy 1%er) which had been previously against all clubs' bylaws. Clubs just got too obsessed with the money and, of course, everything that goes with that kind of money, came to the clubs (Invader Shaggy 1%er). The competition for drug profits, territory, distribution networks, the lucrative nature of the drug trade, other illicit activities, club ideology, and personal vendettas between club members was marked by a series of conflicts and wars among various 1% OMCs. These wars were quite bloody.

The 1% OMC Wars

Most notable of the conflicts between 1% OMC nations were those between the Hells Angels and the Outlaws MCs. These conflicts primarily occurred in the United States and Canada but also had ripple effects in other parts of the world. These wars included shootings, bombings, and ambushes resulting in casualties among club members and innocent bystanders leading to heightened public and law enforcement scrutiny and the transformation of their reputations as bad boys acting out into legitimately feared OMCs as they are seen as today.

Outlaw Bikers vs Outlaw Biker Criminals

The wars between 1% OMCs and their criminal activities fueled by men seeking power, wealth, and greed blurred the line for many, especially those outside of the biker club community and in law enforcement, between the meaning of being an outlaw biker in an outlaw MC and being a criminal biker in a 1% OMC where some members are drug dealers, gun runners, pimps, murderers, and conspirators, but most members are not. The line became increasingly fuzzy when the actions of a few caused many entire 1% nations to be classified as Outlaw Motorcycle Gangs (OMGs) by the Department of Justice (DOJ) and vast governmental resources were expended and new laws written to arrest, prosecute, and imprison these problematic OMCs. As a result, today when someone says, "Outlaw Biker" or "Outlaw MC" folks immediately think of killers in OMGs and not bikers who embrace freedom and shun society's norms and live life by a different standard than what is recognized generally by the public in MCs. This type of lifestyle is not illegal it is just different, referred to as "being an outlaw" In biker circles. So, for the record, there are outlaw bikers in outlaw clubs that are members of OMCs and 1%ers in 1%er OMC nations that are also outlaws that have no dealings in criminality whatsoever. And then there are brothers in those same clubs who do.

Ideological Differences

Ideological differences also contributed to the conflicts between OMCs. Each club had its own set of values, rules, and codes of conduct. Conflicts often occurred when these ideologies clashed. Some clubs maintained a strict hierarchy and adhered to a code of conduct within their club while others had a more decentralized structure and resisted the dominance of larger clubs. These ideological differences, combined with the desire to expand their influence and protect their clubs' reputations heightened tensions and led to violent confrontations.

Hollywood Cashes in on 1% OMC Culture

As many outlaw clubs started to transform into 1% OMCs resulting in wars with one another, railing more against society, falling under increased police scrutiny, embracing violence, selling guns and selling drugs, the old demons from the Hollister Riot continued to echo making society began to be more apprehensive if not terrified of them. MCs couldn't shake the negative stereotypes new reports and articles portrayed of them. The emerging biker club wars from the 1960s through the 1980s depicted on the evening news further damaged the reputation of bikers and bikers in clubs. But nothing was more devastating than the Hollywood movies of the time.

Bikesploitation Films

Hollywood and filmmakers worldwide discovered a financial bonanza in making sensationalized "bikesploitation" movies depicting clubs taking over towns, raping, and pillaging women while terrorizing citizens, this led to the greatest scrutiny against MCs. Starting in the 1960s and throughout the 1970s biker films became one of the most popular staples for drive-ins and grindhouses (GrindhouseDatabase.com). They were essentially a reinvention of all the Westerns that moviegoers loved made for a new generation. These movies told stories of modern rebels and outlaws who roared across the country on two wheels instead of on the backs of four legged beasts. The films delivered all kinds of thrills while taking viewers on wild adventures with the rambunctious gangs of cycle savages who lived life on their own terms (GrindhouseDatabase.com). The anti-hero bikers fought the Fuzz, brawled in bars, drank in droves and got high as hell as they rode the open roads on their hot steel hogs. While the humdrum hippies of the era promoted peace and love, the boisterous bikers seemed to be all about anarchy and mayhem. The roving bands of badass papas and mamas brought their own kind of outrageous counterculture escapism to the silver screen, and it was met with much fanfare (GrindhouseDatabase.com). But these movies burned negative images of MCs and outlaw biker culture into the minds of societies worldwide and indelibly turned them against all clubs as much as OMCs railed against society. The Hells Angels MC was possibly maligned the most as so many of those movies included "Hell(s)" or "Angel(s)" in some part of their titles. But it was probably part of what made that club one of the most famous and well known in history. Still, King of the B rated movies filmmaker Roger Corman claimed the club threatened to kill him for his depiction of them in his wildly successful low budget 1966 drama "The Wild Angels," which was one of the highest grossing B films of all time. During a videotaped interview for the Creative Media Master Class at the University of Hawaii West O'ahu (OHWO) November 6th, 2014, with interviewer Dr. Stanley Orr, and in an article written by Stephen Galloway for the Hollywood Reporter on May 5, 2017, Corman said, "The Hells Angels did not like the way they were presented in the movie," [Corman actually hired real members of the club to shoot scenes]. "They announced that they were suing me for $1 million for defamation of character, on the basis [that] I had portrayed them as an outlaw motorcycle gang, whereas they were actually a social organization, dedicated to the spreading of technical information about motorcycles," said Corman. "Then they announced that they were going to kill me." Corman picked up his phone to find the head of the Angels, Otto Friedli, on the line. "Friedli said, 'Hey man, we're going to snuff you out,'" Corman recalled. "And I said, 'Otto, think about this. You have announced publicly that you're going to kill me. If I slip and fall in the bathtub, the police are going to come after you. Plus, you're suing me for $1 million. How do you expect to collect $1 million from me if you kill me? My advice to you is, forget the momentary pleasure of snuffing me out, and go for the $1 million.' He thought a minute and he said, 'Yeah, man, that's what we'll do. We're going to go for the $1 million.' So, I'm still living."

Below is a list, though not exhaustive, of at least three decades of them. You can tell by their titles how they helped to develop extreme prejudice against MCs:

- *The Motorcycle Gang* (1957)
- *The Hot Angel* (1958)
- *Scorpio Rising* (1963)
- *The Leather Boys* (1964)
- *Motorpsycho!* (1965)
- *The Wild Angels* (1966)
- *Hells Angels on Wheels* (1967)
- *The Glory Stompers* (1967)
- *Devil's Angels* (1967)
- *The Born Losers* (1967)
- *The Wild Rebels* (1967)
- *Hell's Chosen Few* (1968)
- *Savages from Hell* (1968)
- *The Savage Seven* (1968)

- *She-Devils on Wheels* (1968)
- *The Hellcats* (1968)
- *The Mini-Skirt Mob* (1968)
- *Angels from Hell* (1968)
- *The Angry Breed* (1968)
- *The Sweet Ride* (1968)
- *Scream Free!* (1969)
- *Sisters in Leather* (1969)
- *Run, Angel, Run!* (1969)
- *Hell's Belles* (1969)
- *The Sidehackers* (1969)
- *Easy Rider (1969)*
- *Satan's Sadists* (1969)
- *The Cycle Savages (1969)*
- *Hell's Angels '69* (1969)
- *Naked Angels* (1969)
- *Devil Rider!* (1970)
- *Hell's Bloody Devils* (1970)
- *Rebel Rousers* (1970)
- *Stray Cat Rock: Delinquent Girl Boss* (1970)
- *The Losers* (1970)
- *Angels Die Hard* (1970)
- *Stray Cat Rock: Wild Jumbo* (1970)
- *Stray Cat Rock: Sex Hunter* (1970)
- *Black Angels* (1970)
- *C.C. and Company* (1970)
- *Stray Cat Rock: Machine Animal* (1970)
- *The Girls from Thunder Strip* (1970)
- *Angel Unchained* (1970)
- *Ride the Hot Wind* (1971)
- *The Jesus Trip (1971)*
- *Psychomania* (1971)

- *The Tormentors* (1971)
- *Stray Cat Rock: Beat '71* (1971)
- *The Hard Ride* (1971)
- *The Peace Killers* (1971)
- *Werewolves on Wheels* (1971)
- *Angels Hard as They Come* (1971)
- *Outlaw Riders* (1971)
- *Wild Riders* (1971)
- *The Proud Rider* (1971)
- *Chrome and Hot Leather* (1971)
- *Bury Me an Angel* (1971)
- *Pink Angels* (1971)
- *Angels' Wild Women* (1972)
- *J.C.* (1972)
- *The Dirt Gang* (1972)
- *The Limit* (1972)
- *Road of Death* (1973)
- *Savage Abduction* (1973)
- *Psychomania* The Death Wheelers (1973)
- *The Black Six* (1973)
- *Stone* (1974)
- *Darktown Strutters* (1975)
- *The Northville Cemetery Massacre* (1976)
- *Cycle Vixens* (1978)
- *Mad Max* (1979)
- *Crazy Thunder Road* (1980)

(GrindhouseDatabase.com)

Law Enforcement Crackdown

The conflicts and criminal activities of 1% OMCs in the 1970s and 1980s drew significant attention from law enforcement agencies.

The escalating violence and public perception of OMCs as criminal organizations prompted increased law enforcement efforts to dismantle these clubs. Government agencies implemented stricter measures, including targeted investigations, surveillance, and arrests, aimed at disrupting the criminal activities of 1% OMCs. These actions often resulted in high-profile court cases and convictions of club members involved in criminal enterprises.

Chopper Subculture

The 1970s and 1980s witnessed the emergence of new popularized and influential motorcycle subcultures. One of the most notable of these subcultures was the "chopper" scene, inspired by the custom-built motorcycles featured in the movie "Easy Rider" (1969) built and engineered by two famous Black bike builders, Ben Hardy and Clifford "Sonny" Vaughs. A chopper is a custom motorcycle which emerged in California in the late 1950s (Chopper Wikipedia). A chopper employs modified steering angles and lengthened forks for a stretched-out appearance. They can be built from an original motorcycle which is modified ("chopped") or built from scratch (Chopper Wikipedia). Chopper enthusiasts modified their motorcycles, often stripping them down and adding custom parts to achieve a unique look. This subculture celebrated individuality, creativity, and a free-spirited attitude towards motorcycle customization (Chopper Wikipedia).

Racing and Competitions

Motorcycle racing continued to thrive during the 1970s and 1980s with road racing, motocross, and dirt track racing gaining popularity attracting both amateur and professional riders. Iconic racers like Kenny Roberts, Freddie Spencer, and Eddie Lawson achieved remarkable success, contributing to the growth of motorcycle racing as a mainstream sport. The increasing televised coverage of races also helped bring the excitement of motorcycle competitions to a broader audience.

Safety and Legislation

The 1970s and 1980s also saw increased effort in promoting motorcycle safety and an introduction of legislation to regulate the industry. Safety organizations and government agencies focused on rider education, helmet laws, and improved road infrastructure to reduce accidents and improve rider safety. These initiatives were aimed to address the growing number of motorcycle riders and the need for responsible riding practices, ensuring a positive public perception of MCs and riders.

Overall, the 1970s and 1980s were a dynamic period for MCs. Mainstream clubs continued to foster a sense of community among riders, outlaw clubs maintained a reputation for independence and new subcultures emerged celebrating customization and individuality. Motorcycle racing flourished and efforts were made to promote safety and legislation to support the growing number of riders.

1990s-Present

From the 1990s to present day, MCs have been marked by both continuity and changes.

1% OMCs Exponential Growth

From the 1990s to the present, OMCs have continued to have a significant impact on motorcycle culture and have seen fluctuations in their numbers and influence.

The 1990s witnessed a proliferation of OMCs, with the existing major clubs expanding their membership and new clubs emerging and popping up on the scene. This growth was fueled by various factors, including the appeal of the biker lifestyle, a sense of rebellion, and the allure of brotherhood and camaraderie. Some would say that possessing the diamond and a three-piece patch has become an irresistible fashion statement to new folks coming onto the sets. With new laws and RICCO predicates being aimed at traditional OMCs who attempt to regulate the set, many standards have been lowered or even dropped. Many clubs that would have never been allowed to wear a diamond are now no longer challenged. New OMCs are appearing every day trying to exert their will and make names for themselves. This causes an unstable environment for everyone.

1% OMC Conflicts and Violence

The 1990s and early 2000s were marked by conflicts and violent clashes between rival OMCs. These conflicts often arose from territorial disputes, competition over criminal activities, or disagreements between club members. Some of these conflicts gained media attention, further enhancing the public perception of OMCs as criminal organizations.

1% OMC Law Enforcement Scrutiny

1% OMCs faced increased scrutiny from law enforcement agencies during this period. Authorities targeted clubs they believed were involved in criminal activities, leading to extensive investigations, arrests, and prosecutions. This scrutiny contributed to ongoing legal battles and attempts to label certain clubs as organized crime groups. In one instance the Mongols MC was targeted for 11 years by federal authorities that took them to court in an attempt to use civil asset forfeiture and trademark laws to confiscate their colors. The club was able to keep their colors, but they were fined and faced other serious sanctions for portions of the case where they did not prevail. Their legal bills were extensive, and a lesser club would have been crushed fighting their legal battles.

1% OMC Internal Changes and Leadership Shifts

1% OMCs continue to experience internal changes, including leadership shifts and power struggles with some clubs seeing a rise in new leaders, while others faced challenges in maintaining their traditional structures and values. These internal dynamics affected the direction and operations of the clubs.

1% OMC Global Reach

1% OMCs expanded their reach globally during this period, establishing international chapters and forming alliances with other clubs around the world. The globalization of OMCs allowed for increased networking, collaboration, and exchange of ideas and resources. It also allowed illegal activities to flourish internationally for some clubs.

1% OMCs Influence on Popular Culture

1% OMCs continued to capture public attention through their portrayal in popular culture, including movies, television shows, and books. These depictions, although often sensationalized in shows like *"Sons of Anarchy,"* contributed to the perception of OMCs as symbols of rebellion, freedom, and the outlaw lifestyle.

1% OMCs Decline in Numbers

While the popularity of 1% OMCs remained significant, some clubs experienced a decline in membership during the late 2000s and early 2010s. Factors such as increased law enforcement pressure, changing societal attitudes, and the aging of club members have been cited as possible reasons for this decline.

1% OMCs Persistence and Resilience

Despite challenges and fluctuations in membership, 1% OMCs have demonstrated resilience and have maintained their presence within the motorcycle subculture. Certain clubs have even expanded their activities beyond traditional criminal pursuits, focusing on charity work, community involvement, and organizing motorcycle events.

1% OMCs Growth and Diversification

1% OMCs continued to grow in numbers and diversity. Not only did OMCs such as the Hells Angels, Outlaws, Bandidos, Outcast, Chosen Few, and Wheels of Soul expand their presence, but new 1% OMCs also emerged, catering to younger bikers with new interests and ideas about operating their brotherhoods.

Popularity of Riding Groups

In addition to traditional MCs, riding groups and social clubs became more prevalent. These groups often focused on riding together, promoting camaraderie, and organizing charitable events or community initiatives.

Women in Motorcycle Clubs

The 1990s to the present witnessed a notable increase in the participation of women in MCs. More women became members of both coed and women-only clubs, challenging the male-dominated image of MCs and fostering a more inclusive environment. Throughout their history, women's MCs have served as social networks, fostering camaraderie, and providing a sense of belonging for riders. They continue to be an integral part of the motorcycling culture in the US, offering opportunities for like-minded women to connect and share their passion for motorcycles. MC set coalitions have even become more receptive to allowing female MCs a seat on their councils whereas in previous times women were often not even allowed to speak in these meetings. Times are changing and women are being recognized!

Riding for a Cause

Many MCs and riding groups became actively involved in charity work and community service. They organized fundraising events, toy runs, and rides to support various causes, showcasing the positive impact of the motorcycle community.

Evolving Riding Styles and Subcultures

Since the 1990s, there has been an emergence in various riding styles and subcultures, such as sport bike riders, adventure riders, café racer enthusiasts, and custom bike builders. These subcultures formed their own communities and clubs, contributing to the diverse landscape of motorcycle culture.

Globalization of Traditional MCs, alternative Biker Groups and Law Enforcement MCs (LEMCs)

Traditional and law enforcement MCs expanded their presence beyond national boundaries as well during this period. The Blue Knights LEMC, for instance, became one of the largest MCs in the world with over 16,000 members internationally, and hundreds of chapters in countries worldwide. Other biker groups like the Ruff Ryders are also international organizations with thousands of members and chapters in countries worldwide. These alliances and chapters of major clubs were established, leading to the formation of global networks and connections between clubs and biker organizations in different countries.

Technology and Social Media Impact

The rise of the internet and social media platforms has allowed MCs and riders to connect, communicate, and organize events more efficiently. It provided a platform for sharing experiences, promoting club activities, and fostering a sense of community.

The Effect of the movie Biker Boyz on the Black biker set

The DreamWorks movie "Biker Boyz," released in 2003, had a heavy impact on the Black club set culture. I was honored to work on the film as a technical advisor and helped bring this iconic movie to the Black biker set and to the world. It told a small story that was part of our biker club experience.

Biker Boyz Storyline

"Biker Boyz" is a mythic motorcycle tale of a father and son, this is the story of Manuel "Pokey" Galloway, also known as "the King of Cali", the president of a MC, whose members are all African American men, mostly white-collar workers who exchange their suits and ties at night and on weekends for leather outfits and motorcycle helmets. The focus of this story takes place at an annual drag-racing event in Fresno, as Manuel tries to retain his championship title (Information Movie Database (IMDB)).

Biker Boyz Increased Visibility

"Biker Boyz" brought greater visibility to the Black motorcycle set culture and showcased the excitement and camaraderie of MCs in the African American community. This exposure helped shed light on a subculture that had not received significant mainstream attention before.

Biker Boyz Inspiration and Empowerment

The movie inspired individuals to join clubs within the Black motorcycle set culture and to pursue their passion for motorcycles more actively. It showcased skilled riders, promoted the spirit of brotherhood, and encouraged Black bikers to chase their dreams and overcome challenges.

Biker Boyz Fashion and Style Influence

"Biker Boyz" contributed to shaping the fashion and style preferences within the Black MC set culture. The movie featured a variety of motorcycle gear, custom bikes, and distinctive aesthetics that influenced the choices and preferences of riders in terms of clothing, accessories, and bike customization of the day.

Biker Boyz Debate and Discussion

The movie sparked debate and discussion within the Black club set culture regarding its portrayal of MCs and the authenticity of the experiences depicted. It encouraged conversations about representation and the dynamics of club life, creating a space for riders to share their perspectives and opinions. Some of the ugly demons of Hollywood bikesplotation tried to rear their ugly heads. For instance, one tagline for the movie on IMDB.com stated:

> "A son of the leader of a legendary group of an urban biker gang tries to retain his championship title."

However, in the movie not one biker gang was depicted or even discussed. Even as a Technical Advisor I couldn't catch it all. But the determination of director Reggie Rock Bythewood to make one of the few African American biker club films a depiction of our greatest attributes, rather than a regurgitation of typical tropes and stereotypes is evident in his portrayal of African Americans entrenched in club life. He created a cult classic and probably to this day isn't even fully aware of how many proud African Americans joined MCs after his beloved movie inspired them to do so. Though the movie received horrible ratings at the time, it has sustained time as a movie with a cult following the nearly every African American riding in a club today swears had a positive impact on them that ultimately led them to biker club life! Which serves as a testament that folks who rate and review movies often have no idea about the impact those movies have on the viewers they were made to attract! Bravo Zulu Reggie Bythewood, Gina Prince Bythewood, Don Kurt, Paul Garnes, Roee Sharon, Tammy Thomas-Garnes and Stephanie Allain.

History of MCs Summary

The history of MCs is diverse and complex, with individual clubs having unique experiences and dynamics. The historical developments mentioned above provide a general overview of the trends and changes that have occurred within the MC culture as a historical reference and is meant to bring you up to speed but is by no means an exhaustive list. There is much more research for you to do to learn even more.

CHAPTER THREE
HOW DO MOTORCYCLE CLUBS OPERATE

Now that you know the history of motorcycles, MCs and how they came about it wouldn't be a bad idea to understand how they operate so that you can matriculate easily around them. This chapter is dedicated to giving you a crash course in MC operations. This information is not exhaustive. For more detailed information about MC protocol and biker set operations, I recommend referencing my other books on these topics and, of course, hanging around a legitimate MC. Nothing will beat the up close and personal experience of tasting the MC life face-to-face. Still, this information will give you a 'basic' working knowledge upon which you can expound. These are observations from my experiences over the past 36 years.

The Makeup of the MC

The greater extended MC family is made up of several components. Not all MCs will have these exact positions or refer to them by the same names. Some will have more, some will have less (depending upon the scope, size, and age of the club); however, you can expect to see your organization look something like this (respectively by order of seniority):

- National Officers (if a national club)
- Regional Officers (if a national or regional club)
- Nomads (if a national, regional, or local club)
- Local Officers (local club or chapter/charter)
- Full patch brothers
- Prospects
- Women's Auxiliary or 'Properties Of'
- Honorary members
- Hang-arounds

- Brother clubs
- Support clubs
- Social Clubs (female support clubs on the Black biker set)
- 'Friends of the Club'
- Supporters

National Officers

National officers will lead a national MC often referred to as the National Executive Board or Committee. You can typically expect to see:

- National President (National)
- National Vice President (National VP)
- National Sergeant at Arms (SAA) or Enforcer
- National Secretary
- National Business Manager
- National Treasurer
- National Road Captain

These are the supreme leaders of the MC. You may hear them called affectionately (or not) "The Nationals" or anyone of them referred to as "National" but that term is generally reserved for the National "P" (Prez) himself. So, it is often acceptable to refer to the National "P" as "National" or anyone you may see wearing a patch indicating "National" on it.

Note: International MCs may have a leadership board one level above nationals and will have the same positions only with the title "International" before the positions.

Responsibilities of the Nationals

The responsibilities of national officers can vary depending on the specific club and its organizational structure. However, there are some common responsibilities you should expect to see:

Leadership

Nationals are responsible for providing leadership and guidance to the club at the national level. They set the overall direction and vision of the club and work to ensure that the club's values, goals, and objectives are upheld.

Governance and Administration

They are involved in the governance and administration of the club. They oversee the club's bylaws, rules, and regulations, ensuring compliance and proper functioning of the organization. They also handle club finances, membership management, and other administration.

Communication and Representation

The National President is the main point of contact and representation for the club at the national level. He communicates with regional officers facilitating the flow of information and ensuring effective communication within the club. He also represents the club in external interactions with other motorcycle clubs, organizations, or the public.

Event Coordination and Planning

National officers coordinate and plan national-level events, such as rallies, rides, or conventions. They work with local chapters to organize these events, ensuring they align with the club's values and provide meaningful experiences for members.

Conflict Resolution

National officers resolve conflicts or disputes within the club and between chapters or charters. They act as mediators and work to find amicable solutions, promoting harmony and unity among members.

Promoting Club Culture and Values

National officers are responsible for upholding and promoting the club's culture, traditions, and values. They foster a sense of camaraderie, brotherhood/brotherhood, and mutual respect among members. They also develop and implement programs or initiatives that align with the club's mission and values.

Growth and Expansion

National officers expand the club's reach by establishing new chapters or affiliations, both domestically and internationally. They evaluate potential new chapters, oversee their formation, and provide guidance to ensure consistency and adherence to the club's standards.

Definition of a National MC

An MC is generally expected to have five chapters or charters in five states and have been in existence for five years before it is recognized as a national MC on the biker club set. And yes, you may know a few clubs that have National Presidents and national officers that don't meet that standard. Often those clubs run into major problems with 1% clubs when they are attempting to expand. But for every so-called rule of MC protocol, there are exceptions so don't be surprised when you see them. It is what it is.

"Chapter" versus "Charter"

The terms "chapter" and "charter" are often used interchangeably in the context of MCs, but they can have slightly different meanings depending on the club and its organizational structure. Some MCs will recognize the differences between a chapter and a charter as follows:

Chapter

In an MC, a chapter refers to a local branch or subdivision of the club that operates within a specific geographical area. A chapter is typically established in a particular city, region, or state. It serves as a local representation of the larger club and operates under the umbrella of the national or international organization. The chapter is usually led by a chapter officer or a chapter President, along with other officers responsible for managing the affairs of the chapter. Chapters often have their own set of bylaws and rules that are in line with the overall club's guidelines.

Charter:

A charter, like a chapter can refer to a local branch or subdivision of a national or regional MC that operates within a specific geographical area, but it most often refers to a branch that largely operates on its own without governance from the central body, National/International President or executive governing board. This structure may protect a club from laws that would make all members guilty of the actions of one or more members if it were in a chapter structure with centralized leadership. The Racketeer Influenced and Corrupt Organizations (RICO) Act is a US federal law that was enacted in 1970. It provides for extended criminal penalties and civil liability for individuals involved in organized crime. RICO is designed to combat racketeering activities, including illegal activities conducted by organized crime groups. Other laws like civil asset forfeiture laws are also designed to target centrally governed MCs. The charter system seeks to avoid those complications by allowing clubs to operate independently without authorization from nationals which frees them, in some instances, from the worries of these laws.

Definition of a Regional MC

A regional MC is a club that may have many chapters/charters in one state or in one region but hasn't grown to the level of a national MC having five chapters/charters in five states.

Definition of a Local MC

A local MC has one chapter in one location. It has a local

- President (Prez)
- VP (VP or Vice Prez)
- Sergeant at Arms (SAA) or Enforcer
- Secretary
- Treasurer
- Business Manager
- Road Captain
- Public Relations Officer (PRO)
- Full patch brothers (full patch sisters in a coed MC)
- Prospects
- Women's auxiliary or 'Properties Of'
- Honorary members
- Hang-arounds
- Brother clubs
- Support clubs
- Social Clubs (female support clubs on the Black biker set)
- 'Friends of the Club'

- Supporters

Note: Not all MCs have road captains, business managers, or PROs. In fact, PROs are almost uniquely on the Black MC set. On other MC sets you'll see the Secretary performing that job.

Traditionally an MC needs five members to get blessed. These members make up the top five officers:

- President (Prez)
- Vice President (VP)
- Sergeant at Arms (SAA) or Enforcer
- Secretary
- Treasurer

Chapter President

The President (or "Prez") of a local chapter is responsible for leading the MC in its direction, traditions, club culture, discipline, public relations, relationships with MCs external to the club and dominant outlaw or 1%er MCs on the set.

In most traditional MCs and 99%er family clubs, the President doesn't vote unless it is to break a tie. This is because more than anything it is his job to reflect in leadership the will and direction of the MC. He is the ultimate servant of the officers and members of the extended family. His job is to deliver to the MC its will as determined by vote. He may provide guidance, leadership, and direction but in the greater scheme of things he is merely a conduit to provide the pathway to ensure the desires of the voting body of the MC are carried out. The voting body of a traditional MC are the full patch brothers in good standing. You may run into an MC with a dictator or strongman as the leader who thinks he is God and is to be obeyed like some kind of king, ruler, or potentate—but that situation is counter to MC protocol and how MCs are properly run.

In some 1% MC nations, and in outlaw MCs things may be run quite differently, however. For instance, you may find that the President is a dictator (not meant derogatorily) with ultimate authority to assign officer positions, lead the direction of the club according to his agenda, mete out discipline, and run the club with complete authority. It is what it is, and the system works well for them because he is still held accountable by his club brothers via the club's bylaws and social construct. If he gets too far out of sorts the brotherhood has ways to deal with him, get him back on track, or delete him.

Note: For detailed information on the President's duties please refer to my book "President's Bible Chronicle I Principles of Motorcycle Club Leadership" and my book "President's Bible Chronicle II Betrayal in the Brotherhood."

Chapter VP

The VP plays a crucial role in supporting the President in the overall management and functioning of the MC and in carrying out his duties. He collaborates closely with him to make decisions, develop strategies, and implement club initiatives. In the absence of the President, the VP will assume his responsibilities and act as the interim leader. The VP assists in overseeing the day-to-day operations of the club. He coordinates club meetings, events, and activities, ensuring that they align with the club's goals and objectives. He is often the "bad" guy being the "heavy" by executing the Prez's orders and initiating discipline so the Prez can remain the "good" guy of the club. The VP ensures the Prez operates in accordance with the club's vote and bylaws. Though he is second in charge of the MC if he does his job correctly, often the club won't notice he even exists. Being a good VP is an art. He is seldom seen or noticed but must be up-to-speed at all times in case he must step in and take the reins if the "P" becomes incapacitated or unable to fulfill his job duties.

Chapter SAA/Enforcer

The Sergeant at Arms (SAA) is an important position within the MC. While the specific responsibilities can vary between clubs, there are some common duties associated with the role of a SAA you can expect:

Club Security

The SAA is responsible for ensuring the security and safety of the club and its members. This includes maintaining vigilance during club meetings, events, and rides to identify and address any potential threats or security issues.

Enforcing Club Rules

The SAA helps enforce the club's bylaws, rules, and codes of conduct. He ensures all members adhere to the established protocols and standards of behavior within the club. This includes addressing any violations or misconduct and taking appropriate disciplinary actions when necessary.

Preserving Club Traditions and Protocols

The SAA upholds the traditions, rituals, and protocols of the club. He ensures that club ceremonies, rites of passage, and secret idioms are conducted with respect and in accordance with the club's bylaws.

Managing Club Property

The SAA oversees the club's property and assets. This can include maintaining and safeguarding club-owned items such as clubhouses, meeting spaces, club equipment, merchandise, and inventories.

External Relations and Security

The SAA represents the club in interactions with other MCs, law enforcement agencies, or the public when it comes to security-related matters. He may coordinate security arrangements for club events and rides and serves as a point of contact for external security concerns.

Conflict Resolution

The SAA assists in resolving conflicts or disputes within the club. He is a mediator, helping to facilitate open communication and finding resolutions that maintain harmony within the club. He also intervenes in situations where conflicts arise during club activities.

Ride Formation and Safety

As I have previously stated, not all clubs have road captains. In those cases, the SAA often plays a role in organizing and leading club rides. He ensures proper ride formation, communicates ride instructions to members, and promotes safe riding practices within the club. He may also coordinate with road captains and assistant road captains or other ride leaders like tail gunners, road guards or others to maintain a cohesive and safe riding experience for the MCs that utilize those positions.

Specific responsibilities and authority of an SAA can vary between MCs. Their exact powers are located in the club's bylaws. The role may also involve additional duties or specific requirements based on the club's culture, size, and internal dynamics. The SAA typically works closely with other club officers and the club's leadership to maintain a strong and unified club environment. In some clubs the President as the SAA specifically pick them will normally be expected to be wherever the President is whenever he moves. In other clubs they are voted in. But next to the President the SAA is perhaps the second most important and powerful officer in the MC.

Note: Refer to my book "Sergeant-at-Arms Bible Soldier/Sergeant of the Brotherhood" for more in-depth information about this position.

Chapter Secretary

The secretary holds a crucial administrative role and is responsible for various tasks related to documentation, communication, and record-keeping. The specific responsibilities may vary between different clubs, but here are some common duties associated with the role of a secretary you may expect to see:

Meeting Coordination

The secretary schedules church, sends out meeting notices to club members, and prepares the meeting agenda.

Meeting Minutes

During church, the secretary takes detailed minutes of the discussions, decisions, and actions taken. These minutes serve as an official record of the meeting and are circulated among club members upon request. The secretary ensures that accurate records are maintained and kept up to date.

Note: Never write anything in a club meeting that could be used against your club in a court of law. Clubs do it and look crazy as Hell when it gets read out to a jury in open court.

Club Correspondence

The secretary handles incoming and outgoing club correspondence and other forms of communication on behalf of the club. He also maintains contact lists of club members and other relevant contacts.

Club Records and Documentation

The secretary is responsible for maintaining important club records and documentation. This can include membership records, bylaws, financial records, event attendance lists, and any other relevant paperwork. He ensures that these records are organized, secure, and easily accessible.

Membership Administration

The secretary manages the MC's membership administration. He oversees membership applications, member emergency contract information and other documentation as needed. He may also manage prospect administration, provide membership requirements documents, and facilitate the onboarding process for newly patched brothers.

Financial Record-Keeping

In some clubs, the secretary may assist in financial record-keeping. He works closely with the treasurer and business manager to maintain accurate records of club finances, including income, expenses, and dues. The secretary may also help prepare financial reports and assist with budget planning and tax preparation.

Reporting and Documentation

The secretary may be responsible for preparing various reports and documentation on behalf of the club. This can include monthly or annual reports, event summaries, membership statistics, or any other documentation required by the club's leadership, governing bodies, or external entities.

General Administration

The secretary may assist in general administrative tasks as needed, such as organizing club files, managing club calendars, and coordinating club-related logistics. He may provide support to other officers and club members with administrative needs or inquiries.

The role of secretary in an MC requires good organizational skills, diligence, and effective communication abilities. He plays a vital role in maintaining club records, facilitating communication, and ensuring smooth administrative operations within the club.

Chapter Treasurer

The treasurer holds a critical role in managing the club's financial affairs and ensuring the proper handling of funds. Here are some common duties associated with the role of a treasurer:

Financial Record-Keeping:

The treasurer is responsible for maintaining accurate and up-to-date financial records for the club. This includes tracking income, expenses, and any other financial transactions. He must ensure that all financial activities are properly documented and recorded.

Budget Planning

The treasurer often plays a key role in budget planning for the club. He collaborates with other club officers to develop a budget that outlines projected income and anticipated expenses. He helps monitor the club's financial performance against the budget and provides financial insights to guide decision-making.

Membership Dues and Finances

The treasurer manages the collection of membership dues and fees from club members. He maintains records of member payments, tracks outstanding dues, and provides regular reports on the club's financial status. He may also work closely with the club secretary and business manager to ensure accurate membership records.

Financial Reporting

The treasurer prepares financial reports and statements for the club's leadership and members. This includes regular reports on income, expenses, account balances, and financial trends. The treasurer presents these reports during club meetings or as requested by the club's governing bodies.

Banking and Financial Transactions

The treasurer handles banking activities on behalf of the club. This involves opening and maintaining a bank account in the club's name, depositing funds, writing checks, or authorizing electronic payments, and reconciling bank statements. The treasurer ensures that financial transactions are conducted securely and in accordance with the club's policies.

Fundraising and Sponsorships

In some cases, the treasurer may be involved in coordinating fundraising efforts or seeking sponsorships for club activities and events. He may collaborate with other club members to identify fundraising opportunities, maintain donor records, and manage funds raised. He may also work within his responsibilities to manage the club's charitable fundraising and giving efforts.

Financial Compliance

The treasurer ensures that the club's financial activities comply with relevant laws and regulations. He may be responsible for filing any necessary tax forms or reports, as well as maintaining proper documentation for auditing or financial review purposes or managing the club's non-profit status.

Financial Planning and Advice

The treasurer provides financial advice and recommendations to the club's leadership. He analyzes financial data, identifies trends, and offers insights to support informed decision-making. The treasurer may also assist in financial planning for future club initiatives, such as purchasing new equipment or organizing larger events.

The role of a treasurer requires financial acumen, diligence, and a strong sense of responsibility. He plays a crucial role in maintaining the financial health of the club, ensuring transparency, and supporting the club's overall objectives.

Chapter Business Manager

The business manager position is very common on the Black MC set but not as popular among outlaw, 1% or White MC sets. The office can be seen as a variation of the treasurer's job and in many MCs his duties will be divided between the treasurer and the secretary. But in clubs that do have the business manager position he typically handles various administrative and operational tasks to ensure the smooth functioning of the club with an emphasis and specialized knowledge of business management as opposed to a secretary who will be more administrative in his specialty, or a treasurer that will be more slanted toward accounting and fiscal responsibility. Here are some common responsibilities associated with the role of a business manager:

Financial Management

The business manager is responsible for overseeing the club's financial affairs. He may manage the club's budget, track income and expenses, manage club investments, handle financial transactions, and ensure that proper financial records are maintained. The business manager may work closely with the treasurer to ensure accurate and transparent fiscal management.

Club Business Operations

The business manager is involved in managing the day-to-day business operations of the club. This can include coordinating meetings, club events and business opportunities. He handles logistics, such as securing venues, buying equipment, and coordinating with external vendors or suppliers as needed.

Club Business Communication

The business manager will be responsible for club communication and correspondence regarding business matters. He handles internal and external business communications on behalf of the club, including emails, newsletters, announcements, and other forms of communication. He ensures that club members are informed of important updates regarding all business matters.

Documentation and Record-Keeping

The business manager maintains club business records and documentation. The business manager ensures that these records are organized, accessible, and up to date.

Business Contracts and Relations

The business manager handles external business relations on behalf of the club. This can include establishing and maintaining rental agreements, managing club properties, evaluating contracts the club may enter, and managing financial dealings with attorneys, realtors, or other professional services the MC may require. The business manager may look after the club's intellectual properties, handle lawsuits, hire attorneys, accountants, assist with tax documents preparation or other services the MC may need. The business manager represents the club in external meetings, events, or collaborations to ensure the best fiscal interests of the MC as it conducts business.

Club Administration

The business manager may assist in general club administration, providing support to other club officers and members as needed. This can include assisting with event planning, managing club resources or assets, coordinating club merchandise, or branding, and addressing administrative needs or inquiries.

The role requires sharp business acumen, organizational skills, diligence, and the ability to handle multiple tasks and responsibilities simultaneously.

Chapter Road Captain

The road captain plays a vital role although he is the junior officer in the MC as this is the lowest ranking officer position in many MCs. The road captain is responsible for how the MC looks and rides on the road! In many MCs' bylaws this junior officer assumes the authority of the President while the MC is on the road. In this capacity he is responsible for various duties related to planning, coordinating, and executing rides. Here are some common responsibilities associated with the role of a road captain you will see in many MCs that have them:

Ride Planning

The road captain is involved in planning club rides, including selecting the route, determining the duration and stops along the way, and considering any specific requirements or preferences of the club members. He takes into account factors such as road conditions, traffic, weather, and the skill levels of the riders to create an enjoyable and safe riding experience.

Pre-Ride Briefing

Before each ride, the road captain conducts a pre-ride briefing for all participating club members, guests, cars, trucks, chase vehicles, support clubs and all others who will be in the pack. This includes reviewing the planned route, highlighting any potential hazards or points of interest, discussing riding formations and signals, and addressing any specific instructions or guidelines for the ride. The road captain ensures that all riders are well-informed and prepared for the journey.

Leading the Ride

During the ride, the road captain takes the lead position in the group formation (in some MCs in others it is the President or SAA). He sets the pace, maintains proper spacing between bikes, and follows safe riding practices. The road captain acts as a role model for other riders, demonstrating responsible and defensive riding techniques.

Group Management

The road captain is responsible for managing the group dynamics during the ride. He ensures that riders stay together as a cohesive unit, maintain proper spacing, and follow the established riding formations. The road captain may also assist in resolving any issues or conflicts that arise within the group during the ride. In many club bylaws he is able to levy fines, discipline, and suspensions while on the road. Woe be to anyone who may cross him on a trip or be foolish enough to "act-a-fool" or "cut-up" in the pack!

Safety and Traffic Management

The road captain prioritizes the safety of the riders during the ride. He keeps a vigilant eye on the road conditions, traffic, and potential hazards. He may make decisions regarding route adjustments or stops to ensure the safety and well-being of the pack. He communicates vital information, such as road hazards or upcoming turns, using established hand signals or communication systems.

Communication and Coordination

The road captain maintains effective communication with the riders throughout the ride. He may use hand signals, radios, or other communication devices to relay information to the group. He coordinates with other club officers or road crew members to ensure a smooth and organized ride experience.

Ensuring Rider Compliance

The road captain enforces club riding rules and guidelines during the ride. He monitors the behavior and adherence of the riders to ensure that everyone follows safe riding practices and respects the rules of the road. He may provide guidance or reminders to individual riders when necessary.

Ride Evaluation

After each ride, the road captain may conduct a post-ride evaluation or debriefing. This allows for feedback and discussion about the ride experience, identifying any areas for improvement or adjustments for future rides. He may gather input from the riders and incorporate it into future ride planning.

The position of road captain requires strong leadership skills, knowledge of safe riding practices, and effective communication abilities. He plays a critical role in ensuring the smooth operation of club rides, promoting rider safety, and fostering a positive riding experience for all club members. He ensures that "MC" means "move-the-crowd" on two wheels, looking good, safe, smooth, and professional. He must be an exemplary rider, one of the best in the MC. When people exclaim how sharp the MC looks while pounding the ground on twos, it is to the road captain that the club owes its gratitude.

Chapter Public Relations Officer (PRO)

The PRO is a fairly new position found almost exclusively on the Black MC set. Many clubs have a distorted view of what a PRO truly is focusing this position on setting up parties and networking between clubs. This is a poor usage for the position. For clubs that use them the public relations officer (PRO) is responsible for managing the club's public image and handling external communications. Their role involves promoting positive relationships with the public, media, external MCs, and other organizations. Here are some common responsibilities associated with the role of public relations officer:

Media Relations

The PRO serves as the primary point of contact for media inquiries and facilitates interactions between the club and the media. He coordinates press releases, interviews, and media coverage related to club events, activities, or community involvement. The PRO ensures that accurate and positive information is communicated to the media.

Public Image Management

The PRO works to maintain and enhance the club's public image. He develops strategies to promote the club's positive reputation, values, and contributions to the community. The PRO may coordinate public relations campaigns, social media presence, and other promotional activities to shape public perception of the club.

Community Engagement

The PRO plays a key role in fostering positive relationships with the local community. He seeks opportunities for the club to engage in community service, charity events, or other initiatives that contribute to the well-being of the community. The PRO may coordinate with local organizations, government entities, or charitable causes to establish partnerships or collaborative efforts.

Club Representation

The PRO represents the club in external events, meetings, or public forums. He may attend community meetings, motorcycle rallies, charity events, or other gatherings to represent the club and promote its values and activities. The PRO ensures that club members present themselves professionally and positively during these engagements.

Online Presence and Social Media Management:

In today's digital age, the PRO often manages the club's online presence and social media accounts. He creates and shares content that highlights the club's activities, events, and positive contributions. The PRO may engage with online followers, respond to inquiries or comments, and ensure that the club's online presence aligns with its image and values.

Crisis Management

In the event of a crisis or negative publicity, the PRO plays a crucial role in managing the club's response. He works to minimize damage to the club's reputation, address concerns or misconceptions, and handles media inquiries or statements. The PRO may collaborate with club leadership and legal advisors to develop appropriate crisis communication strategies.

Internal Communication

The PRO also facilitates internal communication within the club. He may coordinate newsletters, club updates, or announcements to keep members informed about upcoming events, news, or other relevant information. He ensures that internal communication channels are effective and efficient.

Branding and Merchandising

The PRO may be involved in branding initiatives and merchandise management. He helps develop and maintain the club's visual identity, logo usage, and branding guidelines. The PRO, working closely with the business manager, may oversee the production and distribution of club merchandise, ensuring quality control and adherence to licensing requirements, if applicable.

The role of a public relations officer requires excellent communication skills, a positive and professional demeanor, and the ability to effectively represent the club to the public and media. He plays a crucial role in managing the club's reputation, building relationships, and promoting a positive image both within the motorcycle community and the wider public.

Note: Refer to my book "MC Public Relations Officer's Bible" for more in-depth information about this position.

Nomad

In the context of an MC, a nomad is generally a very senior officer of a national or regional MC who does not have a fixed chapter or geographical area and generally answers only to the National President or nomad chapter President. It is not someone who rides around the country on nomadic journeys and trips, even though that's what many of them do to fulfill their job requirements. They are banished from the MC into nomadism either by choice, club necessity or as a result of disciplinary action. They have the freedom to travel and represent the club in different regions or territories but must have the experience, strength of character, MC protocol knowledge, maturity, mental acuity, and toughness to represent entirely on their own for extended periods, often in enemy territory, without support or resupply from the MC. You will typically only see nomads in OMCs and 1% OMC nations. The role of a nomad within a motorcycle club can vary, but here are some general aspects of their responsibilities:

Representing the Club

Nomads serve as ambassadors of the MC, representing its values, traditions, and brotherhood wherever they travel. They may attend events, visit other chapters, or establish connections with other clubs or individuals on behalf of the MC.

Building Relationships

Nomads focus on establishing and maintaining relationships with other chapters, clubs, and individuals in the motorcycle club community. This involves fostering positive interactions, promoting unity, and facilitating cooperation between different entities.

Support and Assistance

Nomads are often called upon to provide support and assistance to other club members, chapters, or allied clubs. They often travel great distances, wherever required to accomplish these tasks.

Reporting and Communication

Nomads play a crucial role in keeping the club informed about the activities, dynamics, and developments in the regions they visit. They provide valuable information and insights into competing clubs' leadership and members, facilitating informed decision-making in the MC.

Maintaining Club Standards

Nomads uphold the club's standards, policies, and code of conduct, ensuring that the club's reputation and integrity are maintained wherever they go. They serve as examples of loyalty, respect, and commitment to the MC's values. They may be assigned to discipline rogue elements within the MC or Presidents who are challenging national authority.

Flexibility and Adaptability

Nomads embrace a lifestyle of flexibility and adaptability. They are comfortable being on the road and away from a fixed chapter, adjusting to different environments, and integrating themselves into various MC communities.

Nomad Chapters

Some clubs have an entire chapter of nomads who have been banished there to represent. In some cases, the nomad chapter has a President of the nomads who is generally very experienced and incredibly powerful. In some instances, he can be as powerful, if not more powerful than the National President. In some clubs there is a distinction between the nomad and the nomads who are under a nomad and junior in rank.

*99%er Clubs with Nomads

Many OMC and 1% OMC nations do not recognize 99%er clubs, family clubs, LEMCs or traditional MCs' nomad officers. They contend that wearing the nomad patch or rocker is like wearing a state rocker which is reserved, for the most part, for them. But, just like there are 99%ers, traditional MC, LEMCs and others that wear state rockers, you will find some of these clubs with nomads as well. Whether your club can sustain a nomad officer safely on the set will depend strictly on the stature and respect your club has built and certainly it will depend upon the reputation, credibility and relationships said nomad has as well. But generally accepted MC protocol is against it and therefore wearing it can turn into a situation where a higher tiered club may attempt to remove that patch from the wearer.

*RCs, MMs, MAs, Motorsports clubs, etc. with Nomads

Do not attempt this!

Nomads Summary

The specific responsibilities and expectations of nomads may vary between MCs but generally they work only for the National President and work as enforcers to either fix problems internally or handle problems with other clubs externally. Because they are resourceful and think outside of the box, and because they are usually very experienced with dozens of years in the club, when they move and speak, solutions to problems are quickly found. It is often not a good thing when the nomad or nomad chapter shows up in an area unannounced.

Nomads with Little Experience

I've met nomads with less than five years of experience in their clubs or the MC world in general. I would say few can meet the level of knowledge or experience expected from them by the MC set to be effective or even to be taken seriously with less than ten years in the MC life. This is not a job for an egomaniac or a patch chaser even though many of them wind up with the tab. When a nomad appears, he is expected to move with the grace, professionalism, knowledge, wisdom, and acuity of a National President. Most guys who put that tab on prematurely do not last in that position or even in their respective clubs.

What is a Full Patch Brother

A full patch brother is a member who has earned his place in the MC at the most basic level. He has been voted in by the full membership of the MC (in a traditional MC) and is commonly referred to as "the most powerful member of the MC." Full patch brothers are also referred to as "regular fucking members" (RFMs) and for many it is the only position to which they aspire.

The responsibilities of full patch brothers can vary depending on the specific club's rules, traditions, and organizational structure. However, here are some common responsibilities associated with full patch brothers:

Club Loyalty

Full patch brothers are expected to demonstrate unwavering loyalty to the MC. They are committed to upholding the club's bylaws, values, traditions, and code of conduct. They support the club's objectives and work towards its collective goals.

Club Unity and Brotherhood

Full patch brothers foster a sense of unity and brotherhood within the club. They build strong bonds with their fellow club members and prioritize the well-being and camaraderie of the brotherhood.

They actively contribute to creating a positive club culture and maintaining a sense of unity among the members.

Club Support and Participation

Full patch brothers actively participate in club activities, events, and meetings. They show support for the club's initiatives and contribute to its success. They may take on various roles or responsibilities within the club, such as organizing events, volunteering for club projects, or representing the club in external engagements. They support and uphold their officers in their duties by setting them up for success!

Club Security and Protection

Full patch brothers play a role in ensuring the security and protection of the club, its members, and its extended family. They are vigilant in safeguarding the club's interests, assets, and reputation. They may contribute to maintaining the club's confidentiality, enforcing club rules, and addressing any threats or conflicts that may arise.

Club Tradition, Etiquette and Protocol

Full patch brothers adhere to the club's traditions, etiquette, protocol, and hierarchy. They respect the club's chain of command and follow established rules and traditions. They serve as role models for other club members, embodying the values and standards set by the club. But most of all they embody, value, uphold and promote strict adherence to the MCs bylaws!

Club Representation

Full patch brothers represent the club in a responsible and respectful manner. They understand that their actions and behavior reflect on the entire club and its reputation. They maintain a positive image both within the MC community and the public.

Club Development and Growth

Full patch brothers contribute to the growth and development of the club. They may provide mentorship and guidance to newer members, helping them understand and embrace the club's culture. They actively participate in club meetings, discussions, and decision-making processes to contribute their insights and ideas.

Club Unity in Conflict Resolution

Full patch brothers play a role in conflict resolution within the club. They strive to maintain unity and resolve internal disputes or disagreements in a constructive manner. They mediate conflicts, promote open communication, and work towards finding resolutions that align with the best interests of the club.

Good Standing

Full patch brothers are expected to maintain their status "In Good Standing." This means that they must follow the bylaws to adhere to at least the minimum standards in club membership as required. In some clubs that means to be current on dues, meet minimum ride and club participation rules, make mandatory meetings and club functions, maintain an operating motorcycle, ride a yearly minimum number of miles and other requirements. Not being in good standing can result in a full patch brother being fined, suspended, physically disciplined, or put "OUT BAD" from the MC brotherhood after a trial.

What is an MC Prospect/Probate/Probationary

A prospect in a motorcycle club is an individual who is seeking membership and is in the process of proving their worthiness and commitment to the club. Prospects are essentially probationary members who are working towards earning their full patch and becoming full-fledged members of the club. The job of a prospect typically includes the following responsibilities:

Club Familiarization

Prospects are expected to learn about the history, values, traditions, and rules of the motorcycle club they aspire to join. They study the club's bylaws, code of conduct, and any other club-specific information provided to them.

Club Support

Prospects assist full patch members and officers in various club activities and events. They may help with setting up and taking down equipment, organizing rides, providing support during club functions, or any other tasks assigned to them by the club's leadership.

Club Education

Prospects engage in a process of learning and skill development within the club. They may receive training on motorcycle safety, riding techniques, club protocols, and other aspects of club life. They demonstrate a willingness to learn and improve themselves to align with the club's standards.

Club Integration

Prospects actively engage with the club's members, fostering relationships and establishing a sense of camaraderie. They participate in club meetings and social events, interacting with full patch members and getting to know them on a personal level. They seek guidance from experienced members and show respect for the club's hierarchy.

Club Loyalty

Prospects demonstrate their loyalty to the club and its members. They prioritize the interests of the club and show support for its objectives and activities. They prove their dedication by consistently attending club events, following club rules, learning their damned bylaws! And support the club's reputation.

Club Contributions

Prospects contribute to the overall well-being of the club. They may take on specific tasks or responsibilities assigned to them by the club's leadership, such as assisting with fundraising efforts, community service projects, or maintaining club facilities. They demonstrate their commitment and willingness to contribute to the club's success.

Personal Development

Prospects work on personal growth and character development during their prospect period. They strive to embody the values and ideals of the club's bylaws and social construct both on and off their motorcycles. They may be expected to maintain a certain level of personal conduct and integrity as representatives of the club.

Prospect Evaluation

Prospects are continuously evaluated by full patch brothers and club officers to determine their suitability for membership. The evaluation considers factors such as dedication, commitment, loyalty, adherence to club bylaws, and compatibility with the club's culture. The length of the prospect period can vary among different motorcycle clubs.

Each club has its own unique set of rules, requirements, and traditions for prospecting. The prospect period serves as a trial period to assess the prospect's fit within the club and their ability to uphold its values and standards. It is also important that members of other clubs do not trifle with prospects while they are working. They are trying to gain admittance into the MC and if you are distracting them, or hindering them from excellent job performance, you risk costing them longer prospecting times, punishment (possibly physical abuse), suspensions, and fines. Remember they are always under the watchful eye of their full patch brothers and sponsor. They never get to take a break while operating on the MC set because they are earning their way into the MC. Stay clear of them and let them do their work. That is the biggest favor you can do for them.

Note: It is not considered appropriate to ask most prospects their names in many clubs. Some may only be able to refer to themselves as "P1," "P2," "Probie," or the like. Let them tell you what to call them then respect that.

Note: It is never appropriate to call a 1% OMC prospect by the name "Prospect." 1% OMCs require that their brothers (even their prospective brothers) always be referred to with respect. They also consider their prospects senior to the most senior officers of any club that is not a 1% OMC. So, they will absolutely NOT tolerate a 99%er club officer or member talking "down" to one of their prospects. Don't ever make that mistake as the correction could be very public and highly embarrassing. If you haven't been introduced to them and don't know what to call them then call them by the name of their club until you are asked to do otherwise. For instance, it is far better to say, "Hello Screaming Eagles MC how are you" than it is to say, "Hey prospect what's up!"

Note: Prospects only prospect for their own MCs. Even if you have been in your MC forever you will never be appropriate in attempting to give an order to the prospect of any other MC. You will never and should never have that privilege so don't try to invoke it, even if the sponsor or MC of that prospect gives you permission. They are uninformed and wrong if they do that and just don't know any better.

Women's Auxiliary of an MC

The most protected women on the MC set are women who are associated with a biker club. Those two groups are Properties and Auxiliaries. Unfortunately, If an MC cannot protect its women, then it is useless in a male dominated culture. To that end we will discuss women's auxiliaries first.

A women's auxiliary of an MC is a group within a motorcycle club that consists of female members who support and contribute to the club's activities and objectives. They wear some version of that MC's patch. The women's auxiliary is typically composed of female partners, spouses, family members, or close friends of the full patch brothers. While the specific roles and responsibilities can vary between different motorcycle clubs, the women's auxiliary often performs the following functions:

Support Club Activities

The women's auxiliary provides support to the MC by assisting in organizing and participating in club events, rides, and fundraisers. They may help with event planning, coordination, logistics, and promoting club activities.

Community Involvement

The women's auxiliary may engage in community service and outreach initiatives on behalf of the club. They may organize or participate in charitable events, fundraisers, and volunteer activities to support local causes and make a positive impact in their communities.

Social and Networking Activities:

The women's auxiliary creates opportunities for social interaction and networking among its members. They organize gatherings, social events, and meetings to foster a sense of camaraderie and friendship within the auxiliary group.

Support for the Full Patch Brothers

The women's auxiliary provides emotional support and encouragement to the full patch brothers. They are there to offer a listening ear, provide assistance, and create a sense of unity and support within the larger motorcycle club community. They can also be a source of wisdom to prospects and hang-arounds.

Promoting the Club's Values

The women's auxiliary serves as ambassadors for the MC, promoting its values, mission, and positive image. They may engage in public relations efforts, representing the club at community events.

Fundraising and Financial Assistance

The women's auxiliary may contribute to the club's financial stability by organizing fundraisers, participating in revenue-generating activities, paying dues, and providing financial assistance when needed. This support helps the club fulfill its objectives and maintain its operations.

Communication and Coordination

The women's auxiliary serves as a communication channel between the club members and the broader community. They may facilitate communication and coordination among club members' families, relay vital information, and provide updates on club activities.

It's important to note that the structure and activities of a women's auxiliary can vary between different motorcycle clubs. Some clubs may have formalized auxiliary organizations with established leadership positions and specific bylaws, while others may have more informal arrangements. The primary purpose of a women's auxiliary is to support the MC and contribute to its overall success while fostering a sense of community and camaraderie among its female members. It is important to understand the women wearing the patches of the MC will always be exclusive family and will be protected vehemently.

Properties Of an MC

The property of is a relationship that is not often understood by others who are not in the lifestyle. Why a woman would want to be called a property is not something that everyone can understand. Suffice it to say that the most important thing I would want to convey to you is that it doesn't mean chattel property as in slavery or ownership of someone's soul, body, or spirit. This doesn't mean that women haven't been abused. But even wives have been abused so don't let a word (property) throw you off, it is the symbolism of protection, overwatch, support, love, and loyalty they are given that makes them desire to be properties of the MC nation to which they engage completely. As I have said before they are among the most protected groups on the biker clubs' set. Properties are on both the Black and the White set and they should not be trifled with as the entire club will turn up to protect them if necessary.

Properties of can be found in 99%er traditional MCs, OMCs, and 1% OMCs. I have even known some riding clubs (RCs) that have had properties of, believe it or not. But most often you will see them in OMC and 1% OMCs.

Properties of a Club Member

In the context of an MC, the term "property" can also refer to a member's significant other or spouse. In that case you may see her patch reflect the term "Property of Shady One." It would mean she was the property of a particular member named "Shady One." It is important to note that a property does not have to be romantically involved with a full patch brother to wear his "Property Of Shady One" tag. A property's immediate supervisor is known as her sponsor. In most things he will speak for her especially in matters pertaining to the club. A property of can also have a patch that designates her "Property of the Eagle Cliffs MC." She will still have a club sponsor who speaks for her even though she doesn't bear his name tag. Sponsors can also have multiple properties. They are not limited to just one.

Property's roles can vary depending on the specific club's culture and traditions. Here are some common roles and responsibilities associated with being a property:

Support and Loyalty

The primary role of a property is to support her sponsor who is a member of the MC. This includes being loyal to the club, respecting its rules and values, and standing by her sponsor through the club's activities and endeavors.

Club Participation

Properties participate in club events and functions alongside their sponsors. They attend rides, parties, fundraisers, and other activities organized by the club.

Socializing and Networking

Properties engage in socializing and networking within the MC community. They build relationships with other MCs' properties, adding allies to the family.

Community Engagement

Properties participate in community engagement activities organized by the MC. This can include charity donations, and volunteer work to support local causes and give back to the community.

Supporting Club Functions

Properties assist with various tasks related to club functions, like setting up camps, cooking at field meets, organizing rally events, watching over the children, and providing entertainment around campfires.

Emotional and Physical Support

Being a property involves offering emotional support to her sponsor, especially during the challenges and demands of club life. Properties provide understanding and encouragement to their sponsor to aid in navigating the responsibilities and commitments associated with being a club member. They have also been known to provide physical support including aiding in war and battle. A property will always have her sponsor's back.

Respecting Club Hierarchy

Properties are expected to respect the club's hierarchy and chain of command. They should understand and abide by the club's rules and protocols, recognizing the authority of the club's officers and leadership.

Some clubs may have more defined expectations and guidelines for properties, while others may have a more relaxed approach. Communication and understanding between the sponsor and his property are crucial to ensure a healthy and supportive relationship within the MC community.

Honorary Members of the MC

An honorary member is an individual who is recognized and granted a special status by the club. Unlike full patch members or prospects who go through the usual initiation and prospecting process, honorary members are typically invited to join the club based on their exceptional contributions, achievements, or significance to the club or the motorcycle community. Here are some key aspects of being an honorary member:

Recognition

Honorary membership is a way for the club to recognize an individual's notable accomplishments, support, or contributions to the MC or the broader motorcycle community. It is a mark of respect and appreciation for their involvement and dedication.

Symbolic Inclusion

By bestowing honorary membership, the club is essentially extending an honorary patch or symbol to the individual. This patch or symbol may differ from the traditional club patches worn by full patch members and prospects but represents a special affiliation with the club.

Association with the Club

Honorary members are associated with the MC and often enjoy certain privileges and benefits. They may be invited to attend club functions, participate in rides, or be involved in club activities. They are recognized as part of the club's extended family or support network.

Support and Representation

Honorary members are expected to support and represent the club positively. They may be called upon to act as ambassadors for the club, promoting its values, and contributing to its reputation. This can include attending events, speaking on behalf of the club, or lending their expertise or influence on club initiatives.

Relationship with Full Patch Members

Honorary members develop close relationships with full patch members of the club. Often, they may have a mentor-like role, providing guidance and support to club members, especially in areas where they possess specialized knowledge or experience.

Non-voting Status

In most cases, honorary members do not have voting rights within the club's decision-making processes. Their membership is honorary and does not grant them the same level of privileges in club affairs as full patch members. However, their opinions and perspectives may be respected and considered by the club's leadership.

Each club has its own criteria for granting honorary membership and may define the expectations and privileges associated with this status. Honorary membership is typically an honorary title and does not necessarily entail the same level of commitment or obligations as full membership. You will not see them often on the MC set, but if you do see an honorary member, you can rest assured he did something very special to get an honorary patch others had to prospect to achieve.

Note: In the strictest of terms, retirees, founders, and lifers can technically be considered honorary members once they drop from full patch status and stop paying dues. In this case these are former members who may be allowed to wear the club's colors under certain conditions or restrictions and are given many benefits based upon the club's bylaws. But rest assured, if you call one of these folks an honorary member you may have to fight them, so be careful.

Hang-arounds

A "hang around" is a term used in MC culture to describe an individual who is interested in joining a motorcycle club and is in the process of getting to know the club and its members. A hang around is essentially an informal status that precedes becoming a prospect or a full patch member. Here are some key aspects of being a hang around:

Observation and Familiarization

As a hang around, the individual spends time around the club, attending club events, and getting to know the club members. They observe the club's activities, traditions, and dynamics to gain a better understanding of the club's culture and values.

Building Relationships

Hang arounds use this period to build relationships and establish rapport with club members. They interact with club members, participate in conversations, and engage in social activities to develop connections within the club community.

Club Etiquette and Respect

Hang arounds are expected to adhere to the club's rules, protocols, and customs. They demonstrate respect for the club, its members, and the club's property. Following club etiquette and showing proper behavior is essential during this stage of affiliation.

Support and Assistance

Hang-arounds may assist the club in numerous ways, such as helping with event setup, cleanup, or other tasks as requested. They demonstrate their commitment to the club and their willingness to contribute and be of assistance.

Getting Vetted

The hang around period allows club members to evaluate the individual's compatibility with the club and assess whether they would be a good fit. Club members observe the hang around's character, commitment, and dedication to determine if they should proceed to the next stage of becoming a prospect.

The specific process and duration of the hang around period can vary between MCs. Some clubs may have a structured and formalized hang around period, while others may have a more informal approach. The purpose of this stage is for both the hang around and the club to assess mutual compatibility and determine if the hang around will progress to the next stage of club membership. Most hang arounds do not wear club colors, but they may wear support t-shirts.

Brother Clubs of an MC

A brother club can also be known as a support club or affiliated club but for the purposes of this book it is a separate motorcycle club that has a close relationship and affiliation with another MC that recognizes that club as an equal and respects it enough to call it "brother." Brother clubs often share common values, interests, and camaraderie with their brother MC, and they work together to support each other and promote the MC lifestyle. Here are some key aspects of brother clubs:

Mutual Relationship

A brother club maintains a formal or informal relationship with the brother MC. They have a mutual respect and bond based on shared interests and values within the motorcycle club culture.

Support and Association

Brother clubs provide support to their brother MC in numerous ways. This can include attending and assisting with their events, participating in joint rides or runs, and showing solidarity in club matters. They contribute to the overall unity and strength of the MC community.

Shared Values and Protocol

Brother clubs align themselves with the values, protocols, and expectations of their brother MC. They adhere to similar club customs, rules, and codes of conduct, reinforcing a sense of brotherhood and common identity within the MC culture.

Patch or Colors

Brother clubs will have their own distinctive patches or colors, separate from those of their brother MC. These patches typically display their club's name, logo, and other identifiers. However, brother clubs often wear a "brotherhood" patch or a specific patch indicating their affiliation with their brother MC.

Relationship Dynamics

Brother clubs maintain a respectful and cooperative relationship with their brother MC. They understand and respect each other and work in harmony with them. The level of involvement and collaboration can vary depending on the specific arrangement and dynamics established between the clubs.

Autonomy and Independence

While brother clubs have an affiliation with their brother MC, they maintain their own autonomy and independence. They have their own leadership structure, club activities, and decision-making processes. However, major decisions or actions may be discussed or coordinated with the brother MC to ensure alignment and support.

It's important to note that the specifics of brother club relationships can vary between different motorcycle clubs. Each club has its own policies and agreements regarding brother club affiliations. These relationships are based on mutual respect, support, and shared values, enhancing the sense of brotherhood and community within the MC culture.

Support Clubs of an MC

A support club, also called a satellite club or puppet club by law enforcement, is a separate motorcycle club that has a formal affiliation with a dominant 1% MC which governs it to a greater or lesser extent. Unlike a brother club (as explained previously), which maintains autonomy, a support club exists primarily to provide direct support and assistance to the dominant MC, but they can be considered a brother club and are treated as such in many instances because they are so closely tied to their dominant. One of the main differences between a brother club and support club is that from a support club a member can be and often desires to be promoted into the dominant club eventually whereas in a brother club there is seldom that expectation or desire. In fact, support clubs are often the only legitimate way into some dominant 1 OMC% nations as they are used like farming teams in professional baseball. Here are some key aspects of support clubs:

Relationship with the Dominant MC

A support club has a close and formalized relationship with the dominant MC. They are established as a subordinate club to the dominant MC and operate under their authority and direction.

Support and Assistance

The primary role of a support club is to provide various forms of support to the dominant MC. This can include assisting with club events, security, fundraising efforts, and other tasks as required. Support clubs are dedicated to serving the interests and needs of the dominant MC.

Patch or Colors

Support clubs typically wear patches or colors that clearly indicate their affiliation with the dominant MC. These patches often include the dominant MC's name or logo, along with the support club's own identifiers. The patches and colors signify the support club's allegiance and dedication to the dominant MC.

Hierarchy and Structure

Support clubs operate within a hierarchical structure, with the dominant MC holding the highest authority. They follow the rules, protocols, and customs established by the dominant MC and are subject to their directives. The support club's leadership may have direct communication and coordination with the leadership of the dominant MC.

Relationship Dynamics

Support clubs maintain a subservient role to the dominant MC. They work closely with the dominant MC's members and support their initiatives and activities. The relationship is characterized by loyalty, respect, and a sense of shared purpose within the MC community.

Limited Autonomy

Unlike brother clubs or independent MCs, support clubs have limited autonomy and independence. They operate under the guidance and supervision of the dominant MC, and major decisions or actions are often made in consultation with the dominant MC's leadership.

The dynamics and arrangements between support clubs and dominant MCs can vary between different MCs. The specific roles, responsibilities, and expectations of support clubs are determined by the dominant MC, and support club members are expected to prioritize the interests and goals of the dominant MC above their own.

Social Clubs (SCs) on the Black biker set

SCs are unique to the African American biker club experience. SCs are groups of women (mostly African American) who operate their clubs on the Black biker clubs' set, in support of Black MCs while simultaneously doing charitable work for their communities at large. As such, they have etched themselves into a place of existence among Black biker clubs not customary for women on any MC set no matter the race. That is because women are not often included in today's male dominated world of biker clubs and their voices are consequently muted. Black women's SCs; however, have flourished on the MC set because they have learned to understand the MCs around them and found their role as support clubs therein enriching the MC set with their beautiful presence. Many of these SCs are set up administratively much like the MCs they support. Some even have the same officer positions, ranking structure, operational standards, and traditions as MCs—including prospecting their sisters before allowing them to become members which is wildly unheard of on other biker sets.

SCs are heavily regulated on the set by both dominant 1% OMCs and 99%er MCs and serve the set largely in a support capacity. In many regions they are restricted to wearing certain colors of vests and are required to have a sponsoring male MC to be included within coalitions on the set.

An SC is a separate organization that has a formal affiliation with its sponsoring MC and does maintain a level of autonomy over its own affairs. In many instances an SC will become almost as close to its sponsoring or brother club as an auxiliary club especially if that club doesn't have auxiliaries or properties. An SC consists of female members who support and contribute to the sponsoring club's activities and objectives. They may wear a support patch or other affiliation patch of their sponsoring club. The members aren't necessarily composed of female partners, spouses, family members, or close friends of their sponsoring MC. While the specific roles and responsibilities can vary between different motorcycle clubs, SCs often perform the following functions:

Support Sponsoring Club Activities

SCs provide support to their sponsoring MC by assisting in organizing and participating in club events, rides, and fundraisers. They may help with event planning, coordination, logistics, and promoting club activities.

Community Involvement

SCs absolutely engage in community service and outreach initiatives on behalf of themselves and sometimes their sponsoring club. They organize or participate in charitable events, fundraisers, and volunteer activities to support local causes and make a positive impact in their communities.

Social and Networking Activities

SCs create opportunities for social interaction and networking among their sisters. They organize gatherings, social events, and meetings to foster a sense of camaraderie and friendship within their extended family.

Support for the Full Patch Brothers of Their Sponsoring MC

SCs provide emotional support and encouragement to the full patch brothers of their sponsoring MC.

Fundraising and Financial Assistance

SCs organize fundraisers, revenue-generating activities, and provide financial assistance to the communities they support.

The structure and activities of SCs can vary between different organizations. Some may have formalized organizations with established leadership positions and specific bylaws, while others may operate more informally.

Friend of the Club

The term "friend of the club" typically refers to an individual who is not a member of an MC but is considered a trusted and respected associate or supporter of the club. This person may have a close relationship with one or more members of the club or have demonstrated consistent support and camaraderie towards the club and its members. Here are some key aspects of being a friend of the club:

Trusted and Respected Associate

A friend of the club is someone who is trusted and respected by the members of the MC. They have earned the club's confidence and have established a positive rapport with the club's members.

Support and Camaraderie

A friend of the club actively supports the club and its members. This can involve attending club events, participating in rides or runs, providing assistance when needed, and showing solidarity with the club's activities and causes.

Loyalty and Discretion

A friend of the club understands the importance of loyalty and discretion. They respect the club's privacy, maintain confidentiality regarding club matters, and do not engage in activities that may bring harm or negative attention to the club.

Mutual Respect and Trust

The friendship between a friend of the club and the club's members is built on mutual respect and trust. The friend of the club values the club's culture, traditions, and values and conducts themselves in a manner that aligns with the club's principles.

Limited Privileges

While a friend of the club may enjoy some privileges or benefits associated with their association, such as attending club events or socializing with club members, they do not have the same level of involvement or decision-making authority as full members of the MC.

Recognized Affiliation

The club may formally recognize the friend of the club's association by granting them a specific designation or insignia that indicates their status. This can include a "friend of the club" patch, pin, or other identifiers.

The exact meaning and significance of "friend of the club" can vary between different MCs. The club's bylaws and internal policies define the criteria for recognizing and maintaining such friendships, and the extent of involvement and privileges may differ from club to club.

Club Supporters

A supporter of a motorcycle club (MC) is an individual who is not a member of the club but shows their support and loyalty to the club and its members. Supporters are often friends, family members, or acquaintances of club members who align themselves with the club's values, ideals, and activities. Here are some key aspects of being a supporter of an MC:

Loyalty and Support

Supporters demonstrate their loyalty and support to the MC by actively participating in club events, rides, and activities. They may attend club functions, rallies, or gatherings to show solidarity with the club and its members.

Respect for the MC

Supporters have a deep respect for the MC, its history, and its members. They adhere to the club's code of conduct, traditions, and values. They understand and respect the hierarchy and authority within the MC and follow the guidance of club members.

Representation

Supporters may wear clothing or accessories that identify them as supporters of the MC. This can include wearing club merchandise, such as T-shirts or patches, or displaying stickers or decals on their vehicles.

Relationship with Club Members

Supporters often have personal relationships with club members, whether as friends, family members, or acquaintances. They maintain close bonds and enjoy the camaraderie of being associated with the MC.

Mutual Respect and Trust

The relationship between supporters and club members is built on mutual respect and trust. Supporters understand the importance of discretion and confidentiality when it comes to club matters and respect the privacy of club members.

Limited Involvement

Supporters do not have the same level of involvement or responsibilities as full members of the MC. They are not part of the club's decision-making processes, governance, or leadership structure. However, they may be invited to participate in certain club activities or events based on the club's discretion.

The exact role and expectations of supporters can vary between different MCs. Some clubs may have formalized supporter programs or designated roles, while others may have more informal arrangements. The level of involvement and privileges granted to supporters are determined by the MC and may differ from club to club, but the bottom line is a supporter, or club fan is NOT a member! Your support is appreciated but never make the mistake of thinking you act in any way or speak in any way for the MC. If you desire to support on the level of a member earn a patch.

Summary of Motorcycle Club Operations

Motorcycle clubs operate on an international, national, regional, and local level. Traditional MCs generally have officers on each level. The terms I have used to describe these officers can be different based on the club, its location, or bylaws. For instance, some clubs have state bosses instead of regional Presidents or Enforcers instead of SAA while some clubs have all of those positions. Other clubs call their leaders "commanders" instead of Presidents. In fact, my club, the Mighty Black Sabbath MC Nation once called our Presidents "First Rider" back during our humble beginnings. My point here is that for any rule I may have spoken there is another MC somewhere doing it differently, naming it differently, or calling things different names based on their rules and bylaws. Learn the functions of how MCs operate in your area, and you'll be okay no matter where you travel and experience MCing.

CHAPTER FOUR
BIKER CLUBS, SETS, RELATIONSHIPS, MC PROTOCOL, & MOVING AROUND

Your depth of understanding of the way things work inside and outside of your MC will determine your level of success and perhaps your club's level of success while operating on the set. Your knowledge of MC protocol will dictate your every move, how you are respected, how you are treated and how your club moves, is respected, and treated. Yes, one dumb ass brother can spoil it for everyone acting stupid, so you don't want to be "That Guy!" Be smart enough to know your shit out there on the set. It is a grownup environment for grown men who are wearing their grown man pants, are prayed up, head on a swivel, with eyes wide open. Immature or naïve fools will be eaten alive on the set. "Trust me what I tell you!" Let's start with the most widely recognized icon that separates a biker from a biker clubber. The colors!

Colors, Cuts, Patches, Sweaters, Serapes and Rags

In the beginning clubs started wearing matching dress outfits to display uniformity and solidarity. Some even had their club names stitched on the back of their shirts, varsity jackets, overalls, jumpsuits, or more commonly heavy-duty sweaters—which are still worn by old school MCs today. There is at least one 1% OMC that still wears a serape. The AMA encouraged this practice at their events by giving awards to AMA-sanctioned clubs for "best-dressed club", among other awards. From this was the start of wearing MC patches (Wheelsofgrace.com and test). As MCs became more creative and competitive, their designs eventually led to the one-piece "back patch" (known as "colors") stitched, embedded, or painted on the back of their uniforms. Hence club blessings and the use of club colors started originally as an AMA marketing tactic to help motorcycle manufactures sell more bikes through the kinds of promotions that excited people about the sport of motorcycling. The term "colors" refer to an MC's complete back patch setup which can include one, two, three, four, or five-piece setup. However, there are other terms clubs use for colors depending upon their geographical location or type of club. For instance, some clubs call their colors rags, some call them a cut, cut-off, kutte, or battle vest, and some just say vest.

Traditional Patch Setup

Because many clubbers incorrectly believe the three-piece patch is the traditional patch worn by all serious MCs and only RCs and family clubs wear one-piece patches, there is the misconception among new MCs on the set that having a one-piece patch is insulting or beneath them. They clamor to get a three-piece patch no matter what. The truth is the traditional patch setup was a one-piece center patch worn on the back of the uniform which could be easily seen from the back as the club rode in formation on the street. The center patch incorporated the name of the club at the top, the club's icon or symbol in the middle, and the club's location or territory at the bottom. Three-piece patches didn't come until much later when clubs began to disassociate from the AMA and outlaw clubs were formed. There are many MCs that still don one-piece patches including some 1% OMC nations. So, don't let the number of pieces in a patch cause you to doubt the legitimacy of an MC. One-piece, two-pieces, three-pieces and even five-piece patches exist, and all variants of MCs wear them. You may encounter an RC with a three-piece patch or an OMC with a one-piece patch. Either can be equally docile or dangerous. That is why it is important to respect all MCs on the set.

Post WWII, Disillusionment, Birth of the Three-Piece Patch

Returning veterans began to change the clothing style of MCs, incorporating their war-time roots by introducing patch jackets, flight jackets with wartime patches and leather bombers. These patch jackets have their origins in the U.S. Army Air Corps during WWII, where airmen would sew patches onto their regulation flight jackets. Upon returning home, the practice continued as former airmen became a part of MCs (Cut-off Wikipeda). Their style of clothing presented a tougher looking, hardened biker clad in leathers and denim which was more appropriate and protective clothing for motorcycling. Outlaw MCs began pulling away from the "establishment" (and the AMA) not only in spirit and attitude but also in the way that they looked particularly with the advent of the diamond 13 and eventually how their back patches were configured. This led MCs organizing around one of two philosophies:

1. Square clubs (commonly called "racing," "family" or "traditional" clubs) aligned with the AMA.
2. Outlaw clubs (commonly called "outlaws" or "OMCs") outlawed from the AMA.

Eventually, as these outlawed clubs sought to show outward symbols of their contempt for the AMA structure, they broke their one-piece patch setups into three pieces in protest. This distinguished them visually as being separated from the AMA. In today's MC this is what we see in patches:

In OMC culture, support clubs that sprang from them, traditional and 99%er MCs that were blessed by them, the regalia of the patch has become three separate pieces on the back of a vest that combined are called a three-piece patch. So, technically a "three-piece" patch refers to the number of back patches worn by full patch brothers in good standing of an MC known as their colors. A three-piece patch is not unlike the traditional one-piece patch that

AMA clubs wore in the beginning and many clubs still wear to this day. In fact, they contain the exact same elements. They were simply broken into three pieces to set the clubs that wore them apart from the AMA clubs who wore one-piece patches. Each element of the patch carries significant meaning within MC culture:

Top Rocker

The top rocker usually bears the name of the club and is placed above the club emblem. It signifies the club's name and helps identify its affiliation.

Club Emblem (Center Piece)

The center emblem is the main part of the patch and represents the specific club. It often features the club's logo, symbols, and other identifying elements. This emblem is unique to each club and holds great significance within the club's identity.

Bottom Rocker (Territory Patch)

The bottom rocker typically displays the geographic location or territory of the MC. It usually contains the name of the city, state, or region where the club is based or claims as its territory, but you can see other territorial claims in the bottom rocker as well. Some clubs, for instance, may have North, South, East, West or United States on the bottom rocker while others may have "Nomad."

In other countries, you may see the entire country displayed.

Bottom Rocker Rules

DISCLAIMER: Any club can wear or do anything it wants to wear or do. I am presenting accepted MC protocol and whether you follow it or not, believe it or not, accept it or not, is up to you and your club. I always say, "Do what you and your club can stand on!"

The bottom rocker conveys one of the most important messages to all clubs on the set, so the rules behind what is worn there and who can wear it are often strictly enforced by diamond clubs, OMCs, coalitions, and some strong traditional and 99%er MCs. In other words, a wrongly configured bottom rocker can evoke an ass kicking or uncomfortable gas pump conversation/confrontation from more than just a 1% OMC. It is important to understand what the bottom rocker is telling you or what your club's bottom rocker is telling others.

In the US you may see various presentations of MC colors, but typically OMCs and 1% OMC nations wear bottom rockers that display the state or region in which they reside. Generally, when an MC puts the name of a state on their back, this is known as "claiming territory." Traditional MCs, 99%er MCs, family clubs, RCs and other biker organizations wear the name of their city on their bottom rockers (if they wear any territory distinction at all). Wearing a city rocker is not typically considered to be "claiming territory" as MCs have been wearing city patches since the beginning of wearing colors. But it can be under certain conditions!

When Clubs Can't Wear a City Bottom Rocker

Recently (in the past 7 to 10 years) some diamond clubs have prevented lower-level and new MCs or RCs from wearing city rockers, instead relegating new clubs to wearing abbreviations of cities instead, and in some instances the abbreviations of airports near the cities in which they reside, for instance DFW for Dallas Fort Worth. Some will allow new clubs to eventually "earn" the right to wear their cities based on criteria set up by the diamond or coalition, but in those cases, they have turned it into a process rather than the right of passage it used to be. Older clubs will usually be "grandfathered" however, new clubs may face challenges in these areas.

Motorcycle Club Protocol 101

Can Non-1% Clubs Wear a State Rocker

Some 1% support clubs, traditional MCs, 99%er MCs, and well-respected family clubs are blessed to wear state bottom rockers by the diamonds in their area. This is strictly a respect thing and if your MC has earned it, the diamond or coalition in your area will let you know. Often, military, veterans' and fire rescue MCs are blessed to wear state rockers as OMCs have a lot of respect for these organizations as they are mostly extremely patriotic. In addition, you will likely see many LEMCs wearing state bottom rockers, because no one is going to mess with the police and attempt to force them not to wear state names on their bottom rockers. Some rogue MCs have been known to wear state bottom rockers. One of the most famous or infamous (depending upon how you see them) is Iron Order MC.

Iron Order MC, Rogue MC, or Popup Club

The Iron Order MC (IOMC) was founded in Jeffersonville IN on Independence Day, 2004, by a eight men, "Bad Dog," "Big Rick," "Chief," "Copper," "Doc," "Ice," "Professor," and "Willie Ball." The club quickly expanded into Georgia the following year and established chapters in several other states by the end of 2006 (Iron Order MC Wikipedia). Iron Order MC immediately earned the ire of most diamond, traditional and 99%ers because unlike most clubs they sought no blessings from any club and just appeared on the set patched up and riding with state names on their bottom rockers. This earned them the reputation of being a "popup club," which is looked negatively upon by the MC community at large.

Definition of a Popup Club

A popup club is an MC that "pops up" on the set with neither an AMA blessing (making it an outlaw club), or a blessing by a diamond 1% club, coalition, or traditional MC (making it a popup club). Iron

Order has often been credited with starting the "pop-up-club" trend where new MCs rapidly establish chapters across different regions.

Iron Order MC the Cop Club

Unlike many other MCs, the IOMC is alleged to be openly comprised of a considerable number of current and former law enforcement members, leading to controversy within the set and earning them the reputation of being a "cop club" (similar to an LEMC, which are often severely despised among clubbers).

However, in a phone call I had with the IOMC International President a few years ago, he denied the IOMC was a cop club or even currently had a large police contingent. Their website states,

> "We are not 1%ers, not a Law Enforcement MC, not a veterans' MC, nor are we a riding club. We are simply a Men's three-piece patch Motorcycle Club that is independent and neutral. We mind our own business, and we believe in My Brother Before Me."

But the MC community is not so easily swayed from their assumptions because of the many violent interactions that seemed to leave the club unscathed while members of the 1% OMCs they tangled with got arrested and charged, back in their beginning days. IOMC has clashed with Los Lobos MC, Black Pistons MC, Chosen Sons MC, Hells Angels MC, Pistoleros MC, Iron Horsemen MC, Bandidos MC, and the Mongols MC (Iron Order MC Wikipedia). In those altercations at least eight members of those clubs were shot and three killed including a civilian female who was run over by an automobile (Iron Order MC Wikipedia). In no instance were charges sustained against any IOMC member. These incidents have made them hated among many diamond clubs and the wider MC community as they appear to be able to hide behind the shields of the police officers in the club.

Some view the club as an illegitimate popup MC for never seeking blessings to start up, including law enforcement members among their ranks, and for creating conflict with 1% OMCs, coalitions, and established MCs. Others consider them a rogue MC living MC life on their own terms and refusing to bow to the will of others. Some see them as heroes. According to their website they claim none of that. They say they,

> "Seek to emulate the motorcycle clubs of the 1950s and 1960s, adopting the "non-conformist" attitudes of those early clubs."

They say,

> "We are not an outlaw or 1% motorcycle club, and do not endorse nor condone any form of criminal activity from our membership."

However, both the AMA and the U.S. Department of Justice (DOJ) have labeled the club as being "Outlaw. (Iron Order MC Wikipedia)"

Note: It has been explained to me that in places like the UK MCCs don't wear back patches at all. They wear what they call side patches and what we would call chest patches. I've been told that only 1% OMCs and clubs that are allowed to wear the designation MC can wear back patches.

One-Piece, Two-Piece Patches & Diamonds on Black Set

Not all OMCs or 1% OMCs wear a three-piece patch. In fact, the three-piece patch is seen as more of a standard on the White MC set than on the Black MC set. For the longest time, many African American MCs on the West Coast and dominant OMCs wore one-piece back patches with no state rocker and diamond patches without the "1%" or "1%er" nomenclature. This is, in part, due to the fact that African American MCs have never been affiliated with the AMA; therefore, they had no reason to break apart their back patches in protest. In fact, most African American MCs on the West Coast still have one-piece back patches in the traditional fashion of the early MCs..

Two-Piece Back Patches

Some of the African American 1% OMCs, particularly those from the West Coast, decided to add state rockers to their one-piece back patches. This is because of the symbology that 1%ers run states. Instead of turning their patches into three-piece patches, they merely added that all-important state bottom rocker making their back patch set up a two-piece patch design. There are all-White 1% clubs that have only two-piece back patches with similar setups as well.

More Meanings for Two-Piece Back Patches

A two-piece back patch can show a charter or chapter waiting for approval for a regional or national MC. In that case they may have the top rocker with the club's name. Once they patch in, they typically move to some form of the three-piece patch.

Prospects Often Wear Two-Piece Back Patches

In some clubs a prospect or probie may wear pieces of the patch during various stages of their prospectship, perhaps starting with the top rocker, then moving to the bottom rocker, and finally after the prospect "patches-over" the center piece is added to recognize them as a new full patch brother. While other MCs start with the two-piece top and bottom rocker. And some prospects only get a simple capital letter "P" as a center patch. To add insult to injury, some prospects don't even get a "P" patch, instead they get a few pieces of duct tape cobbled together to make some kind of raggedy ass looking "P" as a center patch. Those poor bastards!

The MC Cube and Side Rockers

The "MC Cube" is a small (often diamond shaped) patch placed near (above, below, left, or right) of the center patch that contains the initials "MC" to signify that the club is a motorcycle club. This "MC Cube" (also known as the "MC diamond") holds different meanings depending upon its arrangement. This "MC Cube" can be referred to as a "Four-Piece" patch or (if the M and the C separated on either side of the logo patch) as a "Five-Piece" patch. However, it is still seen as a three-piece patch setup even though the M and C technically make it a five piece patch.

MC Cube Within the Back Patch

When the MC Cube is incorporated as part of the center patch or emblem of the back patch, it is typically positioned within the design and not separated from the main patch. This arrangement signifies that the club is recognized as a traditional MC, adhering to the protocols and traditions of the MC culture.

Separated MC Cube

When the MC Cube is a separate patch either above or below the center patch on the back patch, it is physically distinct from the main patch and can be seen as a standalone element. This arrangement is typically associated with RCs or social RCs that do not fully align with traditional MC culture. While these clubs may share a passion for motorcycles, brotherhood, or specific interests, they may not necessarily adhere to the same strict protocols and traditions as traditional MCs.

Side Rockers

Side rockers are additional patches that can be placed on either side of the vest which carry additional club information or slogans, such as the club's motto, founding year, or other relevant details. They can also be used to identify a specialized group within an MC. For example, "wrecking crew" might recognize a group of line brothers who prospected at the same time or accomplished a certain milestone.

NOTE: In some territories only OMCs and 1% OMC nations are allowed to wear side rockers, and these OMCs and 1% OMCs have been known to remove side rockers from lesser clubs who have them with extreme prejudice.

Accomplishment or Title Patches

Heart Patch

Many MCs wear a heart patch on their left front over or near the heart. Often it is some combination of the back patch in miniature with the name of the MC, perhaps the chapter location and the year the club was established. If your club wears one often no other patch can be placed above it.

NOTE: In some territories only OMCs and 1% OMC nations are allowed to wear heart patches.

NOTE: In some European countries, heart patches (called "side patches) are worn by MCCs and RCs because only 1% MCs are permitted to wear back patches.

Officer Patches

Officer patches (often called "officer tabs," "tabs," or simply "I love me patches"), as opposed to the back patch which is commonly referred to as the "I love the club" patch, signify the rank and status of an officer in the club.

NOTE: Some OMCs and traditional MCs don't wear officer patches at all. They don't see the need for anyone outside of the MC to know the ranks of its members. This tradition also comes from the battlefields of WWII where officers often did not wear their insignia during battle to avoid being killed by snipers attempting to take out command elements of the enemy during battle. When an MC runs this setup others cannot differentiate between members, and it helps to shroud the club in anonymity and mystery. This is often called "running outlaw style."

Ride Patches

Ride patches signify accomplishments achieved during a ride or event either in the MC or as part of another club's run. Some ride patches indicate a number of miles ridden (e.g., "miles per year" or "miles in a 24-hour period"). For example, "1K in a Day" would indicate a rider rode his/her motorcycle 1,000 miles in 24-hours.

Honorary Patches

Honorary patches are used to signify an honorary status conveyed upon a member that offers privileges that are not necessarily covered in the bylaws. For instance, you may see a founder of the club wearing a founder patch when there may not be an officer position called "founder" in the bylaws. The founder may be afforded privileges or have sway in decision making that there is no basis for in the bylaws. There are some clubs that also allow members to wear retired patches. These are technically honorary patches as well and allow a member to be a part of the MC without having to make the mandatory rides and pay dues. Naturally, some clubs offer no recognition for so-called retirees as they deem individuals are only affiliated with the MC as long as they pay their dues and meet minimum requirements.

NOTE: Sometimes the holders of these honorary positions may take unfair advantage of the club or hold the club hostage unnecessarily. There have been many wars between founders and presidents where founders have attempted to exude power in the club above the President even though the bylaws clearly state the President is the most senior officer in the MC. This can lead to club civil wars and even splits. In one instance, I was called in by the club to mediate when the founder went so far as to attempt to remove a President with whom he disagreed citing that he owned the club's trademark and that granted him ultimate power over the club because he could shut the entire organization down and remove his permission for it to wear his trademarked patches. So, you can see that honorary patches can be both boon and curse to the MC.

Award/Recognition Patches

Some MCs have patches that recognize members for accomplishing goals beyond riding that are important to the club. For instance, some clubs have patches that award brothers for their sexual exploits! These "I love me" patches have great meaning to the brothers who win them. They can be awarded for accomplishing significant milestones within the club as well.

Cut-Off Blue or Black Denim Cuts & Leather Cuts

Family and racing MCs wore matching uniforms to win contests at AMA hosted events. The AMA was created, in part, to help motorcycle manufacturers generate interest in the sport of motorcycling in an effort to sell more motorcycles. When the AMA started awarding "best dressed" trophies and prizes, MCs began to design uniforms to win these prizes, and this is how uniforms became a thing that all clubs did. The original clubs of the day wore sweaters, jumpsuits, overalls, and matching kinds of uniforms that looked like what one might call today, "ice cream suits." Eventually some (especially racers) began wearing leather and denim because of the protection and safety they provided (Cut-off Wikipeda). In fact, before WWII Schott was manufacturing his iconic Perfecto motorcycle jacket which was an expensive riding suit that was made of leather (Cut-off Wikipeda). A lot of folks think that "Outlaw" clubs started the denim and leather phase of biker clothing but before the "Outlaw" clubs broke away from the so-called "family clubs," bikers had begun to wear denim and some cut the sleeves off their jackets to make them more comfortable, especially in summer weather (Cut-off Wikipeda). They were called "cut-off vests," or *"cuts,"* for short. Clubbers attached their *"colors"* to them. But it wasn't until returning veterans hit the set wearing bomber leather jackets, khakis, and denim in the postwar period that this biker clothing became incredibly popular to the younger new guys hitting the set (Cut-off Wikipeda). The look was new, cool, and well-liked among clubs in the late 1940s that wanted to break away from the standard look that had been around since 1924. Denim and leather vests made sense for their versatility and could offer a modicum of protection even in the summer when it was too hot for the full sleeved bomber and denim jackets (Cut-off Wikipeda). This made a perfect look for "Outlaw" clubs that began to adopt the look fervently especially after the Hollywood movie craze we spoke of that featured every outlaw biker club wearing it.

Now referred to as "colors," "rags," "kuttes," "cuts," and "cut-offs," these cuts began as denim, then leather, and eventually pre-made without sleeves (Cut-off Wikipeda). Because so many of the "Outlaw" clubs adopted this look, especially by the 1970s, it has become synonymous with OMC and 1% OMC culture and is still standard issue for some OMCs and 1% OMCs. And the cut off premade leather vest has become standard issue for almost everyone else including most OMCs and 1% OMCs. But many clubs, especially those that started in the 1950s, 60s, and 70s can show you pictures of their founders dressed in denim cuts.

Today's MC Protocol Involving Denim Cuts

Today on many sets only OMCs and 1% OMCs are allowed to wear denim cuts. They believe it is part and parcel to "Outlaw" culture and frown heavily on new RCs, 99%ers and family clubs (especially clubs founded after the 1990s) and block them from wearing denim. I have seen more than one popup club forced to remove their colors from denim cuts or have them confiscated during a terse interaction with an angry 1% OMC; however, I've also seen 1% OMCs bless 99%er clubs to continue wearing denim, especially for clubs older than 30 years old.

Patch Summary

Generally, the three-piece patch is considered a significant symbol of membership within the OMC and greater MC community. It signifies the commitment, loyalty, and brotherhood among club members. Wearing a three-piece patch without the proper authorization from a recognized OMC, 1% OMC nation, powerful 99%er or coalition, is seen as disrespectful and may lead to conflicts or misunderstandings within the MC community. Although the three-piece patch is not restricted to OMCs, it is often perceived this way in many areas as RCs, MMs, SCs, Women's MCs, family MCs and non-traditional organizations generally wear a one-piece patch, but there are many 99%er clubs, traditional, nontraditional, specialty MCs and RCs that have been blessed to wear three-piece patches. There are meanings to the placement of all patches, with subtle differences in each category that the untrained eye might not recognize.

A Deeper Look at the "Set"

The term "biker club set" refers to the subculture or community of MCs and their associated activities, values, and lifestyle. It encompasses the network of clubs, riders, and enthusiasts who participate in MC culture and engage in activities such as group rides, social gatherings, and club events.

The biker club set is characterized by a strong sense of camaraderie, brotherhood/sisterhood, and shared interests among its members. It revolves around the passion for motorcycles, riding, and the unique culture that has developed within the MC community.

Within the biker club set, there are different clubs with their own distinct identities, structures, and affiliations. These clubs range from traditional MCs, which adhere to a strict set of protocols and hierarchies, to RCs, SCs, or support clubs that cater to specific interests or demographics.

Overall, the biker club set is a vibrant and diverse community that fosters a strong sense of identity and camaraderie among its members. It provides a space for motorcycle enthusiasts to connect, share experiences, and engage in the unique lifestyle and culture associated with MCs.

Everywhere you are that clubs operate, visit, ride, hang out in, party at, or pass by regularly is part of the biker club set.

Hierarchy of Clubs on the Set

There is a pecking order of biker clubs on the set. It is vitally important that each participant understands exactly what their station is in that pecking order. This is known as the hierarchy of the biker clubs set. There can be some argument between the biker club scholars at to exactly what the hierarchy is so below I will provide you with my opinion as to what that organizational chart looks like:

- 1%er OMC Nations
- 1%er Support MC Nations (brother clubs)
- Supporter MCs

- OMCs (Diamond Clubs)
- Law Enforcement MCs (LEMCs)
- Traditional MCs/99%ers (male)
- Veteran's MCs
- Non-Traditional MCs
    - Christian MCs
    - Masonic MCs
    - First Responder MCs
    - Sober MCs
    - Coed MCs
    - Biker SCs
    - Charity MCs
    - Vintage MCs
    - BACA and Anti Child Abuse
- Female MCs
- Motorsports Clubs
- Riding Clubs
- Patriot Guard and Specialty Biker Groups
- Motorcycle Organizations
    - Motorcycle Safety Organizations
    - Motorcycle Enthusiast Groups
    - Motorcycle Rights Organizations
- Women's Social Clubs (on the Black biker set)

Understand that the pecking order of clubs has been well established in US history. There are many people that will argue that it "shouldn't be that way," or "Who died and made any one organization more important than another." And while these arguments may be true and make a lot of sense, the bottom line is that as an MC, instead of being involved in any or all of those arguments on the MC set, get to know how things are first, before worrying about how they should be. Reality is real so make sure to always keep it real. There has been plenty of bloodshed establishing these parameters and there are those willing to go to great extremes of violence to preserve these customs. Take the time to learn and understand the customs, traditions, values, and hierarchies that you will be held accountable to know as your MC operates on the set.

In the biker club set, particularly within the traditional MC culture, the hierarchical structure defines the relationships and roles among different clubs. Here is a general outline of the hierarchy commonly seen in the biker club set:

1% Outlaw Motorcycle Club (OMC) Nations

1% OMCs (or "1%ers") are considered the top tier of the hierarchy. These clubs have a well-defined structure, established bylaws, and a reputation for being independent and nonconformist. They often have multiple chapters and follow a strict code of conduct. 1% OMC nations have their own set of rules and protocols and are known for their distinct patches and colors. They run the MC set sometimes by violence if it comes to that. There is much you will learn about dealing with 1% OMCs. Learn MC protocol and follow it and you will not have much to fear from 1% OMC nations.

1% MC Designated Support Clubs

Support clubs (also called "puppet clubs" by law enforcement, "feeder clubs," or "brother clubs") are affiliated with a specific 1% OMC. They have a close relationship with their 1%er brotherhood and support its activities and values. Support clubs often wear patches or colors that show their affiliation with their designated 1% OMC and may assist the 1% OMC with tasks such as security, fundraising, or other club-related activities. They are considered an extended family of the 1%er OMC nation to which they are affiliated, which makes them part of that nation. They are not to be trifled with by lower-level clubs or other 1% OMC nations because the 1%er they support will turn up to defend them at all costs. They often go to war against the same enemies as their 1%er and are called in whenever additional muscle or backup is required, and they are often relied upon to do the bidding of their 1%er in its stead.

Example of a Support Club Supporting the 1%er

A former Rhode Island Hells Angels MC chapter President was imprisoned after a gun incident in a neighborhood near his clubhouse. When he was paroled, one of the conditions for his release was that he was forbidden to associate or hangout with any known Hells Angels MC members or Prospects. When a notorious mafia boss of a top New England crime family in his area died he vowed to attend the funeral as a sign of respect. Though forbidden from being seen with any of his brothers, he was escorted to the funeral, in colors, flanked by Red Devils MC full patch brother bodyguards wearing full regalia serving as his personal entourage. The media was taken aback by the exhibition and the story was sensationalized internationally. The courts were outraged, and he was immediately arrested after attending the funeral (White).

The Red Devils MC is a designated support club of the Hells Angels MC Nation (Department of Justice) and they had shown up in support of their brother. The courts could not sanction him because he was not consorting with known Hells Angels though the message was sent to all that he was still supported by the nation. By sending their support club, the Hells Angels had indeed sent an extension of themselves conveying a chilling message to law enforcement, the news media, and the courts, plus they had shown support to the deceased, his family and organization. That former president's parole was amended to prevent him from associating with any known support clubs as well (White 2), but the added sanction was really too little too late. The message had already been conveyed.

NOTE: Two 1% OMCs can be brother clubs on equal levels, and one is not a support club of the other. In that case the two clubs have established a brotherhood of equality, respect one another, perhaps fight together, and back up one another.

Supporter MCs

Supporter MCs are a newer phenomenon on the MC set. These are support clubs but not on as high a level as a brother club or a designated support club. They normally wear a support patch of the 1% OMC and enjoy their protection but are not expected to operate on as high a level of commitment. A lot of these kinds of clubs were not allowed to operate on the set unless they put on a support patch. They still enjoy a high status on the set because they are protected and carry out the interests of the 1% OMC.

Outlaw, OMC, or Diamond MCs

There is another class of OMC out there that is not considered a 1% OMC but still wears a diamond patch. They are called "outlaw clubs." They are not necessarily found in all areas of the country. Some will wear a diamond, but their diamond won't have the 1% in it. Though not 1% OMC nations, they move independently and are respected OMCs, able to move without hassle or intimidation from anyone. And this is the power of a diamond in today's MC set.

Note: There are outlaw MCs (OMCs) that wear no diamond at all; however, they are still considered outlaws for the way they move and get shit done. They are not to be underestimated! And there are outlaw MCs that still wear the 13 diamond to represent that they are not affiliated with the AMA, as it has been since the 1930s, and not necessarily outlawed to law enforcement. In fact, you will still see many 1%er OMC nations wearing both the 1% diamond to show OMC status and the 13 diamond to show separation from the AMA.

Note: Some 1% OMC support or brother clubs are given diamonds without the 1% marking in them too. In Texas, New Mexico, and Washington, for instance, it is routine to see Bandidos' support clubs wearing an orange 13 diamond. This shows their OMC status though not 1%ers definitely outlaws.

Law Enforcement MC (LEMCs)

A law enforcement motorcycle club (LEMC) members are primarily current or retired law enforcement officers, including jailers, police officers, sheriff's deputies, state troopers, and federal agents. These clubs are formed by individuals who share a passion for motorcycles and have a background or affiliation with law enforcement.

Purpose of LEMCs

The primary purpose of LEMCs is to provide camaraderie, support, and a sense of community among members who share a common bond through their law enforcement careers. LEMCs often engage in various activities, including group rides, charity events, fundraisers, and community outreach programs.

LEMC Patches

Their patches almost always incorporate law enforcement symbols, such as badges, emblems, guns, handcuffs, and sheriff stars to reflect their background and affiliation with law enforcement.

LEMCs versus Law Enforcement Agencies

LEMCs should not be confused with official law enforcement agencies or departments. LEMCs are independent social and recreational organizations composed of active duty and retired law enforcement officers and affiliates who come together voluntarily to pursue their shared interests in motorcycles and promote fellowship among fellow law enforcement professionals. They don't represent police departments and operate on their own time night department time. But one thing you will be smart to remember when encountering them, is that they are off-duty police, which makes them police 24 hours a day, 7 days a week. Trifling with them in a drunken fueled barroom fight can end up sending your MC to the calaboose with the off-duty officers (members of the LEMCs) uncharged in the fray. Consider this when making your decision to confront and challenge them.

LEMC Operations

LEMCs typically operate in accordance with local laws and regulations. Their activities are focused on promoting positive relationships within the law enforcement community and the broader community they serve.

LEMCs Hated by the Set

It is important to know that LEMCs are almost universally hated by traditional MCs, especially OMCs 1% OMCs, and their support clubs, and almost all others. Often LEMCs are accused of trying to be "cops in the day and act out their passions as tough guys at night" but then arresting MCs while on-duty and breaking the very laws the night before while acting like thugs. Whether or not that gripe is valid it is a topic for great debate, but the allegations are there. LEMCs often operate entirely on their own and aren't included in biker coalitions, COCs, or other kinds of traditional biker organizations or 1% clubs on the set.

Warning: If your MC gets too chummy with an LEMC, it will most likely be ostracized off the biker set.

Most MCs hate LEMCs because they do not have to follow any protocols to be blessed, exist, ride, or operate on the MC set—kind of like Iron Order MC which stresses they are absolutely not an

LEMC, although the MC set considers them an LEMC because they will openly admit cops into their brotherhood. No dominant MC is going to mess with a group of off-duty cops that is in their right mind, so dominant MCs leave them the hell alone. It is believed they hide behind their badges when confronted, which may or may not be true, but that's what it is.

Traditional MCs / 99%ers

Traditional Motorcycle Clubs refers to a club that follows the established customs, values, and protocols commonly associated with the MC culture. These clubs are male only MCs although they may have women's auxiliaries or properties of as part of their extended families. In traditional MCs women do not have a voice in the operations of the male brotherhood. These clubs can be extremely misogynistic and sexist in nature. They often have a rich history and adhere to a set of traditions, specific protocols, and etiquette passed down through generations that members are expected to follow. Traditional MCs are known for their keen sense of brotherhood, loyalty, and commitment to the biker lifestyle, placing a strong emphasis on motorcycle riding and brotherhood. Group rides, road trips, and attending rallies or events together are common activities that help foster a sense of camaraderie among members. They often organize club events, parties, charity rides, and fundraisers providing opportunities for members to bond and allow the club to contribute positively to their communities.

Traditional MCs typically have a hierarchical structure with specific officer positions such as President, Vice President, Secretary, Treasurer, and Sergeant at Arms. These positions hold specific responsibilities and authority within the club. They have distinct club colors and patches that represent their club identity and affiliation. These patches often include the club's logo, name, and location. The club's colors and patches are considered sacred and should be treated with respect.

Many traditional MCs have a dedicated clubhouse where members gather, hold meetings, and socialize. The clubhouse is often seen as the club's home and serves as a central hub for club activities. Traditional MCs may form alliances or have relationships with other motorcycle clubs, such as being part of a larger federation or maintaining friendly associations with specific clubs. These affiliations are often based on mutual respect and shared values.

Traditional MC Summary

Each traditional MC may have its own unique history, rules, and culture that contribute to its identity. Respect for club traditions and adherence to established protocols are highly valued within traditional MCs.

Veterans MC

A Veterans Motorcycle Club (VMC) is an MC composed primarily of military veterans and active-duty service members. These clubs are formed by individuals who have served in the armed forces and share a bond through their military experience and love for motorcycles. The primary purpose of a Veterans MC is to provide a supportive and brotherhood-oriented community for veterans. These clubs often engage in various activities that promote camaraderie, support for veterans, and community involvement. Some of the common activities include group rides, veteran recognition events, charity fundraisers, and participating in military-related ceremonies or parades.

Their patches may include military symbols, insignias, or flags to honor their military service and showcase their veteran status.

It's important to note that Veterans MCs are not officially recognized or affiliated with any government or military organization. They are independent social and recreational organizations formed by veterans to create a sense of brotherhood, support, and connection with fellow veterans who share a passion for motorcycles.

Veterans MCs often uphold values such as honor, loyalty, respect, and service, which are rooted in military traditions. They may also have specific requirements for membership, such as honorable military service, or may be open to veterans from all branches of the military.

Veteran's MCs Summary

Veterans MCs play a significant role in providing a supportive network for veterans, promoting awareness of veterans' issues, and engaging in activities that honor and remember those who have served in the armed forces.

Non-Traditional MCs

Non-traditional Motorcycle Clubs refers to clubs that deviates from the conventional norms and practices commonly associated with traditional MCs. These clubs may have alternative structures, values, or activities that differentiate them from the traditional MC culture. They may be coed and allow women to be officers even rising to the level of President. Here are a few examples of non-traditional motorcycle clubs:

Christian MCs (CMCs)

Members of a Christian motorcycle club (CMC) are individuals who identify as Christians and have a shared passion for motorcycles. These clubs combine their love for motorcycles with their Christian faith, creating a community of riders who seek to live out their faith while enjoying the biker lifestyle. The primary focus of a CMC is to promote fellowship, brotherhood/sisterhood, and outreach within the context of their Christian beliefs. They typically incorporate elements of worship, prayer, Bible study and spiritual growth into their club activities. Some CMCs also engage in charitable work, community service projects, and missions to spread their Christian values and help those in need.

Many CMCs engage in evangelistic efforts to share their faith and the message of Christianity with others. This can involve participating in rallies, events, and rides where they have the opportunity to interact with non-Christians and share their personal testimonies. They often participate in community service projects and charitable initiatives, organizing fundraisers, supporting local charities, or engaging in outreach activities to help those in need within their communities.

CMCs foster a sense of brotherhood/sisterhood among their members. They create a supportive and inclusive community where riders can connect, build friendships, and encourage one another in their Christian walk. While some CMCs do not allow women to become members, operating more traditionally, others do.

CMCs typically have a code of conduct that aligns with Christian values and ethics. This may include guidelines on behavior, language, respect for others, and adherence to traffic laws.

CMCs Summary

CMCs may have different denominational affiliations and theological perspectives. While they share a common belief in Christianity, the specific expressions of their faith and club activities can vary. The primary goal is to create a community where Christian bikers can come together, support one another to live out their faith in the context of their shared love for motorcycles. CMCs must do everything traditional MCs have to do to get their blessings to operate on the set. Even though they may be religious they are still human. Many are recovering from alcohol and other life vices. Don't be surprised to see them acting out on the set like other MCs - drinking too much or fighting. A criticism that has been aimed at them throughout the years is that they may not act as holy as some would like. Remember they are people too and also remember they are bikers not choir boys – even though they may actually sing in the choir.

Note: Other religions (including Seik, Muslim and Hebrew) have MCs dedicated to their religious structures as well. Like CMCs they serve their communities and biker communities from a religious context.

Masonic MCs

A Masonic Motorcycle Club consists of members who are Freemasons. Freemasonry (sometimes spelled Free-Masonry or simply Masonry) includes various fraternal organizations that trace their origins to the local guilds of stonemasons that, from the end of the 14th century, regulated the qualifications of stonemasons and their interaction with authorities and clients. Freemasonry is the oldest fraternity in the world and among the oldest continuous organizations in history (Freemasonry Wikipedia). Masonic MCs focus on moral and spiritual development, personal growth, and philanthropy by bringing together Freemasons who share a love for motorcycles. These clubs provide a platform for Freemasons to connect, ride together, and promote the values and principles of Freemasonry within the motorcycle community. The specific activities and focus of Masonic MCs may vary, but they typically incorporate elements of brotherhood, charity, and community involvement.

Masonic MCs usually incorporate Masonic symbols, such as the square and compass, into their club patches, apparel, or other branding. They may also incorporate Masonic rituals or ceremonies into their club activities to maintain a connection to the traditions and values of Freemasonry.

Masonic MCs uphold the values and ethics of Freemasonry including principles such as integrity, truthfulness, compassion, and respect for others. Members are expected to conduct themselves in a manner that reflects these values both on and off their motorcycles.

Masonic MCs Summary

As a whole, Masonic MCs are not officially recognized or endorsed by Freemasonry. They are independent social and recreational organizations formed by Freemasons who share a passion for motorcycles and desire to connect with other Freemasons in the motorcycle community.

First Responder MCs

First Responder Motorcycle Clubs are composed of active or retired first responders, including police officers, firefighters, and paramedics as well as other emergency personnel. These clubs bring together individuals who share a common bond of serving in these demanding and often high-stress professions. The primary purpose of First Responder MCs is to create a supportive community for first responders who have a passion for motorcycles. These clubs provide a platform for members to connect, ride together, and support one another both on and off the road. They offer a sense of camaraderie and understanding among those who have experienced the unique challenges and rewards of serving as first responders.

Many First Responder MCs engage in charitable initiatives to give back to their communities. They may organize fundraising events, participate in charity rides, or support causes related to first responder support, public safety, or community well-being. Some First Responder MCs also advocate for issues affecting first responders and promote awareness of the challenges they face by participating in public events, fundraisers, or campaigns to raise awareness about the importance of supporting first responders.

First Responder MCs emphasize the values of respect, service, and commitment to their profession and communities. Members are expected to uphold high standards of integrity, professionalism, and ethics both in their first responder roles and as representatives of the club.

First Responders MCs Summary

Each First Responder MC may have its own specific structure, rules, and activities, as they are independent organizations. However, they share a common bond as first responders and these MCs allow them to come together to enjoy their love for motorcycles and support one another in their challenging professions.

Sober MCs

Sober Motorcycle Clubs are composed of members with a focus on maintaining a sober and drug-free lifestyle. These clubs bring together individuals who have chosen to abstain from alcohol and drug use and provide a supportive community for those seeking a sober way of life. The primary purpose of Sober MCs is to create a safe and supportive environment for members who want to enjoy the camaraderie and brotherhood/sisterhood of motorcycle clubs without the presence of alcohol or drugs. These clubs often organize activities and events that promote sober living and provide opportunities for members to connect, ride together, and support one another on their sober journey.

Many Sober MCs engage in outreach and service activities to support the recovery community and raise awareness about the benefits of a sober lifestyle. They may participate in community events, charity rides, or support organizations that provide resources and assistance to those in recovery. By promoting a positive and healthy lifestyle, members strive to uphold values such as integrity, accountability, and personal growth.

Sober MCs Summary

Each Sober MC may have its own specific structure, rules, and activities, as they are independent organizations. The common goal among these clubs is to provide a space for individuals to connect, ride, and support each other in their maintaining their sobriety.

Coed MCs

Coed Motorcycle Clubs (also known as a "mixed gender MCs") welcome both male and female members. Unlike traditional MCs that may have separate chapters or clubs for men and women, coed MCs embrace inclusivity and offer equal membership opportunities to riders of all genders. The primary purpose of a coed MCs is to bring together individuals who share a common passion for motorcycles and riding. They embrace diversity and welcome riders from diverse backgrounds, regardless of their gender, race, ethnicity, or age and provide a supportive and inclusive environment for riders to connect, socialize, and participate in motorcycle-related activities. Coed MCs promote gender equality and do not restrict membership based on gender. They provide equal opportunities for men and women to join, participate, and hold leadership positions within the club even allowing women Presidents.

Members of coed MCs often enjoy group rides, attend motorcycle events and rallies, and engage in various social and community service activities. Coed MCs prioritize social interaction among members by organizing group rides allowing members to come together to explore scenic routes, enjoy the freedom of riding, and bond with fellow riders. They may organize regular meetings, social gatherings, and events that provide opportunities for riders to connect, share experiences, and build friendships within the club. Many coed motorcycle clubs engage in community service and charitable activities and may organize fundraisers, participate in charity rides, or support causes that are important to their members and the local community.

Coed motorcycle clubs often promote safety and offer educational resources to their members. They may conduct riding clinics, share tips on motorcycle maintenance and safety gear, and encourage ongoing learning to enhance riders' skills and knowledge.

Coed MC Summary

Specific activities and culture of coed MCs can vary. Some clubs may have a specific focus, such as adventure riding, sport biking, or cruiser riding, while others may be more diverse in terms of riding styles and interests. Ultimately, coed MCs aim to create an inclusive and supportive community for riders of all genders to enjoy the camaraderie and thrill of motorcycle riding.

Biker SCs

Biker Social Clubs are motorcycle-oriented groups that emphasize socializing and networking among members. These clubs may focus on creating a welcoming and inclusive environment for individuals who share a passion for motorcycles. They may organize social events, gatherings, and rides to foster camaraderie among members.

Charity MCs

Charity Motorcycle Clubs primarily focus on philanthropic activities and community service. These clubs use their passion for motorcycles to raise funds for charitable causes, participate in charity rides, and organize events to support their chosen charities. The emphasis is on giving back to the community rather than strictly adhering to the traditional MC culture.

Vintage MCs

Vintage Motorcycle Clubs center around a shared love for vintage or classic motorcycles. These clubs focus on preserving and celebrating vintage motorcycles, organizing rides and events that showcase these historic bikes, and providing a platform for enthusiasts to connect and share their passion.

Bikers Against Child Abuse and Anti Child Abuse MCs

Bikers Against Child Abuse (also known as "BACA," "B.A.C.A.," or "B.A.C.A. International, Inc.") is a worldwide charitable motorcycle organization that works to protect children from dangerous individuals and situations across 18 countries. Founded in 1995 in Provo UT, BACA members aim to empower abused children by showing them they are not alone and that they have a support system. They provide emotional support, encouragement, and a sense of security to these children as they work with local and state officials already in place to protect children (BACA Wikipeda).

Members of BACA are motorcycle enthusiasts who use their love for motorcycles and the biker lifestyle to make a positive impact on the lives of abused children. BACA acts as an advocate for abused children by establishing a physical presence by attending court hearings, visitations, and other situations where the child may feel unsafe. They also assist children in feeling secure in their homes and communities. BACA raises awareness about child abuse and works to prevent its occurrence. The organization promotes education and community outreach to spread awareness about the issue and provide resources for prevention and support and offer ongoing support to children and their families. They routinely maintain regular contact with the child, providing a sense of stability and protection.

BACA and Specialty MC Summary

There are hundreds of specialty MC organizations that operate like BACA. They have many different names and missions that range from helping abused children, to helping abused women (Protecting Battered Women MC), helping animals, protecting migrants, and stopping human trafficking. These kinds of MCs operate independently from law enforcement agencies and are not affiliated with any specific religious or political group. Their organizations are solely focused on aiding and supporting abused children and needed causes. They don't engage in illegal activities. BACA chapters and clubs like them are present in various locations around the world, and the organizations continue to grow as more individuals join the cause to fight for world causes and a brighter future for the downtrodden.

Non-Traditional MC Summary

Non-traditional MCs may still have their own set of rules, protocols, and expectations for their members. While they may deviate from the traditional MC culture, they still cultivate a sense of community, camaraderie, and shared interests among their members.

Female MCs

Female (or Women's) Motorcycle Clubs are specifically formed and catered to women riders. These clubs provide a supportive and inclusive community for women who share a passion for motorcycles and riding. Female MCs promote camaraderie and create an empowering space where women can connect, socialize, and participate in motorcycle-related activities. The primary focus of female MCs is to celebrate women in motorcycling and provide a supportive environment for their members.

Female MCs foster a sense of independence, confidence, and empowerment through motorcycling among their female members by encouraging women to pursue their passion for riding and provide a platform for women to support and uplift each other. The camaraderie and sisterhood shared among their members provides opportunities for women to connect, build friendships, and share experiences related to riding, motorcycles, and the biker lifestyle. Female MCs organize group rides and participate in various motorcycle events and rallies allowing women to come together, enjoy the thrill of riding, explore new routes, and create lasting memories. Female MCs often engage in community service and charitable activities by organizing fundraisers, participate in charity rides, and support local organizations that focus on women's empowerment, safety, or other related causes.

Female MCs often offer riding clinics, workshops, and educational resources to help women enhance their riding skills, knowledge of motorcycle mechanics, and safety practices. Some female MCs are involved in advocacy work related to women's issues in motorcycling. They may advocate for increased visibility and representation of women riders in the industry, promote safety initiatives, and support causes that are important to their members.

Female MCs Summary

Female MCs may have different names, structures, and focuses depending on the specific club and its mission. Some clubs may be independent, while others may be affiliated with larger motorcycle organizations. The main goal is to provide a supportive and empowering community for women riders, allowing them to connect, grow, and thrive in the world of motorcycling. They are received with respect on the biker set today; however, this was not always the case. They have won their reputation through superior riding skills, honor, and respect.

Motorsports Clubs (MSCs)

Motorsports Clubs (MSCs) are composed of members with a shared passion for motorsports activities, including car racing, motorcycle racing, off-roading, karting, drag racing, and autocross. MCSs are not considered to be MCs but often hang around the MC set because they do ride motorcycles. You can't typically tell them apart from MCs in their operation and get down. Many MSCs are coed with both men and women riders.

Ruff Ryders MSC

One of the most famous MSC is called Ruff Ryders. Started in the early 2000s, the Ruff Ryders started out as a street production team to promote Ruff Ryders Entertainment projects and artists, they are now bigger than most MCs with international chapters worldwide. Ruff Ryders operate as a fun loving, highly stylized biker organization doing crazy stunt riding, racing, and promotions (Ruff Ryders Lifestyles).

Riding Clubs

Riding clubs are organizations of motorcycle enthusiasts who come together for the primary purpose of riding motorcycles. While they may share a similar passion for riding, they typically do not have the same structured hierarchy as MCs. Riding clubs may have their own set of officers or leaders, but they usually do not have the same level of formality or strict protocols as OMCs, support clubs or traditional MCs.

The requirements for RCs vary, with some wearing back patches, some requiring dues, and some requiring potential members to prospect. In fact, so closely mirror MCs you absolutely can't tell the difference. RCs can hold their own on the biker set, obtaining respect from other MCs in the area. Keep that in mind as you pursue your biker club career.

Patriot Guard Riders and Specialty Biker Groups

The Patriot Guard Riders (PGR) is a volunteer organization in the U.S. formed in 2005, with a primary mission to honor and show respect for fallen military service members, veterans, and first responders during funerals, memorials, and other commemorative events at the invitation of the decedent's family. (Patriot Guard Riders Wikipedia). Initially, the PGR was formed to shelter and protect the deceased's family against protesters from the Westboro Baptist Church, who claim that the deaths of American troops in Iraq and Afghanistan are divine retribution for American tolerance of homosexuality.

They coordinate with the family and event organizers to ensure their presence is appropriate and welcomed. PGR members position themselves to physically shield the mourners from the presence of the Westboro protesters with their motorcade and American flags. The group also drowns out the protesters' chants by singing patriotic songs or by revving their engines (Patriot Guard Riders Wikipedia).

The PGR members often form a flag line, holding American flags, to create a solemn and respectful corridor for the funeral procession or memorial service. They may also provide motorcycle escorts to ensure the safe and dignified transportation of the fallen service member or veteran. The PGR conducts its activities in a non-confrontational manner and operates within the bounds of the law. Their focus is on providing support, respect, and honor to the fallen heroes and their families. They do not engage in counter-protests or confrontations with any opposing groups.

The PGR also extends their support to living veterans, active-duty military personnel, and first responders. They may participate in welcoming home ceremonies, send-offs for deployed troops, homecomings, and other events that recognize and appreciate the service and sacrifice of these individuals.

While the PGR is open to all individuals who support their mission, it has a strong presence within the motorcycle community. Many PGR members are motorcycle riders who use their bikes to honor the fallen and show solidarity. However, participation is not limited to motorcycle riders, and individuals can support the PGR's mission in various capacities (Patriot Guard Riders Wikipedia).

PGR and Specialty MCs Summary

The PGR are just one example of so many specialty groups of MCs that have carved out a space in service to community and mankind. The services provided are varied and plentiful and though they are on a lower level on the MC scale of hierarchy, they are well recognized and respected for their contributions. In the case of the PGR, they have gained recognition and respect for their unwavering commitment to honoring those who have served their country. Their volunteer efforts have made a significant impact in providing comfort and support to grieving families while paying tribute to the fallen heroes and their service to the nation.

Note: I've personally experienced their professionalism as they laid one of our brothers to rest who had fallen due to a motorcycle accident in 2015. They escorted his body on a nearly one-hundred-mile trip to the cemetery and buried him with military honors. It was most amazing to watch how they had coordinated with every police and sheriff's department along the route. Each department escorted our nearly three-mile caravan through their towns and cities, culminating with officers standing at attention with their hats in their hands as we entered their jurisdictions and exited them. The memory causes me to weep as I write these lines. They positioned their motorcycle behind our caravan flying a huge American flag and prevented all vehicles from passing or interrupting our procession. Some drivers got so angry that they threatened to ram them off their motorcycles with pickup trucks, shot them middle fingers, and threatened them with assault. They never wavered, and not one vehicle broke their ranks. All of this thanks to the PGR. To the Mighty PGR, you have my thanks and my prayers for your many blessings and longevity for your assistance in burying our veteran brother with class and dignity. Black Dragon, former National President, Mighty Black Sabbath MC Nation.

Motorcycle Organizations

Motorcycle organizations are groups or associations that bring together individuals with a shared interest in motorcycles and motorcycling. These organizations serve various purposes, ranging from promoting motorcycle safety and advocacy to fostering camaraderie among riders.

Motorcycle Safety Organizations

Motorcycle safety organizations focus promote safe riding practices, rider education, and raising awareness about motorcycle safety issues. They may offer training courses, organize safety campaigns, and collaborate with government agencies and other stakeholders to improve motorcycle safety on the roads.

Motorcycle Enthusiast Groups

Motorcycle enthusiast groups are formed by individuals who share a passion for motorcycles and motorcycling but may not have the formal structure or requirements of MCs or riding clubs. Enthusiast groups often gather around specific motorcycle brands, models, or riding styles and provide a platform for enthusiasts to connect, share knowledge, and participate in events or rides together.

Motorcycle Organizations Summary

The specific nature, purpose, and structure of motorcycle organizations can vary widely. Some organizations may have national or international reach, while others may be more localized or regional. Additionally, the level of formality, membership requirements, and activities can differ from one organization to another.

Motorcycle Rights Organizations (MROs)

Motorcycle rights organizations (MROs) advocate for the rights and interests of motorcyclists. They work to protect the rights of riders by monitoring proposed laws and regulations to promote motorcycle safety, and influence legislation and policies that affect motorcycling. MROs actively engage in legislative advocacy at the local, state, and national levels and work to ensure motorcyclists' voices are heard by lawmakers, providing input, lobbying for favorable legislation, and opposing measures that could be detrimental to riders. MROs may provide legal support and representation for motorcyclists, offering advice, resources, and referrals to riders facing legal issues related to motorcycle accidents, insurance claims, unfair treatment, or discriminatory practices. MROs have also been known to establish legal defense funds to help riders with legal costs and advocate for fair treatment within the legal system.

MROs rely on the support and involvement of individual riders, encouraging motorcyclists to become members and actively participate in their initiatives. They often organize meetings, forums, and membership events where riders can voice their concerns, share input, and contribute to the organization's efforts; providing a platform for riders to connect, share information, and support one another. They offer opportunities for riders to network, exchange ideas, and discuss shared challenges and experiences. MROs often have local chapters or state organizations that facilitate communication and collaboration among members.

MROs often promote rider education and safety initiatives by organizing training courses, workshops, and awareness campaigns to educate riders about safe riding practices, proper gear usage, and defensive riding techniques; collaborating with government agencies, motorcycle safety organizations, and training providers to improve rider safety.

MROs Summary

Examples of well-known motorcycle rights organizations include the Motorcycle Riders Foundation (MRF), American Bikers Toward Education or A Brotherhood Against Totalitarian Enactments (ABATE), National Coalition of Motorcyclist (NCOM), American Motorcyclist Association also known as American Motorcycle Association (AMA) and many others. These organizations, along with numerous regional and local MROs, play a vital role in protecting the rights and interests of motorcyclists and promoting a safe and favorable environment for riders.

Female Social Clubs

Female social clubs (SCs) are unique to the African American biker club experience. Black MC SCs consist of women (mostly African American) who operate independent clubs within the Black biker club set in support of Black MCs, while simultaneously supporting their communities at large through their charitable works. As such, they have etched themselves into a place of existence among Black biker clubs not customary for women on any other MC set no matter the race. Women are rarely included in today's male dominated world of biker clubs and their voices are consequently muted. SCs on the Black MC set have flourished because they have embraced the culture and standards of the MCs they support, thereby enriching the MC set with their beautiful presence. Many SCs are administratively setup much like the MCs they support. Some even have the same officer positions, ranking structure, operational standards, and traditions as MCs—including prospecting their sisters before allowing them to become members. SCs have even been known to attend some MC coalition meetings to have their grievances addressed – an opportunity they never would have been allowed a few years ago.

MC Hierarchy Summary

The hierarchy and structure of the biker club set can vary between different regions and subcultures. Not all motorcycle clubs fit neatly into these categories, and there can be variations and exceptions based on the specific dynamics and traditions of different clubs.

CHAPTER FIVE
INTRA & INTER MC PROTOCOL

MC Protocol

MC Protocol, for the purposes of this book, is broken down to two categories:

- Intra-club protocol (Chapter Six)
- Inter-club protocol (Chapter Seven)

Intra-club MC Protocol

Intra-club MC protocol refers to the set of rules, customs, and traditions that govern the behavior and interactions within the boundaries of the MC -- between brothers. These protocols exist in all MCs (traditional, outlaw, or 1%er) and are the basic building blocks of any MC brotherhood. In addition to the MC's bylaws, the intra-club MC protocol establishes the rights, policies, traditions, and rules of a particular MC above and beyond established MC protocol recognized by traditional MCs.

Inter-Club MC Protocol

Inter-club MC protocol refers to the universal rules of behavior, diplomacy, respect, and politics that exists between MCs that operate on the various biker club sets worldwide. It is peculiar because it is both local and international which means that some things that are done in some areas cannot be done in others but if you know and practice the basics of inter-club MC protocol it can carry you peacefully around the world long enough for you to learn the locally established rules that you don't know without getting into trouble for being new or while visiting a new area.

The combination of rules and modus operandi combined into what has become known as MC protocol has been established throughout the decades to maintain order, respect, peace, and unity within and between members and MCs. If followed, an MC and its members should be able to enjoy peace and prosperity (in most instances, most of the time).

CHAPTER SIX
INTRA-CLUB MC PROTOCOL

The protocols, rules, interactions, and expectations between brothers inside of an MC are known as "intra-club MC protocol." This protocol can coincide or conflict with the most important documents within the club, which are the bylaws. It is important to know that nothing supersedes the bylaws! Even though there are standards of conduct found in all MCs, which dictate how brothers will interact with one another, the bylaws can be written in such a way that any of those protocols won't exist. For instance, most MCs honor the standard of conduct that states "no brother shall sleep with another brother's woman." but the bylaws may state that all brothers will share their women communally. This would, of course, negate the standards of conduct towards brothers' women that most would expect when joining a club, but the bylaws are the directive.

The point is intra-club MC protocol is not as defined as interclub MC protocol. It varies by club, President, or would be dictator. In this chapter, I am writing about the common rules found in most MCs; however, these rules are not engraved in stone. The methodologies in your club's social construct may vary greatly.

Which brings me to my next point. In January 2025, I spoke at the Motorcycle Club Professional Convention in the President's breakout session on the subject of *"Has the MC Set Lost Its Way."* My conclusion was yes it has because of the decaying values of the Presidents who run the sets rather than the members who follow them. I have found that in MCs today, there is too much emphasis on gathering large numbers of new members rather than on gaining quality members who can reflect the great values of honor, respect, brotherhood, unity, and family upon which all the incredible traditional MCs were built. The egos of the "president forever" mindset leaders, who run the MC with a "bylaws be damned, my way or the highway, the rules are for everybody but me, and if I can't lead the MC no one can," mentality cause them to display leadership that corrupts the hearts and souls of the brothers who follow in their footsteps.

Take this from this chapter: If your bylaws are out of step with traditional MC practices, you are setting your brotherhood up for ultimate failure. You are the problem! Your manipulative schemes are the problem! And it is likely that your MC will not pass the test of time, ultimately failing and taking with it all the hard work and sacrifice of those that came before you. I ask today's MC leaders, "What will your legacy tell of your time at the helm? Will you set the club up for success or failure? What will you teach others who follow in your steps? Will you teach them loyalty, honor, and respect? Or will you teach them how to be petulant fools concerned only with self? It takes hard work, love, sacrifice, and honor to do the right things. Do you have it in you Prez?"

There is a basic set of rules followed by bikers around the world that has been coined "The Biker Code." Some authors have gone as far as to write it and share it across social media as memes or pictures. After I read this code recently, I thought about what I would codify into a code for biker clubs were I to write a system. I thought about the standard codes of conduct I've observed in traditional and diamond clubs across the country I've dealt with in the past 36+ years, and I came up with what I call "The Biker Club Code." This "Biker Club Code" illuminates the basic code of conduct for how club brothers are expected to treat one another unless club bylaws demand otherwise. They are as follows:

The Biker Club Code

1. To stay in the club, you must maintain membership in good standing.
2. Protect your MC brotherhood with all your might!
3. One patch, one vote!
4. All grievances are handled at the table!
5. Never sleep with your club brother's old' lady!
6. Always show respect to the club's OGs and severely punish any brother who disrespects them!
7. Never discuss club business outside of the club.
8. Never lie to a club brother or officer.
9. Never steal from club brothers or the club.
10. Always pay back a loan from a club brother or the club.
11. When handling the club's money, always get a receipt.
12. Never exploit the club for personal gain unless all brothers benefit equally.
13. Never get high in the clubhouse.
14. Never make a personal fight a club fight.
15. Never allow the brothers to die for what they believe, instead make the enemy die for what they believe.
16. One fights we all fight! Never abandon a brother in battle.
17. No one talks to cops without at least one witness from the club. If it inadvertently happens the club SAA must be notified immediately.
18. No brother allows rumors to spread about another brother not present to defend himself.
19. No brother is punished, fined, or put out bad without a trial.
20. Never bring disgrace or discredit onto the MC or the colors.
21. Never incite a club war without a club war counsel.
22. Never snitch on the club or on a club brother.
23. IF ever in an incident that involves the police, "No one talks we all walk!"

24. Never divulge personal information on a club brother for any reason.
25. Never allow a club brother to talk disparagingly against the club, its members, its social construct its officers or its president unless at the table.
26. Never write down anything in a meeting that can be used against the club in a court of law.

I will write more about these items later in this chapter but first:

Club Colors and Patches

MCs have their unique colors and patches that represent their club identity. These colors and patches are considered sacred and will be treated with utmost respect. Here are some common MC protocols associated with club colors:

- Only full patch brothers in good standing can wear club colors.
- No patches are for sale. They cannot be bought, bartered, or given away.
- All individuals must prospect, probate, or earn their patches in ways acceptable to the club.
    - The thought that every patch is prospected for is a myth. There can be other ways to earn a patch as long as it is not bought, sold, bartered, or freely given.

    Hells Angels nomad, Jake Sawyer, was patched into the club in his first day as a hang around. As he shared with me in in an interview on my YouTube channel, "*Black Dragon Biker TV,*" on his first day hanging out with the club a few brothers wanted to kick in a guy's door. Although he was against it, the brothers were insistent, so he agreed stating, "Okay well let me be the first one

in the door!" To which they agreed. He kicked in the guy's front door and was shot immediately in the chest. He moved forward, knocked the gun out of the guy's hand and proceeded to pulverize him. He was made a member that day!
- Unauthorized individuals should not wear or display any part of your MC colors or patches.
    o Only full patch brothers in good standing can wear soft colors (t-shirts with the club's logo affixed to the back).
    o Nonmembers cannot wear soft colors. They may, however, wear supporter t-shirts.
- No one outside of your club should handle your colors except in emergency situations.
    o For instance, if you needed to take your cut off for a few minutes you wouldn't normally hand it to someone outside of your club to hold as this would be considered disrespectful to your club.
- Your colors should never leave your possession in public unless closely guarded by a club brother or prospect.
    o Leaving your colors on the back of a chair in a biker bar so you can go use the head is against MC protocol.
- Some clubs require you to fight and or even die before surrendering your colors to an enemy club or even law enforcement; most, however, do not.
    o Most clubs would rather you do everything reasonable to keep from losing them but won't expect you to die trying to keep them.

Respect for Club Hierarchy

Most MCs follow a quasi-military hierarchical structure with designated officers and positions. The reason that I call it quasi-military is because even though you have officers whose orders must be obeyed, you also get to vote in most matters pertaining to the club's direction and social construct, which does not happen in military service. In traditional MCs, these officers are usually voted into office with set limits. Members are expected to show respect and deference to higher-ranking members, including officers and club leaders. It is also important to the brotherhood that you support the club's officers and President simply because if they fail the club fails. By undermining your officers, you risk jeopardizing the entire club. Always remember that an officer can be voted out when his term is over, but he deserves all of the support you can give him while he is serving out his term. In fact, one of the biggest ways that you can support the club is to support the club's officers to your best ability whether you agree with their decisions or not. Practice uplifting and avoid undermining. Your club will benefit from that practice.

NOTE: I'm often asked by brothers of various clubs who have been asked to serve as officers or presidents, *"What if I don't want to serve the club in that capacity? What if I only want to be a regular fucking member (RFM)?"* My answer has always been, if the men have selected you to lead it is no longer about what you want! You exist to serve the MC in whatever capacity the brothers think you are capable. Remember the MC is not about "I," but rather it is about "WE!"

Club Meetings and Communication

A traditional MC is defined by regular club meetings that are held to discuss club matters, make decisions, and maintain communication among members. Part of being a brother in good standing is participating in these club meetings. Most traditional MCs have a minimum number of mandatory meetings that must be attended to remain in good standing. These meetings determine the direction of the club; therefore, it is vital for members to attend and actively participate. Non-participating members who only show up to party, ride, and have fun are a drain on the brotherhood and have no place in the club. Most MCs only keep these non-participating members around to boost their numbers. The brotherhood needs participating members to remain strong. If you can no longer do that take a leave of absence or turn in your colors.

Manage the Money

When MCs break up, suffer splits, or crash and burn, it is most often because of the MONEY and how it is handled! The manner in which the club's finances are handled can be one of the most crucial factors in determining the strength and longevity of the club. The most basic problem is often someone is accused of stealing from the club. Whether it is true or not doesn't really matter. The accusation alone can be the downfall of the entire club. These are some important protocols many traditional MCs use to prevent these accusations:

- The president never handles money.
- Two-person authorization is required for all bank, credit card or financial transactions.
- A financial report is given at all regular meetings.
- Any full patch brother in good standing can request to see the books and financial reports at any time.
- The business manager oversees all contracts, suppliers, and vendors. The treasurer pays the bills.
- If there is no business manager the treasurer works in concert with the SAA or VP.
- A receipt is produced for all monies and transactions received or handled by any brother or prospect.

Dealing with the Patch Maker

The patch maker is one of the most important vendors to the MC because He/she is responsible for the look of the MC. The most common problem among MCs is members refusing to pay the patch maker for their colors or asking the patch maker to do work on projects outside of the scope of the club and not paying for those orders. The patch maker should be treated with great respect and care. When I first became National President of the Black Sabbath MC Nation, The Father Paul 'Pep' Perry taught me some invaluable lessons on how to deal with the patch maker. His teachings served me and my MC well. Here are some of the protocols he taught me for dealing with the patch maker:

- Only one person (perhaps the SAA) deals with the patch maker to submit orders.
- The patch maker is paid in advance for all orders so that he is never left in a bind.
- The patch maker is told in advance that if he/she takes orders from a member for work outside of the club without being paid in advance the loss is on him/her and not the club.

Brotherhood's Responsibility When You go to Jail

As a consultant and counselor to clubs worldwide I've run into so many MCs who have failed to help their brothers in time of need. Perhaps the most disgusting is when clubs do not meet the promised expectations of brothers who go to jail handling club business.

- The club handles the bail.
- The club obtains the lawyer or provides a loan to the brother.
- The club hires the private detective.

- The club takes care of the brother's family, making sure the bills are paid, and the children are secure.
- No brother flirts or tries to move in on a jailed brother's woman. Revelation of anything like this should lead to the most severe consequences for that member.

Brotherhood's Responsibility When You go to the Hospital

Many clubs fail in this area as well, which is hard for me to understand. Many MCs let brothers fall out of sight and out of mind when they go into the hospital and I even witnessed an MC kick out a member who had a wreck with a brain injury for "not riding his motorcycle enough" following the injury with no consideration to his recovery, effects of PTSD, or rehabilitation. Sadly, none of his brothers ever visited him in the hospital after his stay in the emergency room. Sometimes MCs get so busy clubbing and having fun, they miss out on the largest responsibility of all, caring for the family. Support and brotherhood go beyond the flashing lights and the trauma of the emergency room. Support can take years as there are the aftereffects, recovery, and rehabilitation to consider. Here are some protocols to remember:

- The club shows up at the hospital and supports the brother and his family, wife, children, parents, brothers, sisters etc.
- The club provides extended support to the brother throughout the duration of the recovery.
- The club provides extended support to the brother through rehabilitation.
- The club makes the necessary adjustments to welcome the brother back after rehabilitation including allowing a special membership if the brother can no longer operate a motorcycle.

Riding Formation and Etiquette

Traditional MCs ride in formation. This promotes unity, safety, and efficient movement of the club. In good weather on decent surfaces traditional MCs most often ride two up, also known as "parade style" or "suicide style." In this formation the club is riding two-by-two, side-by-side. This is the most aggressive style of group riding and requires training, practice, competence, and communication. Hard riding MCs do not ride staggard unless the weather is poor, the traffic or road conditions necessitate, or there is poor visibility. Members are expected to follow the designated formations and adhere to riding etiquette, including proper hand signals, maintaining formation, and promoting safe riding practices. For clubs who have road captains, standard protocol dictates that the road captain is the President while the pack is on the move. In clubs that do not have road captains, the SAA generally takes on the responsibility of conducting the pack. Usually, the pack moves much faster than the speed of traffic, keeping it safe from inattentive drivers or curious motorists who get too close. In traditional MC formations the club rides by order of rank with the road captain and senior officers forward and succession by rank trailing aft. Here are some common protocols to follow:

- The road captain certifies all hang arounds and prospects before they ride in the pack.
- The road captain certifies all motorcycles are mechanically worthy to ride in the pack.
- No stunting in the pack.
- No one rides drunk or impaired in the pack.
- If two club brothers say a brother is impaired, he must relinquish his keys.
- The road captain can deputize assistant road captains.
- Any brother who cannot ride suicide rides at the back of the pack.

Club Events and Activities

MCs organize various events and activities, such as charity rides, parties, or club runs. Brothers are expected to participate and contribute to these events to support the club and its initiatives. Mandatory events exist to help the club achieve its objectives. Some protocols to follow when supporting club events and activities include:

- Arrive early, on time is late.
- Come prepared to work. The party is for the guests, not the members.
- Stay on your work assignment until you are relieved.
- Do not become inebriated while on duty.
- Be welcoming to all guests and avoid rude or inappropriate behavior. Greet guests and thank them for their support.
- Protect guests and provide security from the parking lot to the venue and back.
- Do not allow any MC to attempt patch policing or conduct their club business against any other MC at your event. It is your MC's responsibility to protect all guests.
- If your MC cannot protect its guests don't throw an event.

Loyalty and Brotherhood

The underlying strength of the MC is the dedication of its members to the bonds of loyalty and respect emphasized by the brotherhood. There is a great expectation of loyalty to the club and its members. Brothers are expected to prioritize the interests and well-being of the club and its members, fostering a strong sense of extended family and camaraderie. In the words of the Father of the Mighty Black Sabbath MC Nation Paul 'Pep' Perry, *"Stop saying I, I, I, and start saying WE!"* If this is the way, there will always be a strong MC.

Club Disciplinary System

Like tribal communities handle all issues within the tribe, MCs handle all issues within the MC. This includes disciplinary actions against members found not to be in compliance with the club's bylaws.

The MC's justice system holds all persons within the extended family accountable for their actions via its bylaws. This only works as long as the club is fair to everyone in exercising its judicial practices. Unfortunately, many MCs are not fair, nor do they offer justice for all. Instead, they devolve into fiefdoms led by egotistical strongmen bent on manipulating everyone around them and corrupting the club. These men reward corrupt patches and officers who help them hijack the brotherhood causing members to become powerless as these leaders imbed themselves too deeply to be removed. This corruption and coercion can be prevented if full-patch brothers hold tight to the bylaws and disallow would-be dictators to corrupt their club.

In most MCs, the justice system is overseen by the SAA. If he remains independent and on his business, the system will remain fair and just for everyone. My book, "Sergeant at Arms Bible Soldier Sergeant of the Brotherhood" covers the subject of the club disciplinary system in detail but here are some basics:

- There must be formal written charge(s) by the aggrieved party accusing the alleged violating party of an infraction for there to even be a case. A verbal complaint won't get it.
- The charge(s) must represent an actual violation of a club bylaw or code of conduct the brother would have advance knowledge he was violating before the occurrence of the act and not be something "made-up" suddenly to satisfy an agenda.

Motorcycle Club Protocol 101

- The Sergeant at Arms (Enforcer in some clubs) conducts an initial investigation examining the evidence and witnesses to determine if the charges have merit. After which he certifies whether the proceeding can advance to a trial also called in some MCs a committee hearing or simply a committee.
- If the SAA deems the proceeding will move forward a committee of neutral full patch brothers in good standing, who are not a party to the matter in any way, will be assigned to hear and judge the trial.
- The accused brother will then be notified of his trial date of which the SAA will officiate.
- During the committee formal charges will be read for adjudication along with the bylaws, constitution, or standards of conduct violated. The accused brother is presented with the opportunity to confront his accusers, vet the veracity of their evidence, question their witnesses, as well as present evidence and witnesses on his own behalf.
- The committee will end with a guilty, innocent, or not guilty verdict.
    - **Innocent:** No, or bogus evidence, accusations maliciously brought, or accusation never should have occurred in the first place.
    - **Guilty:** Evidence proves guilt beyond reasonable doubt.
    - **Not Guilty:** Evidence could not prove guilt beyond reasonable doubt.
    - **Note:** It is important to note that in many MCs the verdict must be UNANIMOUS, especially in trials that could result in a brother's removal from the club.

- There may be a separate committee for awarding punishment if the result of the trial is guilty or it can be handled at the end.
- There should be a method for appeal, at least to reexamine the process to make sure all steps were followed correctly by the MC and that the punishment is in line with similar cases.

Punishment

The meting out of punishment should be just as formal as the committee. It can occur at the end of the committee or scheduled for another time. For instance, the committee may need to reconvene to consider the extent to which punishment will be administered based on the case. In any event the SAA (Enforcer in some clubs) should perform the ceremony:

- The meeting is brought to order which may include only the members of the committee or a meeting of all full patch brothers in good standing.
- The SAA reads charges.
- The SAA reads the guilty verdict.
- The SAA reads the punishment.
- The guilty brother will comply with the punishment by paying fine, or arranging to pay fine in installments, etc., turning in colors for suspension period, or turning in colors for good.

Common Punishments

- **Fines** (yep, they'll take your money! Expect it).
- **Demotion** (all the way back to probationary or prospect in some cases).
    - Sometimes when you are demoted you may not be able to hold office again for some period of time.

- **Suspension** (you may have to surrender colors to the SAA for some period of time if you are suspended).
- **Physical Exercises** (1,000 pushups for a prospect for example).
- **Work Detail** (paint the clubhouse for example or wash every full patch brother's in good standing bike).
- **Ass Kicking** (some clubs will kick your ass, black your eye, bust your lip, Charlie horse your arm, or other physical punishments if the infraction is serious enough—like sleeping with a club brother's woman or stealing from the MC—it can get brutal).
- **Leave of Absence** (this normally lasts longer than a suspension).
- **Dismissal from the club** If things are bad and a suspension or leave of absence won't quite cut it).
    - Confiscate your motorcycle or other belongings (This does happen when you are dismissed, depending on the MC things can get nasty. Don't break the rules).

Brother's Responsibility After Trial, Appeal, Punishment

If the club disciplines you and you didn't deserve it, FIGHT LIKE HELL, appeal, let your voice be heard, gather your witnesses. But be wise enough to know when you are in a fight you cannot win. Then you might have some decisions to make.

If the club disciplines you and you deserve it, accept it, acknowledge the wrong, and move on. I once knew a guy who prospected for his club five different times. It's okay. Put it behind you.

- If you are fined pay it or make acceptable arrangements to pay.
    - If you must claim hardship, then do that.

- - Not paying is disrespectful to the authority of the MC.
- If you are suspended accept the suspension.
  - Sit out the required time, then come back and start anew.
  - It is respectful to show deference to the authority of the MC!
  - This is the contract you agreed to when you accepted membership.
- If you are dismissed accept your dismissal.
  - Don't get pissy and make the club chase you down for your colors. No one had to chase you down to give you your colors so be an adult when turning them in. Feelings are hurt, especially yours, but accept authority and carry yourself like a man.
  - Don't mail in your colors. That shit is so fucking lame! You didn't get your colors in the mail (at least not from a traditional MC) so don't send them back in the mail. It is your responsibility to meet the SAA and turn those patches back in face-to-face, man-to-man, just like you got them, in good condition, showing respect to the club for which you worked so hard to become a member—even if you can't stand those #$@#$%.

What to Do If Expelled/Dismissed from the MC

Turn in everything.

- Patches
- Hats
- Colors
- T-shirts
- Stickers on your car and bike

- Specialty items you had made for your bike like breather covers, etc.
- Club trinkets
- Bylaws
- Memorabilia
- EVERYTHING!!!!! That has the club's logo!!!! EVERYTHING!!

You may be angry and hurt but MC protocol requires you to:

- Never divulge club secrets or club business to which you were privy while a member.
- Never talk negatively about club brothers or the president.
- Never expose club business to the public.
- Never snitch to the police about former club brothers.
- Never capitalize on club intellectual property, ventures, or business ideas.
- Never join another MC before six months have passed unless you have permission from both presidents (new MC and old MC) to do so. If not, you will be considered a club hopper.

Out Bad

If you've ever been in the military, you know that there are levels to separation from service that range from an honorable discharge to a bad conduct discharge and hundreds of reasons in between. At the highest level of separation, a prior service member has benefits and rights and at the lowest level, a prior service member has no benefits or rights (not even the right to be buried as a veteran).

The MC also has levels of discharge, of which the worst is being put "OUT BAD" from the MC. In the MC community this form of expulsion is tantamount to being labeled an outcast and the community may shun you as bad as a pedophile may be shunned in prison. In fact, in some instances it can be physically threatening to be put out bad from a club as your club and its allies, supports, and affiliates will be forced to have no contact with you, and you will not be allowed to join any MC in your area.

MCs that may consider taking you in, after contacting your old club and finding out you are out bad will retract their offers of membership. You will become a cancer on the biker club set, and no one will interact with you. Out bad status is reserved for the worst crimes on the set which is generally considered:

- Stealing from the club.
- Sleeping with a club brother's woman
- Snitching to the police on a club brother or the club.
- Killing a brother in the club.
- Harming or sexually abusing a child.
- Raping or beating a woman.
- Using or selling hard drugs.

Unfortunately, modern era clubs have stopped using out bad for the worst offenses and have started putting members out bad for dumb shit like political differences, blocking people from running for office, jealousy, pettiness, and immaturity. Instead of meeting a brother behind the clubhouse and settling things heads up, a cowardly President will instead exert his power to put the member out bad, failing to recognize the harm interjected into the entire MC set. Consequently, the "out bad" status has lost its bite, and clubs now swap out bad members among each other like baseball trading cards. These days clubs no longer disassociate the moment they find out you are out bad and instead ask, "Why are you out bad?" They figure they'll make the decision themselves because they no longer trust the credibility of the former club's punishment because so many have proven to be so janky when handing it out.

I've been told that it's so bad that COCs and coalitions across the country are looking to redefine the rules surrounding the out bad label because so many clubs have turned it into a tool of revenge and sabotage, and it no longer has validity on the MC set. Until there are new definitions the term will continue to be useless. Use out bad for its intended purpose! That's the best way to help the set!

Brother's Responsibility if the Club Violates Its Bylaws

There are times when clubs violate their own bylaws to get rid of a member they don't like. A cowardly President ejects a brother he doesn't like out of the club without a trial, and oh yeah... he's out bad too while they're at it. The surreal part is that brothers who could stop such a thing from happening will often sit silently afraid of repercussions that may come their way. In my opinion a club makes a contract with you when they ask you to prospect your ass off to become a member. They promise you that everyone will follow and be bound by the rules espoused in the bylaws. You have absolutely no responsibility to be civil to a club that is not following their own bylaws keeping everything fair for all as was promised when you prospected. As far as I'm concerned, "If you can make up the rules as you go then so can I." You have no duty to play by the rules when no one else is saying, "Fuck 'em!" Split the club! Fight with all your might. Allow nothing to be taken you aren't willing to give freely. If you've obeyed the rules, you have just as much right to the colors as any asshole that would try to remove them from you.

Founding Members and Presidents Forever

One of the biggest problems I see in clubs today are would-be dictators who want to be president forever or founders who want to reign over the club throughout their retirement. In traditional MCs, presidents serve for a term as specified in the bylaws and are voted into office. Many tricks are often played by egotistical power mongers who subvert the bylaws to stay longer than they should, but if the club is to survive good brothers must step up and stand up to ensure the system does not get rigged.

In my experience, there are a few strategic actions performed by corrupt underhanded presidents designed to keep their power:

1. They corrupt their officers to back them up in their shady dealings within the club.
2. They suspend parts of the bylaws, changing the way brothers vote giving themselves the advantage.
3. They prevent full patch brothers in good standing or even whole chapters from voting, using fabricated excuses.

As for these founders who have grown too old to participate in the day-to-day activities of the club, but want to make all the decisions at the meetings, I believe the protocol is simple... there is no leader more supreme than the President in a traditional MC. If the founder wants to be the supreme authority he should run for President and participate on a day-to-day level. No amount of muscle flexing should be tolerated of founders who want to overrule the voting body of the MC.

The Biker Club Code Explained

1. Maintaining Membership in Good Standing

Membership in good standing means meeting the minimum requirements for membership in the club as defined in the bylaws. This could be:

- Being current on all dues.

- Meeting all mandatory runs and events.
- Meeting minimum mandatory attendance at church.
- Meeting minimum miles requirements for membership.

2. Protect Your MC brotherhood with all your might!

Do everything in your power to be a credit to your MC and not damage it with your actions (in or out of your cut). Remember cell phones and CCTV cameras are everywhere! Assume that everything you do is being recorded and documented. When in your cut do nothing to discredit your MC. In your personal life do nothing that would bring dishonor to your brothers.

3. One Patch One Vote

All full patch brothers in good standing get a vote in a traditional MC. Anything less than that for any reason is bullshit.

4. All Grievances are Handled at the Table

If you have a problem with the club, an officer, or a brother, handle it at the table. Too many clubs allow side bars and cliques within the club to cause disharmony and conflict. If brothers are whispering about brothers on phone calls so that they can build a hit squad to go after a brother, they are not doing the club any good. Bring your issues to the table and confront a brother face-to-face. You don't need a hit squad to go after a powerful brother if you are an honest man with integrity. This is the only appropriate way to settle grievances in the MC. Even going out in the back yard to handle it fist to fist should first be agreed upon at the table.

5. Never Sleep with Your Club Brother's Old Lady

Too many brotherhoods are broken up by this simple bullshit. One of the biggest milestones of crossing over from adolescent to man is being able to control your basic instincts and not let your little head do the thinking your big head is responsible to do. There are too many women in the world to fixate, pursue, or covet your club brother's woman.

6. Always Show Respect to the Club's OGs and Severely Punish any brother who Disrespects them

A club's history is just as important as its future. The OGs are its past, the current brothers are its present, the hangarounds and prospects are its future. Every component is important. As much as you've put into the MC imagine that the OG put in just as much or maybe even a hell of a lot more yester year ago. You must show deference and respect to those who paved the way because if it were not for them there would be no you. And also, one day, if you live long enough, you'll be the OG desiring the respect you may refuse to give today. If you don't believe me just keep on living. Punish severely those who disrespect an OG.

7. Never Discuss Club Business Outside of the Club

MCs are secret societies so what happens inside the MC must stay within the walls of the clubhouse sealed within the lips of the brothers. The U.S. idiom "Loose lips sink ships," meaning "beware of unguarded talk" and its unintended consequences is relevant on the MC set as in the U.S. Navy. It is against MC protocol to discuss club business with anyone who is not in the club. This means you don't talk to priests, significant others, cops, or anyone else about what goes on in your MC.

8. Never Lie to a Club Brother or Officer

The MC is a brotherhood and an extended family. Membership requires one to practice achieving the highest levels in personal conduct, integrity, loyalty, and honesty toward the brotherhood. It is against MC protocol to lie to a club brother or officer.

9. Never Steal from Club Brothers or the Club

The MC is a brotherhood and an extended family. Membership requires one to practice achieving the highest levels in personal conduct, integrity, loyalty, and honesty toward the brotherhood. Therefore, it is against MC protocol to ever steal from the club brothers or the club.

10. Always Pay Back a Loan from a Club Brother or the Club

The MC is a brotherhood and an extended family. Membership requires one to practice achieving the highest levels in personal conduct, integrity, loyalty, and honesty toward the brotherhood. Therefore, it is against MC protocol to take advantage of the club or club brothers and not pay back personal loans that are extended.

11. When Handling the Club's Money always get a Receipt

MC protocol calls for receipts as a regular practice in doing club business. Receipts are proof that expenditures went where they were supposed to go, and you will be expected to provide one for every transaction.

12. Never Exploit the Club for Personal Gain unless all Brothers Benefit Equally

Exploiting the club for personal gain is against MC protocol. This has been a long-held tenant of MC life. If your idea will benefit all brothers of the club, it will most likely be accepted for the benefit of all. In the MC, the goal is WE not I.

13. Never get High in the Clubhouse

Getting high in the clubhouse can bring cops there and bring down unnecessary heat to the brotherhood, especially if the clubhouse is having an open house or other gathering where guests can witness bad actions. Go out back and get high on the porch if you must but keep the dope out of public view in the clubhouse. Also don't store drugs, illegal weapons, or other contraband in the clubhouse. That way the club will be safe if served with a search warrant.

14. Never Make a Personal Fight a Club Fight

I'll say it again; the club is about "WE" not about "I." If you have a personal beef handle it yourself. Do not involve the club in situations that can bring heat on it if things go wrong. Don't start shit if you can't handle your business. Too many people think the MC is their personal army to sick on people to aggrandize themselves. Protect the club instead of jeopardizing it.

15. Never Allow the brothers to Die for what they believe, instead make the Enemy Die for what they Believe

The purpose of the MC is to keep brothers alive, not sacrifice them. Dying for the club is not nearly as beneficial for the club as negating the club's enemies from carrying out their nefarious intentions. Presidents should prevent their brothers from dying for the club at all costs!

16. One Fights We All Fight! Never Abandon a brother in Battle

It is against MC protocol to run from battle if attacked. If one brother is attacked, we all fight until we win or none of us are left to continue on. We must also all fight together if there is a war council and the club votes to affirm the war. Even if you are against the war the majority vote wins. If you don't like it, then depart the club. But when a brother decides to initiate an action on his own without a war council this does not mean you are responsible to put your life or freedom in jeopardy for a brother who wishes to start shit on the set without any authorization on a whim. You also have a first responsibility to your wife and children who depend upon you for support. Allow no brother to put that in jeopardy just because he cannot control his temper or conduct himself maturely.

17. No One Talks to Cops Without at least One Witness from the Club

No one talks to the cops without at least one witness from the club. If it inadvertently happens the club SAA must be notified immediately. The president will not meet with law enforcement alone. He must always avoid even the appearance of impropriety.

18. No Brother Allows Rumors to Spread about Another Brother Not Present to Defend Himself

If a brother is spreading a rumor about another brother, it is against MC protocol to participate in that discussion without insisting that brother be called or brought to the conversation where he can defend himself. The only appropriate place to speak negatively about a brother is at the table when that brother is present.

19. No Brother is Punished, Fined or Put Out Bad without a Trial

It is against MC protocol to punish a brother or put him out bad without a trial, an opportunity to defend himself, face his accusers, present evidence, vet evidence used against him and question witnesses who have accused him of violating the club's bylaws. This is a right of every brother no matter how hated or maligned.

20. Never Break the Law in Club Colors

Never commit any crime while wearing colors.

21. Never Incite a Club War without a War Counsel

The MC is not about I it is about WE. Therefore, it takes a vote of all brothers to declare war. It is against MC protocol for you to incite a club war without an affirmative vote from the war counsel. It is not your right to put all brothers in jeopardy on your decision alone.

22. Never Snitch on the Club or on a Club Brother

It is against MC protocol to snitch on a club brother or on the club. If you are involved in dirt with your brothers, if you are caught you are expected to take it to the grave.

23. If the Police Question the Club; No One Talks, we all Walk

Never speak to the police in an interview room without an attorney present for any reason.

24. Never Divulge Personal Information about a Club Brother for Any Reason

People will try all kinds of tricks to get you to give out a brother's information. Never trust it. "I had the brother's number, but I lost it, can you give it to me?" This question has gotten so many brothers hemmed up. The bottom line is if someone doesn't know that information you cannot volunteer it. You can give your brother their number, but you cannot give out any of his personal information to anyone in the world—unless he tells you to do that.

25. Never Allow a Club Brother to Speak Negatively Against the Club or its Officers in Public

It is against MC protocol to criticize your club in public. If you see a brother doing this shut him down immediately. As I have said before, negative talk is reserved for the table.

26. Never Write Down Anything in Church that can be Used Against the Club in a court of Law

Never write down in church minutes or anywhere else any incriminating evidence that can be used against the MC. Not everything should be memorialized on paper.

Intra MC Protocol Summary

Learn how MC protocol works within your club, and you can move in it respectfully and safely through almost any interaction with your brothers.

CHAPTER SEVEN
INTER-CLUB MC PROTOCOL

External club interactions occur when your MC is operating on the set or hosting visitors at your clubhouse or other club functions. MCs should follow MC protocols throughout these interactions to ensure MCs coexist in peace and harmony. If not, violence is sure to erupt. MC protocols are based primarily on showing respect to other MCs, maintaining proper conduct during encounters, communicating when there are problems between clubs, having sit-downs to find solutions that prevent violence from occurring and adhering to established rules, agreements, and treaties. Inter-club protocol between MCs refers to the set of rules, customs, and protocols governing the interactions and relationships between MCs operating in the same territory, to promote mutual respect, maintain order, and minimize conflicts. Many of these rules are unwritten and as such are passed down from mouth to mouth among generations like traditions and heritage in tribal communities. All members and officers are greatly encouraged to learn, follow, and respect MC protocol as it is in the best interests of the brotherhood to do so. Here are some common elements of MC protocol between MCs:

Respect for Club Colors and Patches

MCs place a high value on their club's colors and patches as symbols of their identity and allegiance. It is important for members of one club to show respect toward other clubs by not handling or touching the colors or patches of another club without permission. Even if a member of another club leaves his colors unattended it is not another MC's responsibility to teach that member a lesson by confiscating his colors. Inform the member of where his colors are if they are not in jeopardy and leave them alone. Many clubs have warred over this sort of thing. Police your colors and leave others' colors alone.

Returning a Club's Colors

There may come a time when you or your club comes into possession of another club's colors. MC protocol is that you return them safely to the MC as quickly as possible. If you incur an expense in the process the receiving MC is expected to cover them as a show of respect and appreciation.

In one example, one of our club brothers "Shellshock" was killed on his bike in San Bernadino CA. Paramedics had to cut off his colors to treat him and inadvertently left them on the side of the road. A passing clubber pulled over, retrieved our colors and returned them to our SAA in a dignified manner. Consequently, we were able to bury him in his cut, which is our tradition. For that we are eternally grateful.

In another example, when one of our members died, his family sold our colors to a collector in the United Kingdom of all places. The collector auctioned them on eBay and a clubber saw them, purchased them, and returned them to the club. He was reimbursed for his expense.

Permission and Courtesy While Traveling

When traveling outside of your territory to make long distance runs, visit another MC's territory, attend annuals or events it is customary for members of the travelling club to notify the dominant club(s) in advance that they will be traveling through and/or visiting their area – especially in areas you don't frequent. This demonstrates respect and helps maintain good relations between clubs. This is known as "getting a traveling pass" or "obtaining a pass to travel."

Pass Pin, Pass Thru Pin or Pass Through Pin

A "pass pin" or "passthrough pin" is a big safety pin (traditionally about 5" long used to close laundry bags issued by the military to soldiers, airmen, and marines from WWII all the way to at least the 1980s when I joined the Navy, and maybe still issued today) worn by MCs when passing thru another club's territory. It signifies that you're passing through an area and are not there to start another chapter or create any problems. In some MCs if it is worn across the heart (parallel to the ground) it means you will be gone by dark ("Cross my heart I'm gone by dark!"). If it is worn straight up and down (perpendicular to the ground), it means you will be sticking around for a brief stay but quickly moving on ("If it's straight up and down I'm sticking around"). Other MCs may wear it on their back at the top left so that clubs approaching from behind may see it. There are also reports that some wear it on their bottom rocker or side rocker.

NOTE: Though the pass thru pin signifies those intentions you still need to make a phone call and let the other clubs know you will be riding through their territories for two reasons:

1. It conveys respect and clearly illustrates your intentions, then if you get jammed up you will have a name you can use to ensure your pass through.
2. Not everyone knows or honors what the pass pin stands for or they might be ignorant of its use and should therefore be used as a last resort.

How to Call Ahead

I'm frequently asked, "How do I call ahead when I don't know anyone in clubs where I'm going and certainly don't know anyone in clubs in territory I may be passing through?" Simply put ... "Network and research!" If you want to do things right, it probably won't be easy. If you are a 99%er, reach out to your dominant(s). Explain your route and trip plans and ask them if they can help you reach out to make the appropriate arrangements. They may even make the calls for you. Typically, no one is going to mess with you on the highway as you are traveling through, but it does happen (and often)!

Case in point, a few years ago, a couple of guys flew to Hawaii and decided to wear their cuts and hang out on the local biker set. They obviously had not properly secured their traveling passes before making their decision to wear their cuts, so when they showed up to a Luau they were approached and attacked by the local dominant, stripped of their colors, and beaten.

In another incident, I was called by a dominant to verify the authenticity of a 99%er MC that was traveling across the South a few states over. A diamond club had jammed them up at a gas station and wanted to know who gave them a traveling pass through their territory. When they called their club brothers in Atlanta, they couldn't get anyone on the phone, so they called me and asked me the club's status. I verified that I knew they were a solid club in this area blessed by the Georgia council, and they were allowed to proceed. None of this would have been necessary if they had taken the steps to follow MC protocol to make their travel plans known BEFORE their trip.

If you want to fly your colors in other clubs' territories and hang out on their biker sets, make sure you obtain your pass. In fact, my may discover you have some new friends when those clubs invite you to stop in for fellowship on your way across country.

NOTE: If you are traveling to other countries make damn sure you've handled that business before daring to wear your colors abroad. It is a commonsense thing to do!

Greetings and Acknowledgment

When members of different clubs encounter each other, it is customary to exchange greetings and acknowledge each other's presence. This can include hand gestures or a nod to show recognition and respect. On the Black biker set we often hug. Hugs are plentiful and they are everywhere. Men hug women who are not their own, women hug men they do not know. Men hug men and different club brothers hug each other. People outside of the Black biker set are often blown away when they are received with love and hugs from everyone they meet. After all, it is NOT customary for a male on the White biker set to hug the woman or property of another MC. On the Black biker set it is done without thinking. A word to the wise, when you bring your significant other on the set, educate them that hugs are given in abundance if you plan to fellowship on the Black biker set. Be prepared to give and receive them.

Removing Helmet and Glasses

Whenever you meet a biker in another club it is protocol to remove your sunglasses, gloves, and full-face helmet and greet them eye-to-eye like men. 1% MCs expect this protocol whenever dealing with subordinate MCs, but the respect should be extended both ways between men. In other words, if you remove your glasses and helmet to greet, he should also remove his. Common courtesy is a requirement for mutual respect. I'm not taking off my gloves if you aren't taking off yours.

NOTE: Removing half shell or open face helmets is not necessary as your face can be seen.

Full Patch Greeting a Full Patch

In a formal greeting between patch holders, it is protocol to identify yourself by Club/Chapter/Position/Name. For example, "Hello, I'm

Black Sabbath MC Nation, Atlanta Chapter, President, Black Dragon." In this naming convention the club's name is first (nothing is bigger than the MC), the chapter location is second, the member's rank or position is third, and finally the member's handle. If you have no rank, this greeting would be revised to "Black Sabbath MC Nation, Atlanta Chapter, Black Dragon."

NOTE: This formal greeting protocol may vary (such as a different order) between clubs.

Whose Hand(s) do You Shake First

When visiting a clubhouse, it is protocol to greet, shake hands and/or hug all patches in attendance. At a major public event or open house, it may not be possible to greet all, but it is respectful to greet as many patches as you can. This is also a good way to form alliances and make friends.

So, whose hand do you shake first? Is this even a thing? Believe it or not, it could be. Many 1% clubs expect that at a minimum you should always greet them, if no one else, and some feel like you should always greet them first as they are the senior club in the room! Some will give you grief for not greeting them first and take it as a sign of disrespect. My approach is to handle greetings on a "first come, first served" basis. I greet the people I cross paths with first as I am working my way around the room, not forgetting to greet the diamonds out of respect as I get to them, but also not passing up full patched brothers of other MCs and showing them disrespect. If there are several diamonds attending some may actually look to see which one of them you greet first and may give you shit about it later feeling disrespected that you didn't greet one of them "first." By going out of my way to meet and greet as many folks as I possibly can, I hope to avoid any perceived slights and jealousies. There's no right or wrong answer to this question except to say that your club should give some thought and prior planning on how to properly handle this situation, so things flow smoothly when it arrives.

After you've gained status on the set, developing relationships and acquiring respect among some diamond clubs, you may find they come up to you first to seek your greeting as a sign of respect to you or your club. You may wonder how that can be a bad thing, but as with many things on the set a situation like that can turn sour. In one incident, several diamond clubs greeted me first because of the relationships and respect they had for me and my club, but there was one diamond club in attendance that did not feel I was worthy of such attention, so they sat back and waited for me to come to them. I never did because they were over in a corner looking sour and I didn't want to deal with their negative energy. Consequently, I never did end up going over to greet them and that's when a couple of patches came over to chastise me for "cozying" up to the other diamonds but refusing to pay them the respect they were due. Now, you may be thinking, "That shit those dudes were on was childish as hell," but these things happen frequently on the biker set. When insecure dudes want to prove that their patch means way more than anyone else's, attitude and child behavior abounds.

Prospect Greeting a Full Patch

In a formal greeting between a prospect and a patch holder, the prospect should always identify himself first.

Some 1%ers Won't Shake Your Hand

If you extend your hand for a greeting and it is not accepted do not take it personally. Some folks don't like to touch other people. Others are overly invested in making themselves or their club look tough. Some 1%ers won't shake the hands of prospects of 99% clubs. Expect it and don't buy into it as a point of contention. There are many mental head games happening on the set. Don't waste your time with any of them. It just isn't worth the energy.

Interrupting Two Full Patches Talking

Generally, you should avoid interrupting two full patches who are speaking privately, especially if they are on the set and from two different clubs. They may be conducting business vital to the clubs' best interests. It is also against protocol to interrupt two officers from different clubs who are conversing privately unless you are a senior officer acting on club business. Stand where you can be seen, recognized, and invited into the conversation or given a moment to interrupt.

Embracing When Meeting

When embracing during a greeting avoid touching the center patch of someone from another club unless you know you have that kind of relationship with the person and a full embrace will be welcomed.

WARNING: Some full patches, especially older 1% and OMCs may kiss you on the cheek, forehead, or even your lips in a meeting embrace. This is a demonstration of great respect among clubbers in this culture. If a 1%er kisses you it is not a homosexual act. There is nothing that says you have to accept another man kissing you, of course, but understand it for what it is without becoming offended or becoming uptight. The kiss greeting is an older custom. I'm not sure if it is really in use anymore. It was started to offend the general public and scare people away from the 1% community more than anything else.

The Term Brother

The term "brother" or "bro" has a special meaning within the MC culture. It is not a term to be tossed around lightly. Since an MC is an extended family, we consider our male members brothers and our females sisters. These people have earned the right to be referred to as "brother," "bro," "sister," or "sis." You should refrain from calling a Patch or Prospect from another club "bro" or "brother," or another club's property or old' lady "sis" or "sister" as this may be taken as an insult and bring about a stern, verbal rebuke. On the Black biker set there is a greater acceptance for the use of these term as they are commonly used among African American males in general. Still, you should avoid using these terms to address patches you don't know even on the Black biker set.

This is not to say that patches of different MCs don't call each other brother. In MC culture it is not against protocol to call men outside of your club "brother," but it will occur most often after a relationship is built and that term of endearment has been earned.

Some Clubs Have Problems Meeting & Greeting Women in MCs

Women MCs are not new to the MC community, but their presence was almost invisible for many decades. Women MCs of today are gaining their respect again in leaps and bounds. There are still many men in MCs who don't regard women well, so be prepared for some bullshit when greeting males in MCs as the egos are big on the biker set. I will say that women are treated much better than they were even 10 years ago when they were barely recognized or spoken to at all. In many places women officers of women MCs weren't even allowed in coalition meetings but I see a lot more access offered to women these days. Prepare yourself to be hugged too long or other kinds of disrespectful behavior as it is still out there and exists.

NOTE: Women officers, especially Presidents and SAAs are generally more respected than full patches and prospects of women's MCs.

Motorcycle Club Protocol 101

Communication and Diplomacy in Settling Beefs

If issues or conflicts arise between clubs, it is important to address them through open and respectful communication and diplomacy. This can involve designated club representatives or leaders engaging in negotiations to find amicable resolutions. Most MC problems, misunderstandings and conflicts can be resolved at the table in what is formally known as a "sit-down." If this cannot be done, the results can be physical altercations steeped in violence and club wars will occur.

Non-Interference Prevents Most Conflicts

MCs generally respect each other's privacy when it comes to internal affairs and decisions. Clubs should refrain from interfering with the internal matters, disputes, or conflicts of other clubs unless invited or interference is necessary to maintain peace and order (such as when a 1% MC steps into a subordinate MC's affairs to keep the set from getting hot). The general protocol here is to stay out of other clubs' internal affairs!

Don't Speak Negatively About Other MCs on the Set

Whatever you do, do NOT discuss other clubs' business on the set. Gossip is rampant on the MC set, which seems kind of counterintuitive given that the set is supposed to be comprised of alpha males, but alas these men can cackle worse than hens as news and rumors scurry about the set rampantly. It is best you remember that the walls have eyes and ears on the set. You never know is listening when you are running your mouth out on the set! The old man nursing his beer at the bar could be the ex-National President of a major club that you are squawking about and that can result in trouble.

Many set wars have been started by careless bantering so don't speak negatively about any person or club on the set—especially when it comes to spreading a rumor you heard from someone else's flapping their lips. If you must repeat a rumor or talk negatively about another MC, save that for your clubhouse when you are with your club brothers and there are no visitors around to hear and spread. If for some reason you find yourself on the set with your brothers and you simply must say something negative, take your club brother outside, whisper it lowly so no one can overhear, communicate the message in as few words as possible, then SHUT UP ABOUT IT—especially if you are not in a powerful club that can backup what you are talking about if discovered. Common sense should always prevail on the set.

Have the Receipts or See them Before You Spread the Lie!

MCs require receipts before believing in or spreading rumors. It is one of the truly unique requirements in true MCing. We demand that if a person spreads a rumor about a patch or an MC, that individual is able to provide the "paperwork" (often refer to as "receipts") on the person or club they are talking about. This is because the wrong rumor (such as this person or this club is a rat) could result in someone being severely fucked up or even eliminated – especially if enough people believe it. Producing receipts is paramount in the MC lifestyle. In fact, it is against MC protocol to spread a rumor about someone if you haven't personally seen the receipt(s). There can be severe consequences against you if you do.

What is a Receipt

A "receipt" refers to a document that serves as evidence of a transaction. But on the MC set, is seen as proof or evidence. In an MC, these "receipts" (or "paperwork") can come from trial manuscripts, depositions, warrants, recordings of phone conversations or photo or video evidence.

Who Uses Receipts

On the MC set, the term "receipt" is formal and used worldwide to refer to showing proof of evidence of what one is presenting as true about someone or a club. Receipts are increasingly being used in positive ways as evidence that someone is genuine and can truly back up what they claim.

These days you will see people produce their own receipts when making claims, so you don't have to do all the research yourself. In this way they can legitimize their claims instantly by supplying the proof with the claim to remove all doubt before it can really even occur. This is the procedure used by biker news podcasters like me when producing stories about bikers and clubs so that our research is on the table before it can be accused of being defamatory, conjecture, or producing "fake" news. One of the quickest ways to shut haters down in a club meeting is to produce your receipts at church on the table for all to see.

Receipts vs Bullshit Subterfuge Designed to Confuse

As with everything else, dishonest people will try to throw "defecation into the roto oscillator" (i.e., "shit into the fan") to spread confusion and sow the seeds of hate in any situation they feel like they can manipulate and control to make people believe their lies. Since manipulators know that everyone is looking for receipts, similar to how juries are looking for DNA evidence in every murder or rape case after watching shows like *Forensic Files,* these manipulators will try to manufacture receipts to convince the lazy and gullible that their accusations are true. Be careful that you are looking at independently verifiable evidence rather than some bullshit from a dishonest idiot.

Example of Bullshit Receipts

In October 2024, the National President of the Black Sabbath MC, Curtis 'Cee Cee' 'Ride or Die' Hill (along with several of his top lieutenants), decided he could no longer stand the disapproval aimed towards him by the former National President and Lifer Black Dragon. (Yes, I'm talking about myself here.) So, 'Ride or Die' collaborated with East Coast Regional President Jason 'Ol' Skool' Monds, East Coast Regional Vice President Derek 'Hardcorp' Belser, National SAA 'Offset' from the Olympic City Colorado Springs chapter, San Diego VP 'Kool Kat,' and several others to collectively figure out how to get rid of the old man. A 'charging document' they were sure would destroy my name and credibility among my subscribers, followers, fans, and readers was leaked to the world. They were convinced that to illegally put me out of the club they first needed to destroy my name on social media.

In their initiative to throw the first stone, before I could strike and make them look bad, 'Ride or Die' authorized 'Offset' to leak this 'charging document' to an ill-informed podcaster named 'Wrecking Ball Bob' who eagerly ran with the bullshit, telling everyone he had "receipts" on Black Dragon proving I had been put 'OUT BAD' from the Black Sabbath MC Nation. The story was picked up by another clueless podcaster named Marcell 'Big Cell' Tillman who claimed to have received other "receipts" which he broadcasted to the world as absolutes. What these fools broadcasted as "receipts" to the world were nothing more than editable MS Word documents printed up by people with an agenda.

A real receipt is irrefutable, independently verifiable and stands on its own without need for explanation (such as a court transcript). And with the advent of artificial intelligence, clubs will now have to consider deep fakes, voice fakes, video fakes and other manipulative techniques as potential manipulators manufacture "receipts" to achieve their own agendas.

Protocol at Events

When multiple clubs gather at events or rallies, club brothers stick together! Whether on the road in formation or walking together at events, the MC in movement displays numbers which exudes its strength and muscle. You are of no value to the projection of the club's power if you are off on your own dallying and not engaged in the business of the MC. When you are in public, especially when you are in your colors—you are on a stage! Someone is always watching—especially with CCTV cameras and the public with those record-all cell phones in abundance. And don't be fooled, other MCs are watching, too, waiting to see your club slip and fail. Keep your order of formation at events. SAA protects the President and assigns prospects and others to fill in where necessary. Come together, hang out together, and leave together. If you want to hang out alone then go alone. When with the club, be with the club! This keeps your brothers from being singled out for attack. Follow the directions of the SAA and have a meet up point in case of danger. For more suggestions get my book Sergeant at Arms Bible at blackdragonsgear.com, Amazon, Kindle or Audible.com.

Elements of a Neutral Club

If your MC is going to be neutral, be neutral. You can't claim to be a neutral MC if you are hanging out at one diamond more than another in your area. If you hang out at one diamond's party, you damn well better make sure to give the other diamonds in the area equal respect and participation. If you can't, don't go to anyone's party. Another thing to be careful of is what we call "fence riding." Fence riding is when one tries to play one diamond against another. It seldom works because these clubs communicate with one another far more than you might think, even when they are at war. If one diamond tells you no, going to another diamond to get a yes is never appropriate. Work out the issue with the diamond you started with, as this is manly and respectful thing to do. This underhanded tactic is most commonly exhibited when trying to start a new MC. When one diamond club says no, the prospective club attempts to seek the blessing from another diamond in the area. Sometimes it works, but you will always have problems with the first diamond you contacted, and you will never ride in peace.

Your claim to be a neutral must persist in wars, frays, and conflicts between MCs. To remain neutral, you must not take position on either side in any other MC's affairs. This can mean limiting your contact with either of the two clubs at odds. Hanging out with either club during their conflict can put you in the cross hairs of retaliation, rebuke, or violence due to misunderstandings. When you learn that two clubs are warring avoid them, their support clubs, and their functions until you know their situations have been resolved.

Avoidance of Territory Disputes

MCs often have established territories or areas where they have a presence. It is generally expected that clubs respect each other's territories and avoid encroachment or territorial disputes to maintain harmony. If you are going to be in another MC's territory, be respectful and let them know. This is not asking for permission it is letting them know. If you are going to set up in another MC's territory, try to work it out at the table before encroaching to keep the heat off the set. And yes, showing up at another MC's hangout or bar uninvited can and will be seen as an act of war.

This was evident in 2017 in El Paso TX when members of the Kinfolk MC showed up at a known Bandidos hangout, resulting in the members of the Kinfolks MC getting touched up a bit and being made black and blue. At the point where the fight was just ending, the President of the Kinfolks MC showed up, ran into the club, and started shooting. He killed one Bandido, paralyzed one and shot a third. He then ran out of the bar with one Bandido hot on his heels, chasing after him even before he stopped shooting. That brave soul caught him at the door and nearly stopped him, but he slipped away into the night. The resulting trial found him guilty with a sentence of 56 years for murder, 15 years for engaging in organized criminal activity and 15 years for engaging in organized criminal activity with a weapon (KTSM.com News) (KTSM El Paso News). This could have all been avoided by not encroaching on an MC's territory without an invite.

The MC Sit-Down

MCs in dispute with one another employ a sit-down to solve their problems, negotiate outcomes, compromise, and stop wars. No matter what goes down between MCs or for how long, eventually they will have to come to the table for a sit-down because that is ultimately what is best for the brotherhood.

The protocol for a sit-down with an MC on the same level as yours, OR an MC with which you have a problem is:

1. Meet in neutral territory. Never meet on their territory!
2. The President, VP, and Sgt at Arms should attend, at a minimum.
3. A backup van full of patched brothers should be waiting around the corner with the necessary instruments of war or a 40 brother escort (or however many brothers you have for an "all hands on deck") should be on bikes waiting outside until the meeting is over.

Protocol for Two or More Clubs Riding Together

When two clubs ride together, there are protocols for riding in formation, order, and communication to ensure safety and coordination. The protocol for two clubs that have respect for one another is that they ride side-by-side. One club on the left, the other on the right in a two-by-two formation with the road captain from each club conducting the pack. Hand signals and communication should be agreed upon before the ride begins. Even 1% OMCs will ride side-by-side with a 99%er club if they have respect for the club on that level, but it all depends on the relationships the clubs have built with one another.

Dominant Clubs Riding with Subordinate Clubs

If you are riding with a dominant club that sees your club as subordinate, the dominant club will ride in the front, while the subordinate club brings up the rear. The dominant club's road captain will lead the pack and dictate the conduct of the pack to all subordinate road captains.

I never rode the Black Sabbath MC behind any MC during my period as President or National President. Any club that did not recognize us as equals on the road was not a club we needed to ride with. We would meet them at the destination and ride at our own pace and under our own leadership as an independent MC nation. No one led a Black Sabbath pack except Black Sabbath. That is until the Patriot Guard led the Black Sabbath to bury one of our brothers who was killed on his bike.

The Patriot Guard are well qualified to lead your pack for that one somber occasion. They know what they are doing when they are conducting the funeral pack. There's nothing like having a professional funeral conductor moving your pack during such a somber event. You wouldn't be disappointed if you allowed that to occur.

Passing 1% and Other MCs

Since there is a hierarchy among MCs on the set, you should be well advised to know that it carries over onto the roadways and highways upon which MCs operate when traveling from, to and between locations on the set, including interstate travel. MC protocol requires respect and deference be displayed between all clubs as they encounter one another to hold down conflicts and miscommunication on the road. All MCs, RCs, and other groups riding together should observe the protocols of passing MCs, especially 1%ers.

1%er OMC nations face many challenges while moving about the highways including possible violent attacks from rival clubs. In fact, on April 14, 2023, 5 Bandidos MC brothers were shot and 3 were killed while on their motorcycles in Texas (KHOU-11). In 2021 in Florida , Sin City MC and Thug Riders MC had a bloody confrontation that left a mother shot off the back of a Sin City Deciples' bike and killed on the highway (Fox 13 Tampa Bay). These realities automatically put many 1% OMCs on high alert so they can be particularly moody when encountering other MCs on the road or passing bikers. Most clubs should refrain from approaching them to pass at all because usually they are moving so fast that you would need to be flying a spaceship to safely pass them; however, there are times when your club is moving faster than theirs, and you need to pass them so you can get down the road to your business at hand. In that event I have used the following procedures to safely pass 1% OMCs and any other MC that we have needed to pass:

1. Approach the back of their pack and hold at a respectable distance.

2. Your road captain should break from the pack to approach their tail gunner.
3. Your road captain parallels their tail gunner, and hand signals his desire to pass their pack.
4. Their tail gunner will acknowledge the hand signal and either deny or grant the request to pass.
5. If the request is denied, your road captain will drop back to his pack and remain behind at a respectable distance.
6. If the request is granted, your road captain will move forward to their road captain at the front of their pack.
7. Your road captain should parallel their road captain and hand signals to their road captain his desire to pass.
8. Their road captain will acknowledge the hand signal and either deny or grant the request to pass.
9. If the request is denied, your road captain will drop back to his pack and remain behind at a respectable distance.
10. If the request is granted, your road captain will drop back to his pack, gather it, and pass at a respectable speed.
11. Your pack may wave a greeting of acknowledgement while passing.
12. After the pass has been completed safely, your road captain will signal hammer down and the pack will resume the desired speed.

Patch Overs and Club Flips

When MCs want to acquire new MCs, one of the quickest ways to do so is through a "patch over" or "club flip." Patch overs are usually voluntary, whereas club flips are thought to be hostile takeovers, which can occur by threat, intimidation, or at the pointed end of a gun. Recently a major 1%er MC was indicted for surrounding a 99%er's clubhouse, holding them at gun point, stripping them of their patches, and forcing them to flip over to their club. This was an extreme example of a club flip, but it does happen. In a less extreme case, a club was threatened or given few options to exist beyond the flip.

A patch over is less intense. Usually, the club patching over does so at its own behest and under more accommodating terms. The standard protocol for patching over a club is:

- The club patching over must have 5 or more members.
- All colors must be retired or returned to the mother chapter, in the event the club patching over is a charter or chapter of a National MC.
- There is generally no requirement for members of the club patching over to probate or prospect for the new club.
- Officers often keep their same positions as a charter or chapter of the new MC.
- The new members are generally given full voting rights.
- The clubhouse and other assets are transferred to the new MC.

NOTE: Great care should be taken when bringing new members into your MC brotherhood, particularly individuals you don't know. Many clubs are destroyed by the very flips and patch overs they so desperately sought because of a shift in the balance of power that can occur as a result.

Taking Former Members of Other Clubs

Another way to grow your MC grow is to ingesting former members of other clubs. And notice I used the preparatory word "former" before I used the word "member," because that is how things should be. I have seen many clubs pitch membership to potential brothers who are still members of other clubs. It is against MC protocol to do this because it is highly disrespectful of the sovereignty of the MC upon which you are infringing. Remember respect is everything in MC protocol. When you tell someone who is in another club that you have a home for him, you are violating this respect for his current MC. In short, never have discussions with anyone wearing colors about them coming into your club until they have relinquished the colors of their former club and returned all of their former club's property, entirely! Here are some other standards:

- It is protocol for the president or SAA to call the former club and make sure the member left in good standing. Leaving in good standing is:
  - Dues paid up to date.
  - Fines paid.
  - Suspension time and other sanctions met.
  - Colors turned in.
  - All former club property returned.
  - Tattoos removed or covered over.
  - Not put out bad.
- The potential member must have been separated from former club at least six months prior unless both presidents agree to early transfer.
- The potential member must not be prospecting or hanging around another club.
- The potential member must not be a "club hopper."
  - A club hopper is anyone who is trying to join a new MC without spending six months unaffiliated from their former MC.
  - A waiver is given if both presidents (the new club and the old club) agree to less time.

Many of you have told me that 1%ers and OMCs have attempted to coax your members into joining them all the time. My response to this is, just because they are diamond clubs does not make it any less disrespectful for them to attempt to poach your members! When another club believes they are superior to my club and that they don't have to follow the normal and just tenants of MC protocol, it doesn't mean I have to stand by and allow the disrespect to continue. I have and will disassociate my club from any MC that doesn't show us the respect we deserve. Shaggy 1%er of the Invaders 1% MC once told me *"all relationships are built on communication, participation, and respect. If I'm not getting any one of those three components then I have no relationship and I will remove myself and my club from any negative influences that threaten our sovereignty."*

Inter-club MC Protocol Summary

It's important to note that MC protocol between MCs can vary based on the specific clubs involved, regional customs, and the relationships between clubs. Communication, respect, and a willingness to adhere to established protocols are key to maintaining positive relations and minimizing conflicts between MCs.

CHAPTER EIGHT
HOW TO START A MOTORCYCLE CLUB

Starting an MC seems to be the next logical step for any group of friends anywhere in the world who are hanging around one another, riding together, enjoying their friendship, and desiring to take their fellowship to a new organizational level. At least that is how things happened in the beginning (as you may recall from the "The History of the Motorcycle in the United States" in Chapter 2—people who wanted to take their commitment to a deeper level did just that by starting their clubs.. So, why not just do it!? The answer is in two parts: First, because of internal forces that are naturally stacked against new MCs, it is difficult if not impossible to start a club. Second, because the external climate has changed and, in many instances around the world, established clubs have implemented significant challenges to block the way of any new clubs from getting started.

In fact, it is so difficult for new clubs to get started that when I speak on the biker club lecture circuit, I often warn attendees that 50% of all new MCs last less than 3 years. And of those that survive the 3-year mark, only 50% of them last another 2 years. Since knowing MC protocol is paramount to successfully getting a club up and running, in today's climate starting an MC that will live beyond 3 years is likely going to be one of the most challenging things you've ever done—which seems crazy because you don't have to be a rocket scientist to start a biker club.

Why has it become so difficult? Let's examine some of the reasons:

Internal Challenges to Starting Your MC

Among the internal challenges to starting an MC include:

- Even in the best of circumstances, finding 5 members to transition from guys hanging around and riding together to establishing a credible brotherhood is quite a difficult task. For most, since many potential brothers will claim to want to be in an MC and will be all for starting one, few have what it takes to actually do the work. As you are trying to put together a new MC, you will soon discover that folks love the idea of being in an MC but shun the actual workload.
- Getting potential brothers to ride on a consistent enough basis to form the bonds of a brotherhood presents its own challenges. There are no rules or requirements for hanging out together and riding for fun, but when you try to start a MC, many potential brothers will shy away from the idea of rules, dues, and responsibilities. A lot of bikers don't want anyone telling them how when or where they will ride their bikes.
- Many potential brothers are terrified of having meetings with coalitions and 1%ers—which is required in the locality in which you are seeking a blessing.
- It can be exceedingly difficult to bring a disparate group of folks together to form a successful club, especially if you are new to an area and don't really know or have a pre-existing relationship with people with whom you are trying to start an MC! admire the founders who pulled this one off successfully.

External Challenges to Starting Your MC

- Local MCs don't want new competition. In many areas, MCs believe that there are just too many MCs already; therefore, they are averse to allowing a new MC to come in and compete for resources. They often make excuses to prevent new MCs from starting, believing:

- New MCs take away from the number of qualified riders that could support and sustain established clubs that have been around for decades—especially those that are struggling to survive or dying out because of old age and are actively recruiting. They don't appreciate a popup club depleting the pool of qualified candidates.
- New MCs that get popular quickly often take away patrons from established MCs' bike-nights, parties, and annuals which bring a considerable amount of income they have grown accustomed to enjoying. And simply put, they don't want to share that revenue!
- New MCs comprised of younger undisciplined males often bring unwanted heat to the MC set due to their antics and lack of knowledge of the MC protocols that keep the set from getting hot with police. Established clubs don't have the patience to wait around for those younger clubs to "grow up" and stop messing things up on the set. They will bind together to prevent a new MC from starting.
- New MCs are comprised of younger riders who don't respect the old ways and would rather start their own MC than go through the prospecting and probationary periods and earn their way into established MCs. This belief often makes established clubs loathe any new MC in the area.
- There are simply more than enough clubs on the set, in most cases too many, competing for bike nights, sharing annual dance days, and the calendars are simply too full to welcome new MCs into the area, and they don't want any. They believe that the new MC could easily find an established MC to join and there is no need for any new clubs.
- 1%ers often target new MCs with restrictions and often won't let a new MC startup unless vowing to become a

support club to the 1% OMC which attaches a stigma many mom and pop clubs decline to encumber.

Most 1% OMC nations, coalitions, club councils, COCs, established clubs and MC protocol podcast experts, will advise people seeking to start their new MC not to even try. They will say it is in bad taste; it is deemed disrespectful or try to persuade you it won't last. New MCs are often referred to as "pop-up" clubs and many on the MC set despise them. In my opinion a pop-up club is a club that fails within the first 3 years. And you don't know if a club is a pop-up until it fails to exist. I often advise new clubs not to worry about any classification someone else attempts to put on them. In my opinion every club was a pop-up club at one point in their existence until it lasts long enough to prove it isn't. Everyone is a new kid when they first arrive on the block, so who is to say that one group or another won't make it as a club?

I say the biker club set should welcome all new clubs trying to establish themselves and give them the opportunity to make it on their own merits. After all, any group that stops growing starts dying and the biker club set is not impervious to this. New clubs are the life's blood of the greater MC culture. If we stop new clubs from forming, the entire MC set will begin dying. The belief that there are plenty of clubs for folks to join and support therefore there is no need to start a new club is a belief. Beliefs are not facts they are just beliefs. If you want to have your own MC—start it! But do so knowing it won't be easy. You need to be prepared for that. Learn as much as you can about the protocols in your area necessary to make it happen effectively.

This book is a good start, but it won't teach you everything.

There are Several Ways to Start an MC

There will be several ways to start an MC, and we will examine a few of them. Remember no two areas are the same. The actual protocol in your area will be up to you to discover, learn, and most of all obey. If you successfully follow the protocols your MC will get its blessing to operate in your area. If you don't then you will be starting your MC without a blessing. There have been many clubs that started without a blessing, just know that there can be dangers associated with choosing this path. Below is a warning for those who wish to heed it:

WARNING: If you attempt to start an MC ignoring the protocols that exist in your area, you may run into life-threatening or life-ending situations. For some this warning will go unheeded. Some folks believe they are above or exempt from the gatekeepers because they are bad asses, "live in a free country," or are ignorant of the protocols. As I may say several times in this book, "A belief is not a fact, it is merely something you believe." Facts are real and if you make decisions without regard to the consequences that could occur based on the facts associated with them, you will experience these consequences. These consequences may include an embarrassing verbal correction, a beat down, a shootout, death, or imprisonment. The gatekeepers (whomever they may be) are invested in guarding the gate. They have proven time and again they are worthy of the task. If you make the decision to start an MC according to your own path, ensure you and your brothers are worthy of the task. You'll need to be united, vigilant, tough, and as we say in the submarine Navy, "steely-eyed." There is nothing to say that you have to follow the protocols in your area, but if you choose to take the risks involved in doing things your own way you must accept the risks associated with this decision. Following the protocols installs your MC peacefully, without drama, and with the respect of other MCs in your area. My advice to you is that you follow the protocols and if they don't work, try again. If after the 3rd failed attempt, you are still determined, go your own way as you see fit. That way you can at least say you tried doing things the accepted and respectful way.

What is a Blessing

A blessing is simply a nod by the dominant MC (usually a 1% or OMC or a well-established traditional MC or 99%er). In some areas, a coalition is authorized to give a blessing by the dominant or a combination of dominants and powerful 99%ers that says they are okay with you starting your MC in their area and respect your club's right to exist. A blessing is a guarantee that in most cases you won't experience any negativity, violence, or opposition within the community. Your patches, colors and design will be respected and your participation in set activities will be accepted, such that you will be welcomed at the functions of other MCs as a recognized member of the community. It basically means you will get started without enemies. For some, this is optimal, and they seek a blessing before getting started.

A blessing can come in many forms and may simply be a verbal acknowledgement or a highly formalized and ritualized process. It can be an invitation to join MCs in the area or could be a "you stay on your side of the tracks, and we'll stay on ours," situation that means "Your MC won't be invited to hang out with our coalition, but we won't wage war against it either."

Is Getting a Blessing Asking Permission to Exist

One of the biggest oppositions to getting a blessing voiced by many attempting to start a new MC, is the idea of asking for "permission" to exist and these new members aren't about to ask for permission to exist! Depending on the strength of your organization it doesn't have to be all that. In its purest form, getting a blessing is merely informing the dominant or coalition, traditional and family MCs in your area that you will be forming up in their territory in a respectful manner. The best way to do this is to arrange a sit-down with the dominant or coalition of MCs in your area and let them know you are starting a new MC. This alerts them that you are coming, which is considered respectful and conveys your intentions in their territory. It would be like the United States Navy informing other country's that they will be conducting training operations in a certain part of the ocean. This keeps tensions down and prevents the wrong intentions from being conveyed. The United States isn't asking North Korea's permission to conduct training operations with South Korea when they inform them that they are coming. But it does let them know the United States is not invading them with all of the ships and planes that will be in the area next week. They might not like the fact that they are there, but you can't say that they were disrespected.

Informing MCs that you are getting started is not a slight to your right to exist, nor is it groveling, and it's not asking permission. It is being respectful to the community and demonstrating that you aren't coming to step on any toes—you just want to do your MC thing in harmony. And yes, even 1%ers will meet with other 1%ers that are already in an area to let them know they are coming so they can have as smooth a transition as possible in many cases. In some cases, they don't, and just barge on in and, well, then it's on! An agreement beats a war any day.

When I started the Black Sabbath MC Atlanta chapter, I went to every existing MC I could find in Atlanta and told them I was starting the chapter. When I informed the dominant, I was blessed without opposition. I recognize that things were different back then, as there was no coalition in Georgia on the Black biker club set and there was no idea of "getting permission." You just told other MCs you were starting up and that was thought to be respectful and there were no hassles. By the time I was getting chapters started in Florida, the rules and expectations were changing. The dominant was looking for me to ask permission to bring the Black Sabbath MC into the area, so when I simply informed them, "*I wanted to respectfully inform you that we will be getting started in Florida,*" there was some immediate push back. "*What do you mean 'inform' us? You are supposed to be 'asking' for a blessing not 'informing' us that you are coming.*" When I kindly mentioned, "*That's not MC protocol and you know that.*" The dominant thought about it for a second and then said, "*Okay. Then you have our blessing.*" In most situations, knowing your shit often proves helpful. I was able to spread the Black Sabbath MC across the United States without starting a war, paying tribute, donning a support patch, or changing our colors by simply knowing MC protocol. Of course, my club was already 30 some years old when I became National President and my journey of spreading an established San Diego-based MC will be much different than someone starting a brand-new MC and getting it blessed anywhere in the world. I admire founders who possess that passion, drive, and persistence to start a wholly new MC. It's much easier to spread a nation built by founders who passed the club down to you than it will ever be to start something from scratch and making it flourish. Bravo Zulu to all MC founders, originals, and firsts!

Getting a Blessing can be an Exercise in Bullshit, if it is, You Know What to do!

In today's environment getting an MC started can be an exercise in bullshit in some areas. Many dominants, especially new ones—or the new kids in old dominant MCs attempting to establish themselves, are expecting potential MCs to go through excruciating levels of bullshit to get blessed. Some have turned the "informing" part of getting a blessing into a "begging" session that ends with,

"You can't become a club unless you put on our support patch, or if not, pay us," revelation at the end. I cannot advise you as to how to handle this negativity except to say, as a grown man in a club full of grown men you know what you can stand, what you can stand up to, what you cannot, what you will accept, and what you won't. For some, doing what is necessary to get the blessing—including putting on a support patch, if that's the only way—is fine. "Give us our blessing and let us be on our way." For others, these demands will never suffice, and they simply aren't going to be doing that. Some have the kinds of jobs that will not tolerate their employees associating with an OMC or 1% OMC nation in the form of a support club and will fire any employee who makes that commitment when they find out about it. Organizations like militaries around the world will demote you or even put you out dishonorably for becoming a support club for a 1% OMC nation.

I once did a story on my news podcast "Black Dragon Biker TV" on YouTube about an SAA in the Netherlands who was kicked out of the military just for communicating with 1%ers on behalf of his traditional MC (which is the job of a SAA to ensure that he keeps his brothers and his MC safe). But the military was not having it, and they put him out. So, you have to make up your mind how you will handle that situation if it should arise based upon your circumstances and personal beliefs. Make up your mind what you are willing to accept before you even go to the meeting. Preparation is everything.

Starting Your MC in Areas dominated by 1% OMC Nations

In areas dominated by 1% OMC nations:

1. Gather your prospective club brothers together and form your MC privately.

    I have encountered too many individuals who approach a dominant MC or coalition to "ask" if they can start a club. I'll tell you know, the answer is almost always, "No!" It is much better to approach the dominant with your club intact. You need to have everything together and operating as an MC if you expect to be respected when you get to the table. A single guy showing up talking about, "Hey, do you guys mind if I start a club," rarely works. There is strength in numbers and being alone at the table is not operating from a position of strength in the MC world. Have your MC brotherhood together, formed, well oiled, riding formations rehearsed, all parts working, officers elected, culture voted on—bylaws written—everything assembled long before you ever popup on the set, hangout at a biker bar, go to an annual dance, or show up at an open house, announcing to anyone that you are starting a club—most especially not a dominant!

    The hard fact is that no one wants to see a new MC startup, so running your mouth on the set about your "plans" to start the next greatest MC is an effective way to never see it come to fruition. Most areas will shut you down or maneuver you into starting a support club that you will never fully control. Establish your MC brotherhood privately, outside of the prying eyes of others. Then, when you are ready, seek your blessing by showing up with all of your brothers in a position of strength. This means it is silly to recruit off the set. You're going to want people who've never been on the set. This prevents bad habits, bad reputations, and bad people with shitty agendas from poisoning your brand-new MC.

2. Establish the mission of your brotherhood Together as One (TAO).

When you get your prospective brothers together, get to know them. Ride together, hangout together, build your bonds of brotherhood! Play pool, work on projects, help each other do chores, paint your brother's house. In other words, build your lives together as one (TAO).

You didn't see me write anything about hanging out on the set, did you? You don't need to be a set junkie to start an MC. The longest running MCs started out with friends or friends and families growing up together or hanging out together for years, riding motorcycles together and out of this friendship, and motorcycle enthusiasm, grew a bond of extended family wrapped around the insatiable passion of life shared between brothers on two wheels which prompted them to start their own MCs.

If you form your new MC correctly there will be nothing like it in the world. It will be pure and simply one of a kind. That's why when people ask stupid shit like, *"Why can't you go and join one of the clubs that's already established,"* you know like I know that you don't have a bond with those folks like you have with the ones with which you want to start up your club. These guys are already your brothers and now they are your perspective club brothers. *"So, why don't you guys just go join a club that's already formed and needs new people? Why are you trying to reinvent the wheel?"* Simply put, *"Because we don't want to. We like the guys we have. We are just fine forming our brotherhood with ourselves. If we wanted to join another club, we wouldn't be at the table informing you that we've started our own!"* This concept can be hard for people to understand, especially those who have never had the dream of building their own club, so they will never comprehend why you will want to build your own.

There will be roadblocks and challenges to prevent you from accomplishing your dreams of setting up your own MC. Allow for haters in your planning, so that when you encounter them (and you will), you won't be surprised, you'll just move your new club forward until it becomes a recognized MC, RC, MM, COED MC, Women's MC, 1%er MC, OMC, or whatever else you want to call it. As I've said previously and I'll say it several times throughout this book, I have deep respect for founders. You are the pioneers of the new life's blood of MCs. The established MCs have a future, but they are NOT the future of the MC set. The future of the MC set, and any other organization created by man will always be in the new blood.

3. Decide what kind of biker organization you want to be.

Are you going to be an RC, MM, child protection group, LEMC or Traditional MC? Take a vote among all original prospective brothers.

The kind of club you are going to start will be just as important as the people you are going to ask to join it. Remember, you don't have to measure up to anyone's standards other than those who will be your potential club members. So, if being an RC seems comfortable to you and your prospective brothers, then be an RC. Don't push to step up to something that's not in your heart. If you have a passion for spreading God's word, then start an MM. Remember, nothing is set in stone. You can start as one type of club and shift into another as your club sees fit. Many MCs started out as RCs, while many OMCs started out as traditional MCs.

4. Vote for your Ranks.

Now this is always the part where things start to get interesting. A lot of folks who start clubs, especially alpha men, think they should be the one making all of the decisions for the club. They should be the President just because they came up with the idea to start the club. They get offended if someone were to suggest a vote for the officers. Remember, just because you got the thing started doesn't mean you should be the president. Put it to a vote.

Master Chief Tommy "Hog man" Lewis, former National Vice President of the Mighty Black Sabbath MC Nation once told me, "the warrior conqueror doesn't always make a good king!" He said, each job involves two different skill sets and few people possessed both. A conqueror has to defeat the enemies of the throne, kill subversives, take over territory, rally troops, allies, and armies then secure new lands by overthrowing standing kingdoms. And these are all admirable skills to have, but the king has to govern! He must deliver the mail, make sure the sewer carries away the waste, collect taxes, operate the budget, ensure the water, electricity, and police departments are working, fill potholes, control the senators, and fill the arenas with gladiators to keep the citizens entertained. It is the rare man who possesses all of those skills.

A word to the wise is to never be afraid of a fair vote. If you have what it takes, you will win. If not, you don't deserve to win.

5. Name your club!

When you've been with your prospective brothers a while, the most important thing for you to do as a group is to choose your club's name wisely. Sure, one man can come up with the idea, but all original patch holders should help to decide the name. The more people who contribute the more they feel like the brotherhood is part of them. The more they want to work hard to make it a success! Put it up to a vote!

I wouldn't recommend going after the first name that pops into your head because it has most likely already been taken. I can assure you that someone else has come already come up with the names "K9 MC," "Aces MC," "Four Aces MC," "Aces over Deuces MC," or some other variation. so, use your imagination. Contrary to popular belief it is not against MC protocol for multiple MCs to have the same name, but I guarantee you there is a club out there that's not going to allow a new MC to take their name. And now a days, many clubs trademark their names to prevent others from using it, so even though it is not against MC protocol for two clubs to have the same name you can be sued or get your ass kicked for trying it (and I do mean get your ass kicked quite literally).

Around 2015, I was in Tulsa OK when two 99%er MCs had the same name. One of the clubs had members show up for a big roundup. When they took a busload of brothers over to the other club, things got heated and fists started flying.

In the end only one club was left with the name. The other club was either shut down or forced to change their name. I say this only to point out that clubs are serious about their names and even a 99%er MCs will physically fight for it. Do your research before choosing a name, you won't be sorry.

6. Design your colors with respect and research

   For the same reasons that you want to put a lot of thought into naming your MC are exactly why you want to put a lot of thought, respect, and research into designing your prospective colors. There will most likely be some MC using anything you find floating around on the internet either free or bought. When designing your colors and your patch setup much thought should be employed to the process. Almost anything you think of initially will have been created before, unless you are incredibly original, so getting a picture of a bulldog off the internet will have your patch looking like hundreds, if not thousands of others, putting you in jeopardy of offending other MCs in your city or somewhere else in the world you happen to travel. The best bet is to avoid free images you want to incorporate into your patch design because of the high probability the art is copyrighted, which means you can be sued for copyright infringement if you use it without permission and the likelihood that some other lazy dude thought of using that design as well, which can create problems for your new MC when you run into them on the set. I suggest that you spend the damned money to hire an artist! The lesson here is use originality in your artwork designs so you will be different from anything else on the set.

   Thought should also be put into your use of actual colors (red, blue, green, etc.) displayed in the area. Almost every color in the rainbow has been used by someone, but you want to be careful not to use the color patterns of dominants and other well-established MCs if you can help it. Admittedly this may be a next to impossible requirement to achieve as you may have no choice other than to use a color or two in the rainbow that someone else is using. But at least try to know as much about the patch setups around your new territory as possible so you can avoid duplication. After all, you don't want to use the colors red and gold if you were in Texas because this is the color pattern of the Bandidos 1% OMC. But if you were a U.S. Marine MC you might not have any choice as those are also the colors you find in the U.S. Marines. You should put some deep consideration into what you are doing!

NOTE: If you are starting a new chapter of an established MC then your colors are your colors. It is what it is. I can remember moving the Black Sabbath MC into an area where the dominant's colors were primarily black. They didn't want anyone to start a club in the area with the word "black" in it or have the color black as a part of their patch design. This was tough because our club had the word Black in our name for 30+ years at that time and our colors are black, yellow, blue, and white. We had some uncomfortable sit downs where we were told we would have to change or drop the word black from our name and drop the color black from our patches. Things were terse but we weren't going to change our 30+ year old established name. We stuck to our guns and were accepted peacefully and respectfully as the only exception to that rule in the area. The lesson here is that you can work many things out if you can sustain a meaningful dialogue.

7. Write the club's bylaws, constitution, and mission statement.

Okay, some clubs just have a set of bylaws that handle everything. Others will have a constitution, bylaws, mission statement, and statement of purpose. It just depends on the level of structure your club chooses to employ. The point is that these documents will set the rules, rights, responsibilities, expectations, benefits, and punishments established by the MC.

Bylaws

Club bylaws are your MC's rules of operation. These bylaws establish the formal process by which club activities are managed and handled.

Club Constitution

"*A motorcycle club constitution is a comprehensive document that contains and communicates all the rules and regulations that guide the operation of the club.* (Start an MC AMA, https://americanmotorcyclist.com/organizers/charter-your-organization-getting-started/start-a-motorcycle-club/)" Many clubs just have bylaws and won't have a club constitution so if this seems strange to you, don't worry about it.

Mission Statement

This statement outlines the purpose of your club. It could be as simple as, "*To become the greatest riding MC in America*" to something more detailed like, "*Ensuring no child is ever bullied or hungry in America. We will do this by reaching out to communities at risk whose children need protecting and provide them all of the services we have at our disposal.*" Your club's mission statement defines the goals and values of your MC, its underlying social construct, culture, and principles and gives your members a mantra to strive to achieve daily.

Purpose Statement

While your mission statement describes what your MC does, a purpose statement represents why your club exists.

For my club, the Black Sabbath MC the purpose statement was quite simple: *"A Breed Apart."* There was no definition provided beyond those words by the founders but the power behind the phrase has been a unique bonding agent for members across the United States as each has made up their own minds as to what "A Breed Apart" means to them.

Often, when presidents wanted to encourage Black Sabbath club brothers to take action, they would invoke this rallying cry; *"We are a breed apart! There are none like us and there will never be!"* You can imagine the power of the phrase and the unity and cooperation that followed a speech like that!

Make It Legal

It is best to make your MC as legal as possible as soon as you can. This means taking the time to incorporate or start your 501(c) non-profit in the United States. And there are many kinds of 501(c) nonprofit statuses beyond the normal 501(c)(3). There is one specifically setup for clubs, 501(c)(7) which is a social or recreational club organization that meets Internal Revenue Service (IRS) criteria for tax-exempt status.

Get with your club's accountant to consider what works best for your MC. You also want to trademark your club's name and other intellectual properties. It is not hard to incorporate as it can be done with your secretary of state, but you can have a lawyer cover everything for a paltry sum. The point is if you have this documentation in order—when the club splits and other bullshit starts years later, your club's intellectual property will be protected. No interloper will be able to split your club and keep your colors or a variation of them because those things will be protected. I've seen this occur a thousand times across the set. Take the time and money to invest in protecting your club's intellectual properties according to the laws of whatever country you are in.

8. Get that blessing!

> This will involve a sit-down with the dominant or the coalition in your area. If you've done things correctly, the first time they ever hear of you is when you are approaching for your blessing with your fully intact MC.
>
> In the sit-down you will discover what the requirements are to get a blessing in your area. But getting that sit-down can be difficult. Be prepared for it to take time to make it happen. What do I mean by time? Well, I've had some chapters that have taken as long as 5 years to get up and running from start to finish. Sometimes an area is closed to new chapters for a couple of years.
>
> When I moved the Black Sabbath MC Nation into Colorado Springs CO there was a moratorium against starting any new MCs in that area. Bottom line was that the dominant and local 99%er MCs banded together to prevent new MCs from getting started. But there was one MC that knew of the Black Sabbath and respected our history. They worked hand-in-hand with us standing before the dominant and the

area council to lobby on our behalf. The process took nearly a year and there were many obstacles to obtaining a blessing but, in the end it was accomplished. We will forever be thankful to the Street Soldiers MC for standing strongly behind us. An established MC can help you get into a closed area, so the saying "It is not always what you know but sometimes who you know" is definitely true and can help you reach your goals.

You may run into a multitude of challenges from internal to external while trying to set up your new MC. Be prepared. Have patience and determination. Once your club is blessed your journey into MC protocol has only just begun. Good luck! Be blessed!

Starting Your MC in Areas where there are NO 1%ers

Though it may be hard to believe, there are areas with no coalitions or diamonds from whom you need to seek your blessing. This is especially true in rural areas across the country. While patching a club over to the Black Sabbath MC in Rome GA, I discovered , the members seldom left Rome and never encountered a dominant club in their area. When they started their club, they simply patched up and started riding around town and since they didn't travel as a club outside of their local area they were never questioned about their patches or blessings. I'm sure this still occurs in many rural places in the country.

The proper thing for a potential MC to do is locate a dominant somewhere in the state to seek their blessing—especially if you are going to be in a club that travels. The fact is that if you run into a dominant club anywhere in that state you are traveling in and they question where you got your blessing—if the answer is that you don't have one, there is a good possibility you may be asked to take your colors off, or told when and where you will sit-down to have a very uncomfortable conversation.

Starting Chapters of an Established MC

When trying to start an MC with people you don't know, the challenge is much more difficult. As I was spreading chapters of the Black Sabbath MC across the nation, I wasn't spreading to chapters of prospective brothers I grew up with and already knew. These were disparate individuals in cities where I didn't know these prospective members before we came together to create a new chapter. I had one purpose which was to put together enough people to grow the BSMC Nation one chapter at a time. I had to make these people my friends by getting to know them and establishing relationships with them while simultaneously trying to bring them into the MC. My ideas were focused on growth, which is what I was instructed to do by the Founder and Father Paul "Pep" Perry. A lot of times I would just meet a strange rider on a motorcycle near a gas pump or somewhere in the city and say, *"Hey, I like your motorcycle do you ride in a club? No? How would you like to join my club? I'm starting a new chapter in Atlanta, and you are welcome to come and hang around us and get to know us."*

From my experience, when you take this approach, you will recruit the kind of people that weren't worthy of being in an MC and it may take you years to discover them but eventually they will crash the organization because they were never worth a shit from the day you met them.

The lesson here is beware of who you invite into your prospective brotherhood. Bringing people in you don't know may be cool in the beginning, but would you invite a stranger to live in your home without vetting them first? Some would, but most would not. That's because it is not a safe practice. It's a chance you might not want to take. It's always best to take the time to get to know people the long way before inviting them into your brotherhood. The movie, *"The Bike Riders"* proves this point exactly.

AMA Affiliation

There are many reasons your MC may not want to get a blessing from a dominant MC, or a coalition affiliated with them in the United States. For instance, LEMCs by the nature of having police officers as members would seldom if ever seek a blessing from either of these (although it has happened). The AMA has affiliated clubs it blesses after they meet certain criteria. In some areas, dominants will recognize and accept an AMA-blessed club, especially RCs. If you go that route don't expect to be partying with all the other clubs on the set that didn't. You may find your club isolated and not invited to hang out with the others in the area. Go to the AMA's website for specifics on getting a charter from them.

Starting an LEMC

LEMCs are in a category all their own. They don't answer to OMCs or coalitions as most of their members carry badges and guns. They generally move into an area and start up. Most OMCs will not mess with them because it is said that they truly belong to the largest gang in the world. Follow the steps above, leaving out the final step of getting the blessing to get your LEMC started.

Starting an MM

Motorcycle Ministry clubs are becoming popular and are springing up all across the country. If you are trying to start one you should follow the same process traditional MCs follow.

Starting an OMC or 1% OMC

I have generally seen two kinds of approaches to starting a 1% OMC in the United States over my 36+ years in club lifestyle.

One is the scorched Earth approach where the prospective 1% OMC establishes its club without any agreements from anyone. This can lead to many bloody confrontations. I've seen it mostly when disgruntled members leave their big MCs and establish the new MC in their former MC's territory. Or maybe some guys get together and say, "We're 1%ers and we aren't going to ask anyone's permission and so it goes. Or maybe someone who couldn't get along with any MCs in town now goes out of town and comes back carrying the colors of a 1% OMC from across the country he plans on starting in his town. I see a lot of those clubs spend a lot of their time hiding! They don't ride freely, they never ride alone, and if they get caught out in town only one or two deep, they are getting smashed on sight!

The other way is to get your 1% diamond blessed or handed to you by an already established 1% OMC. Starting your 1% OMC in this manner can bring wider acceptance by the other clubs and diamonds in the area. If you think you have what it takes to build a 1% OMC from the ground floor go for it the right way.

Starting MCs in Countries Other Than the United States

When looking to start an MC in countries other than the United States, you will have to take your time to research the MC politics of that country. It isn't impossible because so many clubs that started in the United States are now transnational including some big 99%er clubs. Use as many of the suggestions above as you find helpful to aid in your navigation of the process of accomplishing that dream. Good luck!

Conclusion

Once you get your club started you will want to secure it, stabilize it, and grow it. Handle it carefully and insist that your brothers follow its traditions, culture, and bylaws. Educate your brothers in MC protocol and the proper use of the bylaws.

CHAPTER NINE
THE BYLAWS

Bylaws are the governing document(s) that run your MC. When I was in the United States Submarine Navy, we had several documents that guided our conduct, rights, responsibilities and duties while serving as members of the most revered fighting force on Earth. The Standard Organization and Regulations Manual (SORM) provided guidance and regulations for the internal operations of the Navy, the Standard Operations and Procedures manual (SOPs) provided guidance and regulations for operating procedures aboard our submarine, and the Emergency Operations and Procedures manual (EOPs) provided guidance and direction for operating procedures needed to survive submarine casualties at sea and other emergent conditions. There were many more, but my point is there were documents to which we could refer that would direct our conduct throughout almost anything the Navy could predict that could go wrong as it had documented in its 200-year history. Your bylaws are your MC's document(s) for conduct, rights, responsibilities, duties, standard procedures, emergency procedures, discipline, and motivation to guide you through almost anything that could befall your mighty MC nation. Whether your bylaws are one page containing fifteen lines, or several documents containing a preamble, constitution, bylaws, and summary of rights, most clubs refer to the combined documents that establish the rules of the club as the *"Bylaws"* and they are the most important document(s) that exist in your MCs social construct because they define the brotherhood and your place within it. Bylaws are the set of rules that govern your MC, and their purpose is to provide clarity, guidance, and stability. They can help prevent conflicts, protect the MC and ensure smooth meetings. At minimum they will establish some of the following:

Motorcycle Club Protocol 101

- The structure of the MC and how it is governed
- Requirements for membership within the MC
- How to become a member of the MC
- Definition of a member in good standing
- Procedures for electing officers and definition of term limits
- Calendar for when elections are held
- Mandatory meetings and runs
- Procedures for conducting fair and efficient meetings
- Procedures for amending the bylaws
- Mission statement of the MC
- Disciplinary standards, punishments, fines, etc.
- How to vote, make motions, and resolve resolutions
- Officer and member job descriptions and responsibilities
- Rules of conduct among officers and members
- Procedures for financial management, banking protocols, and who is responsible for handling money
- Procedures for recording church minutes and reports
- Retirement requirements and benefits
- Honorary membership requirements
- Uniform requirements, placement of club patches, handling of club colors, and uniform violations
- Definition of club communications systems
- Club's drug policy
- Amount of dues paid to the club monthly
- Clubhouse rules and requirements to stand duty
- Leave of absence requirements
- Incarceration procedures, rights, benefits
- Loans and debt procedures when borrowing money from club brothers
- Definition of the race or other mandatory personal characteristics the MC will accept as members
- Definition of who the MC will not accept as members

- Rules and requirements for properties, wives, old ladies, house mamas and other women associated with the MC

The above list is by no means exhaustive but for those looking for more, I cover writing bylaws in much greater detail in my book entitled *"How to Write, Edit, Update, and Revise Motorcycle Club Bylaws"* available at blackdragonsgear.com.

The most important thing to know about the bylaws is that if you don't learn them by heart and know them through and through, you will always be held hostage by those who do. That is because there is an insidious word called politics that worms its way into even the greatest of MCs. And those who wish to control the politics of your brotherhood will utilize the bylaws to exert their ill-will and hidden agendas to manipulate outcomes in the club to their advantage. They will learn and weaponize the bylaws only to use them against anyone who stands against them. Their preferred prey are full patches who are ignorant of their bylaws. Those brothers they victimize repeatedly until they change the club's entire culture and set it back decades. The only protection the MC will ever have against these evil vultures is good brothers who care enough about the sacred traditions to know their bylaws so well that they can stand against the usurpers unscathed by their bullshit. You cannot protect the MC or the brothers within it from the MC and the brothers within it if you don't know your bylaws well enough to stand ten toes down on them. The erosion of the bylaws and consequently the club's culture begins with those who attempt to interpret to brothers ignorant of them, meanings that were not intended by the founders who wrote them. Until you see these folks in action you won't believe how divisive they can be. Their true intentions are to sway others to their way of thinking by misrepresenting the bylaws through misleading, confusing, and intentionally wrong interpretations. They build trust speaking strongly which convinces the weak and unread. Those they seek to manipulate are therefore easily turned. They use their sway and influence to increase their power in the club so they can inflict unthinkable injuries on the club. Ultimately you see these bylaws scholars completely discarding them when they start kicking people out of the club without a trial, interpreting the bylaws in such a way that they convince others that certain brothers or chapters don't get a vote, taking perks to which they are not entitled, and the list goes on! So, as you can see, knowing your bylaws isn't just about protecting and guaranteeing your rights, it's also about protecting your club brothers' rights and the sanctity of your MC.

Study to Shew Thyself Approved

To truly understand your bylaws, you must study them. If the founders who wrote them are still alive you must spend time with them asking them everything you can think to ask. You should be constantly seeking to understand their motivations and intentions for the heart and soul of the brotherhood when they wrote them. This is how you maintain the purity of the organization to which you have dedicated your life. There are some who join an MC to mold it around their agendas. When they get finished you no longer recognize the MC or even how it operates. Only brothers who are strong in their bylaw's knowledge can stand against them.

Beware of Constructing Overly Rigid Bylaws

Bylaws can become overly rigid if thoughtful consideration is not exercised when writing or amending them (Start an MC AMA, https://americanmotorcyclist.com/organizers/charter-your-organization-getting-started/start-a-motorcycle-club/). Be careful not to construct or amend bylaws based on emotion or as a 'reaction' to something. Instead, use bylaws to provide direction in the spirit of the law not absolutes unless necessary. If bylaws become overly rigid, they can make it difficult to adapt to fluid circumstances or add unnecessary complexity to managing everyday operations (Start an MC AMA, https://americanmotorcyclist.com/organizers/charter-your-organization-getting-started/start-a-motorcycle-club/). Instead, seek a balance between direction, guidance, absolutes, and preferences when writing them (Start an MC AMA, https://americanmotorcyclist.com/organizers/charter-your-organization-getting-started/start-a-motorcycle-club/).

Honor the Spirit of the Bylaws

When you gain power remember that no brother is above the bylaws, not even you! As a leader it will always be your responsibility to be more accountable to the bylaws than anyone subordinate to you. A good leader must be a good follower, and a good leader must be capable of being led. Allow the bylaws to lead you not your own personal agendas, and you will rule objectively and with fairness.

CHAPTER TEN
THE PROSPECT'S LIST OF 52 DO'S AND DON'TS

Prospect's Bible

In my book, *"Prospect's Bible"* (available on Amazon), I provide a comprehensive overview of the responsibilities as a Prospect or Hang around within the MC. However, in this chapter I have included a list of 52 Do's and Don'ts for Prospects and Hang arounds in an MC.

One of the most important and incredible journeys you will experience during your MC career is the process of prospecting for your chosen club. The prospecting journey sets the foundation you're your MC life. What you learn during this phase should equip you to build your base to face whatever challenge, loss, or victory you may encounter. It is essential for you to have a successful journey through your prospectship.

Here are some guidelines that will help you prospect for your MC with greater ease and a better understanding of set MC protocol:

1 Prospecting is Getting into The Habit of Prospecting

To prospect correctly you must develop the habit of prospecting. Prospecting is not an easy task. The purpose of prospecting is for the prospect to get to know the MC and the MC to get to know the prospect. Through this process you will prove your worthiness to become a member of the MC, and, in turn, the MC will prove its worthiness to deserve your membership. Prospecting is a complicated relationship that requires fairness and equity on both sides. The MC must realize you are not just cannon-fodder to be used, misused, or abused. By the same token you must understand

and learn the MC's customs, traditions, operations, and bylaws while simultaneously learning how to fit in and become part of the club's social construct. When the club fails to fulfill its obligations or the prospective member fails to prove himself, both sides lose. When prospecting works, the process delivers an invaluable brother to the brotherhood and the former prospect gains an MC family for life.

2 Everyone Goes Through It

It may seem like everything is intentionally set up against you, but that's not the case. If you are prospecting for an MC that follows MC protocol rest assured, everyone has traveled a similar path. This is a necessary process you must complete to call yourself a brother and wear the full patch. It's time to put on your big man pants, grin, and endure.

3 Your Pride May Take a Few Hits

The act of prospecting is a humbling experience. You may find yourself taking orders from a brother you deem to be beneath your level in life, but as a full patch brother of the MC, he is above your level in the MC. In the King James version of the Holy Bible it states, *"Pride goeth before destruction, and a haughty spirit before a fall."* Stash your pride away so that it doesn't cause you to trip and fall. Prospecting is designed to be humbling and at times can be quite distasteful. The silly little tasks demanded of you have the effect of letting others determine your true personality. It gives your prospective brothers the ability to judge whether you have the true grit to be one of them – are you willing to sacrifice for the brotherhood, are you a liar, do you share, can you be depended on when a brother needs you? Prepare yourself to endure a few mildly humiliating episodes. Afterall it's all in good fun and for most folks, prospecting doesn't last longer than a few months on average in traditional and 99%er clubs and as much as a year to a year and a half in OMC and 1% OMCs. There is one certainty – if you cannot bring yourself to suffer through this period of prospecting, you will not make it into the club so, suck it up and hang in there!

4 Never Compromise Your Values

Though everything I said in the previous section is true I must add this caveat for your well-being – know your limits and what you will (or won't) allow to happen to you. With that, I must tell you that at no time during any phase of your prospect period should you allow any person to cause you to compromise your self-worth or spiritual values for any reason. No one should ask you to break the law, invade your personal space or cause physical harm to your body against your wishes, or perform any other acts against you that do not align with the values by which you live your life. For example, if you are not okay with being locked into small spaces don't allow someone to lock you in a closet talking about some prospecting bullshit you need to do to get into the club. If that's not how you get down because it might harm your mental state, then don't let that happen to you. And this I say because some clubs will blacken a prospect's eye or punch him in the nose or lips. Other clubs might make you do pushups or any number of silly or physical things to cause you discomfort. I've never been in a club where a senior has permission to bash a junior in the eye or nose. If a motherfucker put his hands on me, I'd do my best to kill him, but that's me! That might not be you! You may find it perfectly fine to get your eye blackened when you do something wrong, and there are a lot of clubs that do that. You have to make up your own adult mind about how you handle those kinds of situations. Always remember, however, that it's okay to let them have their rags back and go find some other MC for which you can prospect, if your self-respect is ever jeopardized.

5 Not Every Brother Who Wears the Patch Will Be Your Brother

Beware prospect! Not everyone who approaches you wearing the patch you one day desire to wear will be a worthy club brother. Just like you are taking the time for the club to get to know you allow the club to take the time for you to get to know the brothers in it. Ensure that they are as worthy of your trust as you are of their trust. It is easy to get overwhelmed and think that everything is just wonderful and great. But be honest, the world just doesn't work that way, not anywhere in it, and not in your prospective MC either. Only time will tell if a brother is worthy of your trust, so take your time and don't be naïve or too damned trusting. Respect, honor, trust, and love are earned, not just blindly given.

6 Give Prospecting Your Best Effort

Only you know if you have what it takes to prospect. If you think you do, give it your best effort. It takes a willing mind to put oneself in the service of the brotherhood. And remember, that is what is called for when you begin your prospecting journey—Service! If you accept this going in, you'll have a much better experience, I promise. Also remember to have fun and enjoy the ride.

Take a Lesson from the US Navy Submarine Service

When I was in the United States Navy I served in the Silent Service as a submarine sailor. I sailed nuclear powered 688 Los Angeles class Fast Attack Hunter/Killers in wolfpacks projecting United States sea power during the Cold War.

As a submarine sailor you were trained at submarine school in Groton, Connecticut and you were nothing but an accident waiting to sink the entire submarine by doing something stupid or not knowing how to fight a casualty at sea. You were given one year to become "submarine qualified" and receive your coveted dolphins breast insignia.

When you first entered submarine training, you were given a qualification card with over 100 signature spaces on it. Each one of those signature spaces represented a specific skill you had to know while serving on a submarine. To receive a signature from a qualified seaman, petty officer, chief or officer you had to answer a series of questions related to that specific skill. For example, to receive a signature for the high pressure hydraulics system you might have to answer questions about how the high pressure hydraulics systems worked aboard the submarine, where they were located, how they operated, from where they derived their power, how to shut power off to them during a fire, how to properly handle a high pressure hydraulic leak, how to service and maintain the equipment during an emergency, and all of the equipment powered by this system. Regardless of your assignment, you had to know the emergency operations of every system aboard that vessel from the engine room to the torpedo room, galley, topside, sail, bilges, pumps, electronics, high pressure air systems, SONAR, Operations and more. You had to know how to fight fires, stop flooding, shore up bulkheads, equipment sound silencing, nuclear weapons handling, reading gauges, take readings and measurements, communications, emergency escapes at sea, and how to repel boarders.

Now, if you worked hard, you might be able to get through two interviews a week, securing two signatures. At this pace you would hope to finish your qualification card in about a year. Of course, there were overachievers (known as a "hot runner") who could finish a 'qual card' in about six months. In fact, I once witnessed a "hot-runner" finish his 'qual-card' in three months. But just as there are overachievers, there were plenty of lazy dudes who took way longer than a year to finish their sub 'qual cards.' We called these guys "dinks," short for "delinquents." (I've heard the Navy now forbids the use of this term, favoring a software more hands-on approach to qualification). Naturally, "dinks" were hated aboard submarines because as long as you were a "dink" you were a danger to the vessel and the crew because you didn't know what the fuck you were doing!

When there was a casualty on board, like flooding, fire, high pressure leaks, etc. a "dink" was useless – standing around while everyone else pushed past to solve the problem. Keep in mind, on a submarine you have just a few precious minutes to stop a casualty before it overcomes the sub's ability to recover and becomes a disaster.

This is how I feel about "dink" prospects and probates. If you ain't a "hot runner" about your business to get "MC qualified," I will personally have little if anything to do with you and you will never get my vote!

7 Conduct Yourself Responsibly Publicly

Any MC worth a damn is going to have rules, customs, and traditions based around how they carry themselves and how they are seen on the set. Most brothers do not tolerate irresponsible, silly, immature idiots. How you carry yourself will determine how your MC is seen by the clubs with which it interacts.

I'm reminded of a video I saw on Instagram in November 2024. A biker riding a Harley, wearing his cut with only a lower rocker—clearly prospecting—perhaps a 1%er club, refused to allow some kid riding a sport bike to pass him. He kept cutting the kid off and trying to run him off the road every time he tried to pass. It was an asshat move that pissed off everyone on social media and made his club look bad. I shared the video which got over 2.5 million views on my Face Book page alone, so there is no telling how many views it got from its original post, or from other posters who shared it as well. It's possible that 5 or 10 million people viewed this prospect acting out in his club's colors. Imagine the ill-will such a move may have generated for his club. In these days and times people are not looking to be harassed on the streets by clubbers, especially 1%ers, who won't let them perform the most basic functions of using the roadways—which is passing someone safely while traveling. Now, imagine the level of disgust if everyone was to observe that the clubber carrying out this transgression was just a prospect! What the hell right has a prospect to conduct enforcement actions and he's just now arriving on the set? As a prospect your job is to make the club look good especially when you are by yourself in public or on the set patched up (wearing your club's colors). For this reason, many clubs have a policy that prospects cannot wear their patches on the set or in public alone.

Remember your every move is a reflection of your club and the brothers you will be depending on to vote you in! Do your best to never make them look bad. The brotherhood will have little tolerance for men that do not carry themselves in a responsible manner. Being drunk, high or out of sorts on the set is the type of thing that will make a respectable MC get rid of your ass. These men aren't playing about the reputation of their club! You are expected to act in a responsible manner when out representing. One weak brother makes all brothers look weak. A weak prospect makes the club look unprofessional and thirsty to just have anyone be a member. A weak prospect makes the club look desperate and when the club looks desperate the club looks weak! No club is going to tolerate repetitive irresponsible behavior from a prospect. Expect your prospectship to be terminated if your MC cannot trust you to conduct yourself responsibly. As it should be.

8. You Haven't Earned Your Way In Yet

Thinking back to that prospect I mentioned in step 8; one of the problems he was having that day was that he had forgotten his place and was acting like a full patch when he was not. I recognize that telling you to remember your station in life as a prospect can be seen as elitist or highbrow but when it comes to prospecting for an MC you must be told this so that it keeps your head sitting on your shoulders correctly. I will tell you to remember your station in hopes that this advice will stick. Depending upon the MC, the brothers who have come before you have fought, bled, laughed, cried, lived, loved, and in some cases died for the brotherhood. You have not. When you put on prospect colors you have not earned the right to assume any of the protections for which they have fought and died. When you prospect for a big club, you will be treated by many just like a full patch brother by members of outside clubs and the general public. This is good for the MC as it exudes its power when all of its patches are recognized, respected and/or feared. But that's the adulation you get from the outside. Everyone on the inside knows good and damned well that you haven't earned shit yet! So, keep that in mind. You haven't earned the right to coast off the reputations of the members of the brotherhood that have been established over the decades so know your station, know your place, and stay humble. Work hard to add to the allure and mysticism of the MC instead of riding the wave created by it. The biggest thing you can do initially is earn your full patch as soon as possible. The quicker you become a competent full patch the quicker you can contribute to the MC. Concentrate on achieving that above all other things—like partying, chasing the club's women, and looking cool in your prospect vest. You earn via sacrifice not via ego!

9A Take an Example from the Submarine Service

When I was in the United States Navy I served in the Silent Service as a submarine sailor. I sailed nuclear powered 688 Los Angeles class Fast Attack Hunter/Killers in wolfpacks projecting United States sea power during the Cold War. Once you arrived aboard a submarine, though you were trained at submarine school in Groton, Connecticut, you were nothing but an accident waiting to sink the entire submarine by doing something stupid or not knowing how to fight a casualty at sea. You were given one year to become submarine qualified and receive your coveted dolphins breast insignia declaring to the world you were submarine qualified. You were given a qualification card with over 100 signature spaces on it. Each one of those signature spaces was signed off when you interviewed with a submarine qualified seaman, petty officer, chief or officer that tested your knowledge of a system represented by that signature. For instance, for the high pressure hydraulics system signature you might have to answer questions about how the high pressure hydraulics systems worked aboard the submarine, where they were located, how they operated, from where they derived their power, how to shut power off to them during a fire, how to properly handle a high pressure hydraulic leak, how to service and maintain the equipment during an emergency, and all of the equipment powered by this system. You might have to answer questions about backup systems, manual systems associated with it if the automated systems didn't work and everything else. The interesting thing about this is this system might be run by mechanics, and you just happen to be a radioman. Even though you had never been to mechanics school in order to become a submarine qualified sailor you had to learn the emergency operations of every system aboard that vessel from the engine room to the torpedo room, galley, topside, sail, bilges, pumps, electronics, high pressure air systems, SONAR, Operations and more. You had to know how to fight fires, stop flooding, shore up bulkheads, equipment sound silencing, nuclear weapons handling, reading gauges, take readings and measurements, communications, emergency escapes at sea, and how to repel boarders. If you worked hard at getting two interviews per week and secured two signatures per week you would finish your qualification card in about one year or so. A "hot runner" could finish a 'qual card' in about six months. That was a guy who didn't get any sleep during those six months. I once witnessed a "hot-runner" finish a 'qual-card' in three months. That dude was heavy. But there were many lazy ass dudes that took way longer than a year to finish their sub 'qual cards.' These guys we called "Dinks!" which meant being delinquent on your quals. "Dinks" were hated aboard submarines. The thought was, as long as you are delinquent you are a danger to the boat because you don't know what the fuck you are doing!!!! If there is a casualty like flooding, fire, high pressure air leak, high pressure hydraulic oil leak, or other casualty, your "Dink," useless ass will be standing around like a dumb ass bump on a log while the rest of us have to push past your valueless "titts-on-bull" ass and solve a problem you should have been able to solve before it got out of hand. For instance, during some events, you have just a few precious minutes to stop a casualty before it overcomes the sub's ability to recover from it. That's when the casualty becomes a disaster. If a "Dink" sees the problem and can't get it stopped it could mean big trouble for the entire crew. Just think about the Titan that wrecked near the Titanic on 18 June 2023. The Titan ran into a casualty (implosion), which likely occurred in less than one second, from which the sub could not recover, and the resulting shipwreck is now a disaster at the bottom of the sea. So, there was little tolerance for "Dinks" during my time on submarines. They were harassed, hazed, ridiculed, and punished. This is how I feel about "Dink-assed" prospects and probates. If you ain't a "hot-runner" about your business to get "MC-Qualified" I will personally have little if anything to do with you. And you will never get my vote! Capiche?

Note: I have heard through the grapevine that today's modern Navy has forbidden submarine sailors from referring to newbies as "Dinks" favoring a softer, touchier approach to getting folks qualified. I don't know if that's true or not, but I will say that I also see a softening in modern MCs as well in administering their prospecting programs. I won't comment about that as I have nothing good to say.

9B Remember Jake Sawyer Hells Angels Nomad

I wrote about Jake a little earlier in this book but now, I'll tell a little more of the story and how it relates to prospects. I once interviewed a 75-year-old former Hells Angel named Jake Sawyer who had been a nomad. He told me before and during that interview that he became a full patch in just one day. He said that when he met members of the club and hung out with them one day they hatched a plan to kick in a guy's door to handle some business they had with him. Jake told the guys that he didn't think that was such a good idea, but they were sold on it and insisted they were going through with it. So, Jake said, "Okay, well then if that's what you guys want to do, I'll be the one to kick in the front door!" So, this Jake the hangaround leads the Hells Angels brothers through the front door and as he kicks it in, he gets shot right in the chest! He continues forward, takes the gun from the guy, and proceeds to kick his ass. They made Jake a full patch that day or the next. His example was that he didn't sit back and coast on the club's reputation, instead he advanced the club's agenda risking his own skin to get it done. He earned the right to wear that patch and strut just as hard as any other Hells Angel wearing it. I'm not saying your sacrifice should be that radical, it's not the 1970s any longer but I think you get my point. Find a way to be a relevant contributor even if it is just mowing the lawn at the clubhouse (without having to be asked to do it) or guard the brothers' bikes at an event, if that's what it takes. Be creative, figure it out and earn your way!

9C Always Display a Positive Attitude

The biker set is a fun place, but it can also be cliquish. Everyone will know you are "just a prospect," and new to the set, when they see that prospect patch on your back or see you hanging around with no colors at all. As a new person you cannot have a negative attitude and as a prospect you represent the MC. It is extremely possible for one negative brother to start trouble for the entire MC simply by displaying a piss poor attitude on the set. You will be expected to display a positive attitude when out and about. You are a prospect —you don't have the right to have a bad attitude. If someone greets you and you respond with a holier than thou attitude, you may bruise a fragile ego and now your MC has problems. Conduct yourself with class and keep your attitude in check. Being classy and positive doesn't make you look weak.

10 Participate as Much as You Think is Acceptable then Participate More

As Invader Shaggy 1%er of the Invaders MC Nation often says, *"There are three things that make any organization great: Communication, Respect, and Participation."* Your mastery of participation is paramount to your success in achieving your goal to be a full patch brother. By giving maximum participation over the next several months, you will find yourself appreciated and respected beyond belief. This is because one of the hardest things to find in any organization is people who are willing to participate. It seems like an easy proposition—if people love their MC (like they claim) there should be lines around the block with brothers volunteering to handle every need of the club. Unfortunately, for most clubs, this is not the case. Often it comes down to the willing few to get most things done. As a prospect that proves himself to be dependable early in the process, you will be amazed at how quickly your prospect time flies by when you are constantly awarded increased responsibilities. Volunteer and participate and make sure to have fun doing it. This is not to say that you need to forgo your other responsibilities in life as it is important to keep a balance between work, family and the MC, but prospecting takes time and must be given as much priority as possible. If you can give more, always give more! Believe me, it will be appreciated.

11 If You See a Club Brother You Haven't Met Take the Initiative to Introduce Yourself

In traditional MCs, to be voted in you must have a 100% yes vote by the members which means you will have to get to know everyone to a greater or lesser extent because you will need everyone's vote if you want in. You can't be shy about getting to know any prospective brother that will be voting for you. If you see a club brother you haven't met yet, take the initiative to do so. Don't leave it up to a brother to come over and introduce himself to you. He's already in the club that you want to join. It's no skin off his ass if he never meets you because at the end of the day he is still in the club if you don't get in. Be proactive, get up and go introduce yourself! Just remember that during the introduction, to present yourself as "prospect number" or "prospect name," never as your real name unless specifically asked.

Note: In some clubs, prospects do use their real names.

12 Ask to Circulate and Greet Every Patch Holder

It is important to always have your best foot forward in front of prospective full patched brothers. Often, the best place to see them will be at events, parties, and gatherings. Keep in mind that some brothers don't make meetings or don't participate in everything, so get to know them whenever you can. When you find yourself at a club event you will probably be very busy working for your sponsor, but there will always be opportunities to take a break. Use this time wisely. Instead of taking that break to catch a smoke, keep working towards your successful prospecting goals and go meet your potential brothers, especially ones that you've never met or seldom see. Remember that you will also need their votes to successfully cross over from prospect to brother. Creating opportunities for them to get used to seeing you and taking the time to go out of your way to get to know them is absolutely in your best interest. Always be on the lookout at any event to find brothers that you've never seen, introduce yourself, and get to know them.

13 Anticipate Needs, Don't Wait to be Told

In this important lesson of prospecting, you must learn to be sort of a crystal ball when observing prospective brothers. While prospecting, remember functions are not your time to party and chase the women, you are there to serve, work, be seen and not heard. You will see a huge difference in the treatment of the prospect with his head in the clouds—more concerned with the party than being of service to the MC and his brothers— than the prospect who is all about his responsibilities. Let not the lazy prospect be you! You don't want the negative attention he receives from his prospective brothers. Keep in mind that your time to party will come after you have achieved your primary goal and become a member of the club. Keep your eyes open and your mind sharp. Be anticipatory to see if you can predict the needs of your perspective club brothers, then get off your butt and go make yourself useful. It is always better to be working on something rather than to be sitting around waiting to be told to do something. The prospect who is always thought to be working and creating projects on his own will be thought to be resourceful and pragmatic. The one who always has to be told to do something, no matter how willing he is to be of use, will still be thought of as lazy and lackluster.

13A Anticipatory Observation Skills

If you see brother Skull reach for a glass—how impressed would he be if you were handing him his glass before he could even grasp it? That's because you got yourself across the room fast enough to get it for him by being observant. If the President puts his glass down to greet the President of another MC and you are there to put a napkin over the top of his glass and stand with it in your hand protecting it for him—how impressed would he be when he turns around to get his drink only to find out it has been under your protection the whole time? That President will surely be thinking, *"Damn! That prospect really had my back tonight. I'm going to keep an eye on him to see if he deserves increased responsibilities."* Sharpen your skills in anticipatory observations as they will help you to be at the right place at the right time.

Remember Jake Sawyer, the Hells Angels Nomad

Earlier I told you about a Hells Angel Nomad named Jake Sawyer who became a full patch in just one day. As Jake kicked in that door and the shot hits him in the chest, he continued forward to take the gun from the dude and proceeds to kick his ass.

I tell you this again only to remind you that Jake didn't sit back and coast on the club's reputation. Instead, he advanced the club's agenda risking his own skin to get it done. He earned the right to wear that patch and strut just as hard as any other Hells Angel wearing it. Now, I'm not saying your sacrifice should be that radical but find a way to be a relevant contributor! Even simple acts of mowing the clubhouse lawn or guarding the brothers' bikes at an event will get you noticed and move you closer to receiving your patch. Be creative, figure it out and earn your way!

14 Don't Get Overly Friendly with Any Non-Regular Acquaintance of the Club; CYA

One problem with being new is that you don't always know what someone is up to when they approach you to ask questions. All MCs have enemies, and it may take you months to recognize who they are.

For example, someone in another MC may want to find out something sensitive about your club. In this scenario, if the enemy is digging for dirt and spots you (the prospect) minding your business tending bar, what better person is there to ask a fucked-up question than the new guy who doesn't understand what's going on? Consequently, you get setup by a smiling face that is just about to bring you more misery than you ever thought possible because he was out for blood the moment, he spotted your innocent ass at that bar! You must be very careful about being overly friendly so that you don't innocently allow access to information to which folks are not entitled. One of the best ways to avoid this trap is to make it a practice to speak very little at functions and events on the set until you have spent enough time there to know what's going on. You don't have to be rude, after all prospects are not expected to speak very much anyway. If someone asks you a question it is perfectly OK to say, "*I am a prospect and I'm not authorized to speak on any club business. Let me find you a full patch brother to answer your question.*" No one can or should take exception to that. It doesn't matter if it's a 1%er, the President of another MC, or a random person on the set. If you hold to the standard that "Prospects don't talk," you can't say the wrong thing! If you pass along questions, you have no rank to answer, you can't get in trouble for answering the wrong question, or for putting information out you really don't know the answer to in the first place. It's called "covering your ass" (CYA). Having expertise at the CYA skill makes you a wise prospect and will likely allow you to crossover quicker.

15 Brothers' Information Stays in the MC

Never, under any circumstance, should you give out a club brother's name, phone number, address, or any other personal information to anyone outside the MC! It is vital you learn this lesson first and foremost because it can protect your brothers' safety, privacy, and anonymity. The MC is a private club that operates in very public venues. It is easy to be drawn into the idea that everybody is family because everybody is laughing, hugging, and smiling. But never forget there are predators all over the set and they seek prey for many different reasons. They are lurking looking to exploit every gap, miscommunication, weakness, or mistake. One of the worst mistakes a prospect can make is to be caught slipping when it comes to another brother's safety. You can be duped into providing the information that gets one of your brothers hurt, kidnapped, or murdered. And believe me, it can happen in an instant! A perpetrator can be anyone—a National President, regional officer, big-time local celebrity. You can't trust anyone, especially with your brothers' personal information! Don't fall for the President, from another club, who comes up to you and says, "I can't remember brother Jack Rabbit's number and I lost it on my phone can you give it to me real quick?" Don't be taken in by the brother of another club who says, "I don't remember brother Jack Rabbit's address and I have to meet him first thing in the morning can you give it to me please out of your phone?" Consider the idea that, he may be mad at Jack Rabbit because he thinks he's sleeping with his girl and wants his address to go to his house and kill him, and you were the one that was duped into providing it. This kind of dumb shit happens. Do NOT be the reason one of your brothers gets hurt.

15A The Day I Spoke on a Brother's Business

I can remember when such a thing happened to me. Yes, many of the things that I tell you not to do are exactly the things that I have done. In this anecdote, I gave out a brother's information because a very skilled woman was able to pry it from my lips. Let me set the scene ... I was dating a woman and my chapter President decided that he would date her behind my back. The whole time she and I were together, I thought we shared a closeness. Little did I know she was sleeping with my club brother and chapter President behind my back! At this point, I had known this club brother for about 25 years as we had served in the Navy together. He had always been a womanizer during our service, but we lost touch and that was a long time ago. When we reconnected, he assured me his womanizing days were over, and he was happily married and dedicated to his Christian lifestyle. The new him came across as a paragon of loyalty and fidelity, which I accepted as the truth because why would a club brother lie? He came across as the perfect family man to me, and a paragon of virtue.

The truth came out (as the truth often does) when my girl informed me that "Your president and I have been sleeping together for quite some time, and I'm upset because he slapped me in the mouth the other day and called me a bitch." Naturally, I didn't believe her. After all he was the perfect family man and a paragon of virtue. I was so sure she was lying; I got so angry at her I screamed, *"Why would you tell those lies on that man? He's a Christian and he's a married man and he would have no reason on Earth to sleep with you! That's my club brother and I cannot believe you would tell those kinds of lies on him and I no longer want to have any more dealings with you!"*

Little did I know I had just given her the magic potion that she sought. That tidbit of information I let slip from my lips, in a moment of rage, allowed her to know something that she had not known previously. You see he hadn't told her that he was married and learning this from me infuriated her. Revealing his marriage was not something I would have done purposefully (to get revenge even though he was sleeping with my woman behind my back), but by catching me off guard the result was still the same. So, that's how she found out.

15B "Loose Lips Sink Ships"

When I served in the submarine Navy we used the saying "Loose lips sink ships!" And for me in this instance, my loose lips did indeed sink the ship of his marriage. Now armed with the fact that she knew he was married, "Tracy" began following him when he left her home. Eventually, he led her to his home where she took the opportunity to show up on his front doorstep to tell his wife exactly who she was and exactly what they had been doing. I am not proud this was because of me! Deftly, she guided me to the revelation of his greatest secret, and I watched my club brother go through a divorce that occurred partly by my hand.

I say this from great experience—people are experts at manipulation and deceit, they are the kings and queens of subterfuge and espionage. "Tracy" could have shown up on the President's doorstep and killed his wife and family out of jealousy and outrage and that too would have been my fault. Be careful with the phone numbers, marital status, employment status, and any other personal information of your beloved brothers. Treat your brothers' business like club business. Give out no one's information. The proper response to any request is, "Tell you what, give me your information and I will make sure that he gets it."

Never forget: "Loose lips sink ships and sinking ships kill people!"

16 MC's Information Stays in the MC

People say, "keep club business inside the club," but sometimes it can be hazy to fully understand exactly what is "club business?" For example, is a club brother's business club business? The answer is nearly every question you can think of about your club or club brothers is off limits to someone outside the club. Even innocuous questions like "How many chapters do you all have?," "How big is your club?," "How many members do you guys have?," or "Do you have enough chapters to be considered a national MC?" are all questions that aren't anyone's damned business.

Think of your MC like a military unit. You would never tell anyone the exact size of your military defense unit, its capabilities, its logistics or its supply routes, so you should never share similar information about your MC. Think of your MC the same way. You should never answer questions like, "How many members y'all got?" or "How many chapters y'all got?" or "Where do y'all hold y'all's meetings at?" As a prospect it is always okay to say "We never disclose the strength of our organization, it's locations or logistical statistics. Who would ever do such a silly thing?" or to direct any question to a full patch club brother who shouldn't be answering those questions either!

16A One Lies We All Lie

One of the reasons your knowledge of MC protocol is so important is because your ignorance could leave your club open to exploitation! There is nothing more annoying than being around people who think they are so smart but don't know a goddamned thing about MC protocol! You can't tell them anything. Just because they believe something in their minds they act upon it as though it is true. But a belief is not fact it is merely a belief. It doesn't become a fact until it is proven so absolutely!

Several years ago, my club, the Black Sabbath MC Nation, was having a major problem with a 1% OMC Nation in Georgia. We got down to a meeting where things were going really bad. The 1% President fires off a question to me designed to probe our strength to see if our club was too big to intimidate or had enough chapters to put up a resistance to the demands he was making. He yelled out, "Are you guys even big enough to be a national club? How many chapters do ya'll have!?" Arrogantly, I started spouting numbers that were greatly exaggerated well over the number of chapters we really had. Surprised, he yelled back, "You know we are going to check!" To which I responded, "Well, check then!"

On my way home following the meeting, I pulled my bike over and called him to tell him that I lied about how many chapters we had (still not telling him how many we had). He laughed at me and said, *"Yeah I know you did. At first you shocked me, but I figured out pretty quickly you had lied to me."* I asked him how he figured it out. He said, *"Dragon, it was your own guys that told on you man! When you told me how many chapters you had they all looked up in the sky with expressions that said, 'Why in the hell did he tell that 1%er that lie!?' So yeah, your boys gave you away. I just didn't want to embarrass you in front of them. Dragon, you need to school your boys to the game man! In the 1%er world we stand together in the face of opposition no matter what! When one fights, we all fight, and when one lies, we all lie together! We back each other no matter what in public. If there is a problem, we will handle it later at the clubhouse. Your boys were lame because they didn't back you!"*

If my men had been up on their MC protocol or if I had trained and taught them better, they would have known that question was out of bounds and therefore would have known there was no way I was going to answer it truthfully if at all. They wouldn't have given me away because they would have been on the same page. But so many of them thought they knew what they were doing they had refused to listen for so long. They got a chance to see that what they believed was not necessarily what was true! Learn from the beginning how to support your brothers when they face opposition because your life can depend upon it.

17 Stay Alert

The biker club set can be a dangerous place. You cannot afford to be unaware of what is going on around you. Your survival depends on your street smarts and ability to observe and recognize danger when you see it. Your brothers' survival depends on your alertness. If you are in an MC that is under an OMC, you must be even more vigilant as the OMC often has way too much else going on worrying about their own safety than to worry about yours. The fact is most OMCs have conflicts going on with multiple MCs at the same time. They fight amongst these enemies and even kill one another. And while this environment can be fun, exciting, and adventurous, the situation can turn deadly in an instant. A gun battle could ensue when just a few moments earlier everyone was partying, dancing, and having fun. You must have a good intuition about the set and almost "feel" when a situation is beginning to turn so you can grab your brothers and get the hell out of there. It's important to get to the point that you know the vibe of the set—such as who is beefing with who.

When you know that two MCs are not getting along, and you see them both arrive at an event your intuition should tell you it's time to turn on your "Spidey senses" because anything could go down between those two warring MCs. Naturally, it will take time on the set before you are able to fully determine these risks, but before you get to that level of familiarity you should focus on learning how to recognize when an atmosphere changes so that you can alert your prospective brothers that something isn't quite right. Your senior brothers will know what to do because you've alerted them to a problem they might not have seen coming. As a prospect you won't know a lot about why things are going on but that shouldn't stop you from knowing or feeling when something isn't quite right.

17A. Listen to Your "Somethings"

Everyone has an inner sense that tells them when to get out of harm's way. Some call it "intuition," "sixth sense," "premonition," "gut feeling," "Spidey sense" or "something told you." I call it my "somethings" and I always listen to them. Make sure you always listen to yours!

18 Conduct Yourself with the MC in Mind

When in public wearing your prospect colors always remember you represent your MC. No matter where you are or what you are doing the public sees you and by extension your MC. If you show your ass at a restaurant in your MC's colors, the public sees the entire MC showing its ass at the restaurant. A waitress you belittle may see one of your brothers in the restaurant later in the week and decide to spit in his food because of the dumb shit you did, just because he's wearing the same colors. If you are doing something illegal in the MC's colors, it's the same as the entire MC doing something illegal. When in public, everything you do represents the MC. If you start beef with another club, then the entire MC has started beef with another club. The MC has no place for selfishness and ego driven individualism. You are part of a hive and something you do to offend someone could cause trouble for a brother who is completely innocent of your transgression. You must always keep your mind on the fact that you represent something greater than yourself. Conduct yourself accordingly! The public never stops seeing you even when you think no one is looking.

19 We Don't Leave Folks Behind – Like the Military

When you are with the MC, you arrive with the MC, and you leave with the MC. You never allow a prospect or full patch brother to go anywhere alone. Often younger prospects think the older full patch brothers are trying to be their mothers when they are told they aren't allowed to be anywhere on the set alone. But this is the farthest thing from the truth. There are plenty of enemies on the set looking to exploit any situation where there is a breakdown in security or a display of weakness. These are evil people with evil intentions and there is no better target than a lone prospect who isn't paying attention for just a moment in time. This is far less likely to occur if the MC has a policy that keeps the brothers together when out on the set. This means no wandering off. The best way to look at this is, "We came together, we stay together, we leave together, and we report in after we get home safely!"

19A Don't Make Jazz's Mistake and Wander Off during Troubled Times

My sponsor, "Jazz" was having a hard time with a rival MC. We were at a party in another state and the SAA told everyone to stick together. Jazz, however, met a woman and decided to walk her out to her car. That's when the rival MC showed up and caught Jazz alone and away from the pack somewhere near the parking lot alone. They surrounded him and kicked his black ass. By the time the club found him, the rival club was long gone celebrating their victory. When I asked Jazz why he didn't pull his gun (in Arizona we always wore our guns on our hips like cowboys), he said, *"John, everyone had guns, if I had pulled mine, they would have pulled theirs and I'd be dead right now. You can't shoot ten people simultaneously. That was just an ass kicking I had to take that night. I shouldn't have left the club and went out on my own. I was stupidly chasing a tail, and I paid the price."* He was right and you should learn from Jazz's mistakes. Stick together, especially during troubled times!

20 Alert the SAA or Senior Brother to Negative Vibes

If you notice any negative vibes while at a function, alert the SAA or a senior brother immediately. This rule is really an extension of "Stay Alert" as it directs you as to who to report to when you sense or detect a potential problem on the set. The club SAA is the first security officer and should always be reported to first, if possible. A senior full patch brother is also an appropriate alternative so that they can report to the SAA. The SAA will direct the brothers as to what to do next.

21 Sobriety Helps You Keep your Eyes and Ears Open

You can't keep your eyes and ears open if you are so caught up in the party—drinking, smoking, and having fun. Never put yourself in a position to become oblivious to the fact that you are on the set. The set is a place where the MC handles business, makes an appearance and moves on. You can party more comfortably at home in your MC's clubhouse. When out on the set, stay vigilant.

22 You are a Prospect 24/7

Your association with the MC doesn't turn off when you take off your colors or aren't on the set. You are a prospect 24 hours a day, 7 days a week (24/7). You represent the MC even in your personal life. It is expected that the MC becomes part of your inner being such that you operate in the best interest of the MC in all of your dealings including professional, social, and personal. Many MCs are so concerned with their public image they will regulate how their prospects and members conduct themselves even when they are not wearing the colors or participating in club events. Yes, being on Instagram or Facebook threatening people and getting into social media beefs may be an activity you are doing on your own time, but the MC may frown on that behavior enough to put you out over it. Take the time to understand the club culture and the social construct upon which the MC oversees the overall behavior of its brothers. Be knowledgeable about the conduct that it expects from its members. In many cases the MC won't hear "your personal time is your own business if that business can bring undue scrutiny on the club." Make sure you understand the culture you are getting into before you get too deep. Ensure you are a good fit while prospecting for your MC because if you aren't you can easily become dissatisfied with them as much as they are with you.

23 You Are Every Brother's Prospect

In most MCs you will need every member's vote to crossover into full patch brotherhood. You can ill afford to think that only pleasing your sponsor will be enough to get you into the family. Do whatever any full patch brother in good standing asks you to do with pride and a good attitude. Also, if you belong to a national club you may need to do whatever any full patch brother asks you in the nation (this rule might differ slightly in your club).

24 Never Wear Your Colors Out of Your Area Without Your Sponsor's Approval and Never Out of State Unless You are with Your MC

There are many rules associated with how and where an MC can travel or wear its patches. Often the MC must seek permission to fly in an area that is not their home. As a prospect, you will not be familiar with these rules of conduct on the set. You may want to proudly wear your colors but it's not always that simple. Never wear your colors outside of your area without your sponsor's approval and never out of state unless you are with your club brothers.

Let's say you decided to go back to Ohio to visit relatives and you want to wear your colors out on the Ohio set but your MC is not cleared to fly there. Or maybe your MC flies a support patch of an

OMC and the area you are visiting is considered hostile territory for your OMC. In either of these scenarios, if you pop-up on the Ohio set wearing your colors, you inadvertently put yourself in a position to get jumped and even living the very negative experience of having your colors forcibly taken. This puts the whole brotherhood and your dominant OMC in a regional conflict that could conceivably get someone hurt or killed. All because you made the honest mistake of wearing your colors in the wrong area without permission.

Although the scenario may seem extreme it is HAS happened! Another, less dangerous, scenario, but just as serious, let's say someone sees that you are wearing a prospect patch and decides to target you because you are alone without a knowledgeable brother around to head them off. As a prospect, being on the set alone is fraught with pitfalls and the potential for danger, especially if you are out of your area.

Never travel alone out of your area with your prospect colors without your club sponsor's approval, no matter how tempting the proposition.

25 Don't Interrupt Conversations Among Brothers

It is considered incredibly rude to interrupt two full patch brothers when they are having a private conversation. A prospect is expected to wait until their conversation is finished before approaching within earshot. If you see two or more full patch members of any club such as a full patch brother talking to a full patch member of another club do not interrupt. In a crisis or when an urgent situation arises that dictates you have no choice other than to interrupt, stand in a position of visibility, outside of earshot where you can ensure you are noticed. When there is an opportunity for them to pause their conversation, you will be recognized and called close enough to state your intent and purpose. You should profusely apologize for interrupting, state your business, or ask your question, then quickly leave after receiving direction. If possible, get a full patch brother or your club sponsor to intervene on your behalf.

26 The Word "Gang" Should Never Be Uttered on the Set

Terms like "biker gang," "gang," "outlaw motorcycle gang," or "OMG" are inflammatory when used improperly or out of context on the MC set. As a prospect it is easy to misidentify a club's lane or authority. By giving them the wrong designation, you can cause some embarrassing or dicey moments. It's best to refer to MCs by their name instead of any other generalized description. If you don't know their names, you shouldn't be talking about them at all. Remember walls have ears on the biker clubs set. You never know who is looking, listening, watching, or reporting what you say so always keep it general, non-accusatory, and indiscriminate. If you find that you must talk negatively about a club to a brother while you are on the set. Take them outside, to a spot that offers some privacy—out of earshot of others. Whisper your negativity to your brother in a low tone and keep it brief. You never know who anyone is on the set and talking loosely out of your mouth about another MC can cause circumstances to be very uncool.

27 Never Lie to a Member of Another Club

There is a difference between lying and refusing to give up club information on the set. In one instance your club is thought of as liars and untrustworthy, in the other it is seen as tight-lipped and protective of its culture and business. The difference being that a lie was told when the words "none of your business" should have applied.

For example, if someone asks about your club's membership size, it's always acceptable to say, "That seems like club business, and I really can't talk about it." A prospect has every right to say, "I can get you a patch holder to answer your question as I am not permitted to talk about club business." This is much better than telling a lie that can put you and the club in a negative light.

28 Show Equal Respect to Full Patch Brothers of Any Club

Always show the same level of respect to full patch brothers and officers of another MC as you would your own. Although you only prospect for your MC and only full patch brothers of your MC may give you orders or expect you to complete tasks they request from you, it is always appropriate and expected for you to show respect to other MCs. It demonstrates to other clubs that your MC is training its prospects traditionally and with respect.

For instance, if you are in the United States Submarine Navy walking down the pier in Turkey and you pass a senior Turkish officer of the Turkish Submarine Navy—you render a salute. Even though he's not in your chain of command, nor can he give you orders, you show respect to his military rank over yours. If your rank was senior, he would render a salute to you which you would respectfully return. Since MCs follow paramilitary structure, it is customary to show respect up and down the set.

29 Always Carry Pen, Paper, Watch, and Calendar

These are the tools of a prospect in most clubs on the MC set. There may be other tools prospects are required to carry in their prospect kit/prospect bag. No matter what your MC wants you to carry it is important to always have those items with you. In many clubs you may catch a fine or extra prospecting days if you are caught without your kit on your person.

30 Frequently Ask Full Patch Brothers How You Are Doing and If There Is Anything You Should Be Doing Differently

By frequently asking your full patch brothers how you are doing and inquiring about how you can improve or do things differently, you avoid potential pitfalls that may hinder your ability to crossover. Some full patch brothers may hold a grudge against you for reasons you may never know. They don't intend to vote for you and never intend to tell you why. But by checking in with each full patch brother, you disable their ability to hold up your crossover because they told you what they wanted you to change in enough time for you to change it before they could screw up your vote. Keep a running internal report card by asking frequently how you can be of greater service to the MC.

31 Never Ask When You May Be Getting Your Full Patch

One of the quickest ways to add time to your prospecting period is to ask when it will end. It is inappropriate to ask your sponsor or any full patch brother when you will be getting your full patch. You will receive your patch when your club brothers feel you are ready and not one moment before, so don't ask. Patch holders may become quite angry if you do and it's an excellent way to get a few months tacked on to your prospectship.

32 Never Call a Full Patch Your "Brother"

Many MCs do not see prospects as members until they crossover, while other MCs feel prospects as probationary members. Some won't allow you to call a full patch a "brother" until after you crossover, some will. Until you find out how it is in your MC it's best to err on the side of caution and call prospective brothers by their club names until after you've patched over.

33 Never Call a Full Patch or Prospect of Another MC "Brother"

There is a long-held tradition on the MC set that only your club brothers are your brothers. No one outside the MC is allowed to call us "brother" and we don't often refer to a member of another MC as "brother." This is especially true on the White MC set. On the Black MC set, however Black people have a history of calling each other "brother" based on a shared experience of surviving Jim Crow in the hostile South and segregation in the U.S. as a whole, the term "brother" is a bit tricky on the Black MC set. Personally, I rarely call anyone on the biker set that isn't my club brother "brother", but I take no offence if a Black man in another club calls me "brother" simply because that is our tradition as Black people in America. And because I'm a talk show host and author who has connected with millions of people worldwide, I don't get upset when someone identifies with something I've said and calls me brother either. Generally, in the MC world your brothers are members of your MC who wear your back patch. It is important that you know the general rule so that you don't make the mistake of calling someone brother, resulting in an embarrassing dressing down.

Note: This doesn't mean you won't ever call members of other MCs, who have earned your trust, "brother" in the future.

34 Patches are Earned Not Given, No Royalty in MCs

You must work for your patch. There are some who believe they have a birthright into the MC simply because their father was the founder they have some sort of a blood-rite into the MC's membership without putting forth the effort of prospecting. Those fools are sadly mistaken and will find out that there is no blood royalty in the MC or anywhere in the entire MC culture. Everyone must prospect to gain their patch or go through whatever rituals the club's bylaws have established—for the most part. Of course you'll find exceptions to every rule, but for the majority of members of any clubs the only way in is the old-fashioned way. In traditional MCs patches are not purchasable, nor are they ever given (of course it happens but it shouldn't). This is the most basic tenet of this society.

35 Never Bring a Personal Friend or a Stranger Into the Presence of Your Prospective Brotherhood Without Permission

As a prospect you do not have the right to bring guests before the brotherhood. Your prospective brothers are just getting to know and trust you, they are not going to accept strangers you bring before them, no matter your intent, especially if they are not expecting them. On the MC side we often tell prospects to leave their woman at home as well. You won't have time for her while you are working for the club, and you probably don't want her to see you in a subservient role. On the prospect's side I say, "Keep it real!" You really don't know the MC well enough yet to be trusting these strange men around your woman like that so what the fuck is wrong with you bringing your woman to the clubhouse? It takes time to build relationships, trust, and loyalty. Take the time to learn your MC before bringing your woman, wife, family, or friends around. They don't really know you like that, and you don't really know them like that yet. I cannot tell you how many prospects have contacted me on my consulting application (clarity.fm/black-dragon) to tell me how unscrupulous 'prospective' club brothers have texted their women, followed their women's Instagram pictures, and even slept with their women or tried! Why not wait until you get into the brotherhood yourself before exposing yourself unnecessarily, or at least get pretty deep into your prospectship first? That would be my advice!

36 Never Turn your Back on a Patch Holder of Another MC

As a prospect, it is considered disrespectful and inappropriate to turn your back on a full patch member on the MC set. Naturally, this can be difficult if you are at an event with hundreds of people, obviously your back is going to be turned to someone. But the idea is to always remain respectful in your conduct on the set. It is better to back away from a full patch brother than it is to turn your back and walk away.

37 Always Show Respect and Courtesy to Patch Holders of Other Clubs

As a prospect you should always show respect and courtesy to full patch members of any club. Remember you represent your MC on the set and you should be the finest example of how your club should conduct itself. Although the set is fun, there are business aspects which require a level of professionalism. You are not there to be friends with members of other clubs, you are there to earn entry into your MC. Keep your encounters with outside club members short, polite, and professional then move on.

38 Avoid Pillow Talk like the Plague

Prospects are seen as "fresh meat" by nearly every female on the set. Be mindful of any "patch-chaser" (Another term for a "patch chaser" is a female butterfly who jumps from bed-to-bed chasing/collecting patches and piling up sexual bodies on her list. Like club brothers who chase, "I love me patches," they are NOT to be trusted, especially with your club or personal business.) you see bouncing from MC to MC seeking whomever she may devour. These "patch-chasers" gossip and are not to be trusted.

Some clubs will actually send a female to sleep with you just to get club information off your pillow. The bottom line is you don't fucking talk club business on your pillow, to your woman, a patch-chaser, a groupie, a chick you met on the set, your girlfriend, or anyone! "Pillow talk" refers to the intimate conversations you have with someone right before or after you've had intimate relations with them, when everyone is comfortable, vulnerable, and your secrets can get exposed.

39 Prospects Never Partake in Consuming Alcoholic Beverages at any Open Function

Simply put, prospects do not drink or indulge in spirits of any kind on the set. Prospects should be working on the set not getting drunk. Your job is to earn your way into the brotherhood. There will be plenty of time for you to enjoy the party after you have crossed over.

40 Prospects Never Partake in any Unnatural Drug

Simply put, prospects should never get high on the set. Just like consuming spirits, prospects should be working on the set not getting high. Your job is to earn your way into the brotherhood. There will be plenty of time for you to enjoy the party after you have patched over.

41 Never Acknowledge a Full Patch Brother's Woman Especially Upon First Meeting Her

Keep away from full patch brothers' and fellow prospects' women. Do not be overly friendly or even open yourself up to the possibility of an accusation of too much interest in full patch brothers' women.

This is a grown-up world. Conduct yourself like a mature, grown-up man at all times. Absolutely never be foolish enough to flirt with any full patch brother's significant other. Don't follow her on social media, don't look too hard at her during parties, don't speak to her alone in the corner, NONE OF THAT STUPID SHIT! It's a good way to never get voted into the MC or to get your ass kicked or killed by some jealous, pissed off brothers. And avoid a full patch brother's woman who is trying to be too friendly to you too. So many times, that bullshit is just a setup and trouble you don't need. Just a word of advice to the wise. In the alpha male dominated world of men too many act-like bitches when it comes to their egos, feelings, and loss of control of their women. So, a full patch could get mad and want revenge from you when his trollop-ass girlfriend should be the one he gets mad at. Stay away from all of that. You are trying to crossover into the MC. That is your primary purpose so focus on that!

42 Do Not Touch or Sit on a Patch Holder's Motorcycle Unless Invited

In the biker club world, it is unacceptable to ever put your hands on or attempt to sit on a biker's motorcycle for any reason without asking permission or receiving an invitation. Breaking this rule could get you cursed out or physically assaulted. Many on the MC set are over-the-top when it comes to their love of their machines. For them, motorcycles are given almost human-like attributes and their love for their bikes can exceed their love for humans. Never be so bold as to get on someone's bike, take a picture in front of it, examine it, touch it, feel it, overly admire it, lean against it, move it, adjust it, move something from under it, pick it up after it falls, or anything else with another man's motorcycle without asking first!

43 Prospect's Don't Pack But If You Do Turn her Cut Inside Out

In general prospects don't pack! ("Packing" is riding a woman, typically your woman, on the back of your bike.) As a prospect, your back seat (pillion) is reserved for the needs of the club.

The full patch brothers may need you to tote a case of beer, and you can't do that with a girl sitting on your bike. When you are working as a prospect leave your girl at home! Now, there may be times when your prospective brothers are lenient and allow you to pick up a chick or get lucky. If that chick is a property of another club, in a social club, or a female MC and is patched up herself she must take her colors off or turn them inside out. There is an MC protocol that "nothing tops the cut of your MC, (Dragon and Black Dragon)" which means the MC's colors must always be distinctly seen and prominent when a brother is on his bike. This means if any chick is wearing a patch of any other club you must tell her to take her colors off or turn her colors inside out. This is because her colors cannot top yours while she is on the back of your bike. Some chick may say, "Hell no! If I gotta take my cut off or wear it inside out, I don't want to ride on your damned bike," well, then she can walk!

44 Two Dudes Don't Ride on the Same Bike

Okay, in some countries you might see this shit but in the United Sates two dudes don't ride the same fucking bike together as of the writing of this book! I don't know what the future will hold but that is how it is right now! Of course there may be exceptions, such as in an emergency or you are teaching someone how to ride, , or some kind of other crazy assed exception I may not have thought about. But you don't, as a matter of general practice, ever let some dude ride on the back of your scooter! Got it?!

I've seen bros make a brother turn around and face backwards behind them in an emergency when they had to give a brother a ride, you figure it out. But that's the general rule. Let good sense prevail in any situation.

45 It's Not an Insult Not to be Acknowledged on the Set

If you see a brother from another MC that you know personally while you are out on the set, don't be insulted if he doesn't particularly acknowledge you in an overly friendly way—as you might expect that he should. There are a lot of politics going on throughout the set so his club may not be on friendly terms with yours or there may be other reasons outside of your personal relationship that prevent him from being friendly at that moment. If he is prospecting, there may be rules against him speaking while on the set, he may be trying to show loyalty to his brothers, or there are a myriad of other guidelines occurring which may prevent his ability to acknowledge you. Don't take any awkward interaction personally on the set. If it bothers you, get back to him off the set on a personal basis to discuss further.

46 Learn Your Patch Parts and Colors

I cannot tell you how many clubbers I've met on the set that had no idea the meanings behind the colors they were wearing on their backs. Learn what each part of your patch represents and what the different color combinations of each club means. What a waste of your time prospecting is, if you don't even know what the color combinations of your patch mean. You must know what every thread on your patch represents if you are going to know what your MC (and in turn you as a member) stands for. What if you later discover that the blue in your patch meant your MC hates people who lived on the blue islands of the Pacific Ocean? Is that something you could champion? No, but there you were wearing that patch ignorantly the whole time.

Would you believe there are Black men in some Black MCs that wear swastikas on their cuts? Naturally, you'd think there had to be something wrong for a Black man to don a swastika given that most people equate the swastikas with Nazi racist culture and white supremacy. What would you think if his response to the question, "Hey man, why are you wearing that swastika on your cut and what does it mean," was "Heck, I don't know what it means but I liked the club and it was part of the uniform, so I wear it." You would look at him as the fool he was. But what if his response was, "The swastika has many different meanings in many parts of the world and even though the Nazi rendition of the swastika is perhaps one of the most recognized, it is not the only interpretation of the symbol. My club has chosen to recognize a different interpretation of this symbol that I am wholly in step with it which is why I decided to wear this symbol despite what the popular interpretation of what it may be is." Of course, you'd be blown away and your perception of this individual would change, understanding that he knows what his club is about, what he is about, and the direction in which he wants to live his club life. This is why you must know what your club's symbology is and what all its iconology means.

46A Knowing Other Club's Patches and Meanings

The more information you have the easier it will be to navigate smoothly on the set. Get to know as much about the other MCs in your area as you possibly can. Learn their colors, iconology, patterns, beliefs, mottos, and symbology as well. Learn why they do what they do because when you know them and what makes them tick, you will be in the best position to effect positive outcomes for your MC in the future when you become a leader. Let your prospectship time be the building blocks for your successful future

MC career. Build your knowledge base as it will be of great assistance to you in the future.

47 A Prospect Must Do Anything a Full Patch Asks

Of course, within reason and legal limits. Don't be anybody's fool after all your mama didn't raise no idiot! Be prepared to let a mothafuka know they can take them patches and shove them up they mothafukin' ass! If need be. But in general, you prospect for your club. When a club brother asks you to do something, get that shit done without question!

48 Don't Touch Another Club's Colors

The vest and colors are the walking billboard that expresses who and what a clubber is. They tell a history of where he has been, who he is now, and perhaps indicates where he is going. The colors also carry the standard of the MC as a back patch of between one and five pieces. It is considered highly disrespectful by some MCs to touch someone's colors, especially the back patch(es). It is also considered to be highly disrespectful to point to someone's patch, touch it, and ask why they got it or what it stands for. When you hug someone on the set it can be considered an insult to touch their back patch(es). Become adept at hugging without touching a person's back patch. Hug around the neck area perhaps with one hand on the left or right side, rather than wrapping them up with both arms around the back. Clubbers are known for aggressively educating the uninformed about this transgression. Of course, as with all rules on the MC set, this practice is not considered disrespectful by everyone and there are some clubs that do not care about it at all.

49 Prospects Must Show Sincere Interest in the Club

If you are going to prospect, do it right because full patch brothers will be looking for you to display a keen interest in becoming a member of the MC. They know what they put into becoming a member so believe me when I tell you they are not going to have any sympathy for you not putting in the same, if not more effort. As I said before, start out like you can hold out.

50 Stealing is Not an Option

Thieves are not tolerated in most organizations or societies. The ironic thing about stealing from your brothers, is that in most cases, if you had just asked, almost anyone in your MC would give you what you thought you needed to steal. In most clubs stealing is automatic grounds for immediate termination. In others it is an immediate ass kicking too. In rare cases it could get you killed! Bottom line… don't steal from the MC because it will get you kicked out bad!

51 Your Colors Should Never Touch the Ground

Most MCs absolutely prohibit the mishandling of your colors. Your colors are the flag upon which your club is represented. No one is going to tolerate you slinging the colors around in a sloppy fashion, laying them on the ground, leaving them unattended in a chair, showing your ass while wearing them, breaking criminal laws in them, or letting another MC hold them. In many clubs such violations start with a suspension, a fine or both. Folks take these rags seriously and they will show you very quickly what happens when you disrespect them.

52 For Now, Just Follow the Rules & Bylaws

Not every rule in the bylaws will come with an explanation as to why it exists, and you may find that some of the rules are outdated or seem meaningless. Understand that something happened (incident, accident, event, tragedy, or triumph) somewhere in the club that caused those who came before you to write a bylaw you might not understand but are required to follow. It may take you years to find out why some of those silly rules were written. As a prospect you needn't worry about questioning why, for now you do or die! Follow the bylaws as they are written then question them later as you have earned the right to question through your sacrifice, honor, and service to the MC. No one respects a prospect that questions every rule before completing a task.

Summary

As you gain experience in the MC you will begin to see the importance of some of the points discussed in this chapter. You may not understand the reasons for every rule just yet—and no amount of writing can convey all you need to know. The hope is that by learning and following these 52 rules of prospecting—you will at least have a basic understanding to get started on the right foot on your MC journey with a foundation in basic MC protocol. Many MC prospects think the full patch brothers are trying to run them and be their mothers. Nothing could be further from the truth. These men are trying to use their wisdom to help you have the time of your life on the set while not having to relive the same bad experiences they endured.

BEST OF LUCK PROSPECT!

For more information on prospecting, be sure to get a copy of "*Prospect's Bible, How to Prospect for a Traditional Law-Abiding MC*" or "*Prospect's Bible for Women's Motorcycle Clubs.*" Available on Amazon, Kindle, Audacity, and at www.blackdragonsgear.com where you can get an autographed copy.

CHAPTER ELEVEN
DEALING WITH THE 1%, DOMINANTS, DIAMONDS, OUTLAWS, OMGS, AND THE LIKE

A Quick Overview to Bring You Up-to-Speed

This chapter is designed to familiarize you with the 1% subculture. This is by no means everything you should know as I could author multiple books on this subject and still have a million words left to write. For comprehensive knowledge, you will need more information and experiences than this book can provide.

What are they called

1% OMCs

"1%" is the original term used to describe these clubs, "…only 1% are not law abiding…", however, they are colloquially also referred to as "1%ers." These terms are interchangeable; however, I personally tend to use the term "1%" over "1%er."

There are some who will tell you one term is more significant than the other or that by adding the "er" to it somehow adds another element, but I have asked many 1% OMC brothers in clubs across the country, and they all say there is no difference between the two terms. After all, you're not going to treat a "1% MC" differently than a "1%er MC." The term "1%" is sufficient to carry the same weight on the MC set regardless of the variations in terminology.

Dominant OMCs

Since 1% OMCs are considered to be at the top of the MC hierarchy you often hear them referred to as "dominant" clubs or "dominant"

OMCs. Colloquially, they are referred to as "my dominant" or "the dominant."; however, they are also referred to as "diamond" clubs.

Outlaw Motorcycle Gangs (OMGs) Outlaw Motorcycle Clubs (OMCs)

1% OMCs and Outlaw MCs refer to themselves as "OMCs." Police organizations and the media often refer to 1% OMCs, OMCs, and some 99%er clubs that get into trouble with the law as "Outlaw Motorcycle Gangs" (or "OMGs,") simply because law enforcement has classified them on the level of criminal street gangs and refer to them in this way in the news or media outlets.

The DOJ describes OMGs as:

> OMGs are organizations whose members use their motorcycle clubs as conduits for criminal enterprises. OMGs are highly structured criminal organizations whose members engage in criminal activities such as violent crime, weapons trafficking, and drug trafficking. There are more than 300 active OMGs within the United States, ranging in size from single chapters with five or six members to hundreds of chapters with thousands of members worldwide. The Hells Angels, Mongols, Bandidos, Outlaws, and Sons of Silence pose a serious national domestic threat and conduct the majority of criminal activity linked to OMGs, especially activity relating to drug-trafficking and, more specifically, to cross-border drug smuggling. Because of their transnational scope, these OMGs are able to coordinate drug smuggling operations in partnership with major international drug-trafficking organizations (DTOs) (Department of Justice).

Motorcycle Club Protocol 101

The federal definition of a gang as used by the DOJ and the Department of Homeland Security's Immigration and Customs Enforcement (ICE), is:

1. An association of three or more individuals;

2. Whose members collectively identify themselves by adopting a group identity, which they use to create an atmosphere of fear or intimidation, frequently by employing one or more of the following: a common name, slogan, identifying sign, symbol, tattoo or other physical marking, style or color of clothing, hairstyle, hand sign or graffiti;

3. Whose purpose in part is to engage in criminal activity and which uses violence or intimidation to further its criminal objectives.

4. Whose members engage in criminal activity or acts of juvenile delinquency that if committed by an adult would be crimes with the intent to enhance or preserve the association's power, reputation, or economic resources.

5. "The association may also possess some of the following characteristics:" ("CRJ315 Chapters. 6-13 Test Flashcards - Quizlet")

    a) "The members may employ rules for joining and operating within the association." ("CRJ315 Chapters. 6-13 Test Flashcards - Quizlet")

    b) The members may meet on a recurring basis.

    c) "The association may provide physical protection of its members from others." ("This resource was retrieved from the National Institute of Justice Web ...")

    d) "The association may seek to exercise control over a particular geographic location or region, or it may simply defend its perceived interests against rivals." ("This resource was retrieved from the National Institute of Justice Web ...")

e) The association may have an identifiable structure.

(National Institute of Justice)

When referenced in the news, media or press conferences, the terms "OMGs" or "biker gangs" are normally used to identify them.

This is NOT a designation given to MCs by MCs! No MC should be referred to as a "gang!" – they will lose their shit if they hear you call them that, and rightfully so. It is never cool to ask an MC brother some misinformed question like, "To which of these biker gangs do you belong?"

There is a reason for the hatred of this term by clubs. If an MC is designated an OMG (i.e., "gang") then certain gang enhancements will be attached to the group should they ever be charged with a crime. These enhancements can add years to prison sentences or additional fines to their final adjudication. In addition, public perception of a gang is horrible, and the legal consequences are grave.

Your own family may question your judgement when they find out you are hanging out with what they might call those "biker gangs," so always correct them, "They are not gangs and we are not "gang families."

Motorcycle Gang (MG)

At the time of this writing, I know of two clubs that refer to themselves as a "Motorcycle Gang." You may encounter a 1% OMC with a self-proclaimed name of "MG," but it is not usual. And even though their name includes the term "gang," I guarantee you will feel their wrath if you ask them "To which biker gang do you belong."

Today's Diamond Clubs

Most 1% OMCs wear a diamond patch containing the words "1%" or "1%er," which is why 1% OMCs are referred to as "diamond" clubs. However, not all diamond clubs are 1% OMC nations. Some diamond clubs are not quite on the level of hierarchy as a 1% OMC diamond club, but they are still high on the MC hierarchy table and fall just under 1% OMC nations. These clubs are often referred to as "Outlaw" clubs (OMCs) in the United States.

Some 99%er MCs are revered at the same level as OMCs simply by the way they move on the set. They don't generally wear diamonds because their reputations proceed them. They are highly respected and not to be meddled with because they are known to handle business just as seriously as the 1% clubs and run their own affairs as "Outlaws."

Diamond 13 Racing MCs (RMC)

Members of the original 13 RMCs also wear a diamond 13 patch issued by the S.C.O.F. to represent the 13 RMCs outlawed by the AMA in the 1930s.

Other Kinds of Diamond Patches

There are other "outlaw" diamond patches that don't include a "1%" or "13." These include:

Some members of the Chosen Few MC, founded in Los Angeles in 1959 wear a "Take None Give None" diamond with a fist in it, issued before the club adopted their 1% diamond.

Redrum MC, an indigenous, first nations MC founded in 2006, and the Legion of Doom MC established in 1997 wear 13 ½ diamond patches to represent the indigenous perspective on the American judicial system (Redrummc.com). In an interview on Redrum's

YouTube founder, "Cliff" explained, "*13 ½ means one judge, 12 jurors, half a chance. In life, if you're gonna roll that way and subject yourself to the possibilities of having to face that, know that those odds are not in your favor—50%, 50%. [So], unless you have a lot of money to spend on a lawyer, and you are a Black, Brown, Indigenous person, or a poor White person, these odds are not in your favor. One judge, twelve jurors, half a chance is the gamble* (Youtube.com/@Redrumotorcycleclub8836)." Therefore, the 13 ½ diamond patch reminds Redrum members never to put themselves in that position (Redrummc.com).

DC Eagles MC, founded in Chicago IL in 1963, wear a 99% NFG diamond. They were founded in Chicago, Illinois in 1963. The founder was Danny LeDesma, who was known as "DC Danny" (OnePercenterBikers.com/DC-Eagles). Part of the name of the club is rumored to have come from the location where the club was founded, on the corners of [D] Damen Avenue and [C] Cortland Street which are in the Bucktown/Wicker Park area on the Northside of Chicago (OnePercenterBikers.com/DC-Eagles).

Hells Lovers MC wears a 0% diamond in place of the traditional 1% diamond.

Hierarchy Among the 1%

There are major players in the 1% game of which you should become familiar if you are to operate on the biker set. Each 1%er OMC plays a significant role in their area of influence with some 1% OMCs being more "dominant" than others. When you join an established MC, your founder and president should have already figured which 1% OMCs are dominant in your area. If you are attempting to establish a new MC, you MUST determine who's set you are operating in and the dominant MC(s) in the area to which your MC will report.

Keep in mind that there are White, Black, Hispanic, Native American, and other dominant MCs in existence across the United States, many of which you may never have heard of. You MUST learn about ALL of the dominants in your area and know them by sight. The following lists the perhaps most well-known Black or mixed-race dominant clubs in the United States:

- Soul Brothers MC
- Chosen Few MC
- Outcast MC
- Sin City Deciples MC
- Hells Lovers MC
- Thunderguards MC
- Wheels of Soul MC
- Street Soldiers MC
- Phantoms MC
- Hawks MC
- THUG Riders MC
- Ching-a-Lings MC

The following lists perhaps the most well-known White or mixed-race dominant clubs in the United States:

- Hells Angels MC
- Pagans MC
- Mongols MC
- Bandidos MC
- Outlaws MC
- Warlocks MC
- Sons of Silence MC
- Vagos MC
- Galloping Goose MC
- El Forastero MC

Motorcycle Club Protocol 101

- Warlocks MC (there are two separate Warlocks MCs)
- Outsiders MC
- Invaders MC
- Brothers East (B*EAST) MC
- Brother Speed MC
- Gypsy Joker MC

With so many 1% OMCs on both the Black, White, and mixed-race sets, I cannot hope to name them all within this book. New OMCs popping up or disappear every day. Learn the ones in your area and the areas to which you will be traveling.

How Do 1% OMCs Control the MC Set

1% OMCs exert control and influence over the MC set by mutual respect, intimidation, fear, compromise, and violence. MCs and biker organizations must comply with the regulations and protocols set forth by the dominant MC(s) in the area or there will be an accounting. How intense, dangerous, or violent that encounter may be will depend upon the strength of the club and its knowledge of MC protocol. Most non-dominant MCs choose simply to comply. In some cases, the dominant will authorize a council run by respected 99%er MCs to govern the region and run most of their own affairs, with Black councils controlling the Black MC set and White councils controlling the White MC set. These councils have different names based upon the region in which they govern, for the Black MC set this includes the "Georgia Council" in Georgia or the "Chain" in Texas. On the White MC set, this council is often referred to as the "Confederation of Clubs" (or COC). There are hundreds of these coalitions across the country with some states having coalitions for different regions within a state. Typically, dominant MCs will administer the council or even run their own councils.

It is important to remember that even though these dominant MCs don't always get along and often fight and kill one another, they STILL TALK and COMMUNICATE to control the biker set! They will check with each other to ensure the MCs and biker groups operating in the area have been blessed and are operated under someone's control. Generally, if you have been blessed by one of the dominants or their associated council, you will be recognized by all OMCs (Black and White) in your area.

Getting a Blessing Today

All non-dominant MCs, MMs, RCs, MSOs, SCs and others that operate on the set will go through an authorization process called a "blessing" to fly their colors without hassle. Even new 1% MCs or nations moving into a new territory must go through some type of meeting or negotiation to ensure smooth ingress into an area, so believe it or not getting a blessing applies to all MCs to a greater or lesser extent. MCs that refuse to follow this process of receiving a "blessing" (even 1% OMCs) will likely experience physical altercations to maintain their status and existence on the MC set. Compliance will be forced if necessary! If you understand this, you will know how to deal with it. If you are hard-headed it will deal with you!

There are some steps that every MC must follow to be blessed today. These steps will vary based on the state, city, area, or region; however, here are some of the common protocol requirements you may observe:

Members

- Your MC needs between 5 and 10 members to be recognized on the set.
- You may need to turn in a roster with your member's names and officer positions annually.

- You may need to provide contact information for all your club's officers.
- You may need to prove you've maintained your membership count and the appropriate number of working motorcycles required in some states.
- You may be required to perform some social services for the community prior to receiving your blessing.
- You may have to present your bylaws and patches for approval.
- You may need to attend mandatory meetings with the dominant or council.
- You may be required to meet other goals as determined by the dominant or council blessing your club.
- You may be required to have a brother club sponsor and invite your MC into the coalition.
- Be advised, you may run into a situation where the area is closed to new clubs. This is often for a brief period of time (1 – 2 years) so stay persistent and wait until your time comes.

Sponsoring MC (Brother Club)

In some areas MCs are required to be invited into the coalition by a sponsor MC to receive a blessing. The sponsor MC provides guidance on how things are performed on the set in your area. Often, the sponsoring MC must be in existence within the area for an established number of years. Therefore, a new MC will not be able to sponsor another new MC. But if you try hard enough you can overcome adversity and make it happen!

For instance, in the Colorado Springs area the Black Sabbath MC Nation was brought onboard with the guidance of our sponsor MC the Street Soldierz MC. At that time, the area was closed to new MCs and the wait was going to be extremely long. The Street

Soldierz MC went to the Sons of Silence MC dominant on our behalf and got an exception to allow us into the state which could not have happened without their help. To them I am eternally grateful. So always keep in mind there are several ways to get things accomplished if you are truly determined and persistent to make your dreams of starting an MC happen.

The sponsor MC must remain compliant with the council. If the sponsor MC becomes non-compliant, this will likely negatively impact their status in helping you receive your blessing. Prior to partnering with an MC for sponsorship, it is wise to validate the history of the MC to ensure that they have maintained their compliance and have never been sanctioned by the coalition.

Hard Colors vs Soft Colors

Most coalitions won't allow you to wear "hard colors" for a period of time before your blessing. Hard colors include your vest with your insignia on the back. Conversely, soft colors are other articles of clothing, like t-shirts with a version of your colors or logo on it. In many coalitions you can wear soft colors during the blessing process. It is only when you receive your blessing that you are legal to fly. "Legal to fly" means you have been blessed to wear your hard colors at annuals, parties, fundraisers, and in general on the set within the state or region in which you have been blessed.

Once established there can be requirements for how long you must operate before you can throw a party or make money on the set. Some coalitions limit new MCs to one revenue generating event during the first 1 to 3 years of operation. These anti-competition rules can be quite stifling and definitely limits the survivability to only the fittest and most financially viable MCs, but violations of this requirement will assuredly incur sanctions against your MC for years to come (including forbidding all MCs from attending future functions hosted by your MC). You are well advised not to violate the rules set forth by the coalition.

Remember, 50% of all MCs never survive their first 3 years in existence. This is where the term "Popup" club is derived. A club that survives less than three years is here today and gone tomorrow which is the expectation that most MCs have of popup clubs. It will be up to you and your brothers to prove them wrong. Sadly, of the clubs that survive the 3 years, 50% of those survive less than 5 years. Although the odds are stacked against any new club from making it on the set, the more friends and allies you can make the better off your new MC will likely be to survive.

The 1% Clubhouse

Many folks are absolutely terrified of the 1% and for good reason – because they have a bad reputation. Be that as it may, you will still find that you will have to deal with them. Just remember, 1%ers are people too, with feelings, emotions, fears, prejudices, they laugh and cry too. For the most part if you deal with them straight up, they will deal with you the same way. They are not the boogeyman, but they do have a lifestyle not everyone understands, nor can everyone live.

I'll tell you like I tell my own club brothers before we go to a 1% clubhouse. Most of the time if you don't start any shit there won't be any shit! If you don't know how to handle yourself, your temper, or your liquor – DON'T GO! Keep your ass at home! If you are looking for a quick hookup know that many of the good-looking women are already spoken for by the 1% club brothers and are properties. Every property there is spoken for by a male sponsor so if every woman belongs to someone it is safe to assume that flirting with any one of them can land your ass in hot water – especially in a 1%er's clubhouse. So, don't be on the hunt for a Jane to get your

Tarzan on over at the 1% spot. Discretion is the better part of valor when you are visiting any MC's clubhouse.

You may find yourself in a situation wherein you may date a property, have a tryst with her, or have a torrid evening. As I have said previously, not all properties are in romantic relationships with their sponsors. A sponsor may just be a friend, brother, cousin, or an ex-partner that no longer is involved with his property. In that case he may grant you permission to date his property if he is asked correctly and respectfully. This isn't something you should necessarily initiate. Always wait instead to be approached. If she shows interest or asks you to dance, or any of the things women do to inform you that they are interested, it's not crazy to ask if her sponsor is around so that you can get his permission to dance with her or otherwise pursue her. Don't accept the BS that she doesn't answer to anyone because that's a setup for the okie doke that you don't need. That's not why you are there. But this can happen. I've seen it with my own eyes.

As national president, I once had a 1% president call me to let me know that he was allowing one of my club brothers date his property. He told me that he had put down all of the rules, no hitting, no abuse, etc., but he wanted me to know and my club to approve of the union because if things didn't go properly that brother would have a problem. Remember, if one brother has a problem, all brothers have a problem, so our entire Georgia chapters was at risk if this relationship goes sideways. There is no "I" in MC. If you are ever dealing with the property of any club but especially one of a 1% MC nation – if you can't do things right, you put all brothers in jeopardy with your inappropriate behavior.

Not all experiences will be the same in every 1% clubhouse as each has its own rules.

There are two reasons you may find yourself at a 1% clubhouse:

1. To take care of business
   a. Good relations
   b. Bad relations
2. To party

Take Care of Business

Good Relations Business

When at a clubhouse for business and you are on good terms with the 1% MC, you can expect a matter-of-fact conversation to handle the business you came to handle.

- Arrive before the agreed upon time.

    A 1% OMC Nation does not see a 99%er MC as an equal and will not be impressed if you are late. So, don't be late! In the Navy, there was the mantra "Early is on time, On time is late, Late is unacceptable." Always arrive early!

- Have your notes prepared and organized.

    Nothing is more aggravating than a person trying to speak about business in a disjointed and unprepared fashion. You want the dominant to see your MC as squared away with little need for attention on the set. Being prepared and knowledgeable goes a long way in earning respect.

- Control your emotions and yourself.

    Don't ever become visibly upset, unorganized, disheveled, or overly emotional. Men are matter of fact, not emotional.

Motorcycle Club Protocol 101

I once witnessed my national president tear up during a hostile 1% MC meeting. I wrote about this experience in my book "President's Bible Chronicle II Betrayal of the Brotherhood." Naturally, the meeting spiraled downhill and the 1% OMC lost all respect for our cowardly National. Check your emotions at the door and come to the table prepared for the business at hand. Remain calm and effective and never elevate your voice with anger or emotion, no matter what they say.

- Have your appropriate officers with you.

As president, your SAA should be with you at all times. Watch and learn how dominant MC's move on the set, then make sure your MC moves the same way. 1%ers respects power, confidence, and authority. If they see weakness they will pounce. As the spokesperson for your MC, move with authority. Don't try to be something you're not but be confident in who and what you are.

- Remain respectful.

Displaying a bad attitude and snappy replies will NOT be tolerated in a 1% MC meeting. Don't act like you are about that life if your club brothers aren't. Everyone's asses are on the line – even in a good meeting, as they can turn in an instant. Acting like you are 'bout it when your MC isn't is a good way to get your hole card called. Stay away from intellectual low blows as well. In an attempt to gain an advantage, you might find the ignorant sounding 1%er has a degree in molecular biology and is ready to go toe to toe with you in a verbal exchange he will likely win. I had a club brother who used to say, "I just look like this, I'm not actually like this!" Keep conversations professional and about business and it should stay that way.

- Wait until the 1% brother is finished talking before you start talking in each verbal exchange.

    You can't hear what someone is saying if you keep cutting them off. It is a good way to piss people off and turn a good meeting bad (I have done this, so I know exactly what I'm talking about here.) Count to 5 before responding. This pause, gives you time to think. Remember as a visiting MC (especially as a 99%er or traditional MC) you are at a disadvantage. Thinking carefully before engaging can be the difference between a good and a bad negotiation.

- Don't act like a know-it-all.

    Nobody likes a know-it-all. Avoid saying, "I know but..." "I know but..." "I know but...," if you really knew, you probably wouldn't be there for a sit down in the first place.

I know this may all sound a bit cliché, but you must understand you are closer to the barbarian age than you are to the age of enlightenment inside a 1% OMC clubhouse. If you get mouthy you are likely to have the meeting turn on you in a way that you may not have ever imagined possible. In the case where you are meeting to do something like find out what you have to do to get a blessing. The more you appear interested in learning, and desiring to be in alignment with protocol the more the 1% club may want to help you. This does not mean don't be a man and not stand on your principles. Always be firm in what you will and will not accept. But also understand when you have no choice and think of all the pros and cons before you come to the meeting instead of being completely blindsided. Suffice it to say no one gets out of hand at the OMC clubhouse—not men, not women and especially not a visitor.

Bad Relations Business

If you are at a 1%er clubhouse to receive a reprimand, you are already off on the wrong foot. One good thing about the MC set is there are usually plenty of warnings before bad shit happens. Most of the time your initial conversations will be warnings and dress downs before any drastic actions or sanctions are taken. Keep in mind that compliance will be had at whatever the cost.

At a bad relations meeting the goal of the 1% club is to bring you in and communicate to you the direction you will be required to traverse to get back in good graces. There won't be many options, if any, and your acceptance and compliance at that moment will dictate whether or not your day gets worse or better. Of course, you don't have to worry about this if you are in a club full of bad-asses, but if you and your brothers were bad-asses you probably wouldn't be at that meeting in the first place.

This meeting usually happens after many warnings or other attempts at communication have occurred so don't be surprised if the dominant president or SAA is short-tempered, rude, or brutally honest.

During this meeting there may be a time when you're allowed to voice your opinion about your MC's position, to have a say about your wishes, expectations, or to provide an explanation of what actually occurred from your point of view. And then there will be a time when the dominant speak. That will not be your time to speak, interject or interrupt! That will be your time to listen and be silent—to acknowledge you have heard the request (or demand) and to indicate that you will comply.

Just think of it like being in court. When the judge (in this case the dominant) is rendering his verdict, he has already heard what you have to say, listened to the evidence (or not), and has made up his mind. The only thing that remains is for you to hear the verdict and abide by the terms.

Warning to Liars—If you are a habitual liar, you better be a damned good and convincing liar because these 1% MCs have eyes and ears everywhere on the set willing to snitch to them like they are the FBI, CIA, and DEA simultaneously! They are good at catching little liars and like most smart prosecutors only ask you questions to which they already know the answers. On the MC set liars are hated as much if not more than anywhere else in the world. Don't get the reputation of being known as a liar on the set. It won't be good for you, and you'll be ostracized everywhere you go. Be honest and shit and stand on your shit. If you did it, own it. You might not be liked for your honesty, but you'll absolutely be respected. On the set reputation, respect, and your word are all that you have. Live by that!

When the bad meeting is over, take your lumps, make your corrections, and move on. Don't be too embarrassed and don't worry. If you keep a low profile, I guarantee you someone else will fuck up in a week or so and your incident will be forgotten as their MC takes center stage.

1% Party at the Clubhouse

For the uninitiated, your first party at a 1% clubhouse can be utterly shocking to your senses. Be prepared to see adult fun and uninhibited behavior. This is the 1%er's playground. This is their kingdom and you are in their castle where they get to live out their greatest fantasies. If you are a prude, don't go! You will witness all types of elicit and eyebrow raising behaviors – from properties twerking on stripper poles to women in Jell-O® fights or all kinds of other eyebrow raising goings on. Mostly you will see people having an excellent time being themselves. There is no one telling them how to behave, who to be, or what expectations must be met. There's nothing like being the king of one's own domain.

Greetings and Hugs

On the Black MC set, it is customary upon entering a 1% clubhouse to greet and hug as many of the brothers and sisters as possible. You are expected to show love to everyone who is willing to receive it. A brief hug are appropriate and even expected. Don't act like a cold fish when engaging with others because you can become despised very quickly if folks think you are acting better than everyone else.

On the White MC set, this type of greeting is not as common as has been my experience. In fact, when White MCs come to visit a Black clubhouse, they are often blown away and a bit uncomfortable by the love and hugs that they receive. It doesn't take most of them long to warm up and soon they too are hugging everyone.

The larger point here is that it is important to greet everyone that will accept your greeting when visiting. As I have said, take off your glasses, gloves, and half helmets as these things are disrespectful to wear while meeting and greeting people indoors. Look a man in his eyes and execute a proper introduction according to MC protocol.

Proper Introduction

In some clubs this will differ but what is generally acceptable is:

1. Extend your hand for a shake while introducing yourself.
2. Club name, nothing is greater than the club, so the club's name is first. *"Black Sabbath MC"*
3. Club chapter area or territory. *"Atlanta chapter"*

Motorcycle Club Protocol 101

4. Rank within the club.   *"Sgt at Arms"*
5. Set name or club given name.   *"Black Dragon"*

Keep Civilian Males out of the 1% Clubhouse

It is never appropriate to take a non-associated friend, brother, or cousin, to a 1% clubhouse if he is not familiar with the MC set. Since he has no colors, he is completely alone and a target for exploitation even if you are there to protect him. I tell women on the set to leave their boyfriends and husbands at home. If she has a jealous boyfriend or husband a good place for them to wind up knocked-out cold and unconscious on the floor, with multiple fractures is at a 1% clubhouse where they have shown their ass and insulted the brothers in their own clubhouse. Many jealous civilian males cannot understand other men coming up and hugging on their woman—and will take it as a sign of ultimate disrespect and feel compelled to take an action that will get their teeth kicked in! In the case that you are a man, and you want to show your brother or friend the MC set take them to your own clubhouse. So many guys are expecting a fair fight when they insult someone, especially after too many drinks, and that just won't be the case over at the 1% clubhouse. So don't set him up for that kind of failure! If you're a woman and he must accompany you ensure he is schooled up that you will be hugged and maybe kissed on the cheek, sometimes bear hugged, sometimes hugged for a second or two too long (brothers will do that kind of silly shit just to piss your man off)—so if he can't handle it tell him to... "Keep his ass at home!" And if you are a guy with a close friend, do your bonding elsewhere.

You know everything I tell you not to do is because, like a dumb ass I did it! I am giving you this warning from personal experience. My friend, TC Cox almost got his teeth kicked in when I thought it was a good idea for my friend to meet me for drinks over at the 1% clubhouse in Atlanta. TC got drunk and somehow misplaced his phone. He was sure someone stole it and started accusing everyone around him of being a thief. When my back was turned, he stumbled his drunk ass to the microphone on stage and announced, *"I cannot believe in these days and times that a person can't even lay their cell phone down in a place with all of you heathens in it and not expect it to be in the same place he put it when it was time to retrieve it. I've never met such a disrespectful lot of people in my whole damned...."* By that time, I was tackling his ass off that stage and dragging him out. To this day, he doesn't know how close he came to getting the rudest introduction of his life to the 1%ers' lifestyle! Keep unaffiliated civilian males out of the 1% clubhouse!

Properties Of vs Civilian Girls in the 1% Clubhouse

Properties at the 1% clubhouse are at home. As a woman, you never want to mix it up with a property in her clubhouse. Properties know very well how the 1% mindset works—how they chase women, what goes on in the clubhouse, and who is visiting. They ain't trippin' so never trip with a property! Never argue or dispute a property. In fact, leave them the hell alone. I can promise you this, if you tangle with them, in their clubhouse, you WILL NOT win. Unless you got some hardcore sisters that are ready to go back-to-back losing all of their hair, makeup, and breaking their heels to get down on a basic level like that backing you had when you were running the streets, then be on your best behavior and never mix it up with the properties.

Never Run Your Mouth Negative on the Set

There will be no negative talk about any other MC while on the set. This includes other MC clubhouses, functions, or sitting at the bar. Believe me when I tell you – the walls have ears! That nice old man sitting nursing his beer with no colors on could be the retired national president and you and your brothers sitting at the bar talking negative about his club can cost your MC a lot of heartache. Or maybe you're talking about his nephew who belongs to another MC. As you can see, problems arise from loose talk.

In the United States Navy, we used to say, "loose lips sink ships." That was because back in WWII running your mouth in a bar about where a ship was going could be overheard by a Japanese spy. That spy would relay that information back to high command and now the Japanese Navy would know where that ship was going to be and sink it. And your loose lips would have sank that ship. Never run your mouth on the set. Never engage in loose talk especially when you are out on the set at a 1% MC clubhouse. If the wrong person hears what you have to say and doesn't like it, you and your brothers could have hell to pay. Also, you would be wise to shut a brother up that's disorderly and running his mouth in a foul way, drunk, incapacitated, or displaying any other kind of mental inadequacies. Get him out of there quickly. Remember you are your brother's keeper and saving his ass could save your own!.

Staying Sober at the 1% Clubhouse

One of the quickest ways to get yourself into trouble is to not be able to handle your substances or alcohol. Being drunk or out of sorts in a 1% clubhouse is a foolish game you should never play. If you shouldn't be drinking on the set – DON'T!. Generally, you don't have to worry about being hurt or attacked in a 1% clubhouse or party. But you do have to act like you've got some sense.

CHAPTER TWELEVE
MC PROTOCOL AND THE POLICE

Traditional MCs, 1%ers, OMCs, and other biker clubs adhere to a "see no evil, hear no evil, speak no evil" policy, which simply means biker club culture demands that members not cooperate with law enforcement. The adage "Snitches get Stitches!" used among MCs demonstrates how vehemently snitches are detested are on the MC set.

What is snitching? Cambridge dictionary defines snitching as "to secretly tell someone in authority that someone else has done something bad, often in order to cause trouble." Oxford dictionary defines snitching as, "informing on someone." While snitching doesn't necessarily have to be talking to the cops, it can include telling your brother's woman that he's cheating on her or talking about the misdeeds of your brothers to other club members or any bullshit that looks like that.

Let me just say this, "It is against basic MC protocol to snitch on anyone for any reason."

Now let's get down to the reality of what really happens. Clubs and brothers of clubs snitch all the damned time! Most brothers won't snitch on brothers they are involved in crime with to the police but will turn around and snitch a brother out to his girlfriend or wife so she will dump him, and the snitch can screw her! Other brothers wouldn't ordinarily snitch but when they are looking at the federal or RICCO time, they get to telling it all to get a better deal for themselves. Face it, self-preservation is the most basic of human traits.

Another common saying in the biker club world is, "If none of us talk then all of us walk!" I've seen this work many times, but I cover stories every day on my show, Black Dragon Biker TV the Black Dragon Biker News Network, where one 1%er after the other has snitched his whole entire brotherhood out. In this scenario, there is no concern for everyone to walk, instead there is only the selfish concern for that member to walk receiving as little punishment as he can get away with.

It should work like this: When you get arrested SHUT THE FUCK UP! Don't say a word. Don't speak to your brothers locked up with you (you are being recorded in that cell fool, excellent police tactic),. Don't talk to other inmates (they will snitch on you to get a better deal). Don't talk to the police. Don't whisper to your woman over the phone. (its recorded).Don't talk to anyone other than your lawyer! Everything you do and say is being recorded at all times! Don't listen to the garbage, threats, lies, intimidation of the officers, just shut the fuck up until your lawyer comes and gets you. That's how it should work. But no, that ain't how it is working these days— so I say, "Limit your bad deeds to a circle so small that it includes you and only you because the only person who you can really trust to keep a secret is your own self, and no one else!" If you must do dirt, do it alone. You don't need a club to do dirt! That way you won't have anyone else to blame when you take your ass to jail. If you MUST have accomplices – keep the circle small! That's why most OMCs were originally very small when they started dealing dope. Only a few trusted people needed to know about the business of the club. Don't expect or trust that anyone will hold the line when their freedom is on that line. Don't bet your freedom on it.

Motorcycle Club Protocol 101

After You're Arrested What should the Club Do for You

Man, I consult with bikers from every club all over the world especially after they have been arrested. They contact me to tell me their stories to get them out because the lame stream media almost never tells the truth about bikers, especially clubbers (bikers in motorcycle clubs), and almost certainly they never tell the true stories about 1%ers. And when I talk to them the stories are almost always the same. So,

I will share their truths as they were told to me.

1. Most of their MCs never came through for them on the attorney's fees and other responsibilities as promised. In fact, I've only heard of one time when a club came through, and that was a top five 1% dominant OMC and in that instance their relief was a loan. It had to be paid back by the member after his trial was over. It was nice that it was there, but that is the best outcome I've seen yet. Many brothers have told me that the club found a reason to put them out bad so they wouldn't have to help pay their legal expenses. Bad news!
2. If you're in a big club and your incident made the news you are absolutely going to lose your job 99% of the time! No company wants a 1%er being held for aggravated assault in a murder trial on their payroll. You are headed to the beach cause you ain't working there no more! I even met a brother fired from an oilfield and I was sure anyone could work and risk their lives dying in the oilfields! Nope! He was gone.
3. If you CAN make bail by putting your mother's house, grandma's house, uncle's farm, and new truck on consignment – the courts are going to have so many

Motorcycle Club Protocol 101

restrictions on whom you can contact, you won't be able to look for a new job to replace the income you lost from the old job that fired you! They will restrict your phone, who you can hang out with, when you can come, when you can go, how long you can be out, what time you've got to be back, and oh yeah, you'll get the privilege of paying for all of that plus the ankle bracelet monitoring system to the tune of about $300 to $1,000 per month for a guy who just lost his good paying job.

4. As soon as you find a security job paying $15.00 per hour when you were making $64.00 per hour and when they run a background check it's likely back to the beaches cause they ain't fixing to hire your "OMG" ass awaiting aggravated assault charges with all the media and press you've got following you.

5. If you're going through a divorce and the wife doesn't like you, she's showing up at court with your news clippings in her hand, you better believe that! But hey, she might not have to because child protective services may have already shown up, if you had custody, because you are an outlaw biker, and they need to make sure your children are not in a house with violence. I'm telling you what I know here. I interview these guys all the time. So, now you've got the state and your ex-wife trying to take your child(ren).

6. If your wife wasn't leaving you, she might now if you had a cell phone, they confiscated with sexy pictures of your side bitch on it shaking her ass and sending you text messages about how good you hit it the other night. Cause the police are going to call her and bring her in to show her all of your dirty little secrets. You didn't think they got down like that over at the local precinct, but they are all about winning and they are playing for keeps! You don't want to cooperate?

Then they are more than happy to break your happy little family right on up.
7. If you didn't make bail and you're rotting in jail for a year or two awaiting trial, one of your club brothers may be stalking your wife to put something up in her that you can't! Yes, that's against MC protocol too but what in the Hell can you do about it? I cannot count on my fingers and toes how many times I've heard that one from a biker club inmate. It's a tough world out there that you put yourself in.
8. The cops may WILL be listening to your attorney/client privileged phone conversations and leaking information back to the prosecution to help them strategize their case against you, like they did to the Iron Range chapter of the Hells Angels in Eveleth MN in September 2024.
9. You will be forced to move your children, wife, significant other and yourself out of town. There is absolutely no way your kids can go to school in peace when their father is an accused killer, 1% biker gang member who was accused of hurting someone or breaking some kind of law in town, especially a small town. So, with your no-job-having-ass you'll have to put the money together to try to get out of town, where you can't find a job anyway—so that means borrowing money from your mother-in-law who never thought you were worth a shit in the first place… you know how that goes…

All of this before you ever even go to trial, only to have the state botch the whole case and have to set you free like all of those folks arrested at the restaurant in Twin Peaks after months of jail confinement with million-dollar bails. How many of those folks lost their jobs, homes, possessions, families, kids, marriages and who knows what else?

My submarine commanding officer used to say, "The stupid will be punished!" Going to jail for the club is not cute. People snitch every day. Don't test your brotherhood to find its limits. Stay within those boundaries if you can.

Clubs will also snitch on other clubs if it is in the best interest of their club. Say it isn't so, but oh hell yes, it is! In the world of modern warfare, whatever it takes to get to the enemy, I have seen clubs do. In the old days clubs handled issues between themselves and never called the police. Everything was in-house. Now, today's news reports have 1%ers getting into shootouts with one another and Florida Sheriff Grady Judd conduct a press conference on his YouTube channel proudly proclaiming that the victim 1%er MC is fully cooperating with the sheriff's office!

So, if you want to believe that mess that no one snitches in the MCs go on ahead and do it. It is definitely against MC protocol to snitch on anyone but the better MC protocol to follow is, keep your circle small and do your dirt, if you must do it, do it all by yourself.

Assertion of Rights

Interactions between police officers vs club brothers are always risky. Most cops don't like bikers and are very suspicious of us. Many, especially rookies, don't know MC protocol and they don't know the difference between a 1%er and a Christian MM member. As a member of an MC, you will likely have a negative interaction with law enforcement at some time during your club career especially if you are a member of an OMC or 1% OMC nation. But you don't have to be involved in an OMC to have negative interactions with law enforcement. In general, MCs are portrayed negatively in the press, media, by law enforcement, civil bodies, and neighborhood watches. Many rookie police officers can't tell the difference between MCs, so for them one MC is just as dangerous as another.

While interacting with the police can be stressful, knowing your rights and how to assert them calmly and effectively can make a significant difference in the outcome of those interactions. Though not impossible, it is considerably more difficult for officers to violate your rights if you know them and calmly assert them than if you have no clue. Many bikers wind up in a slew of trouble they would never experience if they knew only their basic rights.

For that reason, the following section is based on United States laws and constitution.

NOTE: You will need to know the laws of your own country as the things I wrote in this section will not apply in every country.

That being said, below is an expanded explanation of what you should know and do in various scenarios involving law enforcement interactions in the United States.

Know Your Rights: A Detailed Guide to Protecting Yourself During Police Encounters

If You Are Stopped for Questioning

1. **Understand Your Right to Silence**

   The **Fifth Amendment** protects your right to remain silent to avoid self-incrimination. ("Why Would an Innocent Person Plead the Fifth Amendment?") This applies to both minor questioning and formal interrogation.

   You can calmly say: *"I am exercising my right to remain silent."*

Then shut the fuck up! No matter how much they try to get you to talk, silence is always the best policy. You can't be arrested for incriminating yourself if you don't say anything incriminating.

Exceptions include providing basic identifying information like your name, address, and date of birth which are required in most (if not all) states.

2. **Be Mindful of Your Demeanor**

My mother used to always say, *"Son you can be right, but you can also be dead right! If you get into a pissing contest with a cop and you piss him off enough to murder you, he will get away with it and you'll be right, but you will also be a dead right picture on a T-shirt and there will be absolutely nothing that I will be able to do about it. So don't be a smart ass in an interaction with a cop!"* Mom was right and I pass her words of wisdom onto you.

You don't have to be a smart ass to assert your rights. Pissing a cop off can get your ass kicked and your teeth knocked out, it happens every day. The better strategy is to always remain calm and respectful. Aggression, sarcasm, or resistance may escalate the situation. Remember, your tone matters as much as your words. A shitty tone most often results in a shitty outcome.

3. **Clarify Your Detention Status**

Officers are not required to tell you the truth. They don't have to tell you that you don't have to stay and answer their questions. They can intimidate you and ask you questions and get you to fall for their tricks without any obligation to inform you that you don't have to listen. The Supreme Court backs them in this. Even if you are so scared that you don't ask to leave because you are intimidated, the Supreme Court backs the police saying that you are giving permission to the interrogation as long as you stand there and talk, unless you are being detained. So, when you are being asked questions immediately clarify your detention status. Ask directly at the beginning of the questioning:

"Am I being detained, or am I free to go?" ("KEY PHRASES POLICE INTERACTIONS "Am I being detained or am I") If the officer says you're free to leave, walk, ride, or drive away calmly. End the interrogation on your own terms. And make no mistake about it, when an officer is asking you questions, he is interrogating you. Even if his questions seem friendly, they are not. Officers are trained in subterfuge and misdirection. They have an agenda in their questioning which is seldom targeted at being your friend. If detained, ask for the reason, which must meet the legal standard of reasonable suspicion.

4. **Document the Interaction**

If you suspect misconduct, try to record the interaction discreetly if state law permits. Make note of the officer's name, badge number, and patrol car details if possible. ("When Can Police Search Your Car Without a Warrant?")

During a Traffic Stop
1. **Your Obligations:**

You don't have to answer probing questions, but you will have to communicate enough for the officer to ascertain who you are and if you are legally licensed to drive. If on your bike lift your helmet shield and speak. If in your car, roll your window down enough to communicate and hand over your license, registration, and proof of insurance when requested.

Keep your hands visible on your handlebars or on the steering wheel, if in your car, and inform the officer before reaching for documents: *"I'm reaching into my saddle bag or glove compartment for my registration."*

Fast or crazy movements can get your head blown off, so keep it simple. Police are adamant about going home at night to their families even if that means that you don't. Be calm and matter of fact. De-escalation is always key.

2. **Dealing with Vehicle Searches**

Police need probable cause or your consent to search your vehicle. If they have probable cause they aren't going to ask you shit, other than to get out of the car. If they don't have probable cause, then they are going to try to get your permission to search your bike or car. They may ask:

"Do you mind if I search your bike or take a look in your car?"

Always respond politely but firmly: "I do not consent to any searches."
Remember refusing consent is your right and cannot legally be used as evidence of guilt but it can create a hell of a lot of suspicion and the pressure will be applied to get you to comply. You might hear questions like, "If you have nothing to hide why can't I search?" and all other kinds of probing, accusatory questions like that as the officer becomes more agitated that you are standing your ground. Be pleasant but firm. "No, I do not consent to any searches officer."

3. **Handling Traffic Citations**

If given a ticket, sign it—it's not an admission of guilt but an acknowledgment that you received it. You can contest the ticket in court later. If you don't sign you can and will most likely be arrested. So, sign the damned ticket.

4. **DUI Stops and Sobriety Tests**

While field sobriety tests (e.g., walking in a straight line) are typically voluntary, refusing them may raise suspicion. If you refuse you will often have to take another level of a test. You might even be taken into custody long enough to have a breathalyzer, blood, urine, or chemical test administered. Refusal to take chemical tests (e.g., breathalyzer) after arrest will most likely lead to license suspension under implied consent laws in many states. Weigh the risks carefully based on local laws.

If Police Approach You on the Street

1. **Know When to Stop**

If an officer asks to speak with you and you are unsure if you must comply, calmly ask as the questioning begins: "Am I free to leave?"

If the answer is yes, you can leave. If not, you're being detained, and they must have a reason. You can ask multiple times during the questioning, especially if you aren't answering questions,

"Am I free to leave?"

Again, you don't have to be a smart ass about it, but you are demonstrating that you don't wish to cooperate, and you are not legally bound to do so in many instances.

2. **Searches on the Street**

Police may pat you down if they suspect you're carrying a weapon. This is called a Terry Frisk, or a Terry Stop and is protected by the Supreme court, but it is limited to outer clothing. Some police refer to this as a pat down. However, if they ask to search beyond this, assert your rights:

"I do not consent to a search."

3. **Refusing to Answer Questions**

You don't have to answer questions such as "Where are you going?" or "What are you doing here?" "How many guys are in your club?" "What is your position within the club?" "How long are you guys expecting to be in town?" Respond politely with:

"I'm exercising my right to remain silent." Or "I don't answer questions."

If Police Come to Your Home

1. **When to Open the Door**

You are not required to open the door just because a police officer knocks on it unless he has a warrant. You can speak through the door. Don't be tempted to open the door on the chain either or crack it using your foot as a door stop. Officers have been known to push through the chain or your foot and now they are in your house. Instead Ask through the door:

"Do you have a warrant?"

If they have one, request to see it through a window or under the door. Check that it's signed by a judge, includes the correct address, and specifies the scope of the search.

2. **No Warrant, No Entry**
   Without a warrant, you can refuse entry. Say:

   "I do not consent to a search of my home." And "I'm exercising my right to remain silent."

   Beyond that you don't have to speak at all. Exceptions include emergencies, such as someone in danger in the home or a suspect fleeing into your home.

3. **During a Search**

   If police enter your home with a valid warrant or exigent circumstances, observe their actions closely. Do not interfere but document what they search and seize.

If You Are Arrested

1. **Invoke Your Rights Immediately**

   Upon arrest, state clearly: "I will remain silent, and I want to speak to a lawyer." Avoid discussing anything until your attorney is present.

2. **Understand the Arrest Process**

Officers must inform you of your rights (the **Miranda warning**) if they intend to interrogate you. This includes the right to remain silent and to have an attorney. ("Arrest - FindLaw") If they don't, your statements may be inadmissible in court. But regardless remain silent until you speak with your attorney. That is in your best interest. Realize that you may think that you are smarter than the police, but chances are you aren't. They interrogate suspects every single day of the year. You don't get interrogated every day of the year. The numbers, experience, and laws are on their side, not yours. Your lawyer is trained to protect your rights. Give them the opportunity to do so. Also, an arresting officer cannot make you a promise of leniency as it is the district attorney that calls the shots when it comes to charging you. Any deals will have to come through them with your attorney present, so don't be fooled by statements like:

"Take it easy on yourself and come clean now." Or "Now is the time to own up, be a man, and set this situation right." Or "If you want things to go easier come clean now and we'll work something out." Or the most famous one..." Give us something and we'll let you go home." The Supreme Court has given the police the right to lie to you, fabricate evidence, fake evidence, and deal with you unfairly. However, lying to them can be a felony. So, shut the fuck up!

3. **Phone Calls**

You are entitled to at least one phone call. If it's to an attorney, law enforcement cannot legally listen to the conversation—although the Eveleth chapter of the Hells Angels is going through a case right now where it seems that may well have happened. There is also a strong possibility that their case may be thrown out or dismissed because of violations of attorney client privilege laws. Calls to other individuals will be monitored. So, if you are talking to a loved one on the police station phone, or jail phone, never incriminate yourself. Your conversation is being recorded. Take my word for it!

4. **Avoid Self-Incrimination**

   Do not discuss your case with anyone other than your attorney, not even family or fellow inmates. Anything you say can be used against you. Those visitation rooms are under surveillance. The snitch you discuss your case within the jail cell, will snitch your ass out in a heartbeat just to get a better situation for himself. You don't have any friends inside or outside of the system. You don't know any of those people in there. They are not your friends. Even if you do know someone in there, they aren't your friends either when it comes to your case and your business. Shut the fuck up if I haven't said that in this book before.

Understanding Probable Cause

1. **What Constitutes Probable Cause**

   Probable cause exists when officers have factual evidence or circumstances leading them to believe a crime has been committed. For example:
   - Smelling marijuana during a traffic stop.
   - Seeing illegal contraband in plain sight.

2. **Limits on Searches Without Consent**

   Officers cannot search based on a "hunch." If there's no clear evidence or your consent, they need a warrant.

What to Do After a Police Encounter
1. **Document Everything**

    Write down details immediately after the encounter, including time, location, officer names, badge numbers, and witness accounts. If you recorded the incident, secure the footage safely.

2. **Filing Complaints**

    If you believe your rights were violated, file a complaint with the police department or civil rights organizations. Include all supporting evidence.

3. **Contact an Attorney**

    Consult a lawyer as soon as possible to understand your legal options, whether to contest a ticket, defend against charges, or pursue a complaint.

Teaching Others About Their Rights
1. **Educating Minors**

    The police will not play fairly with your children either, so you must teach them not to answer any questions and to demand the presence of their parents and until such time as their parents arrive, not to say anything. This must be drilled into them and the story I'm going to tell you next is the reason why:

Motorcycle Club Protocol 101

How the Police Egregiously Interrogated and Charged on of my Dearest Friend's Child in 1998

One of my dearest friends and former Navy boss, Command Master Chief Gregg Houser, a former Submarine Chief of the Boat and Nuclear Power Engineer with more than 20 years of military service experienced the nightmare of having his son accused of murder and nearly destroyed by police after 12-year-old Stephanie Crowe was found dead on her bedroom floor on the morning of January 21, 1998. Stephanie had been stabbed 8 times with no signs of forced entry. Her window was found unlocked with the screen in place and no trace evidence around the window. A sliding glass door in her parents' bedroom was also unlocked. No murder weapon was found at the scene and no bloody clothing was found.

Police zeroed in on three boys including Stephanie's 14-year-old brother, Michael Crowe, because they felt it was an inside job and Michael seemed preoccupied and distant after her body was discovered (Wikipedia-Murder-Stephanie-Crowe) and Master Chief Houser's son Aaron Houser after using the Reid method to interrogate Michael without his parents' knowledge and without legal representation (Wikipedia-Murder-Stephanie-Crowe). Micheal denied any involvement hundreds of times during the hours long interrogation but eventually confessed in what is regarded as a classic example of a false confession. ("Murder of Stephanie Crowe - Wikipedia") Aaron was also interrogated with Joshua Tredway in what the papers and a judge later called was such an egregious manner, when other evidence that pointed to a transient schizophrenic who lived in the area was completely ignored that the boys were eventually declared to be "factually innocent by the judge. The Reid method of interrogation was developed in the United States by John E. Reid in the 1950s (Wikipedia-Reid-Technique). Reid was a polygraph expert and former Chicago police officer (Wikipedia-Reid-Technique). The technique was known for creating a high-pressure environment for the interviewee, followed by sympathy and offers of understanding and help, but only if a confession is forthcoming (Wikipedia-Reid-Technique). Since its spread in the 1970s it has been widely utilized by police departments in the United States (Wikipedia-Reid-Technique). Proponents say it is useful in extracting information from otherwise unwilling suspects. ("Reid technique - Wikipedia") Critics say the technique results in an unacceptably high rate of false confessions, especially from juveniles and people with mental impairments (Wikipedia-Reid-Technique).

Police interrogated Crowe multiple times without his parents' knowledge after separating the two surviving children from their parents and taking them to a county shelter (Wikipedia-Murder-Stephanie-Crowe). They were not allowed to see their parents for two days during which time both of them were interviewed by police unbeknownst to their parents and without an attorney present (Wikipedia-Murder-Stephanie-Crowe). Later Crowe was taken to the police station and interrogated on several occasions again without his parents' knowledge or an attorney present (Wikipedia-Murder-Stephanie-Crowe)During the interrogations, police falsely informed him that they had found physical evidence implicating him, that he had failed an examination with a so-called "truth verification" device, and that his parents were convinced he had done it (Wilkens and Saurer). After an intense 6-hour interrogation, he gave a vague confession to killing his sister, providing no details, and saying that he couldn't remember doing it. The interview was videotaped by police; at times Michael is heard saying things to the effect of, "I'm only saying this because it's what you want to hear." He was arrested and charged with murdering his sister (Wikipedia-Murder-Stephanie-Crowe).

Police from Escondido and nearby Oceanside also questioned Joshua Treadway and Aaron Houser, two 15-year-old friends of Michael Crowe. Houser had a collection of knives; one of them was reported missing by Houser's parents. It turned up at Treadway's house; he said he had taken it from Houser. ("Murder of Stephanie Crowe - Wikipedia") Police took Treadway to police headquarters and questioned him continuously for eleven hours from 9 p.m. that day until 8 a.m. the next, telling him that they believed his knife was the murder weapon (Sauer and Wilkens, Haunting questions: The Stephanie Crowe Murder Case. Part 3: The knife). They interrogated him again two weeks later, a 10-hour interview during which Treadway gave a detailed confession to participating in the murder with the other two boys. Treadway was then arrested (Sauer and Wilkens, Haunting questions: The Stephanie Crowe Murder Case. Part 4: More arrests).

Aaron Houser was then arrested and questioned. He did not actually confess and steadfastly denied any involvement, but he did present a "hypothetical" account of how the crime might have happened, under prompting by police interrogators using the Reid technique. All three boys subsequently recanted their statements claiming coercion. The majority of Michael Crowe's confession was later ruled as coerced by a judge because Escondido investigators implied to Michael that they would talk to the district attorney and recommend leniency. Treadway actually confessed twice, the first to Oceanside detectives and a second, identical confession, to Escondido officers. The court ruled that the two confessions were redundant and ordered that the first be suppressed. ("Murder of Stephanie

Crowe - Wikipedia") The second Treadway confession remains admissible. Houser's statements to police were suppressed because police did not sufficiently advise him of his Miranda rights (Sauer and Wilkens, Haunting questions: The Stephanie Crowe Murder Case. Part 6: The bombshell).

The district attorney was going to try Treadway first, but three drops of blood were found on a transient's clothing (Richard Raymond Tuite 28, who had been in the neighborhood during the time of the murder knocking on doors looking for a woman he was angry at for turning him away two years earlier. The police previously thought that he was too incompetent to have committed the murder and dismissed him as a suspect until the discovery of the blood. The prosecution embarrassingly dismissed the charges against the boys with prejudice, refusing to exonerate them.

"The families of all three boys sued the cities of Escondido and Oceanside." ("Murder of Stephanie Crowe - Wikipedia") The Crowes reached a settlement of $7.25 million in 2011. In 2012, Superior Court Judge Kenneth So made the rare ruling that Michael Crowe, Treadway and Houser were factually innocent of the charges, permanently dismissing the criminal case against them (Sauer, Michael Crowe Found 'Factually Innocent' In Sister's Murder).

Master Chief Houser's son Aaron received a settlement too and went on to rebuild his life. Eventually Raymond Tuite was found guilty of manslaughter and an attempted escape which was overturned years later by an appeals court. He was given a new trial and found not guilty.

The police will use unfair techniques against your children to target you or them to get to you or the MC. Therefore, as a biker in a club, you should teach your children to stay calm, provide their name only, and request a parent or lawyer before answering questions. You should teach them to never believe any promises made by police because during an interrogation they are not their friends. Drill into them the strength of character they will need to withstand those pressures.

Also, reinforce that they should never physically resist police, even if they feel treated unfairly.

2. **Empowering Vulnerable Groups**

Bikers, immigrants, minorities, and marginalized communities often face unique challenges during police interactions. In fact, I often tell my white MC brethren, "If you want to know what it's like driving while black (DWB) don a set of colors and ride while biker in a club (RWBIC) through the wrong small town, especially if you are riding in a 1% cut." Marginal groups like club bikers should ensure they understand both their constitutional rights and local policies that may affect them. Your freedom may depend upon it.

Final Note: The Balance Between Asserting Rights and Staying Safe

While standing up for your rights is essential, safety should always be your priority. Officers are trained to assess threats, so remain calm, non-confrontational, and clear in asserting your rights. Legal recourse is available if violations occur, but you will never win a battle with the police in the streets—stay composed and let the law work in your favor. Knowing your constitutional rights and how to assert them empowers you to navigate police encounters safely. The Fourth Amendments protects against unreasonable searches and the Fifth Amendment protects against self-incrimination. While most officers perform their duties professionally, understanding your rights ensures you can address any situation calmly and legally. Always consult with an attorney for specific legal advice following an encounter.

CHAPTER THIRTEEN
MC PROTOCOL FOR FIRST EMERGENCY DEPARTMENT PERSONNEL

How can emergency department (ED) personnel comfortably treat bikers in MCs and maintain order in the ED without fear based on their reputations, law enforcement's characterizations, or media's sensationalism? Many articles I've read over the years were missing the point, so I knew that if I ever got a chance to write a more factual overview about MCs, that may help ED personnel and law enforcement address this potential problem I would! This chapter is my opportunity and actually the last one I wrote for this book. Let's go!

Omgs: Aspects of the 1%er Culture for ED Personnel

In a 2014, a feature called *"Outlaw Motorcycle Gangs: Aspects of the One-Percenter Culture for Emergency Department Personnel to Consider,"* written by Anand N. Bosmia BA, James F. Quinn, PhD, Tod B. Peterson, MD, Christoph J. Griessenauer MD, R. Shane Tubbs, PhD, PA-C, MS was published in Physician's Weekly®. This paper was written to discuss the various aspects of the culture of OMGs so that ED personnel could better understand the mentality of the outlaw biker. It held that if ED personnel possessed knowledge of their symbols, values, and hierarchy this information could be crucial to maintaining order within the ED – particularly when helping injured outlaw bikers who presented there, and how to manage their clubs that showed up in support of them. As a member of an MC for over 36 years and a successful author on the topics of MCs, I found that while the premise of the paper was a good idea, the conclusions by the authors were seriously flawed as the authors clearly did not possess a true understanding of MCs, OMCs or OMGs.

Without direct knowledge of MC traditions, protocols, or their social construct, these authors (MDs and PhDs) sourced the majority of their work from biased internet sites that promulgated common stereotypes attributed to OMCs by the media, Hollywood, and law enforcement. As a result, their paper reads more like it was written for a bunch of terrified victims cowering in a corner trying to figure out how to provide treatment to the gangland biker boogey men rather than an informative piece capable of guiding ED professionals when interacting with MCs while administering emergency treatment. I took issue with the fact that they focused only on OMGs, and their support clubs as defined by the U.S. DOJ, and failed to recognize that all MCs respond similarly to a crisis or tragedy regardless of their affiliation (1% or 99% status). All MCs are capable of operating from a pack mentality when stressed or highly agitated, which can be just as volatile or rowdy as OMGs if disrespected. Also, since not all OMCs wear 1% diamonds or wear their colors all the time, most ED personnel won't be able to differentiate between them or MCs and RCs. It is my opinion that all MCs should be treated the same, which will help ensure positive outcomes for members of all MCs treated in the ED.

The article starts with a warning, *"the ED is at particularly high risk for violence against healthcare workers,"* but this risk is not directly associated with violence from OMGs. Their oversimplified assessment indicates that while reaching for a topic of discussion they are conjuring a problem that might not really exist. They advise ED workers to become more vigilant for violent outbursts when OMG members arrive wearing a 1% diamond which establishes a prejudice and instills apprehension and fear among ED personnel towards bikers before they ever even encounter a biker (OMC or otherwise). Though their paper began speaking about the 33,000 street gangs in America the underlying focus was to address the 300 or so OMGs operated by "outlaw bikers" on the biker club set. They cautioned ED personnel that they could be in imminent danger when treating OMG members in the ED because OMGs were well organized, able to mobilize members quickly to assist injured comrades, were heavily armed, often impulsive, possessed expertise in sophisticated weapons and operated intricate intelligence networks. However, what the paper failed to identify is that in an emergency situation, particularly at a hospital, no OMC (or so-called OMG) is looking to utilize its intricate intelligence network or sophisticated weaponry on ED personnel. Regardless of the number of club members present, an MC's primary goal is to be as cooperative as necessity demands to get their club brother medical attention as quickly as possible.

Their paper further biases ED personnel by stating, *"The 1% patch is worn only by clubs immersed in criminality and large enough to defend the claim to be the "baddest of the bad" against all."* What ED professional wants to knowingly provide medical aid and lifesaving services to a biker who lives a life immersed in criminality, who also just happens to belong to an organization large enough to defend being the 'baddest of the bad'? The truth of the matter is that the overwhelming majority of 1%ers have jobs, families, and many are veterans of the military services. Most don't have criminal records—so how could they be immersed in criminality?

There is an ongoing battle of classifications as these clubs fight hard not to be called "gangs" (OMGs) while the U.S. DOJ fights just as hard to classify them as OMGs. MCs refer to themselves as "biker clubs" not "biker gangs" and vehemently fight not to be classified as such. They draw several distinctions between themselves and street gangs. ED personnel should not make the assumption that a member of a 1% OMC is a criminal waiting to be healed so that he can resurge his life immersed in criminality as soon as he can get well and back to society.

There were several sections of their paper with which I disagreed. I will explain my issues with and responses to their statements as follows:

> **Bosmia, Quinn, Peterson, Griessenauer, & Tubbs:** The emergency department (ED) is at particularly high risk for violence against healthcare workers.
>
> **Black Dragon:** The source cited for this point referred to street gangs in America overall and not particularly about a high risk attributed to the presence of OMCs in the ED. The fact that the ED is at risk for violence doesn't mean that ED personnel should develop bias against bikers even if they are 1%ers. MCs and OMCs acknowledge that there are members among their ranks that commit crimes, as does every society, but that does not make them street gangs. They appropriately point out that law enforcement has a financial agenda in villainizing OMCs in an effort to receive additional grants and funding, which is why these agencies push the negative branding and stereotypes on the reputations of 1% nations. Law enforcement, of course, doesn't see their classification in this way as they define an OMG as an ongoing association of five or more persons that has as one of its primary purposes the commission of criminal offenses (federal felonies involving controlled substances, violence, and conspiracies to commit such offenses), its members have engaged in a continuing series of such offenses within the past five years, and such activities affect interstate or foreign commerce. With this broad definition, five bad apples could cause any MC to be labeled as an "OMG." A patient having never been involved in any crime could be considered "immersed in criminality"

simply because of his affiliation with a worldwide MC who had members who committed crimes in another country.

This fact was proven in a recent case wherein members of the Hells Angels were accused of attacking members of the Vagos on a freeway in Nevada in 2022. The DA put enhanced charges on the Hells Angels chapter for being a criminal street gang. The charter challenged the charge claiming that none of the members of that charter had a criminal record and therefore could not be considered a gang. A circuit court judge agreed with them and dismissed the charge; however, the prosecution appealed to a higher court wherein that court decide the Hells Angels could be considered a street gang based on the crimes committed by other members of their club, though not in their charter, across the country and indeed around the entire world. So that a crime committed by a Hells Angels member they might not even know in Spain could be used to classify them as a street gang in Las Vegas and therefore allow the enhanced gang charges to be added to their cases.

I believe ED personnel should consider the possibility of guilt by association when making judgements as to the character of the OMC diamond wearer they are treating as opinions, attitudes and bias can affect the quality of healthcare provided to individuals as many studies have shown (National Library of Medicine) (Madhusoodanan).

Bosmia, Quinn, Peterson, Griessenauer, & Tubbs: The arrival of an injured gang member should cause ED personnel to become more vigilant for violent outbursts. **Black Dragon:** Here the authors are still citing sources talking about general gang members, not members of MCs, further building a bias against bikers among ED personnel whom they have never encountered.

Bosmia, Quinn, Peterson, Griessenauer, & Tubbs: Outlaw motorcycle gangs (OMGs) are an iconic element of the criminal landscape in the United States, the country of their origin.

Black Dragon: OMCs vehemently resist being labeled as "street gangs" or "OMGs." They acknowledge that they have members who are criminals but deny this is supported by the club. They point out that even police departments have members who are criminals and get arrested every day—but they have not been labeled as gangs, even though they could be based on the definition of the DOJ listed above.

Bosmia, Quinn, Peterson, Griessenauer, & Tubbs: The authors aim to elucidate certain aspects of the culture of OMGs so that ED personnel can better understand the mentality of the outlaw biker.

Black Dragon: None of these authors have offered qualifications or experiences to illuminate their expertise about the mentality of the outlaw biker to the ED community. They are MDs and PhDs citing websites created by jaundiced agencies who regularly target biker clubs, particularly OMCs, some of which they label as OMGs further spreading stereotypes and fearmongering.

Bosmia, Quinn, Peterson, Griessenauer, & Tubbs: OMGs present a challenge to ED personnel in that they are well organized and thus able to mobilize their members quickly to assist an injured comrade and are often impulsive and heavily armed. These gangs have expertise in sophisticated weapons and possess an intricate intelligence network.

Black Dragon: A well-organized MC is no threat to ED personnel. The ability to mobilize members quickly to assist injured comrades should be seen as a boon to the MC and crucial to its social construct. Being heavily armed is completely legal in many states with liberal conceal and open carry laws. No MC is coming to an emergency room utilizing its expertise in sophisticated weapons or intricate intelligence network to harm ED personnel. They are coming to support the brothers seeking desperate lifesaving remedies and services provided there.

Bosmia, Quinn, Peterson, Griessenauer, & Tubbs: Thus, the "1%" patch is worn only by clubs immersed in criminality and large enough to defend the claim to be the "baddest of the bad" against all.

Black Dragon: What ED worker wants to save the life of a criminal who once saved will return to a life immersed in criminal activity? Regardless of whether they are a member of an MC, gang, or independent operator. Most 1% OMCs that have never been listed as involved in criminal activity and even entire charters that have members who have not once been arrested. In fact, one of my best friends is a Bandido and also a decorated veteran of the US Navy Silent Service. He has never been arrested. So, if he appears in an emergency room wearing his vest with the 1% patch, should it be assumed that he is immersed in criminal activity?

Bosmia, Quinn, Peterson, Griessenauer, & Tubbs: OMGs are almost entirely white in the U.S., with the exception of the largely Chicano Mongols MC.

Black Dragon: Throughout this book, I have dispelled this notion, but to the authors' credit, not much was known about Black MCs or Black OMCs when this article was written. This statement alone shows they have no knowledge of the biker set beyond observations they gleaned from jaundiced websites.

Bosmia, Quinn, Peterson, Griessenauer, & Tubbs: Many outlaw bikers are racists, and there are strong links between the respective cultures of outlaw bikers and white supremacists.

Black Dragon Biker TV: This statement seems like just another way to bias ED personnel against OMC bikers. There are White MCs that only allow Whites members, just as there are Black MCs that only allow Black members. But racism is not limited to the biker set. There are racists, bigots, sexists, anti- organizations throughout all aspects of society. and White supremacists as well. But there is also respect shown across the set from one color to the next. Racism exists in the world not just in 1% OMCs. ED personnel wouldn't (and shouldn't) deny a level of service regardless of the hateful intents and ideologies of the people they are there to help, so why should they have a bias towards members of MCs?

Bosmia, Quinn, Peterson, Griessenauer, & Tubbs: Black OMGs exist, but these groups operate within a different milieu and have their own symbols and values. OMGs composed of African American or mixed-race members are less extreme in their entrepreneurialism and organization compared to OMGs composed of White members, and do not use the internet as much as white OMGs do. Most black OMGs are local or regional rather than national or global in their reach and are usually encountered on the East and West Coasts of the US.

Black Dragon: Given that this paper was written in 2013, I can see how the authors may have come to these conclusions as very few OMCs were on the Internet (especially Black OMCs) at that time. This was also written at perhaps the beginning of the expansionism of African American OMCs across the US and in fact the world. However, today there are many Black National OMCs and perhaps as many as 7 international Black 1% OMCs. They no longer use their own symbols. For instance, most African American 1% OMCs wear the 1% diamond in 2025.

Bosmia, Quinn, Peterson, Griessenauer, & Tubbs: ED personnel should be aware of which OMGs are active in their state of practice.
Black Dragon: It is not necessary for ED personnel to know which OMCs (or MCs for that matter) are operating in their area. There is no way they can keep up with this information if they are not active on the set as it is constantly changing. If they concentrate on treating all MCs with the same level of respect, kindness, and professionalism there won't be any need to fear or regard any of them differently from the other. With policies developed around that outlook, an MC is just an MC and should be treated as such.

Bosmia, Quinn, Peterson, Griessenauer, & Tubbs: A biker's colors are integral to his identity as a member of the club. Should a biker's colors be removed during the course of his care in the ED, physicians and staff would be prudent to treat his colors with respect or otherwise risk a hostile reaction from the biker and his associates.
Black Dragon: This is true! And it is true of all MCs and biker organizations not just OMCs, 1% OMCs or so called "OMGs". Clubbers fiercely guard their colors. Some are even taught they should die before accepting dishonor or disrespect toward their colors. Under MC protocol it is seen as disrespect for a person outside of one's club to even touch

another club's colors unless there is an emergency—so imagine what may happen should someone in the ED touch a patient's colors. You may physically have to fight an injured, dying biker to remove his colors and the idea of cutting them off is completely unacceptable to some. Almost every clubber will opt to be treated in his colors if he has a choice rather than to have them removed. Even members of RCs, MMs, female MCs, and MAs will fight you to retain custody of their colors. It makes no logical sense to the uninitiated but that doesn't mean it isn't true. Clubbers are so dedicated to their colors the US District Court, C.D. California Southern Division tried to take the Mongols MC Nation's colors away from the entire club with civil asset forfeiture laws because they thought that action would be the death penalty of the club (https://casetext.com/case/united-states-v-mongol-nation#:~:text=Specifically%2C%20the%20jury%20unanimously%20found,Racketeering%20Act%20Eight%20(distribution%20of)(https://www.mercurynews.com/2019/03/01/federal-judge-rules-against-u-s-governments-first-of-its-kind-effort-to-seize-mongols-motorcycle-clubs-prized-patch-2/). The club spent over a million dollars defending itself in court. So, yes, the colors issues are there but there are ways to handle club members when it comes to colors.

Bosmia, Quinn, Peterson, Griessenauer, & Tubbs: Because there are so many OMGs active in the U.S. it would be impractical for ED personnel to memorize every specific logo or insignia associated with each one. However, the authors advise ED personnel to be familiar with the hues worn by each locally active OMG and its support and satellite clubs, and the ubiquitous "1%" patch.

Black Dragon: This would be impractical even if you are not involved in the MC lifestyle. The authors suggestion is ludicrous. If you treat all bikers (especially MC members) exactly the same, you will never NEED to know anything else about who they are or which clubs they come from.

Bosmia, Quinn, Peterson, Griessenauer, & Tubbs: If a gang member perceives disrespect from anyone, including ED staff, the outcome can be deadly, as gang members have an overarching requirement for respect and for saving face in all encounters and from every individual with whom they come in contact. The gang member will not hesitate to injure or kill someone if he believes that person has shown disrespect to himself or his gang.
Black Dragon: MC life is steeped in tribalism, machismo, and tradition. But it also embraces order and respects authority. There are a series of rules, most unwritten, known as MC protocol that MCs follow to show respect to one another and exist in harmony. A cursory knowledge of some of these rules and the hierarchy of how these clubs operate will help ED personnel steer clear of violating any rules or trespassing in territory that would get them in trouble.

Bosmia, Quinn, Peterson, Griessenauer, & Tubbs: If an injured member arrives at the ED, other members of his club will often arrive to protect him or inquire into his welfare. OMGs are an amalgam of a tribe, family, and corporation, and an ethos of "one on all, all on one" prevails, meaning that to assault or injure one member is to attack the entire club, and restoring the club's honor is a sacred duty to which all members are bound.
Black Dragon: A baseball, basketball, football or soccer team also operates on the amalgam of a tribe and exudes an ethos of "one on all, all on one." You can see it when the

benches clear at a baseball game and every team member and coach meets in the middle of the baseball diamond, each adding their punches to the melee. No one knows whether a punch they throw will prematurely end the life of an unintended member of the opposite side. And if one of them should go to the hospital the entire team will hit that ED filling every chair and overcrowding every hall. Equally so MCs will respond to their brothers in arms, supporters, associates, and allies who unfortunately find themselves in the ED to receive medical attention. ED personnel should not fear managing the ED with them there, instead arm themselves with the knowledge of best practices to professionally manage them and keep order when they arrive.

Bosmia, Quinn, Peterson, Griessenauer, & Tubbs: The fact that OMGs are well-organized and primed to respond swiftly with aggression in the event of a member being injured should make ED personnel alert law enforcement with greater urgency in the event that supporters of the injured biker start to congregate at the hospital.

Black Dragon: The quickest way to annoy clubbers is to target them with unnecessary police involvement when they have done nothing wrong based on your stereotypes of them. Congregating in numbers is not an indicator of pending violence. Large families also congregate in numbers in the hospital. Workplace accidents can also lead to large numbers congregating in the waiting room. Being afraid of someone does not make them a threat. It just means you are afraid or apprehensive of them. Take the time to observe and ascertain before jumping to conclusions that can just make matters worse. MCs, OMCs, and 1% OMCs respond positively to authority, confidence, professionalism, and respect.

Bosmia, Quinn, Peterson, Griessenauer, & Tubbs: As motorcyclists, their mobility aids them in evading law enforcement, and thus police may have a more difficult time detaining members of the club and preventing their arrival en masse at the hospital.

Black Dragon: An MC moving en masse is not capability of evading law enforcement. When the pack travels, although it may move at a high rate of speed, it does so under strict rules of operation which would make it a sitting duck for pursuing law enforcement. MCs try to avoid police involvement with anything that pertains to them at all costs. It is an unlikely case that an MC pack will be evading law enforcement in a flat out run to the ED only to be arrested after they arrive when law enforcement finally catches up.

Bosmia, Quinn, Peterson, Griessenauer, & Tubbs: The cause of the biker's injury must be clarified, as some incidents provoke immense anger from the club (e.g., a citizen ramming into a biker with a car or a biker being assaulted by members of a rival OMG), whereas others evoke only concern (e.g., a single-vehicle accident). If a biker's injuries are secondary to interpersonal violence, the biker may avoid disclosing this fact to avoid attention. The emergency physician should take a thorough history in a non-threatening manner to improve his chances of eliciting these details from the biker and thereby avoid not anticipating dangerous complications of the biker's injuries. For example, a fight bite is a laceration of the hand sustained by striking another individual in the mouth with a clenched fist, and such a wound can result in devastating infections if it is not treated early and correctly. Thus, appropriate antibiotics must be administered if a biker has sustained a fight bite.

Black Dragon: This statement seems reasonable. Simply be matter of fact with clubbers about their injuries or wounds. Let them know that you need to know exactly what has happened to them and why so that you can properly treat them and prevent the kinds of infections, etc., that can cost them their lives.

Bosmia, Quinn, Peterson, Griessenauer, & Tubbs: Outlaw bikers may have weapons hidden on their persons that are discovered as their clothing is removed during the course of care. These weapons are not limited to guns and knives.

Black Dragon: This is true.

Bosmia, Quinn, Peterson, Griessenauer, & Tubbs: Emergency physicians should be particularly cautious of a biker in the ED whose colors bear a rocker reading "prospect," "probate," or "probationary." A biker with such a rocker is a candidate for membership to the club and may be more prone to committing acts of aggression than a full-patch member to prove that he is worthy of membership.

Black Dragon: Perhaps but acts of aggression to prove worthiness are never to bring dishonor and disrespect to the club! Attacking ED personnel is not part of any MCs modus operandi for prospects to gain membership. The club would shun a member who attacked an ED nurse to gain 'street cred' while a full patch brother was lying on a gurney fighting for his life and needed that nurse or doctor to save him. ED personnel should treat everyone with equal respect from prospects to presidents, fearing none but respecting all. That's what MCs do.

Bosmia, Quinn, Peterson, Griessenauer, & Tubbs: Women who support the club can also facilitate violence in the ED. Women are not allowed to be members of the club, but they may wear "property" belts or vests adorned with "property" patches to indicate their affiliation with a specific club. ED personnel should be aware that women who arrive to see an injured outlaw biker may carry weapons or drugs for the biker or members of his club.

Black Dragon: While the presence of a property in the ED may bring violence, properties are intricately woven into the fabric of the MC and are highly valued and trusted. In addition, there are co-ed MCs, female-only MCs and at least one 1% OMC with female members.

Bosmia, Quinn, Peterson, Griessenauer, & Tubbs: Rivalries among OMGs can lead to a war when 2 or more OMGs are vying for territory. If the members of rival OMG meet each other in the ED waiting room, a violent altercation is inevitable. Emergency physicians should inquire as to whether an outlaw biker's injuries are secondary to a conflict with a rival OMG. If members of a rival OMG injured the biker, the biker's adversaries may come to the hospital to finish the job.

Black Dragon: Unfortunately, this is true. If two OMCs encounter one another the ED, violence is likely to occur, especially after a violent confrontation or battle. I would think the ED should be more concerned with members of each side inadvertently winding up in the same ED potentially having adversaries showing up to the same waiting room in support of their injured brothers, rather than a hit squad descending on the ED to finish the job that was left incomplete in the streets. But since both could potentially happen ED personnel should follow policies set forth when two warring factions (or gangs) show up at a hospital if it is determined that injures have been sustained as a result of an MC battle.

Bosmia, Quinn, Peterson, Griessenauer, & Tubbs: ED personnel must be aware that outlaw bikers do not always resemble the stereotypical "drunken, swaggering Hells Angel of 1969." Many outlaw bikers are clean cut, and some even prefer 4-wheeled vehicles.

Black Dragon: Stereotypes of any kind are always eventually proven wrong. The same can be said of bikers. Their colors will identify who they are if they are wearing them.

Bosmia, Quinn, Peterson, Griessenauer, & Tubbs: Many OMGs consider themselves to be in a perpetual state of war with law enforcement. Thus, police officers providing security in the ED, especially if they are in uniform, may have an inflammatory effect on bikers who arrive at the hospital.

Black Dragon: MCs must deal with cops all the time in various settings wherever they go. Cops are at the airport, train stations, patrol the highways, are found at restaurants, and even provide security at runs, rallies, and events they attend. A cop providing security in an ED is no different. Cops know how to handle themselves when providing security. ED personnel should focus on doing their jobs and let law enforcement focus on doing theirs.

Suggested Modern Day Procedures for First Responders and ED Personnel Interfacing with MCs

Here are my suggestions concerning modern-day best practices for first responders and ED personnel.

On the Accident/Incident Scene Be Calm, Professional and Show Respect

When dealing with MCs, first responders should prioritize professionalism and neutrality, focusing on the situation at hand and treating all individuals with respect, regardless of their club affiliation, while remaining vigilant and aware of potential risks. While OMCs and 1%ers and so called OMGs require the most consideration as they can have a propensity towards violence, all MCs have the same potential when stressed because most MCs are made up of alpha men and nearly all operate by similar values and protocols. Treating all MCs with equal respect, care and caution will eliminate the need to try to keep up with whoever is a 1%er and who is not. Maintain a neutral demeanor, avoid unnecessary confrontation, and speak clearly and respectfully to all individuals present. The MC depends upon your professionalism and competence to win the day. In the MC world respect is given where respect is shown. If you are giving respect, you will be shown respect.

First Responders Should Quickly Identify the Situation

Assess the scene quickly to determine the nature of the incident, whether it's a medical emergency, traffic accident, or battlefield. This allows you to consider the challenges each scenario presents so you can move forward immediately.

First Responders Should Focus on the individual

Treat each person as an individual, not as a representative of their club. Do not form bias because they are members of an OMC or 1% OMC.s or so called OMGs.

Motorcycle Club Protocol 101
First Responders Should Prepare for Insulting Iconology

Prepare yourself to see insulting and hateful iconology on club uniforms, such as SS bolts, Nazi swastikas, Gestapo ideology, White power patches, Black power fists, anti-White symbols, racial slurs, anti-LGBQT symbols, sexually inappropriate icons or sayings degrading toward women or insulting to men. In many instances the insignia worn on the colors does not directly represent the injured individual though an injured member may be wearing SS bolts they may not be racist at all. This may be hard to believe but many clubs began wearing those symbols to repulse society rather than to support the movements that originated them. You may even see Black club members wearing swastikas, SS bolts, Nazi symbolism or other White racist anthems and wonder how this can even happen. Misogyny runs rampant on the biker set, so, don't be surprised to see patches that depict women performing sexual acts or other unflattering imagery. In a civilized society one might not expect someone to proudly posting such beliefs or opinions on their clothing without fear; h. However, in the MC world it is a regular occurrence and barely noticed. And it doesn't change the respect level clubs will hold for one another across racial barriers. For example, Sonny Barger, founder of the Oakland charter of the Hells Angels MC was known to be good friends with Heavy founder of the Soul Brothers MC. When each died their club brothers showed up at the respective funerals of each to pay tribute, honor, and demonstrate respect. So don't be surprised to find members of an members of Black MCs to show up for members of a White MC regardless of what appears on their uniforms.

First Responders Should Observe Body Language and Behavior on the Scene

It is always a good idea to be aware of your surroundings. Pay attention to potential signs of aggression or hostility and maintain a safe distance if necessary.

First Responders Should Communicate effectively

Because MCs are paramilitary units, they are familiar with command structure and recognize authority within their ranks. They also respect competence and self-confidence. They hate weakness and ambiguity in leadership and respond negatively to people who exhibit these characteristics. If a first responder is arrogant beyond his capacity and is used to talking down to patients or their loved ones, he/she will find himself/herself natural enemies with any members of a solid MC. Be effective, competent, matter of fact, and well-spoken in your discourse. Clearly state your purpose and intentions and listen actively to the responses from club members. Remember, effective listening is an important part of the two-way street of communication.

First Responders Can Seek Backup from Club Officers

If a first responder feels overwhelmed at the scene knowing some MC protocol can be a valuable tool! Most literature written about this subject is quick to tell you to call for backup police support the moment you feel overwhelmed. This action can bring unnecessary complications to an already chaotic situation. MCs have a command structure in place that can be used to recruit club officers to help you on the scene, if necessary. The most important officers to look for in that situation are the President (who runs the club) and the Sergeant at Arms (SAA) (who handles club security and club discipline). In most clubs, these officers wear small patches, called tabs, on their chests to display their rank. These tabs display identifiers such as "president, "prez," "sergeant at arms," "sergeant of arms," "SAA," or "enforcer" (which some clubs use in lieu of a sergeant at arms). Keep in mind that some clubs opt not to have their officers display their ranks, so do not despair if you don't see tabs. You should simply ask, "Who is your sergeant at arms!?" or "Who is your prez?" and in most cases someone will turn and point to him. Then, ask the officer to assist you in handling their personnel. You will be surprised at how quickly they leap into action and unruly bikers get in line when the SAA or prez speaks. If you are on the road and the club is in a pack there may be no senior officers present, (prez, VP, SAA) but there may be junior officers. Typically, the road captain (the most senior junior officer) is leading the pack and in most MCs has the authority of the president when the pack is on the road. If you can't locate a president or SAA, ask for the road captain, or if any officer is present. If no officers are present, ask for the most senior man at the scene. By engaging the MC's leadership, you are making the MC police itself.

First Responders Should Remove Colors with Caution and Respect

Patched brothers of an MC are ferociously protective of their club vest and patches known as colors. Some would almost rather die than give them up and may be confused enough to tell you they would rather not be treated than allow you to remove their colors, but you cannot be deterred or intimidated by this stubborn behavior. Still, if there is an option to treat the patient without removing his colors, seek this option first. If you find you must remove colors to treat an MC, here are some tips:

- Be clear and direct.

    Inform the patient that you must remove his colors to treat him. Be clear that there is no choice in the matter and that you refuse to allow him to die, remain seriously injured, or experience complications later because you've been forced to delay his treatment over a vest the club will replace if necessary. Be resolute and do not accept no for an answer if the task must be accomplished. Let him know that your job is to treat him, and you will competently perform the tasks to the best of your ability. Let him know that it is not a negotiation. Needless suffering or dying to protect his colors is not an acceptable outcome on your watch.

- Do NOT cut the patches.

    You can comfort the patient if you let him know that you only intend to cut the vest and not the patches on his back, if possible. For the clubber, the most important part of the vest is the patch set up on the back that could consist of one or more patches. Of those patches the center icon is the most important (refer to chapter four for details about patches). If you can manage that you'll be a hero! Reassure him that no one in his club wants him to suffer needlessly over his colors and being seriously injured or in a life and death situation is a valid reason to allow them to be removed. Also inform him that you will ensure that they are returned to the club's SAA respectfully or left with him if possible.

- Cut along the seams on the side of the vest.

    If you can, cut along the seams on the side of the vest. On many vests you'll only be cutting shoestrings or leather strings that keep the vest together. On bullet proof style vests or one-piece vests, you'll be cutting cloth, denim, or leather.

First Responders Should Respect Personal Space

Avoid unnecessary physical contact with club members and be mindful of their personal boundaries. Never get into a pissing contest or some kind of verbal back and forth. Always maintain professional and respectful dialogue. Remember you can always request a senior officer.

First Responders Should Not Engage in Personal Opinions or Biases

Maintain a professional attitude and avoid making assumptions about individuals based on their club affiliation.

First Responders Should Know the Local Landscape

If you want to learn about MC culture and which clubs may be operating in your area, books like this one will help you learn the culture, while websites can help you get informed about specific clubs. There is a lot of negative press about MCs, especially 1% OMCs, so you will certainly be exposed to that. Some of it is true and some sensationalized. Remember that people in MCs, no matter the affiliation, are people just like everyone else. They laugh, love, cry, get sick and injured. They are a tough breed, but they are human.

CHAPTER FOURTEEN
THE WAY FORWARD

It is my greatest hope that this book helps you along your MC journey to learn all you can about our culture, history, traditions, protocols, and customs. Thank you for purchasing my book and spending your valuable time reading it. May you find peace and blessings in your travels and among your mighty MC brotherhoods and sisterhoods. Please take the following as you depart these pages:

1. Stand in power.
2. Choose your standards.
3. Stand united in your brotherhood/sisterhood.
4. The MC is not about I, it is about WE! Stop saying I,I,I, and start saying WE!
5. Allow no member to compromise your bylaws.
6. Support those who support you!
7. Trust but verify! Watch all with a jaundiced eye. Demand proof. Check backgrounds and resumes of every hang-around, prospect, and probie.
8. Know that not every brother who wears your patch is your brother or sister.
9. Be wise enough to listen to those who have walked the path before you. Believe it or not they know WTF they are talking about.
10. Know your bylaws by memory. They are your only guarantee of equality.
11. Conduct yourself with honor, loyalty, integrity, and respect.
12. Have fun! Life is short!

Honorably yours

Black Dragon
Former National President
Former National Enforcer
Former East Coast Regional President
Founder Black Sabbath MC Goddesses of the Cross
Founder Black Sabbath MC Sisters of the Cross
Founder/President/Original 7 Atlanta Chapter
Lifer
Mighty Black Sabbath MC Nation
A Breed Apart
BSFFBS
Since 1974 and still strong…………..///

Bibliography

AmericanMotorcyclist.com. 18 June 2023. world wide web. 2023 June 2023.

—. *American Motorcyclist Association*. 19 June 2023. worldwide web. 19 June 2023.

AOA Outlaws MC Wikipedia. *https://en.wikipedia.org/wiki/Outlaws_Motorcycle_Club*. 1 September 2023. Worldwide Web. 10 October 2024.

BACA Wikipeda. *https://en.wikipedia.org/wiki/Bikers_Against_Child_Abuse*. 9 October 2022. Wordwide Web. 11 July 2023.

Bandidos MC Wikipedia. *https://en.wikipedia.org/wiki/Bandidos_Motorcycle_Club*. 18 May 2023. Worldwide web. 24 October 2024.

Bikerider Magazine. *brm.co.nz/brittan-morrow-the-queen-of-road-rash*. 3 July 2023. world wide web. 2023 July 2023.

BMV. *Bureau of Motor Vehicles*. Indiana: Indiana Government Center North 4th Floor, 2016. 17 March 2016.

Britannica, Encyclopedia. *Motorcycle*. 2020. 29 August 2020.

Burgess Wise, David. *Historic Motor Cycles*. Hamlyn Publishing Group Limited, 1973. 7 December 2023.

C.J. Doughty, Jr. "More on Hollister's Bad Time." 6 July 1947. magazine.

ChatGPT Artificial Intelligence. *ChatGPT AI*. 6 June 2023. Artificial Intelligence. 6 June 2023.

Chopper Wikipedia. *https://en.wikipedia.org/wiki/Chopper_(motorcycle)#:~:text =A%20chopper%20is%20a%20type,%22)%20or%20built%20 from%20scratch*. 10 July 2020. Worldwide Web. 28 July 2023.

Choppers MC Instagram. *https://www.instagram.com/choppers_mc/?hl=en*. n.d. Worldwide Web. 19 February 2025.

Chosen Few MC Wikipeda. *https://en.wikipedia.org/wiki/Chosen_Few_Motorcycle_Club*. 8 May 2016. Worldwide Web. 21 July 2023.

Cossalter, Vittore. *Motorcycle Dynamics*. Lulu ISBN 978-1-4303-0861-4, n.d.

Cut-off Wikipeda. *https://en.wikipedia.org/wiki/Cut-off*. 28 December 2012. Worldwide Web. 21 July 2023.

Cycle Queens of America Wiki. *https://en.wikipedia.org/wiki/Cycle_Queens_of_America*. 24 May 2012. Worldwide Web. 15 February 2025.

Department of Justice. *Department of Justice*. n.d. World Wide Web. 12 December 2023. <https://www.justice.gov/criminal/criminal-ocgs/gallery/outlaw-motorcycle-gangs-omgs#:~:text=Outlaw%20Motorcycle%20Gangs%20(OMGs) %20are,weapons%20trafficking%2C%20and%20drug%20tra fficking Sept. 2023>.

—. *https://www.justice.gov/archives/opa/pr/sixteen-hells-angels-red-devils-motorcycle-gang-members-face-charges-related-violent#:~:text=The%20RDMC%20is%20the%20main,1%2C%*

202023%2C%20in%20Raleigh. 16 October 2024. worldwide web. 16 October 2024.

Dicitonary.com/e/slang/receipts. *https://www.dictionary.com/e/slang/receipts/*. n.d. Worldwide Web. 23 February 2025.

Dobbs, Thomas "Tuggy" "Chopper Tuggy" "Chopper Tugs". *Senior Member Chopers MC* John E. 'Black Dragon' Bunch II. 19 February 2025. mobile phone.

Dragon, Black and Black Dragon. *https://www.youtube.com/watch?v=972nYvLlqYg*. 19 July 2017. <https://www.youtube.com/watch?v=972nYvLlqYg>.

Dulaney, William L. "A Brief History of 'Outlaw' Motorcycle Clubs." *International Journal of Motorcycle Studies* November 2005. Magazine.

East Bay Dragon MC Wikipedia. *https://en.wikipedia.org/wiki/East_Bay_Dragons*. 8 July 2017. Worldwide Web. 21 July 2023.

Fiedler, David. *The Boneshaker - Invented by Michaux and Iallement*. n.d. World Wide Web. 7 December 2023. <about.com>.

Foale, Tony. *Motorcycle Handling Chassis Design ISBN 978-84-933286-3-4*. Tony Foale Designs, 2006.

Fox 13 Tampa Bay. *Fox13News.com*. 9 October 2021. <https://www.fox13news.com/news/female-victim-in-fridays-i-4-motorcycle-gang-shootout-has-died-charges-upgraded>.

Freemasonry Wikipedia. *https://en.wikipedia.org/wiki/Freemasonry*. 10 December 2024. Worldwide Web. 1 July 2023.

Georgia.gov. *https://law.georgia.gov/press-releases/2023-06-05/carr-16-alleged-members-outcast-motorcycle-gang-indicted-bryan-county#:~:text=The%20Outcast%20Motorcycle%20Gang%20has,chapter%20was%20formed%20in%20Atlanta.* 6 June 2023. worldwide web. 6 June 2023.

GovInfo. "https://www.govinfo.gov/app/details/CFR-2010-title49-vol6/CFR-2010-title49-vol6-sec571-3/summary." 24 January 2023. *govInfo.gov Code of Federal Regulations, 49 CFR 57.3 Definitions.* 23 January 2023.

GrindhouseDatabase.com. *https://www.grindhousedatabase.com/index.php/Wild_Riders:_10_Classic_Biker_Movies.* n.d. Worldwide Web. 15 January 2025.

HarleyLiberty.com and Dave Walters. *https://harleyliberty.com/2018/12/06/influence-of-the-motorcycle-on-african-american-culture-east-bay-dragons-chosen-few-richmond-road-runners-and-las-defiant-ones/.* 6 December 2018. Worldwide Web. 15 November 2024.

heddels.com. *heddels.com/2020/01/the-rough-history-of-biker-cuts.* January 2020. worldwide web. 7 January 2025.

Hells Angels Frisco Instagram. *https://www.instagram.com/hamcfrisco/p/COJ_0bqgMaA/?img_index=1.* 7 April 2021. Worldwide Web. 5 January 2025.

Hells Lovers MC Wikipedia. *https://onepercenterbikers.com/hells-lovers-mc-motorcycle-club/.* n.d. Worldwide Web. 1 November 2023.

Information Movie Database (IMDB).
https://www.imdb.com/title/tt0326769/?ref_=fn_all_ttl_1.
December 2003. Worldwide Web. 21 July 2023.

Iron Order MC Wikipedia.
https://en.wikipedia.org/wiki/Iron_Order_Motorcycle_Club.
26 March 2023. Worldwide Web. 15 October 2024.

KHOU-11.
https://www.khou.com/article/news/crime/motorcyclists-shot-north-freeway/285-f57d482d-5419-48fd-9b27-455a1a53f459. 14 April 2023.
<https://www.khou.com/article/news/crime/motorcyclists-shot-north-freeway/285-f57d482d-5419-48fd-9b27-455a1a53f459>.

KTSM El Paso News. *https://www.ktsm.com/local/el-paso-news/kinfolk-biker-accused-of-killing-el-paso-bandidos-leader-says-he-feared-for-his-life/.* 16 3 2025.
<https://www.ktsm.com/local/el-paso-news/kinfolk-biker-accused-of-killing-el-paso-bandidos-leader-says-he-feared-for-his-life/>.

KTSM.com News. *https://www.ktsm.com/local/el-paso-news/jury-finds-kinfolk-biker-guilty-of-murdering-bandidos-leader/.* 3 March 2025. <https://www.ktsm.com/local/el-paso-news/jury-finds-kinfolk-biker-guilty-of-murdering-bandidos-leader/>.

Kuhn, Del. *https://thegrandfathersofmotocross.com/1947-hollister-race/a1c-1948-july-4-riverside-riots-motorcycle-hollister-like-reported/.* 20 March 2015. Worldwide Web. 15 October 2024.

Legion of Doom Instagram. *https://www.instagram.com/lodmc/.* n.d. Worldwide Web. 25 February 2025.

Life. "On Fourth of July Weekend 4,000 members of motorcycle club terrorize Hollister California." *Life* 21 July 1947: 31. Magazine.

Lil-Man-1%er. *Soul Brothers MC Nomad* John E. 'Black Dragon' Bunch II. 12 February 2025. Cell Phone.

Madhusoodanan, Jyoti. *Beyond Bias*. 2024. web site https://www.openmindmag.org/articles/immutable.

Maisano, Keaton. *https://americanmotorcyclist.com/hall-of-famer-spotlight-bessie-stringfield/#:~:text=During%20World%20War%20II%2C%20Stringfield,The%20Motorcycle%20Queen%20of%20Miami.%E2%80%9D*. 13 February 2023. Worldwide Web. 20 November 2024.

MC Historian. *https://mchistorian13.blogspot.com/2015/11/what-does-diamond-13-patch-really-mean.html*. November 2015. worldwide web. 11 November 2024.

Merriam-Webster. *Definition of a Motorcycle by Merriam-Webster*. Merriam-Webster, 2023.

Mongols MC Wikipeda. *https://en.wikipedia.org/wiki/Mongols_Motorcycle_Club*. 17 May 2023. Worldwide Web. 11 October 2024.

Motorcycle Club, Wiki. *https://en.wikipedia.org/wiki/Motorcycle_club*. 12 May 2012. Internet. 20 October 2024.

Motorcycles, Motorcycle Timeline - Evolution of. *www.bicyclehistory.net*. n.d. World Wide Web. 7 December 2022.

National Institute of Justice. *https://nij.ojp.gov/topics/articles/what-gang-definitions.* n.d. Worldwide Web. 23 November 2023.

National Library of Medicine. *https://pmc.ncbi.nlm.nih.gov/articles/PMC8004354/.* 8 March 2021. Worldwide web. 20 May 2025.

OLDEST.org. *https://www.oldest.org/entertainment/motorcycle-clubs-in-the-world/.* n.d. Worldwide Web. 18 February 2025.

One Percenter Bikers. *https://onepercenterbikers.com/hells-lovers-mc-motorcycle-club/.* n.d. Worldwide Web. 21 July 2023.

onepercenterbikers.com. *https://onepercenterbikers.com/soul-brothers-mc-motorcycle-club/.* n.d. Worldwide Web. 12 December 2023.

OnePercenterBikers.com/DC-Eagles. *https://onepercenterbikers.com/dc-eagles-mc-motorcycle-club/.* n.d. Worldwide Web. 25 Februrary 2025.

Outcast Forever. Dir. DeVaughn Hughson. Perf. Outcast MC. 2007. Documentary.

Pagan's MC Wikipedia. *https://en.wikipedia.org/wiki/Pagan%27s_Motorcycle_Club.* 6 August 2023. Worldwide Web. 12 October 2024.

Patriot Guard Riders Wikipedia. *https://en.wikipedia.org/wiki/Patriot_Guard_Riders.* 24 July 2014. Worldwide Web. 24 July 2023.

Prezi.com. *https://prezi.com/2wf4w-glat5o/thunderguards/#:~:text=The%20Thunderguards%20Motorcycle%20Club%20originated,Charlie%2C%20Gordie%2*

C%20and%20Cuppie. 21 June 202. worldwide web. 21 June 2023.

Redrummc.com. *https://redrummc.com/about-2/*. n.d. Worldwide Web. 25 February 2025.

revzilla.com. *https://www.revzilla.com/common-tread/75-years-ago-hollister-began-changing-the-image-of-motorcycling?srsltid=AfmBOorUU54XecDNy8Sd2kzvsBDiSs1vLAAOsBVo1N_ja5bZJqescMYL*. n.d. worldwide web. 2 January 2025.

Ruff Ryders Lifestyles. *https://www.rrlifestyles.com/page/aboutrrlifestyles*. n.d. Worldwide Web. 22 February 2025.

Saia, Anthony M. "The Evolution and Influence of Outlaw Motorcycle Clubs in the American West." Master of Arts Thesis. 2015. Report.

Sam, Sudip Issac. "Hollister Riot: The Event That Changed Motorcycle History." *Medium* 15 August 2021. Worldwide Web.

Sauer, Mark and John Wilkens. "Haunting questions: The Stephanie Crowe Murder Case. Part 3: The knife." *SanDiego Union Tribune* 13 May 1999.

—. "Haunting questions: The Stephanie Crowe Murder Case. Part 4: More arrests." *Union Tribune* 14 May 1999.

—. "Haunting questions: The Stephanie Crowe Murder Case. Part 6: The bombshell." *San Diego Union Tribune* 16 May 1999.

Sauer, Mark. *Michael Crowe Found 'Factually Innocent' In Sister's Murder* KPBS. 2012 22 May. Television.

SCDNation.com. *Sin City Deciples*. n.d. Worldwide Web. 25 November 2023.

Shaggy 1%er, INVADER. Interview. Black Dragon. 07 March 2025. Telephone Interview.

Sin City MC Wikipedia. *https://en.wikipedia.org/wiki/Sin_City_Deciples_Motorcycle _Club*. 7 March 2022. Worldwide Web. 5 November 2023.

Sons of Silence Wikipedia. *https://en.wikipedia.org/wiki/Sons_of_Silence*. 4 April 2022. Worldwide web. 2 November 2024.

Start an MC AMA. *https://americanmotorcyclist.com/organizers/charter-your-organization-getting-started/start-a-motorcycle-club/*. n.d. Worldwide Web. 17 July 2023.

—. *https://americanmotorcyclist.com/organizers/charter-your-organization-getting-started/start-a-motorcycle-club/*. n.d. 17 July 2023. <https://americanmotorcyclist.com/organizers/charter-your-organization-getting-started/start-a-motorcycle-club/>.

StateBurners-woodbridge.com. *https://www.stateburners-woodbridge.com/history*. n.d. Worldwide Web. 22 November 2024.

Thesaurus.com Receipts. *Thesarus.com/receipts*. n.d. Worldwide Web. 23 February 2025.

Vagabonds MC Instagram. *https://www.instagram.com/oakland_vagabonds_mc/?hl=en*. n.d. Worldwide Web. 19 February 2025.

Western Motorcyclist and Bicyclist 1924. "An Organized Minoirty Can Always Defeat an Unorganized Majority." *Western Motorcyclist and Bicyclist* (1924). journal.

Wheels of Soul MC Wikipedia. *https://en.wikipedia.org/wiki/Wheels_of_Soul_Motorcycle_Club.* 8 July 2021. Worldwide Web. 17 November 2023.

Wheelsofgrace.com and test. *https://wheelsofgrace.com/history-3pc-patch-part-1/#:~:text=In%20order%20to%20designate%20themselves,area%20from%20which%20they%20came.* n.d. Worldwide Web. 15 July 2023.

White 2, Tim. *https://www.wpri.com/target-12/ri-hells-angels-figure-to-be-released-from-prison-after-attending-mob-wake/.* 24 September 2024. Worldwide web. 24 September 2024.

White, Tim. *https://www.wpri.com/target-12/ri-hells-angels-figure-joseph-lancia-back-behind-bars-after-attending-mob-wake/.* 12 September 2024. worldwide web. 12 September 2024.

Wikipedia Hells Angels MC. *https://en.wikipedia.org/wiki/Hells_Angels.* 10 September 2024. Worldwide Web. 10 October 2024.

Wikipedia Hollister Riot . *https://en.wikipedia.org/wiki/Hollister_riot.* 18 July 2019. Worldwide Web. 2023 24 October.

Wikipedia. *https://en.wikipedia.org/wiki/Hell%27s_Lovers_Motorcycle_Club#:~:text=Hell's%20Lovers%20Motorcycle%20Club%20(HLMC,founded%20in%20Chicago%20in%201967.* 21 June 2023. worldwide web. 21 June 2023.

Wikipedia Moonshiners MC. *https://en.wikipedia.org/wiki/Moonshiners_Motorcycle_Club*. 2 March 2016. Internet. 1 January 2025.

Wikipedia Pissed Off Bastrds of Bloomington MC. *https://en.wikipedia.org/wiki/Pissed_Off_Bastards_of_Bloomington#:~:text=Then%20on%20July%204%2C%201947,%2C%20they're%20outlaws.%22*. 2016 July 2016. Worldwide Web. 22 October 2024.

Wikipedia-Murder-Stephanie-Crowe. *Murder of Stephanie Crowe Wikipedia*. 21 January 1998. https://en.wikipedia.org/wiki/Murder_of_Stephanie_Crowe#:~:text=The%20murder%20of%2012%2Dyear,morning%20of%20January%2021%2C%201998. 21 November 2024.

Wikipedia-Reid-Technique. *Reid Techniqe*. 28 August 2003. https://en.wikipedia.org/wiki/Reid_technique. 21 November 2024.

Wilkens, John and Mark Saurer. "Haunting Questions: The Stepanie Crowe Murder Case. Part 2: The Arrest." *San Diego Union Tribune* 12 May 1999.

Willett, Trent. *https://www.facebook.com/trent.willett.3/posts/this-is-the-original-drawing-of-the-first-1-diamond-a-man-named-frank-sadilek-wa/1104488900689692*. 7 December 2023. Worldwide Web. 10 February 2025.

Woods, Verrel Elizabeth (Vera). *Black Dragon's Interview with Cycle Queen Founder Vera* Black Dragon John E. Bunch II. 18 February 2025. Podcast Interview.

Youtube.com/@Redrumotorcycleclub8836. *https://www.youtube.com/@redrummotorcycleclub8836*. n.d. Worldwide Web. 8 February 2025.

Index:

(ED) is at particularly high risk for violence against healthcare workers 372
"Chapter" versus "Charter" 118
0% diamond 94, 330
1% clubhouse 336, 337, 342, 343, 344, 345, 346
1% Clubhouse 336, 344, 345, 346
1% Diamond 81, 87
1% moniker 68
1% OMCs 51, 88, 93, 96, 99, 100, 104, 106, 107, 108, 109, 144, 147, 158, 170, 171, 172, 174, 177, 178, 181, 183, 185, 250, 251, 286, 325, 326, 329, 330, 332, 333, 375, 376, 377, 380, 390
1%ers 47, 81, 86, 98, 99, 170, 172, 181, 184, 240, 251, 254, 257, 258, 262, 264, 275, 278, 290, 325, 336, 339, 345, 347, 349, 352, 371, 372, 385, 446, 456, 461
13 .... 297, 329, 436, 463
7%ers 94
    Big Leonard 94
    Joe .... VII, 92, 94
    Lensey 94
    Marvin 90, 94
    Sam 92, 94
    Soul man 94
99%er 96, 120, 138, 144, 147, 158, 166, 168, 169, 178, 237, 250, 252, 261, 269, 274, 278, 286, 326, 329, 332, 338, 340, 433, 459, 461, 462, 463
99%ers 138, 169, 178, 180, 186, 261, 461
A Breed Apart .... I, 392, 469
ABATE 39, 203, 434, 456, 460, 462
administrative 124, 126, 128, 130

African American Clubs *83*
African Americans *450*
After a Police Encounter *362*
After You're Arrested *349*
airmen *166, 236*
always get a Receipt *229*
Always Pay Back a Loan *229*
Am I free to leave *357*
AMA .39, 56, 58, 59, 60, 61, 62, 63, 64, 65, 66, 68, 70, 71, 73, 76, 80, 81, 85, 86, 95, 164, 165, 166, 167, 169, 171, 172, 176, 183, 203, 277, 329, 434, 441, 456
American Bikers Toward Education or A Brotherhood Against Totalitarian Enactments *203*
American Brotherhood Aimed Towards Education *39*
American Machine and Foundry *44*
American Motorcyclist Association *39, 58, 80, 203, 456*
AMF *44*
annual .... *III, 66, 68, 111, 125, 258, 265, 444, 452, 454*
Any full patch brother in good standing can request to see the books *213*
Appeal *221*
Ass Kicking *221*
Assertion of Rights *352*
Auxiliary *52, 114, 145*
Award/Recognition Patches *176*
Bad Relations Business *341*
bank account *127, 440*
bank statements *127*
banking *127, 280*
BD's Mentors and Friends
    Bandido Kenneth 1%er IV
    Boar 1%er IV
    Dolla Bill 1%er IV
    Nakita 1%er IV
    Big Bone 1%er IV
    Big Caz 1%er IV
    Bishop 1%er IV

Bolo 1%er ... IV
Cell Block 1%er ... IV
Chuck 1%er ... IV
Dark Shadow 1%er ... IV
DJ ... IV
Doc ... V
Eddie Kane 1%er ... IV
Heavy ... IV, 92, 386
Invader Shaggy 1%er ... IV, 98, 295
Knowlledge 1%er ... IV
Miles 1%er ... IV
PNut 1%er ... IV
Reef ... IV
Rice 1%er ... IV
Seven 1%er ... IV
Skull 1%er ... IV
Tarzan 1%er ... IV
Teddy Bear 1%er ... IV
Uncle Chucky ... IV
Best Dressed MC ... *51*
Best Looking Motorcycle ... *51*
best-dressed club ... *164*
Biker Boyz ... *VI, VII, 47, 111, 112, 466*
biker club set .. *38, 40, 42, 47, 117, 178, 179, 181, 204, 224, 259, 262, 305, 371*
biker gang ... *45, 112, 311, 328, 351*
biker gangs ... *328, 371*
Biker Organizations
   Motorsports Clubs ... 180, 198
   Patriot Guard ... 180, 199, 250
   Riding Clubs ... 180, 198
Biker SCs ... *194*
Biker Social Clubs ... *194*
biker's rights ... *54, 459*
Bikers Against Child Abuse ... *195*
bikesploitation ... *100*

Bker Organizations
  Specialty Biker Groups 180, 199
Black biker set....42, 60, 61, 84, 87, 89, 111, 115, 119, 157, 180, 238, 242, 443, 444, 450, 468, 470
Black Denim................ 176
Black Dragon Biker TV................ I, III, IX, 210, 264, 348, 376, 467
Black Dragon's Books
  How to Write, Edit, Update, and Revise Motorcycle Club Bylaws 281
  MC Public Relations Officer's Bible 135, 467
  President's Bible Chronicle I Principles of Motorcycle Club Leadership................ 121
  President's Bible Chronicle II Betrayal in the Brotherhood 121, 468
  Prospect's Bible................ 284, 324, 477
  Sergeant-at-Arms Bible Soldier/Sergeant of the Brotherhood.. 124
Black OMCs................ 95, 96, 375, 377
Black Sabbath MC Original 7
  John Kearny 'Black'................ 442
  Alvin Ray 'Stretch'................ 442
  Paul Perry 'Pep'................ 442
  Robert D. Hubbard 'Sir Hub'................ 442
  Solomon 'Sol'................ 442
  William Charles Sanders 'Couchie'................ 442
  Clayton Mitchell "Mitch"................ 442
Black Sabbath Motorcycle Club .. I, IX, 440, 441, 443, 444, 447, 448, 449, 450, 451, 452, 454, 466, 467, 469
bobbed................ 97
bobber................ 97
Bob-Job................ 97
Bottom Rocker................ 167, 168
Branding and Merchandising................ 135
Brother clubs................ 115, 119, 153, 154
Brother Clubs................ 153
brother MC................ 153, 154, 155
Budget................ 126
Building Relationships................ 136, 152
Bunch Media Group................ II, III

Business Contracts 129
business management 128
business manager 125, 127, 128, 129, 130, 135, 213
business operations 129
bylaws .. 39, 61, 98, 116, 118, 121, 122, 123, 125, 130, 131, 139, 140,
  141, 142, 143, 147, 152, 159, 161, 163, 175, 176, 181, 205, 207,
  208, 218, 219, 225, 226, 231, 265, 272, 278, 279, 280, 281, 282,
  283, 285, 315, 323, 334, 391, 432, 455, 461
Bylaws 279, 281, 282, 283
BYLAWS 279
cabaret 51
camaraderie. 48, 53, 57, 65, 76, 83, 96, 106, 109, 111, 117, 139, 142,
  146, 147, 153, 159, 162, 179, 184, 186, 187, 191, 192, 194, 196,
  197, 201, 217
Can Non-1% Clubs Wear a State Rocker 169
Center Piece 167
Central District of California Court 79
Chapter President 120
Chapter Public Relations Officer 133
Chapter Road Captain 130
Chapter Secretary 124
Chapter VP 121
charitable fundraising 127
Charity Motorcycle Clubs 195
Check backgrounds 391
chopped 70, 86, 91, 105
Chopper 90, 105, 457
Choppers 87, 90, 442
chopping our bikes 91
Christian faith 188
Christian motorcycle club 188
church38, 124, 227, 233, 245, 280, 432, 434, 436, 437, 441, 442, 457
civil asset forfeiture 79, 107, 119, 378
Club Administration 130
Club Business Communication 129
Club Constitution 272
Club Disciplinary System 218
Club Education II

Club Emblem 167
Club Events and Activities 217
Club Hierarchy 149, 211
club hopper 458
Club Meetings 212
Club Representation 134, 140
club resources 130
Club Security 122, 140
CMC 188
CMCs 188, 189, 190
coalition ... 38, 168, 169, 178, 204, 242, 261, 262, 265, 274, 277, 334, 335, 336, 441, 457
COC 38, 332
Coed MC 194
Coed Motorcycle Clubs 193
Colors 154, 156, 164, 210, 222, 231, 234, 235, 254, 309, 320, 322, 323, 335, 388, 449, 458
combat fatigue 53
committee 437
Common Punishments 220
Community Engagement 50, 134, 149
confederation of clubs 38
Conflict Resolution 117, 123, 141
constitution 279
Control the MC Set 332
Cop Club 170
correspondence 124, 129
Crisis Management 134
Cut-Off 176
Cuts 164, 176, 178
Daimler Reitwagen 43
DC Eagles MC 330
Death is my sidekick and the highway is my home 94
Demotion 220
denim cuts 40, 177, 178
Department of Homeland Security's Immigration and Customs Enforcement (ICE) 327
Department of Justice 79, 99, 171, 370

Design your colors with respect and research 270
Diamond 13 .... 62, 63, 64
Diamond Clubs 180, 329
Dismissal from the club 221
DOJ 79, 99, 171, 326, 327, 370, 371, 374
dominant club 37, 155, 235, 250, 275
Dominant Clubs Riding with Subordinate Clubs 250
Don't Speak Negatively About Other MCs 243
drill team 84
Dues 126, 254
DUI Stops and Sobriety Tests 357
During a Traffic Stop 355
East Coast 1, 37, 82, 84, 87, 93, 246, 392, 444, 445, 447, 469
Easy Rider 456
ED personnel. 369, 370, 371, 372, 373, 374, 376, 377, 378, 379, 380, 382, 383, 384
Electro-Motive Company 77
electronic payments 127
Elements of a Neutral Club 247
emergency department (ED) personnel 369
endurance runs 57
Enforcer 115, 119, 120, 122, 219, 220, 392, 444, 449, 452
enforcers 138
Enforcing Club Rules 122
evangelistic 189
External Challenges to Starting Your MC 257
FAM 54, 55, 56, 59
federal definition of a gang 327
Federation of American Motorcyclists 54, 59
female 47, 51, 52, 85, 109, 115, 119, 145, 147, 158, 170, 193, 197, 316, 317, 319, 378, 383, 450, 457, 459
Financial 125, 126, 127, 128, 146, 159
financial health 128
financial planning 128
financial records 125, 126, 129
fine 432, 433, 437
Fines 220, 254
First Responder Motorcycle Clubs 191

flight jackets *166*
flip *433, 459, 461*
Four-Piece *173*
Freemasonry *190, 191*
Friend of the Club *159*
Friends of the Club *115, 119*
Full patch brothers *114, 119, 139, 140, 141*
full patch brothers in good standing *120, 166, 210, 211, 219, 220, 226, 227*
Full Patch Greeting a Full Patch *238*
fundraising *62, 110, 127, 143, 156, 181, 192*
Galloping Goose MC *331*
Georgia council *237*
Georgia Council *38, 332*
Get that blessing *274*
Getting a Blessing can be an Exercise in Bullshit, if it is, You Know What to do *263*
Getting a Blessing Today *333*
Getting Vetted *153*
Global Reach *108*
Goldwing *45*
Good Relations Business *338*
Good Standing *141, 226*
Greaser Subculture *96*
Great Depression *43, 62*
guilty *437*
Guilty *219*
Gypsy Tour *66, 68*
hang-arounds .... *II, XI, 146*
Hang-arounds *114, 119, 152, 153*
hard colors *335*
Harley Davidson Inc. *43*
Harley Owners Group *44, 460*
Harley-Davidson *457, 461, 462*
Harley-Davison *43*
Harming or sexually abusing a child *224*
Have the Receipts *244*
Heart Patch *174*

Hierarchy Among the 1%	*330*
Hierarchy of Clubs	*179*
HOG	*44, 460*
Hollister Riot	*66, 73, 100*
Hollywood	*VI, 45, 87, 100, 177, 370, 466*
Hollywood Films	*112*
Easy Rider	97, 103, 105
Soul man	97
The Wild Angels	101, 102
Honda	*44, 441, 465*
Honorary members	*114, 119, 150, 151*
Honorary Members	*150*
Honorary patches	*175*
honorary positions	*175*
How to Call Ahead	*236*
HOW TO START A MOTORCYCLE CLUB	*256*
Ideological Differences	*100*
If Police Come to Your Home	*358*
if the Club Violates Its Bylaws	*225*
Important People	
Don Kurt	113
Paul Garnes	113
Roee Sharon	113
Stephanie Allain	113
Tammy Thomas-Garnes	113
Important People	
Augustus 'Gus' De Serpa	70
Barney Peterson	68
Ben Hardy	105
Bessie Stringfield	84
Big Daddy	85
Billy C.	94
Bobby Johnson	91
Boddie	85
Bruce Gale	79
Buckie	94
Bull	V

Carl Rayburn 73
Champ 89
Charles Metz 43
Charlie 94
Cheyenne 85
Chopper Tuggy 90
Clifford "Soney" Vaughs 105
Coffee 85
Cuppie 94
Dennis Hopper 97
Donald Eugene Chambers 78
Ed Youngblood 61, 95
Eddie Davenport 69, 72
Fishman 94
Frank "Claim-Jumper" Rios 94
Frank Sadilek 81
George H. Perry 55
George M. Hendee 55
Gina Prince Bythewood 113
Gordie 94
Hawk 89
Hildebrand & Wolfmuller 43
Jerry Smith 68
Jerry Telfer 72
June 85
Junkyard 94
Lemoore-Hanford 69
Leonard Lloyd "J.R." Reed, Jr. 79
Lil Frank 89
Lionel Ricks 89
Manuel "Pokey" Galloway 111
Marlon Brando 97
Maverick 85
Michaux-Perreaux 43
Motorcycle Queen of Miami 84
Norman Gaines 61

Otto Friedli 102
Paul Brokaw 71
Peter Fonda 97
Peter Gun 85
Pierre Lallement 43
R.G. Betts 55
Reggie Bythewood 113
Reggie Rock Bythewood .... VI, 47, 112
Roger 74, 89
Roger Corman 101
Roger L. Abbot 74
Shirly Bates 89
Slim 89
Sonny Barger 90
Spartacus 85
Tom Lindsay 80
Wilhelm Maybach 43
William B. Johnson 61
William Berry 80
Willie G. Davidson 44
Bad Dog 169
Big Rick 169
Chief 169
Copper 169
Doc 169
Ice 169
Professor 169
Willie Ball 169
The Father Paul 'Pep' Perry 214
Charlie 221
Master Chief Tommy "Hog man" Lewis 268, 445, 446, 452
Jake Sawyer 210, 294, 298
Cliff 330
Danny LeDesma 330
Sonny Barger 386
Bernard 'Krow' Augustus 445

Wolverine 445
Huggy Bear 445, 446
Big Dale 445, 446
Godfather Washington 452
Bull 454
Keith (Alcatraz) Corley 466
Reggie Rock Bythewood 466
Skull 466
Taa Shon 1%er 468
Pipeline 1%er 468
El Domino 468
Snoop Dogg 468
Three 6 Mafia 468
Akon 468
T-Pain 468
The Game 468
Baby Bash 468
Mr. Criminal 468
Joshua Coombs 468
Nelson Mandella 468
Gottlieb Daimler 43
independent 441
Indian *43, 55*
Indian Motorcycle Manufacturing *43*
Innocent *219, 353*
Inter-Club MC Protocol *205*
INTER-CLUB MC PROTOCOL *234*
Inter-club protocol *205, 234*
Internal Challenges to Starting Your MC *256*
Internal Communication *135*
International *115*
Interrupting Two Full Patches *241*
intra-club MC protocol *205, 207*
Intra-club MC Protocol *205*
INTRA-CLUB MC PROTOCOL *207*
Intra-club protocol *205*

IOMC	169, 170
Iron Order MC	169, 170, 185
Is Getting a Blessing Asking Permission to Exist	261
Japanese motorcycle	44
Jim Crow	47, 84, 86, 314
Johnny's Bar	68
Kawasaki	44
Killing a brother in the club	224
King of Cali	111
Know Your Rights	353
Law Enforcement MC	170, 184
Law Enforcement MCs	110, 180
Leading the Ride	131
Leave of Absence	221
legislation	456
LEMC	170, 184, 185, 186, 267, 277
LEMCs	110, 138, 169, 180, 184, 185, 277
Local MC	119
Local Officers	114
logistics	126, 129, 145, 158, 303
Longest Distance Riders	51
loyalty	448
Loyalty and Brotherhood	217
M&ATA	54, 55, 56, 58, 59
MA	43
Make it Legal	273
Makeup of the MC	114
Manage the Money	213
Managing Club Property	122
Masonic Motorcycle Club	190
Matilda's bar	77
MC Cube	173
MC history	42
MC operations	114
MC Professional Convention	39
PROC	VI, 467, 468
MC Professional Convention (PROC)	467

MC protocol .... III, IX, 284, 285, 303, 304, 319, 324, 332, 343, 347, 351, 352, 377, 379, 387, 450, 461, 467
MC PROTOCOL AND THE POLICE 347
MC PROTOCOL FOR FIRST EMERGENCY DEPARTMENT PERSONNEL 369
MCC 52
MCCs 171, 174
Media Relations 133
meeting 457
Meeting Coordination 124
Meeting Minutes 124
membership requirements 125, 202, 280
MG 328
military 303, 312, 363, 371
Military 53, 64, 306
Mission Statement 272, 451
MM 267, 268, 277, 352, 460
Modern Day Procedures for First Responders 384
Montebello, California 79
Most Attended MC 51
Motor Maids 52, 85
Motor Scooter & Allied Trades Association 60
motorbike 43
motorcycle 43
Motorcycle and Allied Trades Association 54
Motorcycle Club
   Portsmouth Motorcycle Club 53
   San Francisco Motorcycle Club 53
   The Motor Cycling Club 52
Motorcycle Club Protocol .... II, 37
Motorcycle Clubs
   13 Rebels MC 66
   Alpha Motorcycle Club of Brooklyn 54
   American Outlaws Association 63, 77
   Andrew "Poolie" 94
   Angels 81
   Bandidos MC .... IV, 78, 80, 170, 251, 331

Berkeley Tigers MC 60
Black 13's 82
Black Angels MC 91
Black Sabbath . I, 392, 440, 441, 442, 443, 444, 445, 446, 447, 448,
    449, 450, 451, 452, 453, 454, 455, 458, 463, 466, 467, 469
Black Sabbath MC 392, 444, 445, 446, 450, 455
Blue Knights LEMC 110
Boozefighters MC 66
Brother Speed MC 332
Brothers East (B*EAST) MC 332
Buffalo Riders MC 87, 91
Ching-a-Lings MC 331
Choppers MC 87, 90
Chosen Few MC .... IV, V, 87, 89, 329, 331, 446, 468
Cobras MC 87
Cycle Queens of America MC 85
D.O.s 89
East Bay Dragons MC 87, 90
El Forastero MC 331
Flamingos MC 87
Frisco Rattlers MC 87, 88
Galloping Goose MC 66
Gooses 81, 82
Gypsy Joker MC 332
Gypsy Jokers 81
HAMC 77
Hawks MC 331
Hell's Lovers MC 94
Hells Angels 77, 78, 79, 80, 81, 82, 87, 88, 90, 99, 101, 102, 109,
    170, 182, 210, 294, 298, 326, 331, 351, 360, 373, 386
Hells Angels MC 77, 80, 81, 82, 90, 101, 170, 182, 331, 386
Hells Lovers MC 87, 330, 331
Invaders MC .... IV, 295, 332
Iron Horse MC 84, 87
King Cobras MC 87
LA Defiant Ones MCs 87

Legion of Doom MC 329
Louis Costello 79
Market Street Commandos MC 66
Mofos 81
Mongols MC 331, 375, 378
Old Burners 85
Outcast MC .... IV, 87, 92, 93, 331, 466, 468
Outlaws MC .... VI, 63, 77, 80, 82
Outsiders MC 332
Pagan's MC 78
Phantoms MC 331
Pissed Off Bastards of Bloomington MC 66
Presidents .... IX, XI, 81, 431
Rattlers 81, 82, 87, 88
Red Devils MC 182
Redrum MC 329
Richmond Road Runners MC 87, 89
Road Rats 81
Roaring Twenties 81
Salinas Ramblers MC 66
Sharks MC 66
Sin City Deciples MC .... IV, 87, 93
Sin City Desciples MC 331
Skull Riders 81
Sons of Silence MC .... IV, 78, 79, 80, 331, 335
Soul Brothers MC .... IV, VI, 92, 331, 386
Star Riders MC 87, 92
State Burners MC 84, 87
Street Soldiers MC 275, 331
Street Soldierz MC 334, 335
THUG Riders MC 331
Thunderguards MC .... X, 331, 468
Top Hatters MC 66
Tulare Riders MC 69, 72
Vagabonds MC 87, 90
Vagos MC 331

Vampires 81
Wheels of Soul .... IV, 87, 93, 109, 331, 468
Wheels of Soul MC 331, 468
Yellow Jackets MC 66
Yonkers Motorcycle Club 52
Zodiacs MC .... V, 454
motorcycle community *51, 58, 76, 110, 135, 150, 190, 191, 200*
Motorcycle Gang *102, 328, 460*
Motorcycle Ministry *460*
Motorcycle Organizations *180, 201, 202*
   Motorcycle Enthusiast Groups 180, 202
   Motorcycle Safety Organizations 180, 201
Motorcycle Orginzations
   Motorcycle Rights Organizations 180, 202
Motorcycle racing *48, 97, 105, 106*
Motorcycle Riders Foundation *203, 460*
motorcycle tours *57*
Motorsports clubs *138*
Motorsports Clubs
   Ruff Ryders MSC 198
Motorycle Clubs
   Mongols MC 78, 79, 80, 107, 170
MRF *203*
MROs *202, 203, 456*
MS&ATA *56, 60*
Name your club *269*
National Business Manager *115, 448, 452*
National Coalition of Motorcyclists *39*
National officers *115, 116, 117*
National Officers *114, 115*
National President .. *I, IX, 37, 115, 116, 135, 137, 138, 139, 201, 214, 243, 246, 250, 263, 300, 392, 438, 444, 445, 446, 447, 448, 451, 452, 466, 467*
National Road Captain *115*
National Secretary *115*
National Sergeant at Arms *115*
National Treasurer *115*

National Vice President 115, 268, 445, 448, 452
Nationals 116
Navy ... 39, 79, 228, 236, 260, 262, 279, 287, 289, 292, 294, 301, 302, 312, 338, 346, 363, 375, 442
NCOM .... VI, 39, 203
Negro American biker set 60
neutral 170, 219, 247, 248, 249, 385, 450
Never Discuss Club Business 228
Never Exploit the Club for Personal Gain 229
Never get High in the Clubhouse 229
Never Lie to a Club Brother 228
Never Sleep with Your Club Brother's Old Lady 227
Never Steal 229
New York Motorcycle Club 54
Niwot, Colorado 79
No Warrant, No Entry 359
Nomad .... VI, 135, 137, 167, 294, 298, 449, 452, 453, 462
Nomads 114, 136, 137, 138
Non Traditional MCs
   First Responder MCs 180, 191, 192
Non-Traditional MCs 188
   BACA 180, 195, 196
   Biker SCs 180
   Charity MCs 180, 195
   Christian MCs 180, 188
   Coed MCs 180, 193, 194
   Female MCs 180, 197, 198
   Masonic MCs 180, 190, 191
   Sober MCs 180, 192, 193
   Vintage MCs 180, 195
Not Guilty 219
nuclear submarine 39
Officer patches 174
officer tabs 174
OMC 64, 77, 78, 79, 80, 82, 83, 86, 87, 88, 89, 90, 92, 93, 94, 99, 100, 107, 108, 136, 138, 144, 147, 155, 164, 165, 166, 168, 174, 177, 178, 179, 181, 183, 184, 251, 259, 261, 264, 265, 267, 271,

277, 278, 286, 303, 305, 310, 325, 328, 329, 330, 338, 339, 340, 349, 352, 370, 371, 373, 376, 383, 385, 436, 439, 450, 458, 459, 460, 463, 468
OMCs. 68, 76, 77, 78, 80, 82, 83, 86, 87, 88, 95, 96, 98, 99, 100, 101, 105, 106, 107, 108, 109, 136, 147, 166, 168, 169, 171, 174, 177, 178, 180, 181, 182, 183, 185, 199, 241, 251, 254, 268, 277, 305, 325, 326, 329, 330, 332, 333, 347, 348, 370, 372, 374, 376,377, 380, 383, 385, 438, 456, 458, 461, 462, 463
OMG 79, 311, 328, 350, 370, 372, 378, 381, 383, 436, 460
OMGs 78, 99, 326, 328, 369, 370, 371, 374, 375, 376, 377, 378, 379, 380, 383, 384, 385, 456, 462
OMGs present a challenge to ED personnel 374
onboarding process 125
One Patch One Vote 227
'one-percenter 80
one-piece patch 165, 166, 178, 448, 463
Online Presence and Social Media Management 134
Orient-Astor 43
Out Bad .... XII, 41, 223, 231
OUT BAD .... IX, 141, 223, 246
Out bad status 224
Outlaw 62, 63, 64, 65, 70, 80, 86, 88, 99, 104, 166, 171, 177, 178, 181, 183, 326, 329, 369, 374, 382, 433, 460, 463, 468
outlaw bikers 44, 99, 369, 371, 376, 384
outlaw motorcycle club 61
outlaw motorcycle gang 79, 102, 311
Outlaws 326, 329, 331
Outlaws MC 331
parade style 216
paramilitary 54, 312, 387
Pass Pin, Pass Thru Pin or Pass Through Pin 236
Passing 1% and Other MCs 251
Patch Maker 214
Patch Overs and Club Flips 252
Patches .. 164, 171, 172, 174, 175, 176, 184, 210, 222, 234, 314, 321, 329
Paul 'Pep' Perry 452
Permission and Courtesy While Traveling 235

PGR 199, 200, 201
Physical Exercises 221
Polaris 44
Popup Club 169
popup MC 171
post-traumatic stress disorder 53
Pre-Ride Briefing 131
Preserving Club Traditions and Protocols 122
President .... I, IX, 61, 81, 89, 95, 118, 119, 120, 121, 123, 130, 131,
   135, 137, 170, 176, 182, 186, 188, 207, 212, 216, 224, 225, 226,
   239, 246, 247, 249, 250, 268, 298, 299, 300, 301, 302, 303, 339,
   387, 392, 431, 432, 434, 438, 442, 443, 444, 445, 448, 452, 454,
   458, 466, 467, 468, 469, 475
president never handles money 213
Presidents Forever 225
Prez 115, 119, 120, 121, 208
print advertisements 51
PRO 119, 133, 134, 135, 436, 452, 461
Probable Cause 361
Probate 141, 461
Probationary 141, 461
Probie 144, 461
PROC 39
Proper Introduction 343
Properties 114, 119, 145, 147, 148, 149, 345
Property's roles 148
prospect administration 125
Prospect Greeting a Full Patch 240
Prospect's Bible 467, 472
PROSPECT'S LIST OF 52 284
Prospects .... IX, XI, 114, 119, 142, 143, 144, 172, 182, 284, 299, 316,
   317, 323, 447, 448, 451
protocols associated with club colors 210
Public Image Management 133
Punishment 220, 221
Purpose Statement 273
Questioning 353
Racing .... VI, 48, 57, 69, 97, 105, 329, 442

racing clubs 63, 64, 86
racist 61, 95, 321, 386
Racketeer Influenced and Corrupt Organizations 462
Rags 164, 461
rallies 50, 116, 134, 161, 186, 189, 194, 197, 247, 384
Raping or beating a woman 224
RC 165, 267, 436, 447, 461
RCs 138, 147, 165, 168, 173, 174, 178, 179, 199, 251, 268, 277, 333, 370, 378, 461
Receipt 244
Receipts 229, 245, 246
Record-Keeping 125, 126, 129
Refusing to Answer Questions 358
Regional MC 119
Regional Officers 114
regular fucking member 212
regular fucking members 139
Removing Helmet and Glasses 238
reports 73, 75, 100, 125, 127, 213, 236, 280, 352
Representing the Club 136
Respect... 152, 160, 161, 162, 187, 211, 228, 234, 287, 295, 312, 316, 385, 388, 390
RFM 212
RFMs 139
RICCO 107, 347
RICO 118, 436, 462
Ride Evaluation 132
Ride Formation 123
Ride patches 175
Ride Planning 130
riding club 44, 170
Riding Formation and Etiquette 216
riding formations 131, 265
Riverside 446
Riverside Riot 73
road captain 130, 131, 132, 216, 250, 252, 388
rockers 96, 138, 168, 169, 172, 173, 174
Rogue MC 169

role of a public relations officer 135
S.C.O.F. 63, 329
SAA.115, 119, 120, 122, 123, 131, 163, 209, 213, 214, 216, 218, 219, 220, 221, 222, 231, 235, 246, 247, 254, 264, 307, 308, 339, 341, 387, 389
safety 42, 50, 51, 96, 98, 106, 122, 132, 133, 142, 176, 192, 194, 197, 201, 202, 203, 216, 236, 250, 300, 305, 367, 435, 439, 459
Safety 460
San Leon, Texas 78
SC 158
SCs 157, 158, 159, 178, 179, 204, 333
Searches Without Consent 361
secretary 124, 125, 126, 127, 128, 273
segregation 60, 95, 314
Segregation 47
Serapes 164
Sergeant at Arms 467, 473
Sergeant at Arms Bible 467, 473
servicemen 53, 97
Settling Beefs 243
Sgt at Arms .... XI, 249, 344
SHUT THE FUCK UP 348
Side Rockers 173
side-by-side 216, 250
six months 458, 468
Sleeping with a club brother's woman 224
Snitches 347
snitching 347
Snitching to the police on a club brother or the club 224
Sober Motorcycle Clubs 192
Social Clubs 115, 119, 157, 180, 204, 464, 468, 470, 476
Soft Colors 335
Sonny 386
Sons of Anarchy 88, 108
Southern California Outlaw Federation 62, 63
sponsorships 52, 127
Starting Chapters of an Established MC 276
Starting MCs in Countries Other Than the United States 278

Starting Your MC in Areas dominated by 1% OMC Nations 265
Stealing from the club 224
Study to Shew Thyself Approved 282
suicide 435, 439
suicide style 216
Super Cub 45
Support 391, 449, 452
support club 153, 155, 156, 157, 182, 183, 259, 264, 265
Support clubs 115, 119, 156, 181
Support Clubs 155, 181
   brother clubs 181
   feeder clubs 181
   puppet clubs 181
Support MC Nations 179
Supporter MCs 179, 183
Supporters 115, 120, 161, 162
suspension 459, 462
Suspension 221, 254
Suzuki 44
Sweaters 164
Table 15, 227
tabs 174, 387
tail gunners 123
Taking Former Members of Other Clubs 253
tax 125, 127, 129, 273
Territory Disputes 248
Territory Patch 167
the "1%" patch is worn only by clubs immersed in criminality 375
The arrival of an injured gang member 373
The Big Five 78
The Big Four 78
The Biker Club Code 208, 209, 226
The Biker Code 208
The Isle of Man TT race 97
The Liberator 43
The MC Sit-Down 249
The Racketeer Influenced and Corrupt Organizations (RICO) Act 118
The Term Brother 241

There are Several Ways to Start an MC	260
three-piece patch	436
Three-piece patches	165
Thunderguards MC	IV, 87, 94
Top 13	64
Top Rocker	167
traditional MC	441, 452, 472, 473, 474
Traditional MCs	110, 163, 168, 180, 186, 187, 216, 347, 458
Traditional Patch Setup	165
treasurer	125, 126, 127, 128, 129, 213
trial	IX, XII, 282, 437
Trial	221, 231
trike	43
Triumph	45
Two or More Clubs Riding Together	250
two-by-two	216, 250
Two-Piece	171, 172
UJM	44
Universal Japanese Motorcycle	44
Using or selling hard drugs	224
varsity jackets	164
Vehicle Searches	356
Veteran's MCs	180, 188
veterans	44, 53, 61, 65, 79, 83, 98, 166, 169, 170, 177, 187, 188, 199, 200, 371
Veterans MC	187
Veterans Motorcycle Club	187
Vets	53
Vietnam War	98
Vintage Motorcycle Clubs	195
VMC	187
VP	115, 119, 120, 121, 213, 246, 249, 388, 442
Warning to Liars	342
What is a Blessing	261
What is a Full Patch Brother	139
What to Do If Expelled	222
When You go to Jail	214
When You go to the Hospital	215

White biker set 42, 238
Whose Hand(s) do You Shake First 239
WII 53
women 281, 291, 297, 315, 317, 336, 341, 343, 344, 345, 383, 386, 451
Women51, 52, 104, 109, 114, 119, 145, 178, 180, 196, 197, 204, 242, 267, 324, 383, 450, 464, 467, 468, 476, 477
women's auxiliary 52, 64, 145, 146, 147
Won't Shake Your Hand 240
Work Detail 221
World War II 61, 64, 66, 70
WWII 64, 65, 66, 77, 83, 84, 97, 166, 175, 176, 236, 346
Yamaha 44, 465
yellow journalism 71

Appendix A: Biker Set Readiness Test

You should have a firm knowledge of the MC Biker Set. Test your knowledge with the following test. This test is by no means all-inclusive, but you can use it as a guide to begin your research:

1. In what city, state, and year was your MC founded?
2. In what neighborhood was your MC founded?
3. How many members comprised the founding brothers of your MC?
4. What were the names and occupations of the founding brothers of your MC?
5. What is the motto of your MC and what does it mean?
6. What is the birthday celebration of your MC?
7. What is the mascot of your MC?
8. Describe your MC's colors and explain the meanings, origins, and symbols of all the elements of the patch.
9. What was the name of the first brother killed on a motorcycle in your MC? What year did he die, and how was he killed?
10. What is the history of the first split in your MC and what happened to the members who split off?
11. How many years must you be in the MC before you are authorized to wear the MC's medallion or ring?
12. What are the names of the Presidents of all the chapters within your MC?
13. When did the President of your local chapter join your MC? What are the telephone numbers and contact names for all of the chapters within your MC?
14. How often are club meetings generally held throughout your MC and when?
15. How many members are necessary to hold a quorum in

your MC?
16. What is the order procedure for how church is conducted in your MC?
17. What are the real names, phone numbers, email addresses and emergency contact numbers for every member in your chapter?
18. What are the steps to becoming a Prospect in your MC?
19. Who can be a Prospect sponsor within your MC?
20. What are a sponsor's responsibilities?
21. When does a chapter President vote on a motion?
22. What are the main responsibilities of the Road Captain in your MC?
23. What are all the award patches you can earn in your MC?
24. If an MC member suspects that a brother is too drunk to ride what is his obligation to that drunken member according to your MC's bylaws or policies?
25. What is the MC's procedure for one member borrowing money from another member?
26. What is the procedure for solving a physical altercation between two members in your MC?
27. What member of your MC is allowed to physically strike another other member?
28. What members can actually fine other members?
29. What members can actually fine the chapter President?
30. Under what specific circumstances may your colors be taken from you for an infraction against the bylaws?
31. If your president requests your colors what must be done before the president can keep your colors forever?
32. Who comprises your MC's governing Council?
33. What can your significant other wear to support the MC?
34. What is the definition of a member in good standing?
35. What are the main responsibilities of a Prospect?
36. What are the basic rules of conduct for a Prospect?
37. Where are required patches to be worn on the vest of a

Prospect and full patched brothers?
38. What is the quickest way to tell if you are dealing with a 1% outlaw MC Nation member if you greet him face to face and have not seen the back of his vest?
39. How can you distinguish outlaw colors from the back?
40. What is the definition of an Outlaw MC?
41. What is the definition of a 99%er MC?
42. What is a 1% MC?
43. What is the history of 1%er MCs in the United States or in your country?
44. Where did the 1%er diamond originate?
45. When did the diamond 13 originate?
46. Who were the original 13 outlaw racing clubs.
47. Is there a difference between an outlaw MC and a 1% MC and if so, what is that difference?
48. Where did the term 1% come from?
49. What is the philosophical definition that sets 1% MCs apart from traditional MCs?
50. What criminal or civil actions, if any, have been brought against your MC by city, local, or national law enforcement agencies in an attempt to shut down, prosecute, and/or fine your MC during its history, and what were the outcomes of those charges?
51. To whom do the colors, insignia, designs, patches, logos, and other paraphernalia of your MC belong?
52. What is a club flip or patch-over in the MC world?
53. What is a support club?
54. If your MC wears a support patch for a 1% MC Nation, who are their enemies?
55. If your MC wears support patches what areas of town, cities, or states is it unsafe for you to go in your colors without being in the company of your brothers?
56. Why is it important to always remember that you are representing every MC member when you are operating out

in public?
57. What is your MC's consequence to you if you rip your patch off of your vest disrespectfully?
58. What is the consequence for striking another brother of your MC?
59. What are the consequences for stealing from your MC?
60. What are the consequences for discussing MC business outside of the MC?
61. What are the consequences for posting MC business on social media?
62. What are the consequences for cyber-banging on social media?
63. What are the consequences for losing your colors?
64. What are the consequences for disrespecting your colors?
65. Should your colors ever touch the ground?
66. Should you ever let anyone outside of your MC hold your colors?
67. What are all the terms for the vest used to hold your colors?
68. What does the term backyard mean?
69. What is the 80/20 rule in the MC world?
70. What is the AMA?
71. What is ABATE?
72. What are broken wings?
73. Why is it against protocol to show your ass at another MC's clubhouse?
74. What is a cage?
75. What does attending church mean in the MC world?
76. What does the term "Club Hopping" mean?
77. If your President wants to Prospect a hang-around who was a member of another MC, what is the proper protocol he should follow with the former club?
78. What is the proper hand signal flashed to the pack when a cop/highway patrol vehicle is spotted?
79. What is the proper hand signal flashed to the pack when

Motorcycle Club Protocol 101

debris is in the road on the left side of the bike?
80. What is the proper foot signal flashed to the pack when debris is in the road on the right side of the bike?
81. What is the proper hand signal flashed to the pack when the Road Captain wants the pack to assume a single file formation?
82. What is the proper hand signal flashed to the pack when the Road Captain wants the pack to assume a staggered formation?
83. What is the proper hand signal flashed to the pack when the Road Captain wants the pack to assume the suicide (two abreast) formation?
84. When the Road Captain lifts his hand up to indicate a left or right turn what does the rest of the pack do?
85. What is the proper hand signal flashed to the pack when the Road Captain wants the pack to slow down?
86. What is the proper hand signal flashed to the pack when the Road Captain wants the pack to continue while he drops out of the pack to view it for safety?
87. What is the proper hand signal flashed to the pack when the Road Captain wishes to change places with the Assistant Road Captain in the back of the pack?
88. What is the best way for a motorcycle to cross railroad tracks in an intersection?
89. During a rainstorm when is the road the slickest for a motorcycle?
90. Why does the front brake have more braking power than the rear brake on a motorcycle?
91. According to distribution of impact locations on motorcycle helmets during collision studies conducted by Dietmar Otte, Medizinische Hochschule Hannover, and Abteilung Verkehrsunfallforschung in Germany, where are most head injuries concentrated for motorcyclists?
92. What does DOT stand for and why is it important when purchasing a motorcycle helmet?

Motorcycle Club Protocol 101

93. What is a freedom fighter in the MC world?
94. What does FTW mean?
95. What does KTRSD mean?
96. What does LE/LEO mean?
97. What is an OMC?
98. What is an OMG?
99. Are cell phones allowed in your church meetings?
100. What is the consequence for secretly taping your church meetings?
101. What is an MRO?
102. What does the term "On Ground" mean?
103. What does the term "On Two" mean?
104. What does the term "Patch Over" mean?
105. What does the term "Flipping" mean?
106. What is a PRO?
107. What is a probie?
108. What are the major differences between an RC and an MC?
109. What is the RICO act?
110. What is a rocker?
111. What is a run?
112. What is a gypsy run?
113. What is special about a mandatory run?
114. What is a tail gunner?
115. What does the diamond "13" mean?
116. What is the significance of the three-piece patch?
117. What is the significance of turning your back on another MC or patched person?
118. What does (X)FF(X) mean?
119. What does DILLIGAF mean?
120. What is a boneyard?
121. What is a 5%er?
122. What is a 3%er?
123. What is a lick and stick?

Motorcycle Club Protocol 101

124. What does the term "Running 66" mean?
125. What is a vested pedestrian?
126. What is a hang-around?
127. What is a civilian?
128. What is a "Property of"?
129. What is a House Mamma?
130. What is an ink slinger?
131. How often should the financial report be given at your MC's church?
132. Where must your MC's colors be purchased?
133. What are your rights if you ever face your MC's disciplinary committee?
134. What is necessary for you to be found guilty of a charge in your MC?
135. Who are the closest MCs to yours that can be considered to love your MC like brothers and where your MC will always have a home away from home (allies)?
136. What is a dominant MC?
137. Is there a such thing as a dominant MC?
138. It is possible for someone to Prospect for an MC without owning a motorcycle?
139. If you don't like the direction the pack is going you can simply leave the pack, take a shortcut, and catch up to the pack later? Y/N
140. Folks can join your MC without prospecting? T/F
141. It is okay for a brother in an MC to pop a wheelie in the pack? T/F
142. It is okay to leave a brother in trouble on the road if he can't keep up? T/F
143. It is okay to screw a brother's old lady or wife? T/F
144. Can the Road Captain fine a member without a trial for infractions committed in the pack?
145. When can the Road Captain of an MC order a member not to ride their bike?

146. Does the Road Captain have the right to see a member's license, registration, and insurance in your MC?
147. When is it okay to give out personal information about an MC member to someone outside of the MC?
148. It is okay for another MC's President to attend a function thrown by your MC without being searched for a weapon if everyone else is being searched?
149. What is the ranking order for the way your MC rides in formation?
150. Who was the first Godfather of your MC, and what was his contribution to the MC?
151. Who is the Godfather of your MC today?
152. When is the Road Captain considered the President of your MC?
153. What is required to take a leave of absence from your MC?
154. When are you allowed to retire from your MC?
155. Where are standard business cards ordered for your MC?
156. How do you get a MC email address?
157. What duties must a Prospect perform daily in your MC?
158. What is the name of the most honored member within your MC?
159. Does your MC have a National President and if so, what is his name?
160. How many MCs operate in your town and what are the names of twenty-five of them?
161. What is the C.O.C.?
162. What is meant by the term "Top 5" when talking about MCs?
163. Name the OMCs in every state surrounding yours.
164. What is a support MC?
165. It is okay to walk into an MC representing your MC without wearing your colors?
166. Should you have a Set of colors with you no matter where you travel?

Motorcycle Club Protocol 101

167. What is the mission statement of your MC Nation?
168. Does handling a problem internally within the MC relieve you of your legal responsibility to call law enforcement if you think a crime has been committed?
169. What are the rules for all members to stand duty at the clubhouse should your MC have a clubhouse?
170. What are your MC's local website URLs?
171. What is the phone number and password used for your MC's conference calls?
172. How do you jump start a motorcycle?
173. When would you jump start a motorcycle?
174. Can you use a car to jump start a motorcycle safely?
175. How do you push start a motorcycle?
176. How do you pick up a motorcycle if it falls over?
177. Do your MC brothers ride in formation—staggered or suicide?
178. Where is lane splitting legal in the United States?
179. When encountering a tornado on the open road should you take refuge under a bridge? Why or why not? (Refer to http://www.srh.noaa.gov/oun/?n=safety-overpass, especially slide 22 – this may save your life!)
180. What should be done to avoid tornadoes in open country?
181. If on the open highway and you encounter sudden heavy fog, how should you seek to protect yourself?
182. When riding a passenger on the back of a motorcycle cross country in extreme heat (100° F or higher) degrees what is one of the greatest mechanical concerns?
183. When riding a motorcycle cross country in extreme heat (100° F or higher) degrees how can you quickly cool off if you feel overwhelmed by the heat?
184. When traveling cross country through various OMC territories what should your MC do before entering their territory in patches?
185. If riding a motorcycle cross country what auto parts store

will always carry motorcycle batteries?
186. How does the AAA club motorcycle towing package' differ from your motorcycle insurance coverage towing plan?
187. When riding female from another organization on the back of your motorcycle should you ask her to remove her colors or turn them inside out, and if so—why?
188. If your MC is national what is your local chapter's responsibility to your MC Nation?
189. If your MC chapter needs a bank account, is it okay for a member to put that account in his name alone?
190. Why do you want to be a member of your MC?
191. What do you bring to your MC?
192. What do you want from your MC?
193. What can you give to your MC?

For answers to this test send an email to blackdragon@blacksabbathmc.com. Put "MC Test Answers" in the subject. Also, in that email you can let me know how you like the book, or suggestions you may have for additional subjects, corrections, or grammar issues. Thank you.

◊◊◊

Appendix A: Brief History of the Mighty Black Sabbath Motorcycle Club Nation

Mighty Black Sabbath Motorcycle Club Nation

The Mighty Black Sabbath Motorcycle Club Nation is a national, traditional MC whose members ride all makes of street legal motorcycles (cruisers at least 750cc and sport bikes at least 600cc). The Mighty Black Sabbath Motorcycle Club Nation does not belong to any governing organizations like the AMA. It is an independent MC nation that does not wear support patches or coalition support insignia. The Black Sabbath MC derived its name from the Original Seven African American male founders who rode on Sundays after church. When the Original Seven were looking for a name to call themselves—they said, "We are seven Black men who ride on the Sabbath after worship, so let us call ourselves Black Sabbath MC!"

Though we have been asked many times throughout the decades our founders had never heard of the band named Black Sabbath when they started the MC.

History
The Original Seven founding fathers of the Mighty Black Sabbath Motorcycle Club Nation taught themselves to ride on one Honda 305 Scrambler in the hills of a neighborhood called Mount Hope in

San Diego, California in 1972. That bike, given to father 'Pep' by a close friend, was shared between them. The founding fathers mostly worked at the San Diego Gas and Electric Company or were enlisted in the US Navy, some were merchant marines. They practiced evenings and weekends on the Honda 305 Scrambler, until they eventually learned how to ride, and each eventually bought a motorcycle.

Faithfully, they gathered at each other's garages after church on Sundays to ride, tell tall tales, and drink beers. By 1974, their wives united and revolted, demanding that no more club meetings be held in their garages on Sundays because the neighbors kept complaining and the wives felt threatened by the strength of the brotherhood. Undaunted, the founding fathers rented an abandoned bar at 4280 Market Street; where they remained one of the most dominant, influential, and successful MCs on the African American Biker Set since 1974 (nearly fifty years at the time of this writing).

Founding Fathers
The seven original founding fathers were:
- First Rider: Robert D. Hubbard 'Sir Hub' (SDG&E Electrician)
- VP: William Charles Sanders 'Couchie' (SDG&E Electrician)
- Sgt-at-Arms Alvin Ray 'Stretch'
- Road Capt.: Paul Perry 'Pep' (SDG&E Meter Reader)
- Asst Road Capt.: Solomon 'Sol'
- Secretary: John Kearny 'Black'
- Clayton Mitchell "Mitch" (Designer of our colors)

Note: Originally the leader of the BSMC was called "First Rider." We did not adopt the term "President" for many years later.

Racing roots
The Black Sabbath MC was not complicated in its mission during the early years. It was comprised simply of seven men who loved to ride, mostly on Sundays, who were similarly possessed with an insatiable appetite for custom building "Choppers" and unbeatable

drag race bikes. This is still true today. All bike styles are welcomed, and racers are still most cherished in the Mighty Black Sabbath Motorcycle Club Nation.

Battle cry "I came to race"
The MC's battle cry was fathered by Black Sabbath MC legend-fabled racer, Allen 'Sugar Man' Brooks, who once wrecked Pep's motorcycle (early 1970's), on the way to the Salton Sea bike run/race event, without a helmet at over one hundred ten mph. Pep had warned Sugar Man that his bike was not operating properly and was excessively vibrating when it got to one hundred mph—so he told him not to exceed one hundred mph on the bike. Sugar Man still insisted that Pep let him test it. Needless to say, he exceeded one hundred mph and the bike went into a high-speed wobble. He crashed and destroyed Pep's bike. After the accident, Sugar Man was forbidden to compete as the MC deemed that he was too injured to race. The President threatened to take his colors if he attempted to compete in the drag racing the next day. Sugar Man said, "You can take these damned colors if you will, but I came to race!" Sugar Man consequently won the drag racing competition despite his injuries; thereby etching himself into the Black Sabbath MC's history books. His battle cry has been echoed by Black Sabbath racers from that time until now; "I came to race!"

San Diego Mother Chapter
The Mighty Black Sabbath Motorcycle Club Nation's mother chapter clubhouse stood at 4280 Market Street on the corner for forty-three years. During most of that time the MC reined dominant as the most successful MC in San Diego and is the oldest surviving MC on the Black biker set there. For decades, the Black Sabbath MC clubhouse was the only clubhouse on the Black biker set in the city. During that time, all San Diego and Los Angeles MCs came to San Diego to celebrate the Black Sabbath MC's yearly anniversary, which grew to be called "The First Run of the Year." Even to this day, West Coast MCs gather in San Diego for the first run which generally happens around the second or third weekend in February. These

days Mighty Black Sabbath MC Nation chapters around the country send their riders on this great pilgrimage across the United States braving freezing winters to get to this annual celebration. This run was named by Black Dragon as "The Cold Ass Run to The Mother Chapter." Brothers who make this ride are awarded the Snow Bear Disciples patch.

Nationwide chapters

The Mighty Black Sabbath Motorcycle Club Nation has chapters across the United States from coast to coast. Growth was initially slow as the MC never envisioned itself a national MC from its inception in San Diego in 1974. The Black Sabbath MC is also the oldest surviving MC born in San Diego. The second charter was not given until 1989 some fifteen years after the MC started. Club racing legend, Allen 'Sugar Man' Brooks, took the colors to Wichita, Kansas where Knight Rider and Lady Magic (previously members of the Penguins MC) developed the chapter; subsequently becoming the oldest surviving MC on the Black biker set in Wichita.

In 1999, then National President Pep, launched the Denver, Colorado chapter. Not long after, he assigned veteran member, Leonard Mack, to head up the Minneapolis, Minnesota chapter. Two years later, Pep ordered Dirty Red to launch the St. Paul, Minnesota chapter. In 2004, Pep launched the Little Rock, Arkansas chapter with his nephew, Lewis 'Doc' Perry, who became the first East Coast Regional President. Once again, two years later Doc launched the Oklahoma City, Oklahoma chapter with his high school buddy, James 'JB' Baker, as President. In 2008 former mother chapter President, Dewey 'Jazz' Johnson, launched the Phoenix, Arizona chapter. By then, the Wichita, Kansas chapter was all but dead with only a few active members.

Exponential growth was not seen until 2009 when then National Enforcer John E. 'Black Dragon' Bunch II was given the mandate by Father Pep to build the club into a national powerhouse. Pep's dream, as intimated to Dragon, all the way back in 1997, was to construct a legendary national MC known worldwide for hard riding on iron that could one day become a household name. Black Dragon accepted the assignment. His first move was to convince Sugar Man to come out of retirement and together they launched the Tulsa, Oklahoma chapter. Black Dragon then rebuilt the Wichita, Kansas chapter over the next three years, but despite his best efforts it could not sustain the re-launch until Lady Magic tapped her son, 'Pull-it', and grandson, Chris 'Chill' Hill. With the addition of those two brothers the Wichita chapter again soared. Black Dragon simultaneously re-launched the Atlanta, Georgia chapter with former Oklahoma City member, Pappy, who had also grown up with Doc Perry. Later, in 2009, Black Dragon launched the Houston, Texas chapter with Bernard 'Krow' Augustus who became the first Mid-Central USA Regional President.

In 2010, the Atlanta, Georgia chapter (originally launched in 2000 by Dragon) was taken over by Black Dragon's former submarine shipmate, Leon 'Eight Ball' Richardson, who also became the second East Coast Regional President. Black Dragon became National President in 2010, and patched over the Macon, Georgia chapter under Curtis 'Ride or Die' Hill from the Zulus MC Nation under a negotiation with 'Wolverine' then the Zulus National President. 'Ride or Die' became the third East Coast Regional President and eventually rose to become the fourth National President of the Mighty Black Sabbath MC Nation. Black Dragon then patched-over Sic Wit' It MC in Rome, Georgia under President G Man to make Black Sabbath MC among the few clubs to achieve three chapters in Georgia at that time.

Sugar Man's first cousin, Jamel 'Huggy Bear' Brooks, launched the San Antonio, Texas chapter by the end of 2010, and became the first West Coast Regional President assuming command of the Phoenix, Arizona chapter later. Black Dragon instructed then National Vice President Tommy 'Hog Man' Lewis and Huggy Bear to patch over the Inland Empire, California chapter under the leadership of former Regulator MC President 'Big Dale' in 2011. Big Dale eventually became the second West Coast Regional President. In 2012, National Vice President Tommy 'Hog Man' Lewis received a blessing from the Chosen Few MC to open the Las Vegas, Nevada chapter with then West Coast Regional President Huggy Bear, but this chapter never actually materialized. In 2012, Black Dragon launched the Jacksonville, Florida chapter under President 'Prime'. In 2014, Black Dragon instructed West Coast Regional President Big Dale to patch over a former 1%er club that had been shut down due to west coast external conflicts. It launched in Riverside, California as the Riverside chapter under President Bob 'Bob O' Rinaldi. In 2015, Black Dragon opened the Hutchinson, Kansas chapter under President Dizzle. External problems with local 1%ers caused them to have to fly "West Wichita" colors for nearly three years, but eventually, through continued negotiations the Hutchinson chapter finally flew their rightful city once again. In 2015 Black Dragon launched the Colorado Springs, Colorado chapter under President 'G-Ride' which flies under the Olympic City flag today. In 2016 Black Dragon opened the Topeka, Kansas chapter under President Cliff 'Big Red Dog'. Consequently, the chapter bounced up and down for nearly four years and never fully opened until about late 2019. In 2017 Black Dragon launched the Beaufort, South Carolina chapter under President Homesick after nearly three years of negotiations with local 1%ers. In 2017 Black Dragon gave President Jason 'Ol' Skool' Monds the mandate to open the Pensacola, Florida chapter but it took until 2019 to secure all necessary agreements to bring it online. Also in 2017, after nearly four years of work Black Dragon opened the Fort Worth, Texas chapter under President Big Mixx who was the second longest prospecting member of the Mighty Black Sabbath MC Nation. In late 2017 early 2018 Black Dragon launched the RONIN chapter of the Mighty Black Sabbath MC Nation which was the Nation's first nomad chapter. Shortly after that he stepped down from the position of National President. In 2020 Black Dragon consulted with President Big Mixx to open the West Fort Worth chapter and in 2021 Black Dragon launched the North Shore Louisiana chapter under President Cuban and the Frederick Maryland chapter under President Devil. In April 2021

Black Dragon began prospecting the Lagos Nigeria chapter, his third attempt to forge into Africa but he failed to bring it to fruition once again. Black Dragon came out of retirement in 2022 to become the fifth East Coast Regional President and began the patch-over of the Shadow Riders RC to the Columbus Maryland chapter. He also approved the introduction of the new Savannah chapter. During his retirement the Orlando chapter (started by Bones), Wisconsin (started by Loki and Goose), Kansas City (started by), and Spring Texas (started by Miles) chapters were born. Mid-central Regional President Miles also began to re-establish the Oklahoma City, Oklahoma chapter. Hail to the forefathers of the Mighty Black Sabbath Motorcycle Club Nation! We hope they are proud of what their dreams have become. Amen.

Membership

A prospective member is allowed into the Black Sabbath Motorcycle Club as a "hang-around," indicating that the individual is invited to some MC events or to meet MC members at known gathering places. This period could last several months to several years. It is the time for the hang-around to evaluate the MC, as well as for the MC to evaluate the hang-around. If the hang-around is interested, and the Black Sabbath Motorcycle Club likes the hang-around; he can request to be voted in as a Prospect. The hang-around must win a majority vote to be designated a Prospect. If he is successful, he will be given a sponsor and his prospectship begins. The prospectship will be no less than ninety days, but could last for years, depending upon the attitude and resourcefulness of the Prospect. Former National President Black Dragon prospected for nearly five years before he crossed over. The Prospect will participate in some MC activities and serve the MC in whatever capacity the full patched brothers may deem appropriate. A Prospect will never be asked to commit any illegal act, any act against nature, or any physically humiliating or demeaning act. The Black Sabbath Motorcycle Club never hazes Prospects. A Prospect will not have voting privileges while he is evaluated for suitability as a full member but does pay MC dues.

The last phase, and highest membership status, is "Full Membership" or "Full-Patch". The term "Full-Patch" refers to the complete one-piece patch. Prospects are allowed to wear only a small thirteen-inch patch with the letters of the local chapter (i.e., BSSD) and the black cross on it. To become a full patched brother the Prospect must be presented by his sponsor before the MC and win a one hundred percent affirmative vote from the full patched brothers. Prior to votes being cast, a Prospect usually travels to every chapter in the sponsoring chapter's geographic region (state/province/territory) and introduces himself to every full patched brother. This process allows all regional chapter members to become familiar with the Prospect. Some form of formal induction follows, wherein the Prospect affirms his loyalty to the MC and its members. Often the Prospect's sponsor may require him to make a nomadic journey on his motorcycle before crossing over, sometimes as far as 1,000 miles that must be completed within twenty-four hours to ensure that the Prospect understands the Black Sabbath Motorcycle Club is a riding motorcycle club. The final logo patch is then awarded at his swearing in and initiation ceremony. The step of attaining full membership can be referred to as "being patched", "patching in" or "crossing over."

Command Structure
- National President
- National Vice President
- High Council President
- High Council
- National Business Manager
- National Ambassador
- Regional President
- President
- Vice President
- Secretary

- Sgt-at-Arms
- Road Captain
- Treasurer
- Business Manager
- Public Relations Officer
- Media/Web Design Officer
- Full Patch Member
- First Lady S.O.T.C.
- Full Patch S.O.T.C.
- Head Goddess
- Full Patch Goddess
- Support Crew
- Prospect
- S.O.T.C. Prospect
- Goddess Prospect
- Hang Around
- Special officers include Disaster Chief, Nomad/Ronin, National Sgt-at-Arms, Enforcer, Support Crew Chief, Father, Godfather, and Godmother.

Colors

The Black Sabbath Motorcycle Club patch is called the "Turtle Shell". The colors are set out on a white background inside a black circle, inside a black crested shield, with the words Black Sabbath MC encircling the riding man. The crested shield on the sixteen-inch back patch gives the appearance of a turtle's shell when worn as it covers most members' entire back. The MC's colors are white, yellow, black, and blue.

In the fifty-year history of the MC the colors have remained untouched except for the addition of the shield in 1975 and the enlargement of the patch to nineteen inches by sixteen inches in 2009. The adherence to the original patch mirrors their adherence to the core values of the Original Seven founding forefathers.

Racial Policies

Because the Black Sabbath Motorcycle Club was started by African Americans and its membership is primarily African American (90%) it is considered to be on the 'Black biker set" by biker clubs across America. However, the Black Sabbath Motorcycle Club states that even though it was started by seven African American men who rode on Sundays, today it is a multi-racial organization that is accepting of all religions, ilk, creed, class, caste, social status, or financial standing in members, with chapters across the United States from coast to coast. The Mighty Black Sabbath Motorcycle Club Nation is a brotherhood based on a unified lifestyle centered on riding motorcycles, living the biker lifestyle, and embracing one another as extended family- as close as any blood relatives.

Neutrality

The Mighty Black Sabbath Motorcycle Club Nation has followed all MC protocol in setting up its chapters nationwide. To that end, it has secured negotiations to operate by dominants in every area in which it has chapters. As a neutral elite traditional motorcycle-enthusiast riding MC the Mighty Black Sabbath Motorcycle Club Nation wears no support patches as it takes no political sides and does not align itself with OMC politics.

Women in the Black Sabbath MC Nation

A male dominated organization, the Mighty Black Sabbath Motorcycle Club Nation men belong to the brotherhood of the cross. Women fall into two unique categories. Women who do not ride motorcycles belong to our female social club known as "Goddesses of the Mighty Black Sabbath Motorcycle Club Nation". Women who ride motorcycles belong to the "Sisters of the Cross MC of the Mighty Black Sabbath Motorcycle Club Nation".

Sisters of the Cross MC

The Sisters of the Cross MC of the Mighty Black Sabbath Motorcycle Club Nation (SOTC) is a female motorcycle club that rides under the protection of the full patched brothers of the Black Sabbath

Motorcycle Club. The SOTC was established in 2011 by then National President, Black Dragon. SOTC Prospects must be eighteen years old, own a motorcycle and have a motorcycle driver's license. The SOTC are called the "First Ladies of the Black Sabbath Motorcycle Club", and the ranking SOTC is called First Lady. The SOTC MC was created to recognize the achievements of many of the Goddesses of the Black Sabbath Motorcycle Club who were buying, learning how to ride, and getting licenses for motorcycles at an incredible rate. The Mighty Black Sabbath Motorcycle Club Nation sought to reward the hard work and passion to ride these women displayed by giving them their own MC under the auspices of the Mighty Black Sabbath Motorcycle Club Nation.

Goddesses of the Cross
The "Goddesses of the Cross" of the Mighty Black Sabbath Motorcycle Club Nation is the social club auxiliary that supports the MC. Goddess Prospects must be eighteen years old, be of exceptional character and devoted to serve the best interests of the Mighty Black Sabbath Motorcycle Club. The GOTC was created by then National President Black Dragon in 2010.

Mission Statement
1. "To become the greatest riding motorcycle club in the world by pounding down great distances on two wheels, bonding on the highways and byways as family, camping out while riding to biker events or cross country, enjoying the wilderness, racing, competing, winning, and experiencing our extended family by tenderly loving each other more and more each day!
2. To become the greatest motorcycle club family in the world by encouraging diversity within our MC, building strong, lasting friendships among members, instilling a sense of love, pride, and togetherness within our communities, helping those in need through volunteerism, and cultivating a mindset of moral and social responsibility amongst our

members; also, by inspiring our youth to achieve beyond all limitations which will leave a legacy of hope and boundless dreams for future generations of the Mighty Black Sabbath Motorcycle Club Nation to come."

National President

The office of the National President was created by Tommy 'Hog Man' Lewis then President of the mother chapter and former mother chapter President Dewey 'Jazz' Johnson in the summer of 2000. Paul 'Pep' Perry, the last original founding member left in the chapter, was elected the first National President. Curtis 'Mad Mitch' Mitchell was appointed first National Vice President one year later. Pep also created the office of National Ambassador to which he assigned Jazz. The National Vice President position was eventually terminated. In 2010, Godfather Washington of the Mighty Black Sabbath Motorcycle Club Nation died, and Pep retired to become Godfather. National Enforcer and President of the Atlanta chapter, Black Dragon, was summoned to the mother chapter in San Diego and was elected as the second National President of the Mighty Black Sabbath Motorcycle Club Nation during the February mother chapter annual dance. Black Dragon recreated the National Vice President office and recruited then retired former San Diego President Hog Man for the position. Black Dragon created the High Council President office to which he assigned Sabbath racing legend Sugar Man. He also created the High Council which consists of the President and Vice President of every chapter. Black Dragon also created the National Sgt-at-Arms, National Business Manager, Nomad/Ronin, Disaster Chief, Support Chief, and Public Relations Officers (PRO) offices.

Riding Awards and Designations

In order to challenge his MC members to ride harder and to distinguish the Mighty Black Sabbath Motorcycle Club Nation as a superior elite motorcycle-enthusiast riding MC, Black Dragon created the Nomad Rider program. In an article written in the Black Sabbath Magazine, Black Dragon stated, "A historic traditional MC

Nation is nothing if its members do not ride!" The Nomad Rider program recognizes and awards Black Sabbath Motorcycle Club nomad riders for their achievements. Some of the awards include:

- Nomad Rider = 1,000 miles one-way (N1)
- 1 K in 1 Day Nomad = 1,000 miles one-way ridden in twenty-four hours or less (N124)
- Nomad Traveler = 2,000 miles one-way (N2)
- Nomad Warrior = 3,000 miles one-way (N3)
- Nomad Adventurer = 4,000 miles one-way (N4)
- Nomad Wanderer = 5,000 miles one-way (N5)
- Snow Bear Disciple Nomad = one hundred miles traveled in sleet, snow, or 18° F (SBN)
- Poseidon's Disciples Nomad = traveling through three states during continuous driving rain (PSN)
- Great Plains Nomad = riding across the Oklahoma or Kansas great plains (GPN)
- Panhandle Nomad = riding across the great state of Texas (TPN)
- Great Winds Nomad = riding through fifty mph windstorm (GWN)
- 1,000-mile bull's horn = eleven-inch bull's blowing horn, awarded to all Nomad Riders
- 2,000-mile Kudu's horn shofar = twenty-three-inch Kudu antelope's blowing horn, awarded to all Nomad Travelers
- 3,000-mile Kudu's horn shofar = thirty-three-inch Kudu or Blesbok antelope's blowing horn, awarded to all Nomad Warriors
- 4,000-mile horn shofar = forty-inch Kudu, Blesbok or Impala antelope's blowing horn, awarded to all Nomad Adventurers; can be Kudu, Blesbok or Impala
- 5,000-mile horn shofar = fifty-inch antelope's blowing horn, awarded to all Nomad Wanderers; can be any horned cloven-footed animal.

Violence

Violent incidents have occurred in and around nationwide clubhouses.

- In 2002, President 'Bull' of the Zodiacs MC was killed after he pulled a gun on his former Prospect, who was partying at the mother chapter with a new MC in which he was interested. The former Prospect slashed Bull's throat with a knife when he looked away during the confrontation. This was the first killing ever committed at a Black Sabbath MC clubhouse and brought the city of San Diego down on the club. The City Attorney initiated a campaign to shut down the clubhouse nearly finishing the Black Sabbath MC. The clubhouse was subsequently firebombed in retaliation for Bull's killing.
- In February 2010, the mother chapter at 4280 Market Street was again targeted by arsonists who attempted to burn it to the ground right before the 2010 annual. They were unsuccessful.
- In 2010, a man was fatally shot in a hail of gunfire near the Phoenix chapter of the Black Sabbath MC clubhouse during an altercation over a woman. He died a block away while fleeing the scene. This incident caused the closing of the Phoenix chapter clubhouse.
- On 11 May 2012, San Diego mother chapter President, 'Wild Dogg', was murdered in front of the Black Sabbath Motorcycle Club clubhouse at 4280 Market Street during a drive by assassination. The case is still unsolved and open.

Decline of the Mighty Black Sabbath MC Nation

In 2018 the Black Sabbath MC entered an unprecedented period of decline. It is hard to see what the way forward for the club will be. Bylaws have been ignored, members thrown out without trials, presidents demoted without charges and there was even an attempt to throw me out bad without a trial on a podcast in front of the world – breaking long standing MC tradition and protocol. Lies and destruction of brothers' reputations, hearts and contributions has been unleashed by an egotistical grab for the power of 'National President for life' by a corrupt leader who will lie as quickly as he breaths. The erosion of bylaws, personal aggrandizement, and unchecked egos has brought nothing but misery, decline, and embarrassment to the nation. I have written about this tragic betrayal in my newest book President's Bible Chronicle II Betrayal of the Brotherhood where I detail the transgressions of the National President Curtis 'Ride or Die' Hill and his band of buffoons. They have disgraced every advancement the club has made in the past 36 years. I've decided not to go into detail in this book to keep it purely educational but understand this: Knowing MC PROTOCOL IS CRUCIAL TO RUNNING AN MC NATION WITH COMPETENCE!

Epilogue

"Everything that I stand so firmly against today, I once was! It is only through experience, pain, suffering, and being blessed to learn life's lessons that I have evolved to whom I've become. I've lived my MC career making the best choices I could, given the challenges I've faced. Still, I continue to strive at being the best brother I possibly can be.

John E. Bunch II
Black Dragon
Lifer
Mighty Black Sabbath MC Nation

◊◊◊

Motorcycle Club Protocol 101

Glossary

1%er: Initially a description falsely attributed to the AMA to describe some of the MCs that attended Rolling Gypsy race meets. It was alleged that the AMA stated that 99% of the people at their events were God fearing and family oriented. The other 1% were hoodlums, thugs, and outlaws. Non-AMA sanctioned MCs, thus being seen as outlaws, adopted the 1%er moniker and embraced it as an identity. Over time the 1%er designation became exclusively associated with OMGs, criminal biker syndicates, and some OMCs. Though not all 1%ers are criminals it is certain that the 1% diamond designation attracts law enforcement scrutiny like no other symbol on a biker's cut.

5%er: A member of an MRO. Only five percent of motorcyclists are involved with MROs that are dedicated to protecting the rights of the other ninety-five percent of bikers by spending money, dedicating time, and championing pro-biker legislation.

80/20 Rule: A requirement held by some MC councils requiring all blessed MCs within a council's region to demonstrate, via a bike count, that 80% of the MC's members have operational motorcycles at all times.

AMA: American Motorcyclist Association

ABATE: An organization started by Easy Rider Magazine to fight against discrimination toward motorcyclists, mostly helmet laws originally. Once called "A Brotherhood Against Totalitarian Enactments" or "American Bikers Against Totalitarian Enactments", ABATE now has many other names including "American Brotherhood (or Bikers) Aimed Toward Education." ABATE fights for biker rights and champions many issues well beyond helmet laws. Members often help charities. Membership comes with yearly dues and officers are elected from the active membership.

Ape Hangers: Tall handlebars that place a biker's hands at or above his shoulder height.

Backyard: Where you ride often—never defecate there.

Baffle: Sound deadening material inside a muffler that quiets the exhaust noises.

Motorcycle Club Protocol 101

Bike Count: To stem the tide of the so called "popup clubs" some councils require a minimum number of motorcycles to be in a MC before they will allow it to start up in their region. MC numbers are proven when the MC undergoes a bike count of its members; usually with all members present on their bikes.

Black Ball List: A list enacted by an MC coalition or council. It is directed at non-compliant MCs that serve to notify other MCs not to support the "black-balled" chapter nor allow it to participate in any coalition authorized Set functions.

Blockhead: The V-twin engine Harley, 1984 – 2000.

Boneyard: Salvage yard for used bikes and parts.

Brain Bucket: Small, beanie-style helmet (usually not Department of Transportation (DOT) approved).

Broad: A female entertainer for the MC. She may be a dancer or at times a prostitute.

Broken Wings: A patch meaning the rider has been in a crash.

BS: bullshit: NONESENSE usually vulgar: to talk foolishly, boastfully, or idly: to engage in a discursive discussion.

Burnout: Spinning the rear wheel while holding the front brake. (Conducting burnouts while visiting another MC's clubhouse is disrespectful as it brings complaints from the neighborhood and invites unwanted police attention. Make trouble in your own neighborhood and be respectful with noise and other commotion while visiting others.)

Cage: Any vehicle of four or more wheels, specifically not a motorcycle.

Cager: Driver of a cage. (Usually, cagers are thought of as dangerous to bikers because they do not pay attention to the road.)

Chopper: A bike with the front end raked or extended out.

Chromeitis: A disease associated with a biker that cannot seem to buy enough aftermarket accessories (especially chrome).

Church: Clubhouse ("Having church" or "going to church" is referred to as the club meeting at the clubhouse).

CLAP: Chrome, Leather, Accessories, Performance

Clone: A motorcycle built to resemble and function like a Harley-Davidson motorcycle without actually being a Harley-Davidson motorcycle.

Club Name: Also known as a handle. A name given to a MC member by his brothers most often based upon his character, routine, quirks, and/or a noteworthy event that happened in the MC of which that member played a part. This is usually a name of honor and often indicates the personality one might expect when encountering that member. This name is generally accepted with great pride by the member and is a handle he will adopt for a lifetime. For instance, I once became annoyed with a member of the Black Sabbath Atlanta chapter for giving me a hard time when I needed him to break into my house and get the keys to my trailer so he could rescue me from the side of the road in Little Rock, AR nine hours away. He gave me so much grief about my trailer registration, working condition of my signal lights, and notifying authorities before he would break in my place that I frustratingly named him "By-the-Book", instantly changing his name from "Glock." By-the-Book so loved his new name that when he later departed the Mighty Black Sabbath M.C. Nation, he took his name with him and is still called By-the-Book to this very day. It is an honor for the MC to name you and quite improper for you to name yourself.

Club Hopping: The frowned upon practice of switching memberships from one MC to another. Traditional MCs have low tolerance for bikers who "club hop" as this phenomenon breaks down good order and discipline in MCs. In fact, this was seldom done in the early days. Most coalitions and councils regulate club hopping and enact vigorous laws against it. Often, OMCs refuse to allow former members to wear another MC's colors after serving in their OMC. An MC should generally ensure that a club hopper waits at least six months before allowing them to prospect for their MC unless the former President sanctions the move.

Colors: Unique motorcycle club back patch or patches.

Crash Bar: Engine guard that protects the engine if the bike crashes.

CreditGlide: A RUB's Motorcycle.

Crotch Rocket / Rice Burner: A sport bike.

Counter Steering: Turning the bike's handlebars in one direction and having it go in the opposite direction. All bikers should learn this maneuver for safety.

Custom: A custom-built motorcycle.

Cut: Vest containing the MC colors. The name comes from the practice of cutting the sleeves off of blue denim jackets.

DILLIGAF: "Do I Look Like I Give A Fuck?"

DOT: Department of Transportation.

Drag Bars: Low, flat, straight handlebars.

Evo /Evolution®: Evolution engine (V-Twin, 1984 – 2000).

Fathead: Twin-Cam engine (V-Twin, 1999 – Present).

Fender / Fender Fluff: A female passenger who is not an Old Lady but simply a lady a biker has invited for a ride.

Flathead: The Flathead engine (V-Twin, 1929 – 1972).

Flash Patch: Generic patch sold at meets and bike shops.

Flip: Occurs when an OMC takes over a less powerful OMC or 99%er. This can occur against that MC's will and could be violent. The less powerful MC will flip from their colors to the dominant MC's colors.

Flying Low: Speeding.

Forward Controls: Front pegs, shifter, and rear brake control moved forward (often to the highway pegs).

Freedom Fighter: An MRO member dedicated to preserving or gaining biker's rights and freedoms.

FTA: "Fuck Them All."

FTW: "Fuck the World" or "Forever Two Wheels."

Get-Back-Whip: A two-to-three-foot leather braid with an easy release hard metal clip that can be attached to the front brake handle or the clutch handle. Often it contains a lead weight at the bottom of the braid with tassels that just barely drag the ground when the bike is standing still. This ornamental decoration can quickly be released to make a formidable weapon to be used to slap against offending cages that invade a biker's road space (to include breaking out the cager's windows). Either end can be used in an offensive or defensive situation. The Get-Back-Whip is illegal in MANY states.

Hard Tail: A motorcycle frame with no rear suspension.

Motorcycle Club Protocol 101

Hang Around: The designation of a person who has indicated that he formally wants to get to know a MC so he can begin prospecting for them.

HOG: Harley Owners Group.

Independent: A biker who is not a member of a MC, but is normally a well-known, accepted individual of local Biker Set (of a higher order than a hang-around).

Ink: Tattoo.

Ink-Slinger: Tattoo Artist.

KTRSD: "Keep the Rubber Side Down" Riding safely and keeping both tires on the road instead of up in the air—as in having a wreck.

Knuck/Knucklehead: The Knucklehead engine (V-Twin 1936 – 1947).

LE/LEO: Law Enforcement Officer/Official.

Lick and Stick: A temporary pillion back seat placed on the fender through the use of suction cups.

MC: Motorcycle Club.

MM: Motorcycle Ministry (Also known as 5%ers).

Moonlight Mile: A short adventure with a lady friend away from camp.

MRO: Motorcycle Rights Organization. These organizations seek to protect the rights and freedoms of bikers (i.e., ABATE, BOLT, Motorcycle Riders Foundation, American Motorcycle Association, MAG, etc.).

MSF: Motorcycle Safety Foundation.

OEM: Original Equipment Manufacturer.

Old / Ole Lady: Girlfriend or wife of a biker, definitely off limits!

OMC: Outlaw Motorcycle Club.

OMG: Outlaw Motorcycle Gang.

On Ground: Refers to showing up on or riding a motorcycle instead of showing up in or driving a cage.

On Two: Refers to showing up on or riding a motorcycle instead of showing up in or driving a cage.

Pan/Pan Head: The Pan Head engine (V-Twin, 1948 – 1965).

Patch: The back patch is the colors of a MC.

Patch-Over: Like club flipping a patch-over occurs when a MC

changes patches from one MC to another. This is acceptable and not looked upon unfavorably in most cases. 99%er MCs patch-over MCs they acquire instead of "flipping" them because 99%ers do not enforce territory. This will be a peaceful gentlemen's agreement that happens unremarkably and without incident. 1%ers flip MCs.
Pillion Pad: Passenger Seat.
Pipes: Exhaust System.
PRO: Public Relations Officer.
Probate/Probie/Probationary: A member serving a period of probation until he is voted into full patched (full membership) status.
Probation: The period of time a Probie must serve before full membership is bestowed. This is the time distinguished from being a hang-around because the member is voted into the Probie status and is permitted to wear some form of the MCs colors. The Probie is also responsible to follow the MC's bylaws.
Prospect: A member serving a prospectship until he is voted into full patched (full membership) status.
Prospectship: The period of time a Prospect must serve before a vote for full membership is held. This is the time distinguished from being a hang-around because the prospective member is voted into the Prospect status and permitted to wear some form of the MCs colors. The Prospect is also responsible to follow the MC's bylaws.
Rags: Club colors or a Cut.
Rat Bike: A bike that has not been maintained or loved.
RC: Riding Club. A group that rides for enjoyment (perhaps under a patch), but members do not incur the responsibility of brotherhood to the level of traditional MCs, modern MCs, or OMCs. Members generally purchase their patches and do not often Prospect/Probie to become members. Rides and runs are generally voluntary and there is no mandatory participation. RCs are still required to follow MC protocol when operating on the MC Set and would do well to know the MC laws and respect them so as not to wind up in any kinds of altercations.
Revolution™: The Revolution engine, Harley-Davidson's first water-cooled engine (V-Twin, 2002 – Present)

RICO Act: Racketeer Influenced and Corrupt Organizations. Initially, these laws were passed for law enforcement to combat organized crime such as the mafia. They were quickly used to prosecute OMGs, OMCs, and some 99%er MCs.

Riding Bitch: Riding as the passenger on the back of a bike.

Road Name: Also known as a Handle. A name given to a MC member by his brothers and is most often based upon his character, routine, quirks, or a noteworthy event that happened in the MC of which that member played a part. This is usually a name of great honor and often indicates the personality one might expect when encountering that member. This name is generally accepted with great pride by the member and is a handle he will adopt for a lifetime.

Rocker: Bottom part of MC colors which usually designates geographic location or territory, though other information may be contained there such as the word "Nomad."

RUB: Rich Urban Biker.

Rubber: Tire.

Rubber Side Down: Riding safely and keeping both tires on the road instead of up in the air—as in having a wreck.

Run: Road trip "on two" with your brothers.

Running 66: Though rare it is sometimes necessary to ride without the MC's colors showing (also known as "riding incognito").

Shovel/Shovel Head: The Shovel Head engine (V-Twin, 1966 – 1984)

Shower Head: The new Harley-Davidson V-Rod motorcycle motor.

Sissy Bar Passenger Backrest.

Slab: Interstate.

Sled: Motorcycle.

Softail®: A motorcycle frame whose suspension is hidden, making it resemble a hard tail.

SMRO: State Motorcycle Rights Organization. Same as an MRO except defined by the state in which they operate, (i.e., ABATE of Oklahoma, MAG of Georgia, etc.).

Straight Pipes: An exhaust system with no Baffles.

Tats: Tattoos.

Tail Gunner: The last rider in the pack.

The Motorcyclist Memorial Wall: A biker's memorial wall located in Hopedale Ohio where the names of fallen riders are engraved for a nominal fee (www.motorcyclistmemorial.com). Memorial bricks may also be purchased to lie at the beautiful site.

The Motorcycle Memorial Foundation: The foundation that operates the Motorcyclist Memorial Wall. P.O. Box 2573 Wintersville, Ohio 43953.

Thirteen ("13") Diamond Patch: This is a patch commonly worn by some Outlaw MC Nations. The "13" symbol can have several meanings referencing the thirteenth letter of the alphabet, "M," standing for Marijuana, Methamphetamines, Motorcycle, or the original Mother Chapter of a MC. In Hispanic gang culture, "13" can represent "La Eme" (Mexican Mafia).

Three-Piece Patch: Generally thought of as being OMC colors consisting of a top rocker (name of MC), middle insignia (MC's symbol) and bottom rocker (name of state or territory MC claims). Not only OMCs wear three-piece patches, but new 99%er MCs should stay away from this design and stick to a one-piece patch.

Turn your back: A show of ultimate disrespect is to turn your back on someone.

Twisties: Section of road with a lot of increasing, distal, radial turns.

Vested Pedestrian: Is a person who is in a MC and wearing colors but does not own a motorcycle. Often thought of as a person who has never had a motorcycle, rather than someone who may be between bikes for a short period of time (i.e., a month or two).

Wannabe: Someone that tries to pretend to be a part of the biker lifestyle.

Wrench: Mechanic.

XXF-FXX/XXFOREVER – FOREVERXX: Patch worn by MC members to represent their total commitment to the MC and every other member of that MC. XX stands for the name of the MC (i.e., Black Sabbath Forever Forever Black Sabbath).

Thank you for reading my book Social Clubs Bible Revival of the Women's Social Clubs, "Lifting As We Ride!"

John E. Bunch II

About the Author

John E. Bunch II 'Black Dragon' rode on the back of a Honda Trail 50cc for the first time when he was six years old. Instantly, he was hooked! His mother could not afford to buy him a motorcycle so he borrowed anyone's bike that would let him ride- on the back roads and farms all over Oklahoma where he grew up. When he was fourteen his mother bought him a Yamaha 125 Enduro, cashing in the US Savings Bonds his father had given him. By the time he was seventeen, his stepfather, J.W. Oliver, gave him a Honda CX500. He was known throughout the neighborhood as the kid who always rode wheelies up the block (16th street and Classen), and as the kid who always rode wheelies with his brothers, Thea, and Lori, hanging off the back. He took his first long distance road trip at seventeen riding from Oklahoma City to Wichita, Kansas to visit his aunt and uncle. He knew then that he was born to distance ride! The nomadic call of the open road in the wind, rain, cold, heat—under the stars were home to him.

In the late 1980s, he found himself a young submarine sailor stationed in San Diego, California. He got into trouble on the base with a Senior Chief who gave him and his best friend an order they refused to follow. The white Senior Chief did not want to see the young Black man's career ended over insubordination, so he did Bunch an extreme favor. He sent him and his insolent friend, Keith (Alcatraz) Corley, who was similarly in trouble; to see African American, then Senior Chief, George G. Clark III, instead of to a Courts Martial. Senior Chief Clark threatened Bunch and Corley with physical violence if they did not obey the white Senior Chief and worked out a solution that saved both of their careers. Later, Clark invited them to 4280 Market Street when he discovered Bunch had a love for motorcycles. Bunch walked into the mother chapter and was blown away to learn that Senior Chief Clark was also known as 'Magic', former President of the Black Sabbath Motorcycle Club Mother Chapter. His insubordinate ways were not quite behind him, so it took Bunch several years to actually cross over as a full patch brother known as 'Black Dragon' in the Black Sabbath Motorcycle Club Mother Chapter.

In 2000, Black Dragon began advising writer/filmmaker Reggie Rock Bythewood, who co-wrote and directed the Dream Works movie Biker Boyz. Black Dragon went to Hollywood and worked as the Technical Adviser on the film. Biker Boyz has often been credited with re-birthing the African American MC movement in the United States.

In 2000 Black Dragon brought the Black Sabbath Motorcycle Club to Atlanta, GA and was blessed by President Skull of the Outcast MC Nation to start the chapter but the Atlanta chapter never really gained steam until he got serious about it in 2009. He suffered his first setback in Atlanta during a coup d'é·tat that cost him the Presidency of the Atlanta chapter in December 2010. In February 2011, he was elected to the Office of National President and began his nationwide march to spread the Black Sabbath Motorcycle Club from coast to coast. By 2011, the Black Sabbath Motorcycle Club became the Mighty Black Sabbath Motorcycle Club Nation with chapters from the West coast to the East coast.

2002 to 2013 Black Dragon has published several biker magazines including: *Urban Biker Cycle News, Black Iron Motorcycle Magazine, Black Sabbath Motorcycle Newsletter,* and the popular blog *www.blacksabbathmagazine.com.*

In 2013, Black Dragon wrote his first MC phone app, *"Black Sabbath Motorcycle Club."*

In 2014 Black Dragon wrote "Prospect's Bible" which has become required reading for over 3,000 MCs worldwide.

In 2015 Black Dragon wrote "MC Public Relations Officer's Bible" and "Prospect's Bible for Women's MCs."

In 2016 Black Dragon started the wildly popular YouTube channel "Black Dragon National President" which eventually became "Black Dragon Biker TV." It quickly rose to become the number 1 MC protocol and biker news channel in the country. He also created the online news magazine www.bikerliberty.com.

In 2017 Black Dragon wrote "Sergeant at Arms Bible" and was the keynote speaker at the MC Professional Convention (PROC) one of the largest MC education conferences in the United States.

In 2018 Black Dragon was again invited to speak at the PROC.

In 2019 Black Dragon created the podcast "The Dragon's Lair Motorcycle Chaos" on the Spreaker podcasting platform.

In 2021 Black Dragon wrote best seller "President's Bible Chronicle I, Principles of Motorcycle Club Leadership."

In 2023 Black Dragon launched "BlackDragonBikerTV" TikTok and went to 93 thousand subscribers in eight months.

In 2023 November 6th Black Dragon was honored to be invited to participate in the rap 1% unification song … by Taa Shon 1%er (Thunderguards MC) and Pipeline 1%er (Outcast MC). This rap song announced a truce between all major 1% Black and mixed-race OMC nations operating on the Black biker set. Black Dragon had a cameo appearance in the music video which can be found at https://www.youtube.com/watch?v=4eZBEUbLar0. In this video members from Outcast MC, Thunderguards MC, Chosen Few MC, and Wheels of Soul MC can be seen.

In 2023 Black Dragon was honored to be included on the El Domino song "Diamond on my Heart (Outlaw Biker Anthem) featuring Big Buzz and Black Dragon on the El Domino comeback album, "The Preacher The Gangster The Outlaw" featuring Snoop Dogg, Three 6 Mafia, Akon, T-Pain, The Game, Baby Bash and Mr. Criminal. The music video "Diamond on my Heart" was produced by three-time Emmy award winning director Joshua Coombs. Black Dragon did the voiceover in the music video quoting former South African President Nelson Mandella, *"A wise man once said, when a man is denied the right to live the life he believes in, he has no choice but to become an outlaw."*

On December 10, 2023, Black Dragon published "Social Clubs Bible Revival of the Black Women's Social Clubs Movement Lifting as We Climb!" This was his sixth book in the Motorcycle Club Bible series.

In November of 2024, Black Dragon began penning MC Protocol 101 and President's Bible Chronicle II Betrayal in the Brotherhood.

In 2025 January, Black Dragon was again invited to be a featured speaker at the PROC.

In March of 2025 El Domino's song, "Diamond On My Heart" was remixed to feature Snoop Dogg rapping on the song. Black Dragon is now featured on a song with Snoop Dogg as a result.

In March of 2025 Black Dragon published Motorcycle Club Protocol 101 his seventh book in the motorcycle club bible series.

Today Black Dragon is looking ahead to see where he can be of service to motorcycle clubs, riding clubs, social clubs, and biker organizations worldwide. Black Dragon is currently a senior lifer and East Coast Regional President in the Mighty Black Sabbath Motorcycle Club Nation.

      Black Sabbath Forever Black Sabbath
      A Breed Apart
      Since 1974

      www.blacksabbathmc.com

◊◊◊

A NOTE FROM BLACK DRAGON

Now what? You have read the book, and you know the power of the information held within. I want you to know that you can help other bikers and clubs navigate their way through the murky waters of having a successful club life in their beloved MCs.

If you were helped, educated, or informed by this book there are a couple of simple things you can do to join me in remaking the MC world through knowledge, experience, education, and love:

1. If you believe "Motorcycle Protocol 101" has helped you then I ask that you spread the word by buying a copy for someone you think should have one.

2. Setup a reading group to discuss how this book applies to helping to better your MC. You can also write an honest review on social media, your blog, website, or on your favorite bookseller's website. There are countless ways you can help others by spreading this word. "Motorcycle Protocol 101" is not just a book worth reading, it is a vision and a plan worth following for every member to contribute positively to their MC. It is a vision worth sharing.

3. Enrich other MCs by buying this book for your brother MCs on the set with whom you share alliances. Imagine if brother MCs could have the benefit of the knowledge you have attained.

Thank you for your support! Send me an email anytime with questions, improvements, or your best MC tales! blackdragon@blacksabbathmc.com

Buy Prospect's Bible

More from John E. "**Black Dragon**" Bunch II

Bunch Media Group LLC.

Prospect's Bible
Amazon #1 Best Seller

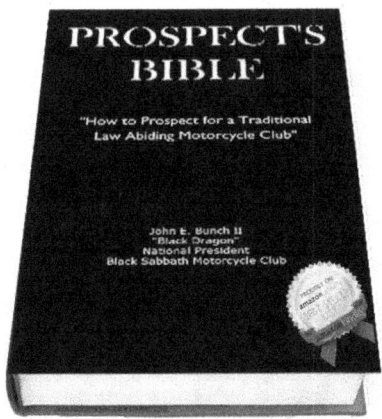

Learn how to prospect for
a traditional MC!
Order 24 hours per day
www.blackdragonsgear.com
Available from Kindle, Amazon.com, Audible, and retail bookstores.

Buy Sergeant-at-Arms Bible

More from John E. "**Black Dragon**" Bunch II

Bunch Media Group

Sergeant at Arms Bible
Amazon #1 Best Seller

Learn how to be the Sergeant-at-Arms for a traditional MC!
Order 24 hours per day
www.blackdragonsgear.com
Available from Kindle, Amazon.com, Audible, and retail bookstores.

Buy Public Relations Officer's Bible

More from John E. **"Black Dragon"** Bunch II

Bunch Media Group

Motorcycle Clubs Public Relations Officer's Bible
Amazon #1 Best Seller

Learn how to be the Sergeant-at-Arms for a traditional MC!
Order 24 hours per day
www.blackdragonsgear.com
Available from Kindle, Amazon.com, Audible, and retail bookstores.

*Buy President's Bible Chronicle I
Principles of Motorcycle Club Leadership*

More from John E. "**Black Dragon**" Bunch II
Bunch Media Group Amazon #1 Best Seller

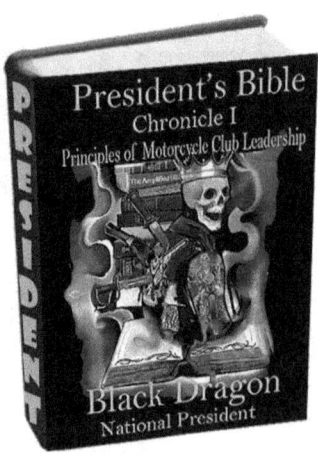

Learn the 17 scientific principles of motorcycle club leadership! Get this number one best-selling book now!
Order 24 hours per day
www.blackdragonsgear.com
Available from Kindle, Amazon.com, Audible, and retail bookstores.

Buy Social Club's Bible
Revival of the Women's Social Club Movement
"Lifting as We Climb"

More from John E. "**Black Dragon**" Bunch II
Bunch Media Group Amazon #1 Best Seller

Social Clubs Bible is a manual that teaches women who are interested in joining or are already part of Black women's social clubs. The book covers the history, rules, and protocols of the Black MC set. It also revisits the history of Black women's clubs and encourages today's social clubs to improve the African American MC set and communities.

Buy Prospect's Bible for Women's MCs
'How to Prospect for a Women's MC'

More from John E. "**Black Dragon**" Bunch II
Bunch Media Group Amazon #1 Best Seller

Learn how to define the MC Set, find a women's motorcycle club, and successfully prospect for it to win your status as a full patch sister in today's MC environment.

Black Dragon's MC Consulting Services

Black Dragon's Motorcycle Club consulting services will help you solve challenges that threaten the reputation, peace, safety, or morale of your motorcycle club or startup.

His services include:
MC/RC/RA/SC startups
1%er - 99%er conflict resolution
MC Crisis Management
MC Reputation Management
Press Releases
Press Conferences
Media Alerts
..and more

Setup an appointment at:

Clarity.fm/black-dragon

If you find you need a motorcycle clubs expert when facing criminal or civil trial don't hesitate to call Black Dragon! My expert witness legal services may be able to help you!

404.692.0336

blackdragon@blacksabbathmc.com

www.ingramcontent.com/pod-product-compliance
Lightning Source LLC
Chambersburg PA
CBHW071233300426
44116CB00008B/1015